Religion in Britain
from the Megaliths
to Arthur

ALSO BY ROBIN MELROSE

*The Druids and King Arthur: A New
View of Early Britain* (McFarland, 2011)

Religion in Britain from the Megaliths to Arthur

An Archaeological and Mythological Exploration

ROBIN MELROSE

McFarland & Company, Inc., Publishers
Jefferson, North Carolina

LIBRARY OF CONGRESS CATALOGUING-IN-PUBLICATION DATA

Names: Melrose, Robin, author.
Title: Religion in Britain from the megaliths to Arthur :
an archaeological and mythological exploration / Robin Melrose.
Description: Jefferson, North Carolina : McFarland & Company, Inc.,
Publishers, 2016. | Includes bibliographical references and index.
Identifiers: LCCN 2016003941 | ISBN 9781476663609
(softcover : acid free paper) ∞
Subjects: LCSH: Great Britain—Religion—To 449. |
Great Britain—Antiquities, Roman. | Great Britain—History—
Roman period, 55 B.C.–449 A.D. | Mabinogion. | Welsh literature—
To 1550—History and criticism.
Classification: LCC BL980.G7 M45 2016 | DDC 200.9361—dc23
LC record available at http://lccn.loc.gov/2016003941

BRITISH LIBRARY CATALOGUING DATA ARE AVAILABLE

ISBN (print) 978-1-4766-6360-9
ISBN (ebook) 978-1-4766-2426-6

© 2016 Robin Melrose. All rights reserved

*No part of this book may be reproduced or transmitted in any form
or by any means, electronic or mechanical, including photocopying
or recording, or by any information storage and retrieval system,
without permission in writing from the publisher.*

Front cover image of Stonehenge © 2016 iStock/Keawpiko

Printed in the United States of America

*McFarland & Company, Inc., Publishers
Box 611, Jefferson, North Carolina 28640
www.mcfarlandpub.com*

Table of Contents

Preface: Routes to the Past   1

Introduction: Celts, Druids and the Age of Arthur   5

1: The Age of Megaliths (1): Stone Monuments and Neolithic Astronomy   15

2: The Age of Megaliths (2): Rich Burials and More Astronomy in the Early Bronze Age   34

3: The Age of Depositions (1): Water, Fire and Earth in the Late Bronze Age   53

4: The Age of Depositions (2): The Sky God and Iron Age Hillforts   78

5: The Age of Depositions (3): Chariot Burials, Lunar Eclipses and Wooden Buckets in the Later Iron Age   111

6: The Romans in Britain: Roman Gods and British Gods, Roman Burials and Decapitated Burials   134

7: The Beginnings of the Age of Arthur: Arthur the Bear-Man   162

8: Arthur in the Underworld   176

9: Arthur the Witch-Slayer, Warrior and King   186

10: Arthur and the Early Medieval World: Holy Islands and the Arthurian Cycle in Cornwall   203

11: Druids and the Early Medieval World: the Bear-Druid of Welsh Mythology   224

Chapter Notes   249

Bibliography   263

Index   275

Preface

A few years ago I wrote a book on the Druids and King Arthur in which I said that the Druids originated in eastern Europe and spread west into Britain some time in the Early Iron Age, around 800 BC. At the time I was following the traditional model of the genesis of the Celts, in which the Celts originated somewhere in Central Europe and eventually spread west to France, Spain, Portugal, Britain and Ireland. However, since then, I have become convinced that this model is wrong. Archaeologists like Barry Cunliffe and Celtic scholars like John Koch have argued persuasively that the Celts originated along the Atlantic coasts of Europe, in Portugal, Spain, Ireland and western Britain in the Late Bronze Age, and spread east, effectively turning the traditional theory on its head.

The present work is about prehistoric religion, and any book about prehistoric religion in Britain must tackle the question of the Druids. In his *Commentaries on the Gallic War*, the Roman general Julius Caesar said that the Druid priesthood originated in Britain, and this makes much more sense if the Celts themselves first emerged in the west rather than the east of Europe. Caesar said that the Druids were experts on "the stars and their motion," and this raises the possibility, cautiously advanced by Barry Cunliffe in his book on the Druids, that druidism emerged in the Neolithic (4000–2500 BC), at a time when monuments with astronomical alignment were being built across Britain and Ireland.

So this book begins with the astronomically aligned megaliths—the great stone monuments like Stonehenge—and with what John Koch calls the Age of Megaliths, which straddled the Neolithic and the Early Bronze Age (2500–1500 BC). After this came what Koch calls the Age of Depositions, when Britons placed offerings to the gods in the earth and in watery places like rivers, lakes and fens. It was early in this period (between 1500 BC and 700 BC) that the first Celts emerged along the Atlantic coasts of Europe, and with them, the first Druids, who inherited the astronomical knowledge of their Neolithic and Early Bronze Age ancestors.

The Age of Depositions came to an end with the coming of Christianity, which was established throughout Britain by the late 7th century. The end of paganism and the beginning of Christianity ushered in what I call the Age of Arthur—a celebration of Britain's pagan past which came to be focused on the figure of Arthur. There may have been one or more "real" Arthurs, but the Arthur of Welsh literature before the Norman invasion of 1066 was largely a figure of mythology and folklore. I will argue that he was originally a British god or gods, perhaps dating back as far as the Neolithic, who went through a series of transformations in the Roman period before assuming his final form. Arthur in Welsh probably means "Bear-Man," and in my final chapter I look at the Fourth Branch of the medieval Welsh *Mabinogion*, the story of Math son of Mathonwy, whose name

Math is a very ancient word for "bear." Math is a magician in the Fourth Branch, and I will show that he is in fact a Druid, and that the earliest form of Arthur may have been a Druid like Math.

Since there are no written records of British religion in prehistoric times (apart from the occasional report of a Greek or Roman writer), we must rely heavily on the findings of archaeology to give us an insight into ancient British paganism. Archaeology can tell us what was buried in the earth or cast into river, lakes or fens, so we can learn a good deal about burial rites, the kinds of offerings that prehistoric Britons made to the gods, and where they lived. What archaeology tells us can be interpreted in the light of the observations of Greek and Roman writers, mostly about Gaul (France), which came under Roman rule in the 2nd and 1st century BC (between about 125 BC and 50 BC).

But the Greek and Roman writers can only take us so far, and perhaps the most valuable source of information about prehistoric British religion is the collection of Welsh tales known as the *Mabinogion*, in particular the four branches of the *Mabinogion*, which were probably composed between 1060 and 1200. The *Mabinogion* was of course written by Christians, several centuries after the last pagan gods were worshipped, but if we can match what we find in the *Mabinogion* with the findings of archaeology, then we can arrive at an approximation of the truth. If we combine the four branches of the *Mabinogion* with Welsh Arthurian tales like *Culhwch and Olwen* (11th century), Geoffrey of Monmouth's fanciful *History of the Kings of Britain* (12th century), and the French tales of Tristan and Isolt (also 12th century), we are afforded a series of glimpses into Britain's pagan past—or rather, how medieval Britons saw their pagan past.

Although archaeology is the most powerful tool we have to explore prehistoric religion in Britain, it is not the only one. Much of this book concerns the Celts, and Celtic languages are still spoken across the British Isles: Welsh in Wales, Gaelic in Scotland, and Irish in Ireland (Cornish became extinct in the 18th century, though there are attempts to revive it). The Celtic languages belong to a family of languages known as Indo-European, which includes most of the languages of Europe, together with some languages of the Middle East—most notably Farsi or Persian—and many of the languages of the Indian subcontinent, including Hindi and Urdu.

Now the main languages of the British Isles, Welsh, Irish and English, only appeared in written form in the early medieval period, but other Indo-European languages have a much longer history. The earliest literary texts in Latin date from the 3rd century BC, and the earliest Greek texts—Homer's *Iliad* and *Odyssey*—date from around 700 BC. But we can go back even further. The Greeks of Mycenae in the Peloponnese used a script called Linear B between about 1450 and 1200 BC to produce a series of texts, mostly lists and inventories. The Hittites of Anatolia (now Turkey) used a Sumerian cuneiform script between the 16th and 13th century BC to produce a wide variety of texts. In the 2nd millennium BC the priests and poets of northern India composed the Vedas, the oldest sacred texts of Hinduism, in the language known as Sanskrit (Old Indian). At around the same time, Zoroaster was composing the earliest sacred texts of the Zoroastrian religion in Avestan, a form of Old Iranian which is very close to Sanskrit.

Thanks to Mycenaean Greek, Hittite, Sanskrit and Avestan, we have some idea of the Indo-European gods worshipped over three thousand years ago across a wide area, from northern India to Greece. We don't know what gods were worshipped in Britain three thousand years ago—or two thousand years go, for that matter—but in the course of this book I'm going to use findings from archaeology to speculate on some of these gods. Often I will draw on what we know about Greek or Vedic Indian gods, but I will also be making use of Julius Pokorny's *Indogermanisches etymologisches Wörterbuch* ("Indo-European Etymological Dictionary"), which was first published in 1959 but has since been updated. The gods I introduce into the discussion may not be the actual deities worshipped in Britain, but they are about as close as we can get to long forgotten gods.

The plan of the book is simple. The first two chapters deal with the Age of Megaliths—Chapter 1 with the Neolithic and Chapter 2 with the Early Bronze Age. Chapters 3 to 6 deal with the Age of Depositions—Chapter 3 with the Middle—Late Bronze, Chapters 4 and 5 with the Iron Age, and Chapter 6 with the Roman period. Chapters 7 to 11 deal with the early Medieval period that I am calling the Age of Arthur—Chapter 7 with the genesis of Arthur, Chapter 8 with Arthur as an underworld figure, and Chapter 9 with Arthur as witch-slayer, warrior and king. In Chapter 10 I bring all these elements together in an attempt to "explain" Arthur, and introduce the story of Tristan and Isolt, which emerged in the 12th century and exists on the fringes of the Arthurian tales. Finally in Chapter 11 I return to the Druids with the Bear-Druid Math son of Mathonwy, perhaps the most ancient incarnation of Arthur.

Introduction: Celts, Druids and the Age of Arthur

The Celts

The prehistory of Britain is usually divided into three main periods, based on the material used for weapons, tools and ornaments: the Neolithic, or New Stone Age (4000 BC–2500 BC), when weapons, tools and ornaments were made of flint, bone, antler or other materials like jet or shale; the Bronze Age (2500 BC–800 BC), when weapons, tools and ornaments were often made of copper, bronze or gold; and the Iron Age (800 BC–43 AD), when iron gradually took over from bronze, especially in the manufacture of weapons such as swords.

However, the Celtic scholar John Koch, in a 1991 paper[1] suggests a different scheme for prehistoric Britain, with just two periods: the Age of Megaliths, that is, the age of great stone monuments like Stonehenge (Neolithic and Early Bronze Age, 4000 BC–1600 BC), and the Age of Depositions, when the focus was on placing offerings to the gods in the earth or in rivers (Late Bronze Age and Iron Age, 1300 BC–AD 43). The powerful central authorities in the Age of Megaliths "may be regarded as theocratic, that is to say that there was an equvalence of chieftainly and priestly functions. The religion had a celestial orientation." In the Age of Depositions, society "became more aristocratic and warlike. Wealth and labour were conspicuously expended upon ornaments, fine metal weaponry, and hilltop fortifications." Now ritual was focused on "deposition of rich metalwork in pits, more often in rivers, pools, bogs and other watery settings.... The orientation of the religion was chthonic." The office of king "entailed the rôle of battle-leader and aimed at domination of the landscape for cultivation and stock-rearing. The priestly functioned now closely shadowed the activities of artisans dealing in fine work in bronze and gold." The Age of Depositions is "recognisably Celtic," while the Age of Megaliths is not.

In Koch's model, the consolidation of Proto-Celtic (the ancestor of today's Celtic languages like Welsh and Irish) is seen in the prestige economy of the Late Bronze Age (1300 BC–600 BC)

> in which an Atlantic Zone with centres in Armorica, South-East England, South Wales, Ireland, and later on, Iberia, was in a continuous close contact with, and generally followed the cultural lead of, Urnfield/ Hallstatt C West-central Europe. A crescendo of wealth, geographical extent and intensity occurred in Hallstatt B3, corresponding broadly to the Irish Dowris A of *c.* 900–*c.* 650 BC.... The chief evidence for our long-term and long-range aristocratic network is found in metalwork, often in subterranean hoards, but also ritual aque-

ous depositions. Ornaments of gold and bronze are relevant, bronze weaponry more so, and the sword most of all.

This early paper hints at a view which began taking shape in the 2000s, that the Celts originated along the fringes of the Atlantic Ocean. So the authority on the Iron Age, Barry Cunliffe, suggests in his book on the Druids that the Celts emerged in Atlantic Europe, in a zone stretching from Algarve in southern Portugal to Britain and Ireland, "gaining a degree of cohesion from the fact that intense maritime activity bound the Atlantic-facing communities tightly together"; in such a context, "a common language would have evolved to facilitate communication."[2] This contrasts with the traditional view—that the Celts originated in central Europe and spread westward to France, Iberia (Spain and Portugal), and the British Isles (Britain and Ireland) during the later Iron Age.

Cunliffe's view of an Atlantic origin for the Celts is endorsed by Koch in later paper.[3] Here he points out[4] that Britain, Ireland, and Armorica were in "direct and intense contact by sea with the western Iberian Peninsula," as can be seen in "shared types of feasting equipment and weapons, reflected, for example, in the contents of the mid–tenth century Huelva deposition" and the iconography of the "warrior stelae."

The Huelva deposition refers to a collection of around 400 objects found in the mouth of the Odiel River opposite the important Tartessian town of Huelva in southwest Spain. The objects included swords, daggers, spearheads, some of them made in Ireland, a helmet, and a number of *fibulae* (safety-pin brooches) from the eastern Mediterranean.[5]

The "warrior stelae" of southwest Iberia are Late Bronze Age monoliths with an average height of between 27 and 39 inches one face of which is engraved with (generally but not exclusively) motifs depicting weapons, often surrounding a central anthropomorphic figure. The most common composition in the warrior stelae depicts a person surrounded by artifacts, which are usually military in character (swords, spears, shields, helmets and chariots), although sometimes other objects are also included (such as mirrors, fibulae and musical instruments).[6] The circular shields, swords and spears depicted on the warrior stelae are types that can readily be found as far afield as Ireland and Britain.[7]

In his *O'Donnell Lectures 2008*, and in a 2009 paper, "A Case for Tartessian as a Celtic Language," Koch shows that one of the earliest references to Celts comes from southern Portugal or southwest Spain. The early Greek historian Herodotus, writing around 430 BC (Book 2, Chapter 34, Book 4, Chapter 48) says[8]:

> I am willing to believe that [the Nile] rises at the same distance from its mouth as the [Danube], which has its source amongst the Keltoi at Pyrene and flows right through the middle of Europe, to reach the Black Sea at Miletos's colony of Istri. The Keltoi live beyond the Pillars of Hercules, next to the Kunesioi who are the most westerly people of Europe.
>
> The [Danube], that mighty stream which, rising amongst the Keltoi, the most westerly, after the Kunetes, of all the European nations, traverses the whole length of the continent before it enters Scythia.

Herodotus was plainly mistaken about the Danube, which he thought rose near Pyrene (the Pyrenees) and flowed across the whole of Europe. However, he may well have been right about the Celts. The Pillars of Hercules refers to the promontories that flank the entrance to the Strait of Gibraltar, the narrow strait that connects the Atlantic Ocean to the Mediterranean Sea, and we know from later sources that the Kunesioi or Kunetes inhabited the Algarve in southern Portugal, and that their eastern limit was at or near the Guadiana River, which forms the southern border between Portugal and Spain. The Roman historian Trogus Pompeius, who flourished in the late 1st century BC, said that the Cunetes inhabited the forest of the Tartessians, who lived in southwest Spain at the mouth of the Guadalquivir River.

Koch believes that the Cunetes are Celtic. The name closely resembles the British place-name *Cunetio*, a Romano-British town near Marlborough in Wiltshire, which corresponds to Medieval Welsh *Kynwydion*, the name of the war band of Dark Age Strathclyde (also known as Alt Clut). The root of these names is Celtic *ku, kuno-*, which literally means "dog," but also metaphorically "warrior, hero." In that case, *Cunetes* would mean "Band of Warriors."[9] The first king of the Cunetes, according to the Roman historian Justin, was Gargoris, who tried repeatedly to kill his grandson Habis, and Koch believes that this corresponds to Old Irish *garg*, "fierce, savage" and *ri*, "king."

The Tartessians may also have been Celtic, or at least influenced by Celtic. Herodotus mentions an expedition to Tartessos around 550 BC made by the Greeks of Phokaia in Asia Minor (now Turkey): "[The] Phokaians were the earliest of the Greeks to make long sea voyages: it was they who discovered the Adriatic Sea, and Tyrrhenia, and Iberia, and Tartessos.... When they came to Tartessos they made friends with the king of the Tartessians, whose name was Arganthonios." The name or title *Arganthonios* is clearly Celtic, based on the word for silver and money *arganto-*, found in Old Irish *airget*, Middle Welsh *aryant*, "silver." *Argantonios*, or "Agent of Divine Silver" is closely comparable to the title ARGANTODANNOS found on Gaulish silver coinage. There could hardly be a more suitable title for the ruler of Tartessos, which was rich in silver.

There are also very early Celtic names for Ireland, Britain and Gaul (France). *Eriu* (genitive *Erenn*) is derived from Proto-Celtic *Iwerju*, "The Fertile Land," related to Sanskrit *pivari*, "fat, rich," Greek *pieira*, "fertile," referring to land (there is a district in the northeast of Greece called *Pieria*)[10] (initial Indo-European "p" was lost in Celtic).

Alba (genitive *Alban*), the Gaelic word for "Scotland," corresponds to Old Welsh *elbid*, "the habitable surface of the world." In an early 11th century Latin text from Brittany, Latinized *Albidia* occurs as the ancient name of Britain. Proto-Celtic *Albiju* (genitive *Albijonos*), "the White One," is related to Latin *albus*, "white," and to the Galatian leader *Albiorix*, "King of the Land." Koch believes that the application of this epithet "white" to the land "may involve a semantic development akin to that of the Greek *alphis/alphitou*, "barley," and points out that "barley has been a popular crop in Britain since the Copper Age."

Letha corresponds to Old Welsh *Litau*, Medieval *Llydaw*, Old Breton *Letau*, Romano-Celtic *Letavia*, all meaning "Brittany, Armorica." The name is cognate to Vedic *Prthivi*, "The Divinized Earth," Germanic *feld*, "field," *Fuld-aha*, "the River Fulda" (a river in Hesse, west-central Germany). An inscription has been found in Narbonne, in the far south of Gaul, MARTI CICOLLUI ET LITAVI, "to Mars Cicolluis and Litavis." "The Gaulish cult of Litavi(s) shows that the name had once designated the divinised land for Continental Celts and that Brittonic and Irish have merely preserved a usage anciently current in Gaul itself. The inscriptional evidence from the far south of Gaul indicates that the name had once covered a region far larger than Brittany."

Eriu and *Albion* may date to the 6th century BC. The *Ora maritima* of Avienus was written in the 4th century AD, but may be based on the *Massiliote Periplus* (possibly 6th century BC), or the *Periplus* of the Carthaginian Himilco, which took place around 500 BC. In the *Ora maritima* we find *gens Hiernorum*, "the race of the Irish," and *insula*

Albionum, "the island of the British," based on the Celtic forms *Iverni* and *Albiones*. By the time of Pytheas (325 BC), Britain and the British had become *Pretannike* and *Pretannoi*, from Celtic *Pritani*, "People of the Forms," corresponding perhaps with the arrival of Early La Tène influences in Britain from the later 5th century BC.

Before I close this discussion, it is fair to point out that there is not universal agreement that the Celts and Celtic came from the west and spread east. For example, the linguist Graham Isaac suggests an eastern European origin for the development of proto-Celtic based on the many innovative morphological characteristics shared by Celtic and Eastern Indo-European languages like Indo-Iranian, Baltic, Slavic, Greek and Albanian[11] ("morphological" refers to the prefixes and suffixes used in language to convey meaning—like the *pre-* of *prefix*). However, his view is probably not widely shared, and there seems to be broad agreement that, archaeologically at least, the Celts originated along the Atlantic coasts rather than in, say, Central Europe.

The Druids

Koch, in his discussion of the Age of Megaliths and the Age of Depositions, refers to the famous Iron Age priests, the Druids, who may have been the successors of the priests who built the megaliths, but did not exercise the same day-to-day power as their ancestors[12]:

> In the transition from the Age of Megaliths to the Age of Depositions. the priest caste was not so much eclipsed, as dislocated from a direct temporal power and central economic position by a rising warlike nobility. The influence of the druids remained one of the distinctive features of Iron Age Celtic civilisation. In the Roman conquest of Britain, for example, dynasts of the tribal aristocracies, such as Cassivellaunos, Caratacos, and Boudica, spearheaded the resistance, but the Druidic sanctuary of Anglesey was also a centre of anti–Roman influence and treated as a military objective. And though the priests called druids officiated at depositions and did not build great astronomical monuments, Caesar (in *De Bello Gallico* VI) tells us that they "have many discussions concerning the stars and their course, the size of the universe and of the earth, and the strength and properties of the undying gods...." Some prehistorians have have concluded that the druids continued the megalithic priesthood.

Later Koch elaborates on the role of Druids in the Irish social order, linking them to artisans. According to Caesar, the main god of the Gauls was Mercury, who has been identified with Lugus, who was most associated with the "peripatetic professional class or, in Old Irish, the *aes dano*." They comprised "smiths and wheelwrights as well as bards, jurists and storytellers. The Irish laws were cast after the conversion, but it may be inferred from the sagas and the classic ethnographies of the Celts that the druidic priesthood had been the summit of the pre–Christian professional orders."[13] The *aes dano* were the "people of the arts"—Old Irish *dano*, "arts" is perhaps related to Old Indian *damsana*, "magic power, witchcraft," Avestan *dahma*, "expert, inaugurated in religious questions,"[14] while Old Irish *aes*, "people" is related to Oscan genitive *aeteis*, "part," *aittium*, "portions."[15]

As Koch says, Julius Caesar spoke of the Druids in his *Gallic Wars*, written during his Gaulish campaign (58–51 BC). At this point, a note on terminology might be useful. Gaul refers to a region which today includes France, Belgium, and those parts of the Netherlands and Germany which lie to the west of the River Rhine. According to Caesar, three groups of people lived in Gaul: the *Aquitani*, who lived in the southwest and correspond to the Basques; the Gaul or Celts; and the *Belgae*, who lived in France to the north of Paris, as well as in Belgium and parts of the Netherlands and Germany, who were possibly Celts with a German origin.[16] The Druids were the priests of the Celts in Gaul (it's not clear whether the Belgae had Druids, and there is no mention of Druids among the Celts of Spain or Portugal).

In Gaul, says Caesar,[17] there are two order of men, the knights and the Druids. The Druids "are engaged in things sacred, conduct the public and the private sacrifices, and interpret all matters of religion." The Druids "assemble at a fixed period of the year in a consecrated place in the territories of the Carnutes, which is reckoned the central region of the whole of Gaul. Hither all, who have disputes, assemble from every part, and submit to their decrees and determinations." The institution "is supposed to have been devised in Britain, and to have been brought over from it into Gaul; and now those who desire to gain a more accurate knowledge of that system generally proceed thither for the purpose of studying it."

Caesar says very little about the teachings of the Druids, simply saying[18]:

> They wish to inculcate this as one of their leading tenets, that souls do not become extinct, but pass after death from one body to another, and they think that men by this tenet are in a great degree excited to valor, the fear of death being disregarded. They likewise discuss and impart to the youth many things respecting the stars and their motion, respecting the extent of the world and of our earth, respecting the nature of things, respecting the power and the majesty of the immortal gods.

Caesar implies that the Gauls practiced human sacrifice[19]:

> The nation of all the Gauls is extremely devoted to superstitious rites; and on that account they who are troubled with unusually severe diseases, and they who are engaged in battles and dangers, either sacrifice men as victims, or vow that they will sacrifice them, and employ the Druids as the performers of those sacrifices; because they think that unless the life of a man be offered for the life of a man, the mind of the immortal gods can not be rendered propitious, and they have sacrifices of that kind ordained for national purposes.

As Koch says, Caesar names Mercury as the main divinity of the Gauls, but also mentions Mars, the god of war[20]:

> To him, when they have determined to engage in battle, they commonly vow those things which they shall take in war. When they have conquered, they sacrifice whatever captured animals may have survived the conflict, and collect the other things into one place. In many states you may see piles of these things heaped up in their consecrated spots.

Caesar also mentions another important god[21]:

> All the Gauls assert that they are descended from the god Dis, and say that this tradition has been handed down by the Druids. For that reason they compute the divisions of every season, not by the number of days, but of nights; they keep birthdays and the beginnings of months and years in such an order that the day follows the night.

Dis or Dis Pater was the Roman god of the underworld, originally a god of riches, fertile agricultural land and underground mineral wealth, and later identified with the Greek god Pluto. This of course was the Roman name of the god, and there is no agreement on what the Celts called this god, though I will be addressing this problem in Chapter 3.

Julius Caesar was not the only classical writer to mention the Druids. The Greek writers Diodorus Siculus ("Diodorus the Sicilian"), in his *Historical Library*, written between 60 and 30 BC, mentions not only the Druids but also bards and diviners[22]:

> Among [the Gauls] are also to be found lyric poets whom they call Bards. These men sing to the accompaniment of instruments which are like lyres, and their songs may be either of praise or of obloquy. Philosophers, as we may call them, and men learned in religious affairs are unusually honoured among them and are called by them Druids. The Gauls likewise make use of diviners, accounting them worthy of high approbation, and these men foretell the future by means of the flight or cries of birds and of the slaughter of sacred animals, and they have all the multitude subservient to them.

Diodorus Siculus also says of the Gauls[23]:

> it is their custom, even during the course of the meal, to seize upon any trivial matter as an occasion for keen disputation and then to challenge one another to single combat, without any regard for their lives; for the belief of Pythagoras prevails among them, that the souls of men are immortal and that after a prescribed number of years they commence upon a new life, the soul entering into another body.

A little later Diodorus Siculus mentions the famous Gaulish "cult of the head"[24]:

> When their enemies fall they cut off their heads and fasten them about the necks of their horses; and turning over to their attendants the arms of their opponents, all covered with blood, they carry them off as booty, singing a paean over them and striking up a song of victory, and these first-fruits of battle they fasten by nails upon their houses, just as men do, in certain kinds of hunting, with the heads of wild beasts they have mastered.

Another Greek historian who touches on the Druids is Strabo (64 BC–AD 24). In his *Geography* Strabo writes[25]:

> Among all the Gallic peoples, generally speaking, there are three sets of men who are held in exceptional honour; the Bards, the Vates and the Druids. The Bards are singers and poets; the Vates, diviners and natural philosophers; while the Druids, in addition to natural philosophy, study also moral philosophy.

Strabo, in the same chapter, also refers to the "cult of the head":

> when they depart from the battle they hang the heads of their enemies from the necks of their horses, and, when they have brought them home, nail the spectacle to the entrances of their homes. At any rate, Poseidonius says that he himself saw this spectacle in many places, and that, although at first he loathed it, afterwards, through his familiarity with it, he could bear it calmly.

Poseidonius was a Greek philosopher, historian and geographer who travelled through the south of France in the early 1st century BC and left an account of his travels which has now been lost.

There is some evidence for this "cult of the head"—and possibly for human sacrifice—in the south of France. The *oppidum* (defended settlement) of Entremont near Aix-en-Provence was founded at the beginning of the 2nd century BC as a small settlement of about two acres, and was enlarged around 150 BC. Between 125 BC and 100 BC, a monumental hall 65 feet long and 16 feet wide was erected. The ground floor of this building was a hypostyle hall with a packed mud floor. The pillars of the facade rest upon a stylobate (platform) made up of reused elements from at least one earlier religious sanctuary. These elements, which may date to as early as 500 BC, include representations of human heads without mouths, and cephalic concavities destined to receive human skulls or parts of skulls. Around twenty skulls of aged men, which were pierced for suspension, were found dispersed around the stylobate of the hall. They were probably originally attached to the wood of the facade. The only remains found on the floor are fragments of Italian amphoras, which suggest the practice of libation rituals.[26]

In 1817 three blocks sculpted in bas-relief were discovered at Entremont in a small house in the center of the plateau. The sculpted blocks show armed cavalry soldiers caracoling (executing a half turn to the left or right), an unclothed person standing in front of a building or door, and human heads, isolated or in pairs, sometimes integrated with vegetal motifs. The heads may be skulls of the deceased, not necessarily representations of war trophies, but more likely "allusions to cycles of the Afterworld or reincarnation."

There is only one reference to Druids in Britain. In AD 43 the Roman emperor Claudius launched an invasion of Britain, and for almost 300 years Britain as far north as Hadrian's Wall was part of the Roman Empire. The Welsh resisted Roman rule for some years, and in AD 61, the Roman governor Gaius Suetonius Paulinus prepared to attack the island of Mona (Anglesey in north Wales), which had a powerful population and was a safe haven for fugitives. The attack is described in blood-curdling detail by the Roman historian Tacitus.[27] The Romans crossed the Menai Strait that separates Anglesey from the mainland:

> On the shore stood the opposing army with its dense array of armed warriors, while between the ranks dashed women, in black attire like the Furies, with hair dishevelled, waving brands. All around, the Druids, lifting up their hands to heaven, and pouring forth dreadful imprecations, scared our soldiers by the unfamiliar sight, so that, as if their limbs were paralysed, they stood motionless, and exposed to wounds. Then urged by their general's appeals and mutual encouragements not to quail before a troop of frenzied women, they bore the standards onwards, smote down all resistance, and wrapped the foe in the flames of his own brands. A force was next set over the conquered, and their groves, devoted to inhuman superstitions, were destroyed. They deemed it indeed a duty to cover their altars with the blood of captives and to consult their deities through human entrails.

But we don't just have Tacitus's word for it that Anglesey was important to the Druids. In 1942 a hoard of over 150 objects of bronze and iron was discovered at a small lake called Llyn Cerrig Bach in the northwest of Anglesey, during construction of the RAF airfield at Valley. The finds are "primarily military" and included eleven swords, eight spearheads and parts of a parade shield. Equipment from several chariots was also present, both the harness and parts of the structure[28]:

> Up to 22 chariots can be recognised from the wheels discovered, but this might indicate the offering of wheels alone (which are known to have been sacred to one of the Celtic gods) rather than complete vehicles. Some items were locally manufactured, a few came from Ireland but a great many originated from southern England; a possible sign of trade, plunder captured from war or suggestive that the lake was more than a shrine of local importance. The dates of the finds are also of interest. Some of the swords are of types current in the 2nd century BC, others are of later designs, but nothing later than AD 60 can be identified.

Clearly Llyn Cerrig Bach was a shrine of national importance which was in use from the 2nd century BC till the 1st century AD, when the Druids were suppressed by the Romans.

There were also sacred lakes in Gaul, as we learn from Strabo in his *Geography*. Strabo, in discussing the *Tectosages* of southwest France, reports that they were involved in the sack of Delphi in 279 BC. When the Roman statesman and general Caepio plundered

Llyn Cerrig Bach, the lake on the island of Anglesey, north Wales, where weapons were offered to the gods in the Iron Age, January 29, 2011 (Richard Keatinge).

the temples of Tolosa (Toulouse in southwestern France) in 105 BC, part of the treasure he stole came from Delphi, which led to a series of misfortunes for Caepio. However, says Strabo, "the account of Poseidonius is more plausible: for he says that the treasure that was found in Tolosa amounted to about fifteen thousand talents (part of it in sacred lakes), unwrought, that is, merely gold and silver bullion; whereas the temple at Delphi was in those times already empty of such treasure."[29]

To which he adds that *Celtica* was full of treasures, and "it was the lakes, most of all, that afforded the treasures their inviolability, into which the people let down heavy masses of silver or even of gold."

Koch mentions in passing that the Druids may have continued the Neolithic priesthood, and this is very much the view of Barry Cunliffe. In his book *Druids; A Very Short Introduction*, Cunliffe discusses Neolithic and Bronze Age religious practices and says, "it is a reasonable assumption that the beliefs and practices that constitute druidism began earlier and were deeply rooted in western European prehistory."[30] Later he elaborates on this:

> The rich fabric of prehistoric belief, revealed by the archaeological evidence in especially in Britain, Ireland, and Armorica [= Brittany], could only have been maintained by specialists—a group with coercive authority capable of abstract though, philosophical speculation, and scientific observation, who passed on their learning from one generation to the next."[31]

And he concludes with a rhetorical question: "Could it be that the Druids, who are known to the Classical world from the 4th century BC, had their roots deep in prehistory—that the accumulated wisdoms which they guarded and taught were the legacy of learning and practice going back into the 2nd and 3rd millennia BC?"

The Age of Arthur

The Romans suppressed the Druids in Gaul and Britain, and by the end of Roman rule in Britain around AD 410, Christianity was on the march and paganism was in retreat ushering in what I call the Age of Arthur. Arthur was probably not a real person, or at least a single individual, but he played a considerable part in Welsh life from the 7th century until the Norman Conquest in 1066, and gained a wider audience in the 12th century with the publication of Geoffrey of Monmouth's *History of the Kings of Britain*. It is my belief that Arthur was originally, in part at least, a pagan god or gods who took on a human shape in the Christian era. So I'm using the term "Age of Arthur" as a shorthand for traces of earlier beliefs which still persisted among newly converted Christians, and which came together in the first Arthurian stories and in the Welsh mythological tales known as the *Mabinogion*.

These mythological tales belong to the areas of Britain where Celtic languages survived longest (or still survive today)—Cornwall (where Cornish was spoken until the 18th century), Wales (where Welsh is still spoken today), the English counties bordering Wales, and northern England/southern Scotland (where a Celtic language called Cumbric was spoken until the 12th century). For this reason, perhaps, Arthur is most commonly associated with Cornwall, Wales, the English Midlands, northern England and southern Scotland, and only marginally with Scotland north of the Forth and Clyde. I would love to explore early medieval Scotland with the Picts and their mysterious symbol stones, and at times I will go north of the Forth and Clyde, but neither the Picts of eastern Scotland nor the Irish of western Scotland have left any stories of the legendary Arthur, and their story belongs to a different book.

Stories of Arthur and tales from Welsh mythology cannot bring back the prehistoric religion of Britain, but they can give us glimpses of pagan belief and help us to resurrect the Druids, who continue to intrigue and baffle us two millennia after the last Druids were slaughtered by the Romans on Anglesey and their groves "devoted to inhuman superstitions" were destroyed.

CHAPTER 1

The Age of Megaliths (1): Stone Monuments and Neolithic Astronomy

Megalithic Astronomy

Iberia

Cunliffe and Koch say that Celtic peoples and language may have developed along the Atlantic coasts of Iberia, France and the British Isles in the Late Bronze Age, but the Atlantic played a significant role in Britain as early as the Neolithic. If, as Cunliffe implies, the Iron Age Druids originated in the Neolithic, then it was certainly among the megaliths—structures made of large stones—which proliferated along the Atlantic coast and were often aligned on important events like sunrise or sunset on the summer or winter solstice.

Some of the earliest megaliths are to be found in the southwest of Iberia. Indeed, one of oldest megaliths in Europe is the Almendres Cromlech, on a hillside near Evora in the Alentejo region of southern Portugal. The monument was built in several phases between 5000 BC and 4000 BC, and consists of two stone circles, with over 90 stones forming an oval 98 feet by 196 feet. Some of the stones are engraved with cup marks, spirals and circles. Most of the stones have "flattened" faces which all seemingly face towards the sun. In the Mesolithic (the period which precedes the Neolithic) the main focus of settlement was around the estuaries of the Tagus and Sado rivers, well to the west of the Almendres Cromlech. In the Neolithic, on the other hand settlements were in areas of Central Alentejo where there were notable granite outcrops, which may have been seen as "natural megaliths," or as "ancestral monuments in ruins." For example, there was a Neolithic settlement on a hill to the east of Evora, near large granite outcrops which have now been reduced by quarrying. So its possible that the early Neolithic settlers "appropriated places" which may have been sacred to the Mesolithic people settled in the Tagus or Sado estuaries.[1]

The sun was also the focus of the seven-stone *antas*, a group of megalithic dolmens (tombs) of distinctive design that were built in the southwest of the Iberian Peninsula during the 4th millennium BC. The range of orientations of these monuments corresponds almost exactly to the range of possible sunrise positions during the year, providing remarkably strong evidence of an association between these tombs and the sun.[2]

There are 177 seven-stone *antas* in central Portugal and neighboring parts of Spain. In such tombs only the backstone is a true orthostat; the next stone to either side leans on the backstone, the next to either side leans on its predecessor, and similarly for the third and last stone to either side. The tombs are concentrated in the Alentejo region of Portugal, and are spread over a region that measures some 125 miles from east to west and from north to south. Every one of the 177 faces east, and the astronomer Michael Hoskin remarks[3]: "It seems impossible to imagine any means by which such uniformity could be achieved, over this vast and very flat region, except by reference to the sky." Every tomb "faced within the range of sunrise, the great majority towards sunrise in the autumn and winter."

France

Carnac is on the south coast of Brittany in northwest France, and is famous as the site of more than 10,000 Neolithic standing stones. The Tumulus de Saint-Michel, on a hill 98 feet above sea level on the northern edge of Carnac, is a large burial mound 410 feet in length; the central burial chamber has dry-stone walling and a roof made of one capstone. It was first excavated in 1862, when 39 polished stone axes, 11 of them of Alpine jadeite, were found. They were embedded vertically in the deposit, with their cutting edges uppermost, and were accompanied by nine pendants and 101 beads of Iberian variscite, two flint flakes, and small beads of bone or ivory.[4] Burnt bone from the central chamber suggests that that the Tumulus was built around 4700 BC. A short distance to the east there was another focus of monumental activity, with the passage grave at Gavrinis, and the two horseshoe stone settings at Er Lannic. The stones at Er Lannic were probably raised during the 5th millennium BC, and it is possible that work began on the Carnac stone rows at around the same time.[5] The passage grave at Gavrinis was constructed in the 4th millennium BC, and is famous for its decoration—of the 29 slabs making up the walls of the central chamber, 23 are decorated, and 21 are almost entirely covered on their visible face.[6]

Ireland

One of the earliest megaliths in the British Isles is Newgrange, a passage tomb in County Meath, Ireland, just over half a mile north of the River Boyne (a passage tomb consists of a narrow passage made of large stones and one or more burial chambers covered in earth or stone). It was constructed around 3200 BC by a farming community that prospered on the rich lands of the Boyne Valley. Newgrange is a large kidney shaped mound covering an area of over one acre, retained at the base by 97 kerbstones, some of which are richly decorated with megalithic art. The 62-foot-long inner passage leads to a cruciform chamber with a corbelled roof. The amount of time and labor invested in construction of Newgrange suggests a well-organized society with specialized groups responsible for different aspects of construction. The tomb is carefully aligned so that at dawn on the day of the midwinter solstice the rays of the rising sun would shine through a slot in the roof and along the passage to light up a triple spiral carved on an orthostat set at the back of the central chamber.

Newgrange is part of a complex known as Bru na Boinne that also includes the Neolithic tombs of Knowth and Dowth. Knowth is the largest of all passage graves situated within the Brú na Bóinne complex. The site consists of one large mound (known as Site 1) and 17 smaller satellite tombs. Essentially Knowth (Site 1) is a large mound about 40 feet high and 220 feet in diameter, covering an area of over two acres, which contains two passages, placed along an east-west line. It is encircled by 127 kerbstones (three of which are missing and four of which are badly damaged). The large mound has been estimated to date from between 2500 and 2000 BC. The west-facing passage captures the setting sun on the spring and autumn equinoxes (March 21 and September 21), while the east-facing passage is lit up by the rising sun on the same days. The main passage of nearby Dowth is aligned west-southwest, and may have been "designed to capture the setting sun on the winter cross-quarter days (November and February) half way between the equinox and solstice"[7] (the cross-quarter day in November is Samhain, which coincides with All Saints' Day or Halloween, while the cross-quarter day in February is Imbolc, which falls at the same time as Candlemas).

The decorated backstone in the passage grave known as Cairn T, Loughcrew, County Meath, Ireland (M&K Davison—megalithics.com).

To the northwest of Bru na Boinne, also in County Meath, are the Loughcrew passage tombs, which also date to the later 4th millennium BC. The site is spread across three hilltops, Carnbane East, Carnbane West and Patrickstown. In 1980 the Irish American researcher Martin Brennan discovered that Cairn T in Carnbane East is directed to receive the beams of the rising sun on the spring and autumn equinox, with the light shining down the passage and illuminating the carvings on the backstone.[8]

Scotland

One of the oldest megalithic structures in Britain is Callanish stone circle on the island of Lewis in the Outer Hebrides, northwest Scotland. The stone circle, built around 2900 BC, is a cross-shaped setting of stones, centered on a circle of tall stones. At its heart stands a solitary monolith almost 16 feet high. Lines of smaller stones radiate from the circle to east, west and south. From the north runs an avenue 272 feet long, formed by two lines of stones that narrow as they approach the circle. Within the circle is a chambered tomb.[9] Nobody knows why Neolithic Britons built Callanish, but the most plausible explanation is that it has something to do with the moon. At Callanish Stones, every 18.6 years at the time of a major lunar standstill (when the moon rises at its most northerly point and sets at its most southerly), the moon appears to rise out of the hills of the "Sleeping Beauty" and to skim the horizon. Some hours later, for viewers standing at the north end of the avenue, the moon sets, then briefly re-appears between the stones of the central circle.[10]

Maeshowe on the island of Orkney, northeast Scotland, which dates from around 2800 BC, is one of the largest tombs in Orkney; the mound encasing the tomb is 115 feet

Callanish stone circle on the island of Lewis in the Outer Hebrides, northwest Scotland, August 16, 2012 (Petr Brož).

in diameter and rises to a height of 24 feet. Surrounding the mound, at a distance of 50 to 70 feet is a ditch up to 45 feet wide. The grass mound hides a complex of passages and chambers built of carefully crafted slabs of flagstone weighing up to 30 tons. The tomb is aligned so that the rear wall of its central chamber, held up by a bracketed wall, is illuminated on the winter solstice. Intriguingly, this phenomenon does not occur only on the shortest day of the year[11]:

> A similar phenomenon occurs daily from more than a month before the solstice until more than a month after it, and the same would have been true in prehistory. In fact, a most impressive light phenomenon occurs about twenty-one days (twenty-two to twenty-three days when the tomb was built) before and after the solstice. On these days the sun, having set behind the top of Ward Hill, on the adjacent island of Hoy, reappears briefly to the side of the hill a few minutes later, suddenly striking the back of the chamber for a second time.

Interestingly, this two-month period before and after the winter solstice corresponds to the two-month period of Yule, a Germanic festival first mentioned by the 8th century Anglo-Saxon monk and historian Bede, in *The Reckoning of Time*.[12]

Wales

Bryn Celli Ddu is a passage grave on the island of Anglesey, north Wales, which was constructed around 3000 BC. It consists of an outer circular stone kerb 85 feet in diameter, with an inner stone arc, both of which encircle a simple passage tomb whose entrance lies on the east side. The passage tomb is one of the finest of its kind in Wales. The 23 foot long inturned forecourt and stone-lined entrance passage gives access to a central polygonal chamber made of large slabs. In the north angle of the chamber is a 5 foot high smoothed stone pillar, interpreted as a "protectress" or tomb guardian in the style of Breton tombs, or a phallic symbol. One of the chamber stones bears a small spiral carving which is probably Neolithic. A central pit contained the most richly decorated Neolithic carved stone in Wales, which has patterns variously described as "serpents" or "meanders."[13]

A solar alignment on midsummer sunrise, first postulated by Sir Norman Lockyer in 1909, was finally proven and documented by Dr. Steve Burrow of the National Museum Wales in 2005. Burrow is quoted as saying of the midsummer sunrise at Bryn Celli Ddu: "It's stunning," he says. "First there is a

A replica of the decorated stone standing outside Bryn Celli Ddu on the island of Anglesey, north Wales, July 12, 2008 (Booaug11).

The southwest side of Bryn Celli Ddu, showing the decorated stone and back of chamber, September 2008 (Ijanderson977).

The interior of Bryn Celli Ddu, Anglesey, north Wales (M&K Davison—megalithics.com).

sparkle through the trees, then the sun rises out, it's quite exhilarating." The rays light up a quartz-rich stone at the back of the tomb.[14]

England

Britain's most famous megalithic monument, Stonehenge, started life between 3015 BC and 2935 BC as a bank and ditch enclosure measuring about 360 feet in diameter. Within the outer edge of the enclosed area was a circle of 56 pits, each about 3 feet 3 inches in diameter, known as the Aubrey holes, after John Aubrey, the 17th century antiquarian who first identified them. Recently Mike Parker-Pearson and the Stonehenge Riverside Project investigated the Aubrey Holes and found 60 cremation burials dumped in Aubrey Hole 7 by William Hawley when he investigated Stonehenge in the 1920s. Hawley had initially decided that the Aubrey Holes once contained small standing stones that were later pulled out, but had subsequently changed his mind. In the bottom of Aubrey Hole 7 the Stonehenge Riverside Project found the undisturbed residue of a layer of chalk packing and a patch of crushed chalk caused by the weight of a standing stone. They concluded that Hawley was right in his initial estimate, and that the Aubrey Holes once contained bluestones, meaning that Stonehenge was a stone monument from the beginning.[15]

For much of the 3rd millennium BC Stonehenge was a cemetery. Cremated bones have been found in all but eight of the 34 Aubrey Holes so far excavated and on the basis of cremations found in Aubrey Holes and ditches, Mike Pitts has estimated that there could be as many as 240 people buried at Stonehenge.[16] Recently the Stonehenge Riverside Project has obtained radiocarbon dates on eight samples of human bone collected at Stonehenge, five of which date to the third millennium BC. The earliest date was for the

1: The Age of Megaliths (1)

Distant view of Stonehenge near Amesbury in Wiltshire, with a least three pairs of sarsen stones topped by lintel stones (trilithons) clearly visible (author's photograph).

Close-up view of Stonehenge, showing a pair of sarsen stones topped by a lintel stone (trilithon) in the foreground (author's photograph).

cremation burial of an adult from the lower fill of Aubrey Hole 32—this cremation dated from 3030 to 2880 BC. A cremation burial of a young or mature adult from the middle fill of the Stonehenge ditch dates to 2930–2870 BC. Human skull fragments from the northern ditch fill and from the eastern ditch fill date to 2890–2630 BC and 2880–2570 BC respectively. Stonehenge's ditch was re-cut (partly dug out) during the period 2560–2140 BC and the third cremation burial—that of a 25-year-old woman—was placed in this new ditch on the ditch's northern side (in layer 3893). Its date of 2570–2340 BC places her death within or after the period when the sarsens were erected.[17] These radiocarbon dates suggest that Stonehenge was used as a cemetery over a period of 500 years—this amounts to one burial every two years, and suggests they were drawn from a very small and select living population, interred there "because of their special status as members of an elite dynasty of rulers."[18]

Stonehenge is aligned on the midsummer sunrise, when the sun rises not above the Heel Stone (as many people think), but along the axis of the sarsen monument to its left. The Heel Stone is now known to have been one of a pair, one on each side of the axis, and there were further upright pillars between these two outliers and the sarsen circle. This arrangement would have given the impression of the stones forming a corridor along which solstitial sunlight would have shone into the center of the monument. However, its alignment to the midwinter sunset may be just as important: the Altar Stone is oriented to the southwest, and the ceremonial approach along the Avenue is from the northeast, that is, toward the midsummer sunset.[19]

Stonehenge is a unique monument, but it can't be understood without reference to the nearby henge of Durrington Walls, just two miles to the northeast of Stonehenge (a henge is an earthwork enclosure surrounded by a bank and a ditch inside the bank).

The Heel Stone at Stonehenge. The sun rises to the left of this on the day of the summer solstice (author's photograph).

Durrington Walls is the largest henge in the British Isles, over 42 acres in area and surrounded by a chalk-cut ditch 16 feet deep with a large bank outside. Excavations at Durrington Walls in 1967 uncovered two timber circles: the smaller Northern Circle and the Southern Circle, over 130 feet in diameter and set just inside the henge's east entrance. The 1967 excavations at Durrington Walls also uncovered enormous quantities of Late Neolithic Grooved Ware pottery and animal bones whose minimal breakage patterns have been considered as evidence for large-scale feasting. Most of the bones were of domestic pigs, and more recent work has demonstrated that some of these had been shot with arrows and barbecued.[20] Outside the Southern Circle's entrance, the 1967 excavations located a gravel and chalk platform on which a large fireplace had been set. This might have been the fire on which pigs were roasted.[21]

Like Stonehenge, Durrington Walls has a solar orientation. The southeast entrance of the Southern Circle at Durrington Walls was aligned precisely on the midwinter sunrise. In 2005 the Stonehenge Riverside Project discovered a monumental avenue linking Durrington Walls henge to the River Avon. It was originally about 328 feet long and its estimated width is over 65 feet. In contrast to the midwinter sunrise orientation of the Southern Circle which it approaches, the avenue's solsticial alignment is in the opposite direction, within 1.5° of the midsummer sunset.[22] Together with the Southern Circle's midwinter sunrise axis, the Durrington Walls avenue provides a complementary arrangement to that at Stonehenge where the avenue and stone circle are aligned on the midwinter sunset in one direction and the midsummer sunrise in the other.[23]

Boskednan stone circle, also known as Nine Maidens, is near Madron in the West Penwith district of west Cornwall. It consists of 11 stones, 3 recumbent, though it originally featured at least 19. From Boskednan the sky is dominated by Carn Galver, a hill half a mile to the northwest, and the profile of another hill, Carn Kenidjack, is prominent in the distance three miles to the southwest. The two highest stones on the northern side of the circle, over six feet high, would originally have flanked Carn Galver when observed from the center of the circle. A menhir a short distance to the northwest of the circle, a cairn placed immediately to the south-southwest, and a series of cairns situated on a slight ridge to the northwest all indicate the orientational axis and processional route to Carn Galver from the circle. This is also the direction of sunset at the summer solstice,[24] when the sun set to the north of due west.

Earthworks and Timber Structures with Astronomical Alignments

As Durrington Walls shows, not all astronomically aligned monuments in the Neolithic were built of stone. Marden henge in the Vale of Pewsey is one of the largest henges in Britain, with an area of some 35 acres. It is set hard against the floodplain of one branch of the River Avon, which rises nearby at Beechingstoke and is supplemented by a number of small rivulets fed by springs in the immediate locality.[25] Springs appear to have been incorporated within and around the Marden enclosure, and even today the enclosure ditch still holds water for part of the year. Within the southeastern entranceway was a series of compact flint gravel layers clearly forming a deliberately laid surface and sitting within a shallow linear cut. The gravel deposits were made up of three distinct re-metalling episodes and may well form a routeway into and out of the henge; if so, the projected line would lead southeast down to the River Avon—this may be comparable to the gravel routeway identified leading from the southeast entranceway to the river at Durrington Walls. It is possible that the southeast routeway may have been aligned on the solstice, or sunrise more generally.[26]

Marden henge was first excavated in 1969 by Geoffrey Wainwright, who identified Neolithic remains including antler picks, flintwork, and the skeleton of a young female near the north entrance, as well as a possible circular timber structure. The henge was again excavated in 2010 by English Heritage. In the southern part of the henge is a circular enclosure 295 to 312 feet in diameter, with an internal ditch and an external bank some 3 feet high. Here the English Heritage team excavated a "well-preserved rectangular chalk building surface, which had a large sunken area containing evidence for a hearth in its centre." The surface measured 24 feet 3 inches long and 16 feet 5 inches wide, while the sunken area within the surface was roughly square (12 feet 5 inches by 10 feet 10 inches).[27] The central part of the sunken area within the building contained evidence for a circular hearth; intense burning had modified the color of the chalk within the hearth, turning it a pinky-orange color. A discrete deposit of over one hundred sherds of exceptionally decorated Grooved Ware from a minimum of seven vessels was recorded on the southeastern side of the floor surface and clearly indicates a placed deposit, possibly in the entrance of the building. Outside the building and on the northeastern side was another hearth, this time filled and surrounded by a thick layer of charcoal. Leary and Field say[28]:

> The presence of two hearths, one internal and the other external, is interesting. One interpretation is that the structure formed a sweat-lodge like building, whereby stones heated in the external fire ... were brought into the structure and placed in the central hearth; water, perhaps obtained from the henge ditch or the Avon, could then be poured on these stones to produce a steam bath or sauna effect, likely as part of a purification ritual.

On the opposite side of the building, and immediately outside, was a midden deposit, dominated by animal bones, mostly pig and representing joints of meat. The midden also contained 135 sherds of Grooved Ware from a minimum of thirteen vessels. The sherds were large and well preserved, and are exceptional in terms of their decoration. Three bowls are represented, all with neatly executed internal decoration, as are several decorated jars. Two lug handles are present, one of which may be anthropomorphic. Leary and Field say[29] that the midden "clearly originated from a single event that involved the preparation of a large amount of food, and it is tempting to see it as the result of a feast, presumably associated with the use of the building or part of a closing ceremony when the structure was demolished."

As we'll see in Chapter 3, sweat lodges, often known as burnt mounds, became widespread in the Bronze Age and were probably used in religious rituals or ceremonies, as the midden outside the building suggests.

Sometimes, monuments with astronomical alignments were neither megaliths nor timber structures, but massive earthworks. One of the most spectacular Neolithic monuments in Dorset is the Dorset Cursus, a cursus monument around 6.25 miles long which runs roughly southwest-northeast between Thickthorn Down and Martin Down in northeast Dorset (a cursus is a long and relatively narrow earthwork enclosure). Narrow and roughly parallel-sided, it follows a slightly sinuous course across the chalk downland, crossing a river and several valleys. The monument in fact is made up of two cursuses laid out end to end. The earlier southwestern (Gussage) portion terminates on Bottlebush

Down; the northeastern (Pentridge) cursus then continues on a slightly different alignment, adjusting its course slightly on a few occasions before terminating on Martin Down.[30] The cursus is aligned with the movement of the sun at the mid-winter solstice[31]:

> The North-Eastern end of this monument terminates just below the ridge on Bottlebush Down. Observers standing here and looking back along the course of the Cursus, which would have presumably been kept clear of vegetation, could watch the mid-winter sunset directly behind the silhouetted long barrow on Gussage Hill.

There was a Neolithic ritual complex at Dorchester-on-Thames, Oxfordshire, where the River Thame meets the Thames. Perhaps the earliest monument on the site is the long enclosure known as Site VIII, which was excavated in the 1940s. Finds were few—part of a human jaw was found within the site, prompting suggestions that it may have been a mortuary enclosure.[32] This was followed by the Dorchester-on-Thames cursus, which was probably constructed in the second half of the 4th millennium BC. It consisted of two broadly parallel ditches some 194 feet apart, running for at least a mile in a more-or-less northwest-southeast direction. The western section of the cursus was oriented upon the midsummer sunset.[33]

At Godmanchester near Huntingdon in Cambridgeshire, there was a large trapezoidal ditched enclosure 249 yards across at the open end, 367 yards long, with an "entrance" 183 yards wide, which included a cursus extending to the River Ouse. The site was carefully excavated and recorded during the late 1980s under a rescue archaeology program by English Heritage's Central Excavation Unit. The site included 24 large post pits set inside an internal bank with an external ditch 13 feet wide. Charcoal from post pipes within the post pits was carbon-dated to the beginning of the 4th millennium BC. Paired posts "offered accurate bearings to a nearby low-lying horizon at possibly significant astronomical azimuths. Calculations and analysis demonstrate that the post-hole alignments did indicate a full set of the limiting positions of the Sun and Moon at the solstices, equinoxes, and major and minor lunar standstills to very good accuracy."[34]

The Thornborough Monument Complex is on the River Ure at West Tanfield in North Yorkshire, some 6 miles north of Ripon. The first monuments were constructed during the Early Neolithic. At least one cursus, but possibly two, and a triple-ditched round barrow known to have covered human burial deposits, are thought to date to the 4th millennium BC. This early complex was superseded during the Late Neolithic by three massive double-entranced henges, each sited about 546 yards apart on a northwest to southeast alignment. The henges are evenly spaced from one another, are almost exactly identical in both their size and design, and possess double entrances broadly aligned upon one another. The southern causeway of the central henge was located very exactly over the earlier cursus, whose largely denuded ditches would have carefully delimited the entrance's inner and outer extent.[35]

The eastern end of the main cursus is aligned on the midsummer sunrise, while its western terminal would have framed the three setting stars of Orion's main belt around 3300–3000 BC.[36] All three henges can be associated with the rising of Sirius in 3000 BC[37]: "as the star rises over the eastern edge of the central and southern henges as viewed from the center of the northern and central henges, respectively, and the eastern bank terminal as viewed from within the southern henge, Orion's Belt would have been above the western bank terminal of all three southern henge entrances." Orion's Belt "would have first become visible toward the end of summer, initially in mid–August for an hour or so, but by mid–September for much of the night, at a time of year when the landscape had begun to change."[38]

The rising and setting of Orion and Sirius have been significant events since the earliest times. The Greek poet Hesiod, who lived around 700 BC, refers to Orion in his *Works and Days*[39]:

> when the Pleiades and Hyades and strong Orion begin to set [i.e. at the end of October], then remember to plough in season. But if desire for uncomfortable sea-faring seize you; when the Pleiades plunge into the misty sea [i.e. again towards the end of October] to escape Orion's rude strength, then truly gales of all kinds rage.

Hesiod also mentions Sirius:

> When the piercing power and sultry heat of the sun abate, and almighty Zeus sends the autumn rains [October], and men's flesh comes to feel far easier,—for then the star Sirius passes over the heads of men, who are born to misery, only a little while by day and takes greater share of night.

Of course Hesiod was writing over two millennia after the construction of the Monument Complex, by which time the rising and setting times of Orion and Sirius had changed.

No timber circles have been discovered in the Thornborough henges, but adjacent to the southern henge a double pit alignment was excavated in 1998–9. It is at least 382 yards in length, with pits every 16 to 23 feet. The rows of the alignment are between 32 and 36 feet apart. The existence of post-pipes (the remains of upright timbers) and stone packing suggested that most contained post settings. There was a gap of some 98 feet in the eastern line of pits, where it passed closest to the northern entrance of the southern henge, suggesting that the monument was part of a processional route which incorporated the earlier henges. One of the excavated pits contained the upper half of an inverted Deverel-Rimbury vessel and another three sherds of Collared Urn. A radiocarbon date of 1750–1590 BC was obtained from a small charcoal fragment in one pit, indicating that the double pit alignment was constructed in the Early Bronze Age.[40]

Burial in the Neolithic

Chamber Tombs and Long Barrows

Classical writers said that the Druids believed in reincarnation and practiced a "cult of the head," so clearly it is important to know how Neolithic Britons treated their dead. In 3rd millennium BC Stonehenge, cremation was the norm, but during the Early Neolithic (4th millennium BC) burial practices were very different. At this time, the most common form of burial was in long barrows or chamber tombs. Long barrows consist of a large mound of earth, trapezoidal or oval in shape, rarely more than about 164 feet in length and up to 82 feet in width, often constructed over a timber mortuary chamber. Chamber tombs are megalithic structures built of large stones then covered with earth. Stones often form a passage or corridor leading to the chamber and there is frequently a monumental façade at the entrance. Occasionally the tomb will have side chambers called transepts.

Neolithic tombs are found throughout Britain, from northern Scotland to southern England. A good example of a chambered tomb in northern Scotland is the Tomb of the

Eagles, or Isbister Chambered Cairn, on South Ronaldsay in the Orkney Islands, where the disarticulated remains of 342 individuals were found. The chambered cairn is known as the Tomb of the Eagles because during excavation of the tomb, the bones of white-tailed sea-eagles were found in a compartment at the south end of the chamber. The earliest activity at this site has been radiocarbon dated to around 3150 BC and the tomb continued in use until about 2400 BC, when the chamber was deliberately filled in and sealed. At around 1600 BC a cist burial, containing the remains of three individuals, was inserted into the rubble mound,[41] indicating that the tomb continued to be used into the Early Bronze Age. This is reinforced by further investigation of the eagle bones. The archaeologist Mike Pitts says[42] that among the bones, which included some 16,000 human fragments, "were 725 from birds, of which Don Bramwell identified 641 as white-tailed sea eagle representing at least eight birds." The sea-eagle bones were thought to have been placed there when the tomb was constructed around 3000 BC, but recent tests have shown that the birds died between 2450 BC and 2050 BC, in the Early Bronze Age.

One example of along barrow in the north of England is Willerby Wold Long Barrow in North Yorkshire, a few miles from Scarborough, which was excavated by Greenwell in the mid–19th century, and shown to be one of the crematorium long barrows peculiar to Yorkshire. From 1958 to 1960 a more extensive excavation was undertaken to clear the whole eastern end of the mound. The barrow was a trapezoidal mound 122 feet long, 35 feet broad at the east end and flanked by ditches on the north and south sides. It had been erected over the site of a trapezoidal mortuary enclosure which had had a post-set facade at the eastern end incorporating a ritual-pit at the center and another set behind. Bones of several bodies had been placed in the crematorium deposit and had been cremated by the firing of the deposit after the erection of the mound.[43]

One of the best examples of a Neolithic tomb in Wales is Parc Le Breos, a transepted long cairn at Ilston in the Gower Peninsula, not far from Swansea. Parc Le Breos, named after the great medieval deer park in which it now lies, was excavated in the early 1960s, and "samples have recently been subjected to radiocarbon dating in the most complete dating programme undertaken for any chambered tomb in Wales." The tomb was in use for as long as 800 years, from 3800 BC, or for as little as 300 years. Human remains recovered from the chamber represent an estimated min-

Cathole Cave near the chambered tomb at Parc le Breos, Gower Peninsula, south Wales, which may have been used for excarnation in the Neolithic. November 9, 2008 (Daicaregos).

imum of 40 individuals. Some skeletal remains showed evidence for scavenging by carnivores. Bodies may have lain exposed for various periods of time, possibly in nearby caves like the Cathole Cave, and were deposited as defleshed parcels of bone, not bulky bodies. A passageway deposit showed no such damage and was therefore placed in the tomb as a fleshed corpse.[44]

Among the Neolithic tombs in southern England, two stand out. The Neolithic long barrow at Ascott-under-Wychwood in Oxfordshire was excavated between 1965 and 1969. The excavators found at least five discrete, burial deposits, three of which were contained inside stone cists defined by large stones, arranged in an unusual manner across the long axis of the barrow towards its narrower, western end. Provisional totals have reached a minimum of twenty individuals, many represented only by a few bones—a feature which is consistent in tombs of the same period in Britain and which is generally attributed to a practice involving the burial or exposure of corpses elsewhere before final interment in the barrow. Preliminary examination of the remains has shown that their deposition took place when the bones were partially, and in some cases completely, free of tissue attachments.[45]

The most famous Neolithic tomb in Wiltshire is West Kennet Long Barrow at Avebury, to the west of Marlborough, excavated in 1859 by Thurnam and in 1955–6 by Piggott. The chambers of the long barrow were constructed of large sarsen boulders with drystone walling and contained the remains of at least 46 individuals including both inhumations and cremations. Many of the burials were incomplete—some bones were missing, while others had been grouped together in particular parts of the barrow. For example long bones and a quantity of vertebrae had been placed by the rear wall of the north west chamber. Radiocarbon dating indicates that the barrow was built between 3670 BC and 3635 BC.[46]

Causewayed Enclosures

Burials are occasionally found in causewayed enclosures, which are Early Neolithic earthworks surrounded by discontinuous ditches separated by causeways. One of the

Entrance to West Kennet Long Barrow near Avebury in Wiltshire (Wikimedia).

best known causewayed enclosures is Windmill Hill at Avebury, near West Kennet Long Barrow. Windmill Hill encloses an area of 20 acres, making it one of the largest causewayed enclosures in England. The enclosure has three circuits, defined by the inner, middle and outer ditches. The smallest, inner ditch has no trace of a bank, and the northwest part probably had an entrance. The middle ditch is circular, and may have traces of an inner bank, and a possible entrance in the form of a wide causeway, slightly offset from the entrance in the inner ditch. The largest, outer ditch has a bank which in parts survives to 2 feet 3 inches high and 16 feet 5 inches wide.[47] Windmill Hill was first excavated by Alexander Keiller between 1925 and 1929, and most recently by Alasdair Whittle in 1990. Huge quantities of pottery, worked flint and animal bone—including whole skeletons of a dog, a pig and a goat—were found during the excavations, mainly in the ditches, as were smaller amounts of human bone, worked chalk, other worked stone and charred plant remains. The pottery included pieces of about 1,300 different pots, while the excavations produced approximately 95,000 pieces of struck flint. The bone has been radiocarbon dated, and according to the archaeologist Rosamund Cleal,[48] most of it belongs to the period 3600 BC–3300 BC:

> Analysis carried out in preparation for the eventual publication demonstrated how exotic some of these items were. Some of the pots, it turned out, had been made in the extreme south-west of Cornwall, on the Lizard, some 115 miles from Windmill Hill. Some of the stone axes had travelled a similar distance from Cornish sources, while others, in later Neolithic levels, had come from sources in North Wales and the Lake District.

Cleal says that Windmill Hill was clearly a great gathering place:

> The predominance of cattle bones and apparent absence of domestic structures led Piggott to interpret it largely as a corral and market for cattle. More recent interpretations have focused on evidence for ritual activity, notably on certain types of structural deposition of artifacts in the ditches, and the recurrent association of certain types of objects with one another.

The people there, she says, "almost certainly engaged in feasting and other ceremonies which reinforced their sense of identity."

As for the burials at Windmill Hill, human remains were found in the ditch, mostly as single, scattered finds. Three individuals were represented by more or less complete skeletons: an adult male, a child and an infant. Several children were represented by skulls only.[49]

Another well known causewayed enclosure is Hambledon Hill near Blandford Forum in Dorset. The enclosure was excavated in 1977 by Roger Mercer, who found that the causewayed ditches of the enclosure, and the inner ditches of cross-dykes 1 and 2, contained deposits of animal bone and pottery, as well as the remains of about 25 human skulls and two infant burials. Many had been placed under flint cairns, as primary deposits, and suggest that the site was used for funerary rituals.[50]

Human skulls have also been found at Etton causewayed enclosure at Maxey in Cambridgeshire, which was excavated between 1982 and 1987 in advance of gravel extraction. This causewayed enclosure occupied a floodplain "island" within a relict stream meander in the Welland valley at Maxey, in the far north of Cambridgeshire near the border with Lincolnshire. The enclosure is defined by a single circuit of interrupted ditches enclosing an area 196 yards east-west by 153–174 yards north-south. Three principal entrances were noted to the north, east and west, but none could be located to the south because the southernmost part of the enclosure had been destroyed by a broad drainage channel, the Maxey Cut. The excavations recovered large quantities of waterlogged material from the ditches. Human remains, pottery, animals bone and lithic artifacts forming apparently structured deposits, typically occurred at the ends of ditch segments. Recent research into the dating of the enclosure suggests that Neolithic activity at Etton started probably in 3725–3670 BC. The primary use of the enclosure ended probably in 3310–3210 BC.[51]

The human remains found in the enclosure ditch included a cranium found near the butt end of the ditch at causeway G, a skull fragment found at causeway H, the frontal bone of a skull found at causeway K, fragments of a skull found at causeway M, the right parietal of a skull found at causeway M and a number of thigh bones. All the human remains show evidence of damage caused by exposure to an abrasive environment, and this probably occurred in an open-air or surface context. This interpretation is supported by the high frequency of canid gnawed bones (50 percent), which suggests that human remains were available for scavenging by carnivores such as dogs or foxes.[52]

The structured deposits at Etton included two particularly striking ones: a human cranium placed rightside-up and "facing" the causeway, together with a red deer antler object (perhaps a "baton") and the bones of other animals[53]; and an inverted fox head alongside an inverted Mildenhall bowl, an antler comb, and another complete vessel, but this time rightside-up.[54]

Burial Rites in the Early Neolithic

The disarticulated state of human remains from the long barrows, chamber tombs and causewayed enclosures shows that bodies were not simply buried in the Early Neolithic, but subject to a process known as excarnation, or de-fleshing, in which the body is allowed to decompose, and the "dry" bones are then given a second burial. This may seem like a macabre practice to us, but it has a very clear religious motivation. Among many people who practice this burial rite, it is believed that the soul of the deceased cannot leave the body until the flesh has decomposed. While the flesh is decaying, the deceased is neither alive nor dead, and is unable to enter the "society of the dead," and leads a pitiful existence on the fringes of human habitation. Once the flesh is decayed, the dry bones are recovered, a great feast is held, the bones are given a second burial, and the deceased is then free to enter the land of the ancestors.[55] Secondary burial may involve all the bones of the deceased, but in Neolithic Britain it was often only selected bones such as skulls and long bones which were reburied.

Evidence for excarnation in Neolithic Britain has been studied by a number of archaeologists, including Martin Smith,[56] who studied the human bone from the long barrow at Adlestrop near Stow-on-the-Wold in Gloucestershire. Amongst the identifiable fragments of bone, 76 (20 percent) exhibited evidence consistent with scavenging by vertebrates. The most likely agents responsible for this were thought to be either wolves or domestic dogs. The evidence suggests, says Smith, that bodies were left exposed for a limited period during which time they were accessible to scavenging animals. The remains were then collected as part of a multi-stage mortuary rite ending finally with deposition in the long barrow.

As I said, the scavenger is most likely to have been the domestic dog, and remains of dogs are often found in the Neolithic tombs of Gloucestershire. At West Tump long barrow, Brimpsfield, seven bones from a dog aged less than 6 or 7 months were identified, while at Sale's Lot long barrow at Withington, the femur of a young fox or dog was recovered from the entrance pathway. At Notgrove a large dog mandible (jaw bone) was identified from Chamber A, and eight identifiable fragments were recorded from the "Passage"—four metapodials from fore- and hind-limbs and four phalanges (toe bones) from at least two adult dogs. The largest bone (a 3rd metacarpal from a dog's paw) was comparable in size to a modern female greyhound. The original excavation report for Nympsfield long barrow at Frocester also indicates the presence of at least two different sizes of dogs, in a grave containing parts of at least three human skeletons on the south side of the passage at the west end. Levitan records the presence of a complete dog scapula (shoulder blade) from the north chambered area at Hazleton North, and dog remains were found alongside human remains at Eyford Hill long barrow, Upper Slaughter.[57]

So we might say that the Iron Age "cult of the head" started in the Early Neolithic, except that it was not only the head that was venerated, but a variety of bones, especially the long bones which, like the skull, are the bones that are most likely to survive the ravages of excarnation and exposure.

Neolithic Religion

We can only guess at the religion of the Neolithic people of Britain, but we know that cattle played an important role in the life of Neolithic Britons, including their religious life. For example, Boles Barrow (also known as Bowl's Barrow), at Heytesbury near Warminster in southwest Wiltshire, was excavated in 1801 (William Cunnington), 1864 (John Thurnham), and 1885–6 (W. and H. Cunnington). The excavations indicated that there was a primary deposit of at least 16 skeletons, on a flint pavement at ground level, with heads and horns of oxen, overlaid by sarsens.[58]

A Neolithic long barrow at Beckhampton Firs near Bishops Cannings in Wiltshire was completely excavated by Smith in 1964. A few sherds of Neolithic pottery were found in the mound, and animal bones including the skulls of three oxen were found both in and under the mound.[59]

At Stonehenge, two cattle jaws were found in the terminals of the henge ditch, one either side of the northeast entrance. They are from two different animals, and were deposited as clean bones. The radiocarbon dates of the two jaws were significantly earlier than the dates of antlers from the base of the same ditch, which suggested they had been kept for some time before finally being buried.[60] Thirteen cattle skulls were found at Windmill Hill, Avebury, and ten of these were in the terminals of ditches.[61]

At Sixpenny Handley in the northeast of Dorset, a pit excavated by Pitt Rivers in 1893 contained the disarticulated remains of a human skeleton and, lower down, 12 ox bones "laid out as if placed on a flat surface."[62] Pottery recovered by Pitt Rivers from the feature has since been identified as sherds of Early Neolithic bowls, Peterborough Ware and Early Bronze Age Beaker vessels.

At the large trapezoidal ditched enclosure at Godmanchester in Cambridgeshire, the southern ditch terminal contained an ox skull placed at its bottom, and the northern terminal featured two cattle mandibles on top of the primary fill. A deer antler and a lower cattle limb came from post holes.[63]

We have no idea what cattle meant to Neolithic Britons, but the German archaeologist Axel Pollex believes that cattle in Neolithic Europe were associated with the sun.[64] It is likely, says Pollex, that cattle were used in Neolithic Europe to pull wagons. At Budakalasz in Hungary a clay model of a wagon was found at a cemetery where a cattle skeleton was also excavated; the cemetery was associated with the Baden culture (3600 BC–2800 BC). A pottery vessel from Bronocice in Poland, dated to between 3635 BC and 3370 BC, shows the symbols of rain, water, cereal-ears or lightning. In addition, there is one symbol showing a four-wheeled wagon bearing a circle, which Pollex interprets as a sun-symbol. Pollex concludes: "The Bronocice bowl suggests that the sun played an important role as this is the only sign decorating the wagon motif, and in this object it was probably "symbolically" pulled by cattle."

A Neolithic Priesthood?

The Neolithic was a period when dozens of astronomically aligned monuments were constructed, and it seems highly likely that the construction of these monuments was organized by a body of religious experts. The Scottish archaeologist Euan MacKie has been arguing for the last thirty years or more that during the Neolithic there was a priesthood in Britain responsible for designing and building a range of Neolithic monuments, from Stonehenge in Wiltshire to Maeshowe in Orkney. In this he was inspired by the work of the Scottish engineer Alexander Thom, who spent many years analyzing megalithic sites and concluded that they were built according to a measurement he called the *megalithic yard* (about 2.72 feet), in order to predict events tied to a *solar calendar*. Much of his work is highly technical, but the concept of the solar calendar is fairly straightforward. Mackie, like Thom, believes that Neolithic Britons used a solar calendar which divided the year into sixteen months of 22 or 23 days. The year was first divided into four by the winter solstice (December 21 or 22), the spring equinox (March 20), the summer solstice (between June 20 and 22), and the autumn equinox (September 22). The dates of the "eighths" were calculated by working out the halfway positions between solstices and equinoxes, and may coincide with the four great Celtic festivals at the beginning of February, May, August and November. These festivals are Imbolc (1 February), Beltane (1 May), Lughnasadh (1 August), and Samhain (1 November).[65] The name Imbolc is from Old Irish *i mbloc*, "in the belly," referring to the pregnancy of ewes, and it marked the start of lambing. Beltane probably means "bright fire," and it marked the time when new lambs and calves were turned out to graze. Lughnasadh, "Festival of Lugh," marked the beginning of the harvest. Samhain probably means "Assembly," and marked the time when the flocks and herds were rounded up. The four Celtic festivals survive to a greater or lesser degree up to the present day: Imbolc as Candlemas (the feast of the Presentation of Jesus at the Temple), Beltane as May Day, Lughnasadh as Lammas (the festival of the wheat harvest), and Samhain as All Saints' Day (Halloween).

The End of the Neolithic

The Neolithic was a very productive time in terms of the building of monuments with astronomical alignments and the construction of great tombs for the elite of the community. With the focus on astronomy and the possible birth of a priesthood dedicated to the amassing of astronomical knowledge, the Neolithic may well have been the time when the Druid priesthood first came into being. The Neolithic was a time of great communal projects—the construction of Stonehenge probably involved hundreds if not thousands of people just to bring the stones to the place where they were erected—but this was soon to end. Metal and metal-working came to Britain, and with it came powerful individuals who transformed Neolithic society, bringing new forms of burial and new ways of commemorating the dead.

CHAPTER 2

The Age of Megaliths (2): Rich Burials and More Astronomy in the Early Bronze Age

The Late Neolithic/Early Bronze Age in Europe

The Domestication of Horses

In the Late Neolithic, life in Europe began to change with the domestication of the horse. The horse was probably first domesticated around 3500 BC by the Eneolithic (Copper Age) Botai Culture of northern Kazakhstan.[1] A team of researchers led by Dr. Alan Outram of the University of Exeter examined the teeth of a number of horses from four sites in northern Kazakhstan including Botai, and found evidence for biting damage resulting from harnessing with a bridle or similar restraint. Analysis of organic residues in cooking pots showed that mare's milk was being consumed by the people of the Botai Culture, just as it is today (fermented mare's milk, or *kumis*, is still a traditional drink in Kazakhstan).

It's not clear whether the horses were ridden or used to pull carts, but early Bronze Age burials with the remains of wooden wheels have been found in the Lower Don in Russia, at Koldyri and Kuban. The discovery at Kuban near the Black Sea consisted of the remains of a wagon with wooden wheels approximately 2 feet in diameter. The partial remains of a similar wheeled cart have also been found at Kalymykia near the Caspian Sea.[2]

We don't really know when horses were first domesticated in central Europe. Although it is difficult to distinguish wild from domesticated horses in faunal assemblages, bones found in the Late Funnel Beaker-Baden occupations at Bronocice (southern Poland) around 2900–2700 BC do represent domesticated horses. In Switzerland horses were introduced by the Corded Ware peoples around 2700 BC, while in Greece the first domesticated horses appeared during the Middle Helladic period, 2100–1700 BC.[3]

The Corded Ware Culture

The domestication of the horse and the use of wheeled carts almost certainly enabled the dissemination of two great cultures of Late Neolithic/Early Bronze Age Europe, the Corded Ware Culture and the Bell-Beaker Culture. The Corded Ware Culture (2900 BC to 2400 BC) stretched from western Ukraine through Poland and Germany to the Netherlands, and from southern Scandinavia to the Czech Republic. The beginnings of the

Corded Ware culture, say the Indo-European language scholars Edgar Polomé and Werner Winter[4]

> is defined by a few sites found on the North European Plain from the Netherlands to the western Ukraine. In the Netherlands, the earliest of the Corded Ware graves … can be dated as early as the late fourth millennium.… An equally early presence for Corded Ware graves in north Germany can be inferred from a few graves and a scatter of disputed A-Axes.

Typological comparisons, they say, suggest that the earliest Corded Ware beakers of Malopolska, in the southeast of Poland, and the pre–Carpathian beakers of southeast Poland and western Ukraine may go back to equally early times. The "thin scatter of Corded Ware sites across the North European Plain in combination with the absence of Corded Ware in both southern Central Europe and southern Scandinavia supports the hypothesis of an expansion of steppe elements at the time of the Pit Grave III culture"[5] (the Pit Grave or Yamna culture arose on the Pontic Steppe of western Ukraine and southern Russia in the late Copper/Early Bronze Age). The archaeologist Andrew Sherratt says of Corded Ware[6]:

> Decoration using impressed cord had been known before, on the steppes and more latterly in the eastern half of the North European Plain: but it now it took the characteristic form of a drinking vessel known as a beaker—a tall, handleless pot with an everted rim, holding a litre or so of liquid, and decorated in horizontal bands on its upper half. Such pots are typically found in male graves, accompanied by a stone axe with a shaft hole and a single drooping blade, often called a "battleaxe."

The Bell-Beaker Culture

Origins

Closely linked to the Corded Ware Culture is the Bell-Beaker Culture, a cultural movement that spread over wide parts of Europe between 2800 BC and 1900 BC, from the upper Danube in the east, and Germany between the Elbe and the Rhine, through the Low Countries and France, to Spain, Portugal, Britain and Ireland in the west. The Bell-Beaker culture probably arose on the Atlantic coast of Iberia. Early in the 3rd millennium BC, people living in regions around the lower Tagus River in Portugal began building fortified settlements and smelting copper ore.[7] One such settlement was Zambujal, some 30 miles north of Lisbon, which today is 8 miles from the Atlantic, but at the time was half a mile from an arm of the sea. The settlement was established around 3000 BC, and copper manufacture was carried out at all periods of its existence.[8]

With the establishment of fortified settlements and the manufacture of copper, long-distance exchange systems extending to the Atlantic coast of Morocco developed, in which copper was bartered for exotic commodities like gold, ivory, and ostrich shells. Around the 28th century BC, an elite culture emerged, characterized by a refined ceramic drinking vessel, the beaker, used in daily life and in burial. In funerary contexts, emphasis was placed on the individual whose status was symbolized by the finely crafted beaker and the equipment of the hunter: bows and arrows, a copper dagger-knife, and sometimes a stone version of the wrist guard designed to protect the wrist from the lash of the bowstring. Other exotic items made of gold or ostrich shell might also be buried with the dead.[9]

In the 27th and 26th centuries BC, this "Beaker package" spread widely into western Europe, where it is characterized by the distribution of a particular form of beaker known as the Maritime Bell Beaker. This spread took place over a wide front, overland through the center of Iberia, by sea into the Mediterranean to southern France and beyond, and via the Atlantic northwards to southern Armorica (Brittany).

By 2500 BC the Maritime Bell Beaker and the "Beaker package" had spread throughout western Europe as far as the Rhine valley. It was disseminated by way of major river valleys like the Rhône-Saône and the Garonne-Gironde in the southern half of France, and overland routes like the one leading from the lower Loire valley across the Gâtinais (an area to the south of Paris) to the central Paris basin and from there northwards to the lower Rhine. The 3rd millennium networks are clearly defined by the distribution of Grand-Pressigny flint, a fine honey-colored stone mined in the valleys of the Claise and Creuse in the vicinity of Poitiers, and frequently found in Beaker period burials in the Paris basin and the lower and middle Rhine.[10]

When the "Beaker package" reached the Rhine valley, it encountered communities who had already adopted the Corded Ware-Single Grave Culture. Corded Ware is pottery in which twisted cord was impressed into the wet clay to create various decorative patterns and motifs; the Single Grave Culture was characterized by single burials under barrows, usually accompanied by a stone battle-ax, amber beads and pottery vessels. What emerged in this contact zone was a hybrid culture characterized by a distinctive beaker type, the All Over Ornamented Beaker, frequently found in single graves accompanied by items of Grand-Pressigny flint. From this contact zone ideas and values of the Corded Ware-Single Grave Culture flowed westwards along the lower Rhine-lower Loire axis, merging with Bell-Beaker concepts spreading eastwards from the Atlantic coast. The result was a "highly innovative culture with many regional variants extending in a broad arc from Armorica across northern France to the Low Countries." It was from this zone that Britain was to receive its Beaker culture.[11]

Spread

We don't know for certain why the Beaker people spread so widely across Europe, but they may have been motivated partly by the search for copper. Evidence of Bronze Age copper mining has been found at sites all over Bell-Beaker Europe. The settlement at Mariahilfbergl in Brixlegg, Austria, is located on a hilltop above the middle Inn Valley in the Tyrolean Alps, approximately 30 miles to the east of Innsbruck, and was excavated in 1999. The most remarkable finds were pieces of copper slag found close to a fireplace—the earliest indication of copper metallurgy in the Tyrol. The archaeological association with the Late Neolithic is confirmed by a radiocarbon date of charcoal from pieces of baked clay, partly mixed with green copper minerals (3960–3650 BC).[12]

Elsewhere in Beaker Europe, copper was probably mined at Cabrières (Hérault), in the far south of France. Principal mining sites are Vierge, Broum (a natural cave), Roussignole and Pioch Farrus. At Roussigole an arrow head of the Palmela type has been found which indicates contact with Iberia. A radiocarbon date from the lowest stratum in the Broum cave sets the beginning of the habitation and/or exploitation between 2825 BC and 2300 BC.[13]

As mentioned earlier, copper was worked at Zambujal in southern Portugal, which flourished in the 3rd millennium BC. Since its discovery in 1932, intermittent excavation at Zambujal has produced 900 copper objects weighing 6 to 9 pounds in total. The most numerous items are metal droplets and unidentifiable small, broken or semi-molten tool fragments, while only about 80 complete copper artifacts exist.[14]

Closer to home, excavations at Ross Island on Lough Leane near Killarney, Co. Kerry, in the south-west of Ireland, revealed the site of a Beaker work camp connected with copper mining in the period 2400–2200 BC. Ore-processing sediments, metallurgical treatment pits and a number of hut structures associated with early Beaker pottery have been identified.[15]

The earliest known copper mine in Britain is at Great Orme near Llandudno in north Wales—excavations have shown that copper was being mined there as early as 1600 BC.[16]

Language

It is possible that the people who disseminated the Bell-Beaker culture spoke an early form of Indo-European. The Indo-European family of languages includes all the languages of western and central Europe, apart from Basque and Hungarian, all the languages of eastern Europe apart from Finnish and Estonian, together with Russian and the Indo-Iranian languages, including Persian (Farsi), Kurdish, Urdu, Hindi, Bengali, and Sanskrit (Old Indian), the language of the Hindu scriptures. The only Indo-European languages to have left written records in Bronze Age Europe are Hittite (an extinct language spoken in Anatolia, now Turkey), and Mycenaean Greek (spoken in the Peloponnese, southern Greece, and on the island of Crete). So all we have left of early Indo-European in northwest Europe are river names belonging to a pre-Celtic, pre-Germanic language that the German philologist and linguist Hans Krahe calls "Old European."

A number of Old European river-names survive in Britain. The rivers *Derwent* in Cumbria and Yorkshire are first recorded in Roman times as *Derventio*, and Rivet and Smith, in *The Place-Names of Roman Britain*, suggest[17] that this is a Celtic name meaning "oak-river." However, the linguist P.R. Kitson links *Derventio* to a number of European river names, including *Drewenz* in East Prussia (now northern Poland), *Trionto* in southern Italy, *Drance* in Switzerland, *Durance* in southeastern France, *Trave* in Schleswig-Holstein, northern Germany, *Drava* in Austria, Slovenia and Croatia, and *Drôme* in southeastern France.[18] Kitson believes that all these names are derived from the root *Drav-*, "run,"[19] related to Old Indian *dravati*, "runs," *Dravanti*, "an Indian river."[20]

The Derwent is not the only British river with an Old European derivation. The river *Farrar* in the Scottish Highlands has the same derivation as Old Indian *var*, "water," Old Persian *var-* "rain," *vairi*. "sea," and is related to the *Var* (a river in southeastern France), *Vire* (a river in Normandy, northwestern France), and *Vière* (a river in the Marne department of eastern France).[21] The British rivers *Don* (in South Yorkshire, Lancashire and Aberdeenshire) have the same root as Old Persian *danu*, "river," as do the River Danube and the River Don in Russia.[22] The name of the River *Thames*, says Kitson[23] is derived from a root *ta-*, to melt, dissolve, flow," which also gives Welsh *tawdd*, "molten," Old Church Slavic *tina*, "slime, mud." Kitson believes that *ta-* was specially applicable to muddy rivers, and the Thames in its lower reaches is "conspicuously muddy."

The Beaker People in Britain

It is, of course, impossible to know why the "Beaker package" spread to Britain, but one answer may lie in Cornwall's most famous export, tin, which is an important ingredient in the making of bronze. The very earliest bronze did not contain tin but was a copper-arsenic alloy and tin-bronze only came into wide circulation in Britain around 1500 BC. Tin was a very scarce commodity in Bronze Age Europe, and one of the few sources was Cornwall. Until the Middle Ages, British tin ore was dug up from riverbeds—rather than mined—and archaeological evidence for early extraction is scarce. However, six pieces of tin slag (the waste material from smelting) were found underneath the Bronze Age Caerloggas Barrow near St. Austell in the south of Cornwall.[24] An ogival dagger of Camerton-Snowshill type was also found in the barrow, which dates the barrow to between 1650 BC and 1400 BC.

The most famous early Beaker visitor to Britain is undoubtedly the Amesbury Archer. In 2002 at Amesbury in Wiltshire, three and a half miles southeast of Stonehenge, Wessex Archaeology, during excavations in advance of a housing development, found a rich Beaker burial dating from around 2300 BC.[25] The man buried there, dubbed the Amesbury Archer, was 35 to 45 years old, was buried on his left-hand side, with his face to the north. Tests showed that the man came from the Alps region, most probably Switzerland, but possibly areas of Germany near Switzerland, or Austria. His grave was large and rectangular in shape and probably had a timber lining. On his forearm there was a slate wristguard to protect the arm from the recoil of an archer's longbow. Partly covered by his torso was a copper knife which may have been worn in a sheath on the chest. Within touching distance of the man's face were two Beaker pots, a red deer spatula used for working flints, boars tusks, a cache of flints, and another smaller tanged copper knife. Behind the man's back lay another Beaker pot, more boars' tusks, another cache of flint tools and flakes. Next to them was a cushion stone, upon which the Archer could work metal. Scattered through the grave but at a slightly higher level were 16 flint barbed and tanged arrowheads. Two more Beaker pots lay at the man's feet. By his knees there was another wristguard, another small tanged copper knife, a shale beltring, and two gold hair tresses.

Another grave was found close to the Archer's—the skeleton of a man between 25 and 30, dating from the same time as the Archer. A pair of gold hair tresses were found inside the man's jaw, in the same style as the Archer's. An analysis of the bones later showed that he and the Archer were related as they both had the same unusual bone structure in their feet—the heel bone had a joint with one of the upper tarsal bones in the foot. Analysis of the oxygen content of the enamel in their teeth showed that while the Archer had grown up in the Alps region, his relative grew up in southern England. He may have spent his late teens in the Midlands or north-east Scotland.

Not far from the grave of the Amesbury Archer, Wessex Archaeology found another rich Beaker grave, this time on Boscombe Down.[26] This normal sized grave contained the remains of seven individuals dubbed the Boscombe Bowmen—three adult males, a teenage male and three children. A man who had died between the ages of about 30 and 45 had been buried on his left side with his legs tucked up and with head to the north. Buried close to his head were the remains of the three children. One child, aged between about 2 to 4, had been cremated (though there was barely a handful of their bones in the grave), while the other two had been buried. Matching the seven individuals were eight

Beaker pots. Seven of the eight pots are decorated all over, six with cord, one with plaited cord. Plaited cord is an extremely rare form of decoration on Beakers in Britain (it is much more common in continental Europe), and one of the very few British finds is in the nearby grave of the Amesbury Archer. The other finds include five barbed and tanged arrowheads, some other flint tools, scrapers and flakes, a boar's tusk and a toggle. In continental Europe tusks are often found in the same grave as stones used for metalworking, like the one found in the grave of the Amesbury Archer. Only one other bone toggle has been found in Britain, from a later, and rich, Bronze Age burial at Barnack, Cambridgeshire—most toggles have been found in continental Europe.

Beaker burials are found throughout Britain, from southern England to Scotland. Hemp Knoll Barrow near Bishops Cannings in Wiltshire was excavated in 1965. The mound had been constructed over a group of five Neolithic pits containing flint implements, pottery, antler and animal bone. The primary burial comprised an inhumation with pottery, wristguard and beaker. There were traces of some kind of wooden structure associated with the grave, presumably a coffin. The presence of an ox skull and four feet suggests that the interment had been covered by an ox-hide.[27]

Barnack is in the north of Cambridgeshire, not far from the Neolithic causewayed enclosure at Maxey, and in 1974 and 1976 a leveled round barrow there was excavated in advance of destruction by gravel extraction. The excavation revealed a narrow inner ditch almost 38 feet in diameter, a more substantial middle ditch some 78 feet in diameter, and an outer ditch about 164 feet in diameter. A pair of concentric stake circles were found outside the inner ditch and partially overlapping the infilled middle ditch. The primary "Barnack Man" Beaker burial was at the center point of the stake circles rather than that of the inner ditch. "Barnack Man" is thought to have been an important local chieftain. The remains of 23 individuals were found, 19 of them within the 16 grave pits. All the graves were within the area defined by the stake circles, most of them clustered towards the center, but some were over the inner ditch. The primary burial comprised a flexed adult inhumation. At its feet was a Beaker with yellowish soil spilling out from it over the skeleton's feet. A tanged copper dagger was at the left elbow, and nearby was a bone or ivory toggle and a stone wristguard. The latter had 9 perforations at each end, all fitted with a gold cap. A series of radiocarbon dates from several burials cluster in the Early Bronze Age.[28]

A multi-phase Bronze Age round barrow at Irthlingborough on the River Nene in Northamptonshire was excavated in 1985–86 as part of the Raunds area project. The barrow comprised three concentric ring ditches, measuring 49, 78 and 104 feet in diameter. Each additional ditch appears to have been accompanied by enlargement of the central barrow mound. When excavated, the mound survived only to a height of just under a foot. The primary burial deposit comprised a timber structure within a pit, which contained a Beaker inhumation. The structure was subsequently roofed with timber and covered with a cairn of limestone slabs. This cairn also included the skulls of at least 184 domestic cattle and one aurochs (a type of large wild cattle, now extinct). A small number of pig, sheep/goat and dog bones were also present. Radiocarbon dates concentrate mainly in the 2nd half of the 3rd millennium BC.[29]

At Folkton near Scarborough in North Yorkshire, a round barrow was excavated in 1889 by Greenwell and again in 1969 by Brewster, the latter due to extensive damage being caused by plowing. Beneath the mound, Greenwell located two concentric ditch circuits, though Brewster was only able to locate the outermost of the two. Greenwell found several crouched inhumations. At the center was a disturbed flint cairn containing the bones of an adult male and an adult female, one of them with a Beaker. The barrow is best known for one of the secondary burials. A grave containing a child inhumation was accompanied by three chalk "drums," each decorated with a variety of incised designs. The inhumation would appear to be secondary to, and at best contemporary with, the central Beaker-associated interments, although the decorative motifs incised onto the drums has much in common with those found on later Neolithic Grooved Ware pottery.[30] The three chalk drums are a fascinating example of Neolithic art: each of the drums "bears a unique incised design covering the sides and domed tops. The essentially geometric decoration is organised in panels with stylised human faces looking out from two of the drums. The tops bear concentric circle decoration."[31]

Meadowsweet, which was used in the Early Bronze Age to flavor mead, an alcoholic drink made from fermented honey. July 7, 2013 (Ivar Leidus).

Three or four short cists were discovered in July 1963 during construction work on a housing scheme at Ashgrove farm near Methil in Fife, southeast Scotland. Cist A contained the crouched inhumation, probably of a male age about 55, accompanied by an Early Bronze Age dagger and a Beaker. A deposit of black crumbly matter lay over the skeleton and cist floor, and a layer of plant material, 12 inches by 2 inches, lay in front of the skeleton's chest.[32] The plant material was subsequently analyzed by James H. Dickson, who found that pollen from the burial contained exceptionally high quantities of lime and meadowsweet, possibly due to the presence of mead, perhaps poured or spilled in the grave. This theory was supported by a test analysis of material remaining within the associated Beaker.[33]

Rich Burials in the Early Bronze Age

After the arrival of the Beaker culture, burial customs changed: the elite were buried with grave goods (these were rare in the Neolithic), often in specially constructed barrows (burial mounds). Often these barrows were in barrow cemeteries, which consist of between five and thirty barrows, and are found throughout England, with a concentration in southern England (Wiltshire and Dorset in particular). Although Beaker burials were all inhumations, the burials that followed the Beaker period were a mixture of inhumations and cremations. Perhaps the most famous Early Bronze Age burial is the one at Bush Barrow, in the barrow cemetery on Normanton Down, just a short distance from Stonehenge, which probably dates to 1900–1700 BC. It was excavated in 1808 by Sir Richard Colt Hoare and William Cunnington. In the grave they found the skeleton of an adult male, buried lying on his left side, in the crouched position. In the grave had been placed prestigious weapons including a bronze ax and the two largest daggers to have been

An Early Bronze Age barrow cemetery at Bronkham Hill near Weymouth in Dorset, December 22, 2006 (Jim Champion).

An Early Bronze Age round barrow on Normanton Down, a short distance from Stonehenge. August 10, 2014 (David Smith).

found in a grave of this date. One had a wooden handle elaborately decorated with fine gold-wire pins, and came from Brittany. By the right side of the body was a mace, the head made from a rare flecked fossil stone from Devon, while the handle was embellished with bone zig zag mounts. Three other exquisitely worked sheet gold objects were also found—a large diamond shaped lozenge resting on the man's chest and a large belt-hook lying by his waist, both decorated with delicate impressed linear lines, as well as another small diamond shaped lozenge, which may have been mounted on the handle of the mace. A number of rivets and fragments of bronze found near the skeleton have recently been identified by experts as being from a knife-dagger dating to some 200 years earlier than the rest of the objects found in the grave. This dagger may have belonged to an ancestor involved in the construction of the enormous sarsen stone circle and horseshoe of trilithons at Stonehenge.[34] The most famous and intriguing object from the Bush Barrow grave is the gold lozenge, which measures 7 inches by 6 inches. Four decorative bands, each of four grooves, form concentric lozenges. The space between the outermost band and the second band is filled with a zigzag pattern, and the central lozenge is filled with a lattice design that divides the central lozenge into nine smaller lozenges.[35]

Close to the Bush Barrow burial is another barrow known as Wilsford 7, excavated in the early 19th century by Sir Richard Colt Hoare, who found a primary inhumation with a variety of grave goods, including: a spherical cover of thin sheet gold; a grape cup (incense cup); a collared urn; shale beads and pendant, and four amber pendants. Close to Wilsford 7 is Wilsford 8, also excavated by Colt-Hoare, who found a primary cremation deposit accompanied by a variety of grave goods, including: a gold and bronze penannular ring; two gold-bound amber discs; a sheet gold button cover; a bone pendant with sheet gold cover; a pottery accessory vessel; a halberd pendant of bronze and gold; and 9 amber pendants of various shapes.[36]

Clandon Barrow near Dorchester in Dorset was excavated in 1882, when a cremation burial with an urn, a copper dagger, shale mace head, gold lozenge similar to the one found at Stonehenge, and an amber cup were all recovered.[37] There was a barrow cemetery at Hengistbury Head near Bournemouth in Dorset. One barrow was completely excavated in 1911–12 by Bushe-Fox, who found a cremation within a collared urn, plus two cones of sheet gold, three amber beads, a halberd pendant of bronze and amber, and some worked flints. The cremation was probably of a female aged around 20 years.[38]

Cornwall was a popular place in the Bronze Age because of its tin, so it is no surprise to find a particularly rich burial in Cornwall. At Rillaton near Callington in southeast Cornwall a cist was excavated in 1837. It contained an inhumation with grave goods consisting of a small gold cup (the Rillaton Cup), an urn, bronze knife-dagger, rivet, pieces of ivory and a few glass beads.[39] The cup is thought to date from between

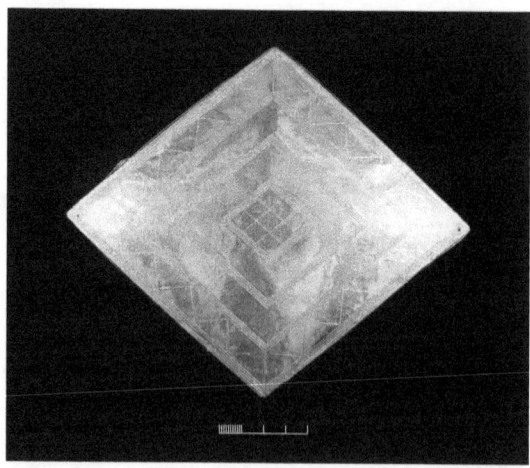

The Bush Barrow Lozenge from Normanton Down near Stonehenge, which dates from the Early Bronze Age (© Wiltshire Museum, Devizes).

1700 BC and 1500 BC. The Rillaton cup has some similarities to vessels found at Eschenz in Switzerland and Gölenkamp near Hannover in Lower Saxony, which may be associated with the Unetice culture of the Czech Republic, and southern and central Germany.[40]

At Gayhurst Quarry on the River Great Ouse near Newport Pagnell in Buckinghamshire, seven Bronze Age barrows were excavated between 1998 and 2000. At the center of the largest barrow there was a massive grave pit, 11 feet 6 inches long and 4 feet 9 inches deep, with a sequence of five successive burials. An extended inhumation of an adult man within an oak-lined chamber, accompanied by only a foreleg of a small pig, was followed by a cremation, a crouched inhumation burial of an older man, also within a small chamber and accompanied by two flint knives and a red-deer antler, a second cremation and, finally, a cremation within a collared urn that had been damaged by plowing. Radiocarbon dating places the burials between 2100 and 1900 BC. In the ditch of the barrow excavators also found a deposit of cattle bones, perhaps containing the remains of some 300 animals, that had been deposited as part of an elaborate funerary practice at the time of the first burial.[41]

Gristhorpe is near Scarborough in North Yorkshire, not far from the Willerby Wold Long Barrow, and in 1834 landowner William Beswick and a group of friends dug into the central and most prominent of a group of three barrows on the cliffs at Gristhorpe. They discovered an intact log-coffin burial which contained a perfectly preserved skeleton, stained black from the oak tannins and buried with a range of grave goods that included a bronze dagger blade and whalebone pommel, a flint knife, and a range of organic grave goods that remains unparalleled in the British archaeological record. These included a bark basket or container and an animal skin within which the body had been

The blocked up entrance to the Early Bronze Age Rillaton Barrow in Cornwall, December 21, 2008 (Eric Foster, CC BY-SA 3.0).

wrapped. In 2005 the skeleton was reassessed by a team of archaeologists from the University of Bradford. They found that the skeleton was that of a man around six feet tall and about 60 years old when he died. He probably originated from the Scarborough area and had a high animal protein diet, obtained from terrestrial rather than marine animals, throughout his life. Radiocarbon dates indicate that he was buried between 2115 BC and 2035 BC.[42]

Rich burials are most common in southern England, but are also found in Wales and Scotland. Bedd Branwen is a Bronze Age funerary mound near Tref Alaw on Anglesey, north Wales, excavated in 1967. At the center of the monument is a boulder or standing stone 4 feet high, at the center of a carefully constructed cairn ring. Eight Bronze Age urns were recovered, and most of these contained cremation deposits. One urn was accompanied by a string of jet and amber beads. Radiocarbon dating of material associated with the cairn ring and cremations produced a date between 1403 BC and 1274 BC.[43]

The site known as the Knowes of Trotty on the island of Orkney is one of the biggest Bronze Age cemeteries between Orkney and southern England. The largest of the barrows was first excavated in 1858 by local antiquarian, and Orkney Sheriff Clerk, George Petrie. Within the earthen mound, a stone cist containing four exquisitely crafted gold sun discs was discovered, along with 27 amber beads and a number of burnt human bones. This find has, to date, been unparalleled anywhere else in Orkney. The gold discs were made from paper-thin sheets of gold, decorated with concentric circles of zig-zags and lines. The largest of the undamaged discs had a diameter of 3 inches and was holed in the middle.[44] Both the sun discs and amber beads imply some connection between Orkney and Wessex, the area that includes Wiltshire and Dorset, where so many rich burials have been found.

The Knowes of Trotty was again investigated between 2001 and 2005 by archaeologists Nick Card and Jane Downes. They found that the cemetery was in use between 2000 BC and 1600 BC, and is made up of 16 barrows arranged in two rows. An excavation of the primary barrow in 2005 revealed that it would once have appeared quite striking in the landscape. The barrow was made up of a stone burial cist, flanked on both sides by two upright stones. It had then been surrounded by a stone cairn, which was in turn covered in earth. The two standing stones inside the barrow are intriguing: they don't appear to have been structurally necessary, and may have had some symbolic purpose.

Astronomy in the Early Bronze Age

Devon

The Neolithic was the high point of astronomically aligned monuments in Britain, but construction of such monuments did continue in the Bronze Age. Bronze Age barrows are not usually associated with the sun, but one exception to this is a group of barrows in the Devon Pebble Beds, which have been studied by the landscape archaeologist Christopher Tilley. The coastal Pebble Bed heathlands of east Devon lie on a long low ridge that forms the watershed between the Exe estuary to the west and the river Otter to the east. The Pebble Beds are visible in the red sandstone cliffs at Budleigh Salterton, and extend inland for a distance of about 8 miles. The Pebble Beds underlie the barren east Devon heathlands, but wherever the vegetation is absent or disturbed, in the stream beds, on exposures on the often quite steep sides of the valleys, and on paths and trackways crossing the heathlands, pebbles are exposed at the surface. It is likely that during the Neolithic and Bronze Age, the heathland would have been used for plant gathering, hunting and pasture for sheep or cattle.[45]

There is no evidence of Neolithic graves from this area of east Devon, and the earliest monuments are round barrows of Early Bronze Age date, almost all in the pebbly heathlands. There are at least twenty-six round barrows, which vary in diameter from 13 feet to 105 feet, and were all constructed from the local pebbles, which show through wherever the thin soil covering is eroded.[46] One of these barrows, at Woodbury near Exmouth, was excavated by the amateur archaeologist George Carter in 1930 and 1936. Carter apparently found that under the surface of the barrow pebbles had been arranged in significant patterns which probably had a ritual significance[47]:

> Under a thin turf layer he reports a surface patterning of large pebbles in various "geometric" forms. The centre of the mound had, according to Carter, surface patterns of a circle and an ellipse. A ring of large pebbles surrounded the edge of the mound. At about ground level a large blue stone overlay a pebble cairn containing another blue stone. Under this was an "ashy layer" resting on the undisturbed Pebble Beds. At the bottom of this ashy layer he discovered decorated beaker sherds, a small pebble of dark-coloured stone, and a barbed and tanged arrowhead. Below this was a further pebble cairn in a pit with blue stones on top and underneath…. Excavations around the cairn revealed that it was surrounded by a pebbled pattern extending "on all sides like a carpet for some distance on the plain of the Common, the overall diameter being about 50 feet."

To the southeast of the mound in this pebble platform/pattern, a Mesolithic ax hammer, dating to the period before the Neolithic, was found at the base of a small cairn and below it a layer of small quartzite pebbles. Carter's report, says Tilley,[48]

> seems to suggest that the large cairn formed a central focus for a patterned pebble skirt surrounding it. Both covered preexisting small pebble cairns in pits, some with especially selected blue coloured stones (rare in the Pebble Beds: they occur in a ratio of 1: 1,000). The central cairn contained an Early Bronze Age Beaker burial or deposit. The presence of Mesolithic material in a small pebble cairn at this location indicates long-term continuities in both the usage of specific locations across the heathlands and a fascination with the symbolic qualities of the pebbles themselves.

Again the pebbles and other stones were being used to make statements about the religious beliefs of those who constructed the barrows.

One of the most distinctive landmarks in the Pebble Beds is High Peak near Sidmouth, which stands out because of its relative isolation, distinctive triangular shape and coastal situation. The site was excavated in the 1960s by Sheila Pollard, who found traces of a possible Early Neolithic causewayed enclosure on top of the hill, virtually all of which has been subsequently destroyed along with the ramparts of a later Dark Age hillfort, by coastal erosion. The pottery recovered was of two principal types and identical to that from Hembury causewayed enclosure near Honiton, to the north of the Pebble Beds. Most flints were of local material but included two pieces of Portland chert and black flint derived from Beer, on Lyme Bay. Amongst the groundstone ax fragments there is more exotic material: a jadeite piece with an Alpine origin and a picrite (basalt) piece from Callington, Cornwall.[49]

It is striking, says Tilley,[50] that High Peak is visible from all of the Bronze Age barrows whatever their position in the landscape:

> It is situated either to the east, or south-east or east-south-east of all the barrows. From most of the Pebble Bed barrows the rising sun would first be seen on the winter solstice

just to the west of High Peak emerging from the sea. Sunrise at the spring and autumn equinoxes would first be visible through the Sidmouth gap between the Peak Hill and East Hill ridges visible from most. Similarly the rising sun on the summer solstice would first be seen through the Honiton gap. The presence of these three gaps to the east of the barrow distribution thus point to the significance of the *rising* sun as seen from the barrows at significant points during the year. The gaps through the hills effectively served to frame and thus dramatize and animate these important celestial events and the brilliant changes in the colour of the sky from red to yellow.

In other words, High Peak framed sunrise on the winter solstice, and sunrise on the spring and autumn equinoxes.

Cornwall

Sun and stones also play an important part in the story of the Bronze Age settlement of Leskernick Hill, on the northeastern edge of Bodmin Moor in Cornwall. Leskernick Hill is an oval hill over a 1000 feet high, enclosed on all sides by higher hills. Leskernick is covered with "dramatic spreads of granite boulders known as clitter, among which the houses and field systems that comprise the prehistoric settlement complex were placed." The settlement consists of the remains of 50 circular stone-wall houses which, together with their associated stone-wall field systems, extend over an area of 51 acres. On the hill above the settlement is a propped stone known as the Quoit, and to the southeast, at the foot of the hill, there is a stone-free plain on which there is a ritual complex consisting of two stone circles, a stone row and a large cairn. Charcoal from house 39 in the southern part of the settlement was radiocarbon dated to 1430–1265 BC.[51]

One of the most northerly houses in the settlement is House 3, which the excavators have dubbed the Shaman's House.[52] This house is "peculiarly isolated and set high up on the slope and levelled into it." The entrance facing west to Rough Tor on the horizon is marked by two fallen orthostats. South of the entrance a large "grounder" (earthfast stone) has been incorporated into the wall. The southwest section of the house wall appears to run up to another large grounder marking the edge of a dense clitter mass to the south of the house. The southern wall is built up against this clitter mass.[53] House 3 is the only house at Leskernick where Rough Tor is visible from the doorway, and it also has a good view of the Propped Stone. On the top of Leskernick hill are great tabular stones, and at some point in the distant past, people climbed to the top of the hill and erected a huge triangular slab 9 feet 2 inches long, 5 feet 11 inches wide, and almost 12 inches thick, which they propped up at an angle with three small boulders. In doing so, they created a peep-hole through which the horizon to the north could be seen. On the longest day of the year, "the dying rays of the midsummer sun shine through the peep-hole just before the sun sinks below the horizon."[54] The Propped Stone can be seen from the Shaman's House, but is also visible on the skyline from the southern stone circle below Leskernick Hill and is just visible from the stone row terminal.

To the south of Leskernick Hill are The Hurlers, three Early Bronze Age stone circles arranged in a line aligned northeast to southwest near Minions on Bodmin Moor, some 4 miles north of Liskeard. Two of the stone circles are linked by a granite pavement which Brian Sheen and Gary Cutts from the Roseland Observatory, Cornwall, and the archaeologist Jacky Nowakowski have dubbed the "Crystal Pathway." The team has confirmed that Bronze Age inhabitants used a calendar controlled by the movements of the Sun.

The Hurlers stone circle near Minions, Bodmin Moor, Cornwall: A view of the North Circle (M&K Davison—megalithics.com).

The four cardinal points are marked together with the solstices and equinoxes. "The Pipers are standing stone outliers to the main circles. When standing between the stones, one to the right and the other to the left, one looks north and south; when lining both up, one faces east and west," says Sheen. "We also think the three circles that comprise The Hurlers monument may be laid out on the ground to resemble Orion's Belt. Far from being three isolated circles on the moor they are linked into one landscape."[55] Interestingly, the axis through the centers of the two northern circles aligns directly on the massive Rillaton Barrow, visible on the skyline to the northeast.

Wales

Crick barrow is a bell-barrow situated near the village of Crick in Monmouthshire, southeast Wales, about a mile northeast of the town of Caldicot, which was excavated in 1940 by Dr. Hubert N. Savory. The mound was found to cover two cremations, both of which were located in pits a short distance from the barrow's center. The primary burial is believed to have been of a young woman; the sex of the secondary was not determined. The barrow was dated, through the finding of two plano-convex knives, to the Early Bronze Age Period III (1750 to 1450 BC).[56]

Beneath the mound was a stone ring 92 feet in diameter. The ring was made up of what Savory called "key boulders," of conglomerate sandstone, with an average height of 2 feet 3 inches, interspersed with a "crude walling" of small stones held together by clayey earth. The ring was considered too unsubstantial to serve the obvious purpose of providing a revetment walling for the covering barrow. Two of the "key boulders" had been decorated with numerous carved circular or oval cup-marks. One of these boulders occupied the southeastern quadrant of the circle. It was the largest boulder in the ring, measuring 5 feet 7 inches long by about 1 feet 11 inches wide, with 23 cup-marks on its outer face. They were mainly clustered on one half of this face, with diameters ranging from one-and-a half inches to three inches, and depths of between a quarter of an inch and three quarters of an inch. The second decorated boulder occupied the northeastern quadrant and was smaller, measuring 2 feet 3 inches long by 1 feet 8 inches wide. Its upper surface had 17 cup-marks, which were also clustered on one half of this face. They varied in diameter from an inch to two inches, and were between a quarter of an inch and half an inch deep.

Martin J. Powell believes that the two cup-marked boulders are astronomically aligned. If a prehistoric observer were standing at the center of the ring and at the surface level of the barrow, that is, before the mound was constructed, the line of sight over the mid-point of the south-eastern boulder would cross an almost level hill almost a mile distant (Crown Hill), in the direction of the midwinter sunrise. The line of sight across the smaller, northeastern boulder faces a gently sloping hill just over a mile distant (Parkwall Hill), in the direction of the sunrise on the cross-quarter days in early May and August (Beltane and Lughnasadh). Powell also draws attention to the way in which the cupmarks are patterned on both boulders:

> On the south-eastern boulder, there is a horizontal line of cup-marks across its centre, with an arc of cup-marks towards its southern edge, where the greatest concentration of markings occur. One could argue that this pattern was a symbolic representation of a succession of sunrises leading up to midwinter's day, the arcing pattern mimicking the actual rising path of the sun. A similar arcing pattern occurs on the north-eastern boulder.

In other words, the lines of cup marks may represent actual sunrises leading up to sunrise on the day of the winter solstice.

Power in the Early Bronze Age

The elite buried with grave goods like daggers and amber necklaces were obviously powerful people, but this is not the only way they demonstrated their power. In 1953 Richard Atkinson discovered a carved dagger and axhead on the inner face of stone 53, one of the imposing trilithon sarsens at Stonehenge. Existing records show about 13 other axes on the same stone, some very hard to see. About 26 axes have been claimed on the outer face of sarsen Stone 4, and three on the outer face of Stone 3, both in the stone circle. Known axes vary from 3 inches to 14 inches long, and all have the blade pointing upwards. In 2012 the stones were scanned with a laser, and 115 axhead carvings were identified.[57]

The carved axheads at Stonehenge are not unique. In 1830, seven clear ax shapes were found at Ri Cruin, in the Kilmartin valley in Argyll, western Scotland. They were located at one end of a stone burial cist, which was covered with a cairn. In contrast to the Stonehenge carvings, the blades point to the right. Close by, the cairn of Nether Largie North revealed another stone cist onto which were carved 14 axes. Like those at Stonehenge, they vary in size, but there is no common orientation; the end slab has two axes whose blades point upwards. The chambered cairn of Nether Largie Mid, also in the Kilmartin valley, contains one other ax. Boscawen-un near St. Buryan in the Penwith district of west Cornwall is a stone circle consisting of nineteen large upright stones, all of granite except for one made of quartz. Just off-center within the circle lies a tall stone said to resemble an ax cutting into the earth with two ax carvings of low relief on its north-east face.[58]

Carvings have also been found closer to Stonehenge. When a round barrow near Badbury Rings in Dorset was excavated in 1845, excavators found within the cairn at least three inhumations, apparently primary, two of them with Food Vessels and one with an ornamental handled pot. Also probably in the cairn were at least fifteen cremations, a few perhaps primary, but most of them secondary, some with Collared Urns. At the center, a huge slab of sandstone weighing half a ton was decorated with cup marks and carvings of daggers and axes similar to those at Stonehenge. We don't know what the axheads and daggers mean but the archaeologist Thomas Goskar says[59] that the axes "are almost certainly crude representations of contemporary Bronze Age metal flanged axheads. The dagger could be compared to examples found in the nearby Bush Barrow. Here an apparently powerful man was buried with an exceptionally rich group of artefacts, including three copper or bronze daggers and an axhead."

The Early Bronze Age in Britain and Indo-European Religion

We know very little about the beliefs of Early Bronze Age Britons, but the gold discs found in Orkney provide us with a clue. Similar gold discs have been found in Wiltshire, Wales and Ireland. In around 1800, a Bronze Age barrow was excavated at Mere, in the southwest of Wiltshire, near the Somerset and Dorset borders. This was a bowl barrow "with [a] primary crouched male inhumation embraced by a younger (female?) inhumation to his right side in a large cist. A tanged copper dagger and slate wristguard lay at his left side with a Beaker nearby. A bone implement and 2 thin circular gold disks (with cruciform pattern) were sewn to his clothes."[60] The discs were "of very thin beaten gold, decorated with a Greek cross etched with horizontal lines encircled by a line and circle of indented dots around the margin"[61] (a Greek cross is a cross with all arms of equal length). These are not the only gold sun discs found in Wiltshire: one was also found in a bowl barrow known as Jug's Grave at Monkton Farleigh, northwest of Bradford on Avon and near the Bristol Avon. The barrow contained a primary interment of two skeletons in a stone cist accompanied by four Early Bronze Age flint arrowheads, probable Beaker sherds, a gold "sun disc" ornament and a fragment of bone ring.[62] The sun disc, like the two found at Mere, has a cross with all arms of equal length.

A gold sun disc was discovered in 2002 during an archaeo-

The Mere gold disc from Mere, Wiltshire, which dates from the Early Bronze Age (© Wiltshire Museum, Devizes).

logical excavation of a Roman and early medieval lead bole smelting site at Banc Tynddol, Cwmystwyth, Ceredigion in west Wales. The disc was one-and-a-half inches in diameter with a repoussé decoration consisting of three concentric circles bordered by circles of punched dots and two central circular perforations. During re-excavation of the site in 2003, an oval-shaped shallow-cut grave 5 feet 9 inches long was identified lying almost directly beneath the find-spot of the disc. Extensive animal burrowing and poor conditions for the preservation of bone meant that almost nothing of the skeleton had survived except for a thin film of tiny fragments.[63]

However, gold sun discs are most commonly found in Ireland. Among the best known sun discs from Ireland are the two found in the hoard from Coggalbeg in Co. Roscommon. The hoard consisted of a gold lunula—a crescent-shaped collar made from thin sheet gold—and two gold discs. The two gold discs featured a cross with arms of equal length surrounded by two circles.[64]

The most famous Bronze Age sun image is the Trundholm sun-horse from Denmark. This extraordinary statue, dated to some time between 1400 BC and 1000 BC, was discovered in a peat bog on the Trundholm moor on the northwest coast of the island of Zealand in southern Denmark. It is a bronze model horse about 10 inches long, drawing behind it a bronze disc taller than itself, over 10 inches in diameter. The disc has a bright side covered with gold leaf, and a dull side. The set was mounted on three pairs of wheels, two for the horse and one for the sun-disc, each wheel having four slender spokes and able to turn.[65]

Almost as famous as the Trundholm sun horse is the Nebra sky disc, a bronze disc depicting the heavenly realm with moon, sun and stars. The Nebra sky disc, dated to 1600 BC, was found on the Mittelberg, a hilltop site near Nebra in Saxony-Anhalt, eastern Germany, along with two bronze swords, two hatchets, a chisel and fragments of spiral bracelets. It is a bronze disc inlaid with gold symbols interpreted as a sun or full moon, a lunar crescent, and stars (including a cluster interpreted as the Pleiades). Two golden arcs along the sides were added later. The Nebra sky disc was first analyzed by the German astronomer Professor Wolfhard Schlosser[66]:

> Schlosser recognized that the two golden arcs each subtend angles of about 82° from the centre of the disc and suggested that this could relate to the fact that, in this part of Germany, the difference in azimuth (degrees clockwise from true North) between the sun on the horizon at midwinter and at midsummer is also 82°. The disc could therefore be a representation of the annual solar sunrise and sunset cycle as seen from near Nebra.

Schlosser also calculated that at the time the Nebra disc was made, the last evening visibility of the Pleiades was on March 10, and their first morning setting was on October 17. These dates, says Schlosser, "describe quite well the beginning and the end of the agricultural year for the region where the sky-disc was found." Lithuanian peasants "observed until modern times the last evening visibility and the first morning setting of the Pleiades as agricultural key-dates."[67] Whatever the Nebra sky disc means, it shows that the people of the Bronze Age had a sophisticated understanding of heavenly bodies.

However, my main concern here is the British and Irish gold discs, and one of the most intriguing features of the sun discs is that they are often found in pairs. The Danish archaeologist Kristian Kristiansen, in a paper on the Nebra sky disc,[68] says that the Nebra sky disc "takes the idea of the Bronze Age sun cult, as represented by the Trundholm Sun Chariot, one step further back in time, and it indicates that the myth of the journey of the sun was anchored in a complex system of astronomic and cosmological knowledge."

This knowledge, says Kristiansen, "was wedded to a shared Indo-European religion, which placed the sun cult and its practitioners in a milieu of dual gods." The most famous of these dual gods were the "Divine Twins," the Ashvins of Bronze Age India and the Greek Dioscuri. The Ashvins are known as early as the 2nd millennium BC—their name means "possessor of horses," and they appeared in the sky before the dawn in a golden chariot; the Dioscuri are Castor and Pollux—they were sometimes called *leukopoloi*, riders on white (i.e. shining) horses.[69] Diodorus Siculus reports that "the Celts who dwell along the ocean [= Atlantic] venerate the Dioscuri above any of the gods, since they have a tradition handed down from ancient times that these gods appeared among them coming from the ocean."[70] In Anglo-Saxon mythology the kingdom of Kent was founded by Hengist ("Stallion") and Horsa ("Horse"), who were clearly Divine Twins.

The Trundholm sun-chariot is not the only Bronze Age model chariot known in Europe. Two bronze wagon models were found in a Late Bronze Age cemetery at Gross Perschnitz, Silesia (now part of Poland); they had been deposited in a pit along with a pair of arm-rings. These, like other examples from the same region, were each drawn by a trio of waterbirds. The more complete of the two ceramic wagon models from Dupljaja, Banat, Serbia, was also drawn by waterbirds and carried a standing anthropomorphic figurine with a bird-shaped head.[71] White swans play an important role in mythology: the Greek sky god Zeus appeared as a white swan to rape Leda, the mother of the Divine Twins Castor and Pollux; and white swans pulled the chariot of the Bronze Age Indian sun-goddess Usha.[72] Swans are also associated with the god Apollo, from the time of Alcaeus, a poet from Lesbos who flourished around 600 BC[73]:

> When Apollo was born, Zeus furnished him forth with a golden headband and a lyre, and giving him moreover a chariot to drive—and they were swans that drew it—would have him go to Delphi and the spring of Castaly, thence to deliver justice and right in oracles to Greece. Nevertheless once he was mounted on the chariot, Apollo bade his swans fly to the land of the Hyperboreans.

The Hyperboreans were a mythical people living "beyond the North Wind"; swans were linked to Hyperborea because whooper swans migrated south to Greece from their summer breeding grounds in Iceland, northern Scandinavia and Russia. The Greeks were probably aware of the far north because of Baltic amber, which is found in numerous Mycenaean graves of the 2nd millennium BC. Amber is mentioned in Homer's *Odyssey*. When Telemachus, the son of Odysseus, visits the palace of Menelaus, King of Sparta, in Book 4, He is awestruck: "Mark the flashing of bronze throughout the echoing halls, the flashing of gold, of amber, of silver, and of ivory. Of such sort, methinks, is the court of Olympian Zeus within." In Book 17 of the *Odyssey*, when the suitors vie with each other in the extravagance of their gifts to Penelope, Eurymachus' contribution is "a richly crafted necklace of god adorned with sun-bright amber."[74]

Cattle continued to play an important role in the ritual life of Britons, as the burials at Irthlingborough and Gayhurst show. The significance of cattle to the early Greeks is demonstrated in the *Odyssey*. In Book 12 the enchantress Circe warns Odysseus about the cattle of the sun god[75]:

> "You will now come to the Thrinacian island, and here you will see many herds of cattle and flocks of sheep belonging to the sun-god—seven herds of cattle and seven flocks of sheep, with fifty head in each flock. They do not breed, nor do they become fewer in number, and they are tended by the goddesses Phaethusa and Lampetie, who are children of the sun-god Hyperion by Neaera. Their mother when she had borne them and had done

suckling them sent them to the Thrinacian island, which was a long way off, to live there and look after their father's flocks and herds. If you leave these flocks unharmed, and think of nothing but getting home, you may yet after much hardship reach Ithaca; but if you harm them, then I forewarn you of the destruction both of your ship and of your comrades; and even though you may yourself escape, you will return late, in bad plight, after losing all your men."

Despite Circe's warning, Odysseus and his men do land on Thrinacia and are stranded there for a month. While Odysseus is absent, his men kill some of the cattle; Helios is enraged and asks Zeus to punish them. When they finally leave the island, they are caught in a terrible storm, and all but Odysseus are drowned.

The *Odyssey* was probably composed in the 8th century BC, recalling the past glories of Mycenae, which flourished in the Bronze Age. Although the tale is Greek, it may well recall a time in the European Bronze Age when cattle were linked to the sun, and confirm that the cattle slaughtered at Irthlingborough and Gayhurst were offerings to the sun god.

The End of the Rich Burials

The rich burials in Wessex came to an end between 1500 BC and 1400 BC, with one of the last being on Boscombe Down, where the Amesbury Archer and the Boscombe Bowmen were found. Here Wessex Archaeology excavated a shallow chalk-cut grave containing the remains of a teenage boy and over 90 amber beads. The style of burial is late within the Wessex 2 grave series (1700–1500 BC), confirmed by a single radiocarbon date of 1530–1430 BC.[76]

The Early Bronze Age was a unique period in British prehistory, when Britain was part of a trading network that stretched from Ireland and Iberia in the west to the Baltic in the north and the Mediterranean in the south, as far east as Mycenae in the Greek Peloponnese. The powerful individuals who benefited from this trading network were buried in barrows with rich grave goods, and in barrow cemeteries that expressed not only the power of particular individuals but the prestige of their descendants. But such a way of life could not last, and in the centuries that followed, many Britons turned away from the burial rites of the Early Bronze Age and chose a very different form of burial, one more in keeping with the practices of their Early Neolithic ancestors.

CHAPTER 3

The Age of Depositions (1): Water, Fire and Earth in the Late Bronze Age

Depositions in Fens, Rivers and Lakes

Fens

With the rich burial of the teenage boy on Boscombe Down near Amesbury around 1500 BC, the Age of Megaliths was drawing to a close, and the Age of Depositions was about to begin. The first Celts were about to emerge along the Atlantic seaboard, and an age when ritual was increasingly focused on "deposition of rich metalwork in pits, more often in rivers, pools, bogs and other watery settings."

It is impossible to know where the Age of Depositions began, but a good place to start is Flag Fen, to the east of Peterborough in Cambridgeshire, not far from the Etton causewayed enclosure at Maxey, the astronomically aligned structure at Godmanchester, and the rich burial at Barnack. The history of Flag Fen starts in the Neolithic at Fengate, an archaeological site on the edge of The Fens, an area of marshland which covers parts of Lincolnshire, Cambridge and Norfolk. Fengate was first investigated by G. Wyman Abbott who made regular visits to Fengate gravel pits during the first 30 years of this century, finding mainly Neolithic and Beaker material. Air photographs taken by Dr. St. Joseph in the 1960s revealed extensive crop marks showing that the area of occupation was much larger than originally thought. Large scale excavations by the Royal Ontario Museum took place between 1971 and 1977 in advance of factory construction. They found that the first clearings in the forest appeared about 3000 BC, when farmers moved in. The first known house was rectangular and stood to the west of Cat's Water and four people, perhaps from this house, were buried in a pit on the site. One of them was found to have a Neolithic leaf arrow head between his ribs.[1]

The actual site at Flag Fen consists of an alignment of wooden posts over half a mile in length and a wooden platform of approximately 3.5 acres. The post alignment extends from the very gently sloping dry land of Fengate settlement to the slightly steeper dry land of Northey "island." The platform sits on the post alignment closer to Northey than Fengate. The platform has been radiocarbon dated to between 1000 and 660 BC, within the Late Bronze Age. The post alignment has been assigned a date of use from between 1300 and 900 BC from dendrochronology (the dating of tree rings) which would suggest that it is slightly earlier than the platform, although there is some overlap in the date ranges.

Flag Fen does not appear to have been a settlement site in the conventional sense owing to the absence of definite domestic occupation layers and hearths. The site appears to have had a defensive and ritual role in the landscape. The large quantity of metalwork found would support a ritual interpretation. Bronze, iron, tin, lead and one gold object were found which showed signs of deliberate damage. Swords, tongue chapes, daggers, pins, fibulae and a spearhead were found dating from the 12th to 5th centuries BC. Most objects seem to have been thrown into the water during some form of religious observances. Some objects, however, may have been buried in shallow scoops. At least two objects were found deliberately concealed beneath horizontal timbers on the platform. One was a complete pottery jar, the second a pegged and socketed bronze spearhead. It is also possible that many of the items were made specifically for deposition in the water—items such as miniature swords and two very small dirks.

The excavator Francis Pryor believes that gradually rising ground water levels during the 2nd and early 1st millennia BC gave rise to social and economic tensions that led to the construction of the post alignment and platform. Thus the two were to form part of a barrier over half a mile long that isolated the landscape of the Fengate/ Northey embayment from the open fen to the north and east.[2]

Rivers

Ritual deposits have also been found in the River Thames, mainly in the upper Thames between Oxfordshire and London. These deposits include a considerable quantity of Bronze Age metalwork: for example, a Late Bronze Age bronze shield at Long Witten-

The River Thames at the Goring Gap, 8 miles upstream from Reading, July 21, 2008 (Motmit).

ham in Oxfordshire; a socketed ax, tanged chisel, gouge, bifid razor (class II), socketed knife, dirk and spearhead at Wallingford in Oxfordshire; palstaves, socketed axheads, spearheads, a socketed sickle, a socketed knife, a sword, a dagger and a rapier at Reading in Berkshire; a Bronze Age bronze sword, a bronze rapier blade, two bronze spearheads, two bronze ferrules, a bronze socketed axhead, and a bronze palstave at Staines in Surrey; and a bronze shield, dated to between 1200–1000 BC, found in the Thames at London. The archaeologist Jill York has studied the metalwork recovered from the Thames above Teddington in the London Borough of Richmond upon Thames. Ritual deposits increased markedly after about 1350 BC, and included spearheads, swords, dirks and rapiers, socketed axes, and palstaves. In the Early Bronze Age no metalwork was deliberately destroyed, but 21 percent of the Middle Bronze Age artifacts and 50 percent of the Late Bronze Age were. Swords show both high levels of use (84 percent) and of deliberate damage (59 percent). Damage took varying forms: some swords were bent in an arc using heat until they snapped, while others had been hit and broken into two or often more pieces.[3]

In addition, a large number of human skulls have been found in the Thames between London and Oxford, including a group of over 100 from Strand-on-the-Green in Chiswick, west London.[4] Richard Bradley and Ken Gordon have examined museum collections and have found that almost 300 skulls still survive from the stretch of river between Oxford and London. Six skulls were radiocarbon dated, and four skulls gave dates in the later Bronze Age. It is clear that the skulls were deposited in an unfleshed condition—there were very few mandibles (jawbones), and other body parts were absent from the museum collections, even though ordinary animal bones had been retained. The skulls showed a bias towards males aged between about 25 and 35.[5] It is possible that the metalwork found in the Thames was deposited as grave goods at the same time as the skulls.

Lakes

Metalwork was also deposited in lakes during the Late Bronze Age. In 1913 a hoard was discovered buried in peat at the bottom of the lake at Llyn Fawr, Rhigos, in the Cynon Valley of south Wales. The Llyn Fawr hoard includes seven socketed bronze axes, three socketed sickles, two of bronze and one of iron, three socketed chisels, a socketed iron spearhead, two bronze cauldrons belonging to the first half of the 7th century BC, two bronze cheek-pieces, three bronze discs or phalerae from harness decorations, and a Hallstatt C (Early Iron Age) iron sword.[6]

A Late Bronze Age hoard was found in 1778 by workmen while dredging for marl from the bottom of Duddingston Loch, Holyrood Park, Edinburgh. The objects came up in the collecting bag with bones, said to be human, and horns of animals. The better-preserved objects were presented to King George III and subsequently lost, others were retained by the family of the owner of the loch, Sir Alexander Dick, and some of these were given to Sir Walter Scott while the remainder were presented to the Museum of the Society of Antiquaries of Scotland. This donation included spearheads, swords, rapier, and a bucket-staple; more swords and one spearhead were acquired by the Museum in 1935, ultimately from the Scott collection. All the spearheads and swords are broken and/or bent, and some have been burnt and partly melted. Types include Late Bronze Age Ewart Park swords (800–700 BC), plain and lunate spearheads, barbed and lunate spearheads, and a ring with staple from a bucket.[7]

Late Bronze Age Cauldrons and Flesh-Hooks

But it was not only weaponry that was deposited in watery places. In 1961 a cauldron was found near Feltwell in Norfolk, at the edge of The Fens; it dates from the Late Bronze Age Penard Phase (1275–1140 BC). In 1928 a large bronze cauldron was found by bathers in the bed of the River Cherwell at Shipton-on-Cherwell in Oxfordshire. It is one of the earliest Late Bronze Age cauldrons known in Britain, and dates to about 1100–1000 BC. It is of a type known as "Atlantic cauldrons" that are found in areas along the Atlantic coasts of Europe: Britain, Ireland, France and Iberia. It is thought that the earliest forms, such as the one from Shipton, were made in England, but that the majority of later examples were made in Ireland and traded along the sea coasts.[8] Another Late Bronze Age cauldron was found in the Thames at Battersea, London, dating to between 800 BC and 700 BC. As I said earlier, two bronze cauldrons were found in the lake called Llyn Fawr, dating to the 7th century BC.

Cauldrons were presumably associated with feasting, but they were not the only feasting equipment in circulation in the Late Bronze Age. Bronze flesh-hooks occur in Britain, Ireland, western France and Iberia and have a long currency from about 1300 to 800 BC. At their simplest they are double-pronged, made from a single bent bar and attached to a wooden shaft using an organic binding, or single-pronged with a socket to receive the shaft.[9] They were probably used to extract food from sheetbronze cauldrons, or possibly buckets, as part of a feasting ritual.[10] The finest flesh-hook in the British Isles was found in the course of peat cutting at the Dunaverney Bog to the north of Ballymoney,

The River Cherwell as it joins the Thames at Oxford, June 10, 2008 (Motmit).

County Antrim, Northern Ireland, in 1829.[11] It dates from between 1050 and 900 BC, and originally consisted of stretches of wooden shaft linking together three tubular bronze segments. One small section of wood that survives is studded with small strips of bronze set in a herringbone pattern. The pair of birds on the butt end can be identified as corvids, perhaps ravens, and the family along the middle portion as a pair of swans with three cygnets.[12] As we saw in Chapter 2, it is likely that swans were associated with the sun-god.

In Britain, a flesh-hook was found inside the Feltwell cauldron, and in 1929 a flesh-hook was discovered in a bog at Little Thetford in Cambridgeshire. Reginald Smith outlines briefly the circumstances of this find, the first complete one in England: "It was found this year about 9 feet from the surface in digging a dyke on reclaimed fen-land at Little Thetford, Isle of Ely."[13] One of the larger timbers that supported the wattle wall or revetment of Row 1 of the post alignment at Flag Fen also concealed a copper-alloy flesh hook; the excavator remarks that "this careful positioning suggests deliberate deposition."[14] The flesh-hook probably dates from around 1300 BC,[15] and is similar to the flesh-hook from Feltwell.[16]

Right: **The Late Bronze Age Dunaverney Flesh Hook from County Antrim, Northern Ireland, with the two ravens, two swans and three cygnets clearly visible (© The Trustees of the British Museum. All rights reserved.).**

Bottom: **The River Great Ouse at Little Thetford, January 18, 2003 (John McCullough).**

The God Apam Napat, Burnt Mounds and Watery Depositions

The Indo-Iranian God Apam Napat

Why did water become so important in ritual in the Late Bronze Age? We know very little of Bronze Age religion, and the only Bronze Age religious texts that are still known to us are the Indian *Rigveda* and the Iranian *Avesta*. In the *Rigveda* there is a sun-god *Savitr*, meaning "the Vivifier," who is associated with bringing the dead back to life.[17] The sun sinks into the Ocean at sunset and emerges from it at sunrise; for this reason Savitr is known as *apam napat*, "progeny of the waters." The fire-god *Agni* is also called *apam napat*, because the waters are one of Agni's three abodes[18]:

> First, Agni is born in the Sky as lightning;
> Second, Agni is born on Earth, as sacrificial fire;
> Third, Agni is born in the Ocean, as the risen sun.

In the *Avesta* there is an analogous figure *Apam Napa*. He is known to have the epithet *auruuat.aspa*, "having swift horses"; otherwise, this word serves only to describe the *huuar-* "sun." There is a parallel in the Rigvedic word *asuheman-* "driving swift horses," which serves as an epithet for Apam Napat. Savitr's chariot is also drawn by horses.[19]

The relationship between the sun and horses is particularly clear in Bronze Age Scandinavia. On bronze metalwork from Denmark, especially razors, there are many pictures of horses, boats and the sun; a great majority of the bronze objects, in particular the razors, are associated with cremation burials. Between about 1600 BC and 500 BC, the same motifs are more widely distributed in Danish, Swedish and Norwegian rock art. The Danish archaeologist Flemming Kaul has made a study of ships on bronze items, and he observes[20]:

> First, the images seem to show the sun being carried across the sky, in association with a boat and often with a horse. Secondly, he suggests that after the sun has set it travels through the underworld until the following dawn. During this period it passes through the sea, accompanied by a snake or a fish.

Here the sun is associated with horses, boats and water, so there is a clear link to the Indo-Iranian Apam Napat.

Burnt Mounds (1): England

This combination of fire and water is typical of a class of Bronze Age monuments known as *burnt mounds*. Burnt mounds are "enigmatic mounds of burnt stones have been recorded adjacent to streams in a wide range of landscape settings from the fens of East Anglia, the southern chalklands of Hampshire to the uplands of Northumberland and Cumbria. Where excavated, burnt mounds have proven to be mostly Bronze Age in date (roughly 2300–850 BC), although earlier and later examples are known." The mounds of burnt stones "often lie adjacent to, or overlie, a water trough which was fed by the adjacent water source." The function of burnt mound is much debated, but there are basically two conflicting interpretations: "firstly that they were specialised sites for cooking food by boiling in water, and experimental archaeology has shown this to be possible; alternatively, it has been suggested that burnt mounds may be some form of sweat lodge or sauna used for ceremonial purposes for ritual purification as can be found in Native American archaeology."[21]

However, the cooking hypothesis "is problematic in that very few sites have produced evidence for food debris (organics or animal bones)." The sauna hypothesis "could be borne out by the lack of evidence for food preparation or settlement debris at the mounds," and their close proximity to water. Although burnt mounds are associated with the Bronze Age, one of the earliest burnt mounds in Britain was at the Late Neolithic Marden henge in Wiltshire, close to one of the sources of the River Avon.

Since Flag Fen was such an important place for watery depositions, I'm going to start my exploration of Bronze Age burnt mounds in the East Anglian fens. Bradley Fen, on the western margins of Whittlesey island and to the south of Flag Fen, a few miles from Peterborough, was excavated between 2001 and 2004. The earliest finds on the site were Beaker pits, one of which contained 20 fragments of a single comb-impressed Beaker.[22] A Beaker settlement was found at a site known as Silt Lagoon, to the south of Bradley Fen. This settlement consisted of a roundhouse, together with pits containing Beaker pottery.[23]

Three burnt mounds were found at Bradley Fen on the edge of Whittlesey island, and one burnt mound at Bradley Fen Farm, to the west of Bradley Fen, all radiocarbon dated to the first half of the 2nd millennium BC.[24] The three burnt mounds at Bradley Fen were found between 55 and 77 yards apart. These three mounds were accompanied by large hollows and watering holes. The mounds were located consistently on the southern side of these features. Whereas the sub-mound features contain burnt stone fragments in primary contexts, the adjacent watering holes and hollows were burnt stone free. Hearths survived beneath two of the three mounds.[25] The three island edge mounds were very alike and shared very similar histories, which included, for instance, deposition of parts of log ladders, tree-stumps, and disarticulated human bone.[26]

Another burnt mound in The Fens is the one near Feltwell in Norfolk. At Feltwell Anchor (also known as Brandon Bank) near Feltwell, fieldwalking as part of the Fenland Survey identified a prehistoric burnt mound. An auger survey was carried which revealed the presence of undisturbed burnt mound material beneath the plowsoil. Excavation of the mound demonstrated that beneath it lay several small pits. To one side of the mound a larger waterlogged pit contained a wooden trough and important environmental evidence. A grave cut into the top of the mound contained a crouched inhumation which had been buried in a timber coffin, hollowed out log or mortuary structure. The skeleton and charcoal from the mound was radiocarbon dated to the Early Bronze Age.[27]

Burnt mounds are relatively rare in Wessex, apart from Hampshire. A large number of burnt mounds have been identified in the New Forest in Hampshire, mostly near the River Avon, but very little is known about them. The best known burnt mound in the region is the one recently discovered at Bestwall Quarry in Dorset. Bestwall Quarry lies to the east of Wareham, between the rivers Frome and Piddle and on the edge of Poole Harbour in Dorset. The earliest activity on the site is represented by four large Neolithic pits dated to around 3700 BC. The location of the pits must have had significance, because they were succeeded by a timber circle (15 irregularly-spaced posts in a ring 39–46 feet across) and then by a ditched, small enclosure surrounding a rectangular timber building. The functions of the building and monument remain unknown. A cluster of pits in the center of the site contained many styles of Beaker domestic pottery;

in one pit were grains of both naked and hulled barley as well as emmer wheat—the first clear evidence of arable farming. Around the mid 15th century BC the first house was built on the site, followed by seven further houses in the 14th century BC. House 1 was partly sealed by a "remarkable series" of "closing deposits" after it was abandoned and dismantled. A fire pit was then constructed, with a contemporary burnt mound consisting of a large kidney-shaped heap of fire-cracked gravel which was spread across the former entrance of the house. Two bronze bracelets of Middle Bronze Age date were carefully and deliberately placed, one in the former house hearth and the other on the base of the fire pit. Three Middle Bronze Age cremation burials in plain pots were also uncovered. Settlenet resumed in the Late Bronze Age: three "farmsteads" were excavated which were occupied from the early 10th century BC until the middle of the 9th century BC. A wide variety of pottery was manufactured throughout the life of the settlement.[28]

Burnt Mounds (2): Wales

In Wales, burnt mounds have been discovered at Llandegai (also known as Llandygai) in north Wales, which lies over a mile from the coast, just across the Menai Straits from Anglesey. This site was first excavated in 1966–7 by Christopher Houlder, who discovered an Early Neolithic rectangular building, two henges with cremation pits, a cursus, and an Early Bronze Age round barrow containing an un-urned cremation and a Food Vessel in a separate pit.[29]

Around 98 yards from the Llandegai henges, another site was excavated in 2005. A second Early Neolithic rectangular building was uncovered, aligned east-northeast to west-southwest, and a number of pits, one of which contained Late Neolithic Grooved Ware.[30] The pottery found in the rectangular building was Early Neolithic, mostly normal "Irish Sea ware" shouldered bowls but very little of any one vessel surviving.[31] Radiocarbon dates indicate that the building was in use from around 3800 BC to around 3600 BC.[32]

The excavators also found scattered across the site 6 significant spreads or mounds of burnt stone of varying dimensions and depth. Most of these had at least one associated pit or trough and these too varied in size and shape. The majority of the mounds were situated either on the wet, clayey, lower parts of the site or along a natural boundary in the geology where the ground water was close to the surface.[33] Few artifacts were associated with the burnt mounds. Embedded in the natural clay beneath mound 2176 was a fragment of an edge-retouched knife with neat scalar flaking. This is a simple form of plano-convex knife indicating a date in the 2nd millennium BC.[34] The burnt mounds seem to have been in use from the Late Neolithic to the Late Bronze Age.[35]

Burnt mounds have also been found on Anglesey. The most interesting is the burnt mound set close by a minor tributary of the Lligwy river at Moelfre on the east coast of Anglesey, which was excavated in 1912/13. This is a crescentic or horseshoe shaped mound about 56 feet in diameter and up to 1 feet 3 inches high, open towards the stream on the south-east. It is largely made up of friable burnt stones. Excavation revealed a slightly sunken rectangular floor about 7 feet 6 inches by 4 feet 3 inches, aligned towards the stream, with three upright stones about its edges. Its north-west end was paved and the remainder was floored with broken stones embedded in the natural clay. This was interpreted at the time as a hearth, but is probably the emplacement for a water trough or tank.³⁶ Not far from the burnt mound is Lligwy megalithic tomb, which was excavated in 1909, when two layers of deposits were recorded, separated by a layer of paving. The deposits contained unburnt bone, human and animal, pot sherds and some flints and the upper deposit was covered by a layer of limpet shells. Between fifteen and thirty individuals were represented in the tomb chamber. Some of the pottery appears to be Bronze Age and at least one of the layers may represent the re-use of the tomb.³⁷

Burnt Mounds (3): Ireland

In Ireland burn mounds are known as *fulacht fiadh*, and have been primarily interpreted as cooking places. The term *fulacht fian* is found in the early Irish literature from at least the 9th century AD, and refers to open-air cooking places in which a water filled pit was made in which to cook meat. The early Irish literature also shows that the word *fulacht* is not only applied to a water filled pit for boiling meat but also to an outdoor cooking pit where meat was roasted on a spit or over an open fire.³⁸

One such burnt mound is the one uncovered at Rathpatrick. Test-trenching in Rathpatrick townland, near Slieveroe, Co. Kilkenny, in the southeast of Ireland, revealed a large mound of heat-shattered stone and charcoal in a poorly drained area close to a small stream. The team of archaeologists from Headland Archaeology, under the direction of Catríona Gleeson, initially presumed that they were dealing with a "run-of-the-mill burnt mound," or *fulacht fiadh* site. As excavation progressed, however, it became clear that as well as "normal" cooking-sized troughs, on its western side the mound of burnt stone and charcoal "covered evidence for much more interesting activity."

The main feature was a circular structure 16 feet 5 inches in diameter, the floor of which was about 1 feet 4 inches m below the surrounding ground-level. Thirty six stakeholes were found spaced regularly around the periphery of the sunken area. No evidence was found for any flooring material. At the eastern side, where the ground sloped upwards, two steps were cut into the subsoil, giving access to the sunken area; the steps coincide with a gap in the stake-holes. Close to the top step was a rectangular, bath-like pit, 9 feet 10 inches long and 6 feet 7 inches wide. Immediately south of the steps a pit formed an annex to the sunken area, and the two were separated by a slight ridge of subsoil and a number of small stake-holes. The excavators found a hearth about 3 feet upslope from the pit, to the southeast.

The excavators believe that the sunken area would have been covered by a hemispherical, tent-like structure. Hazel charcoal was identified in the fill of some of the stake-holes; radiocarbon dating of a sample of this charcoal has shown that it came from a hazel tree that lived in the 7th and 8th centuries BC, in the Late Bronze Age. Hazel rods, being long and flexible, "would have been ideal for forming the framework needed to cover the area." The roof

> could have been made from hides or blankets, thatched with rushes or straw, or covered with sods. It is assumed that the small pit cut into the side of the structure was also covered by the roof. Stones heated in the fire could be easily carried with a tongs, or rolled downslope into the pit, where they would have radiated a significant amount of heat inside the covered area. If, as happens in modern saunas, water was sprinkled on the hot stones, steam would have been created and the temperature inside the covered area would have risen accordingly. Once the occupants of the sweathouse had enjoyed their steam-bath, they could climb the two steps and plunge into the pool outside to cool down.³⁹

From Burnt Mounds to Watery Depositions

What is the connection between burnt mounds and watery depositions? At Bradley Fen prehistoric Britons were constructing burnt mounds in the first half of the 2nd millennium, and by the end of the 2nd millennium they were casting bronze swords and other weapons into nearby Flag Fen. This is speculation, but the connection could lie in the breaking of the metalwork. Swords and other weapons are born from fire, and when the individuals broke the weapons and cast them into the fen, the Britons of Flag Fen may have believed that they were symbolically releasing the fire trapped inside the sword and returning it to the water.

Feasting in the Late Bronze Age (1): Riverside Locations

Washingborough, Lincolnshire

The Late Bronze Age cauldrons and flesh-hooks suggest that feasting was taking place, and occasionally feasting sites have been found at riverside locations. Washingborough in Lincolnshire is on the River Witham to the east of Lincoln, and recently a feasting site was discovered on the north bank of the river. Excavations between 2004 and 2005, discovered the remains of raised brushwood platforms stabilized with roundwood posts, which must have originally covered an area approximately 164 feet by 82 feet. In places the platform had been covered with a stone surface. The site "was in use in the Late Bronze Age 1100–800 BC, a date supported by radiocarbon dates and pottery styles.... It was originally on the north bank of the river, a wetland area with reed swamp which was cleared prior to construction of the platforms. Bones of young sheep and cattle suggest it was used seasonally in the spring/summer. It would have been accessible from land or from the river, by log boat. No other structural remains were uncovered."

Evidence of metal working was discovered,

> including crucible fragments, parts of a mold for making pin heads, and a bronze bar. No casting waste was discovered, suggesting that the actual metal-working was taking place close by, but not in the excavated area. Other crafts including the working of flint, leather, wood, shale (to make bracelets), bone and antler also appear to have taken place on or near the site. A bone weaving implement suggests textile production. There was also evidence for cereal processing taking place in the vicinity on a fairly large scale, probably to produce surplus for exchange. The presence of barley also suggests brewing. Also, animal rearing was taking place for meat, dairy products and wool. Residues from a meat and vegetable stew were discovered on the insides of some of the pottery. Bones of house mice were discovered—this is the earliest occurrence of these animals in Britain. They would have been associated with crop processing and storage over a length of time. A wooden tank was discovered, which would have been lined with skins. Heat-cracked stones were also found, which could have been used to heat water in the tank, possibly for brewing or cooking.

Bridle fittings were found

> suggesting the presence of horses which would have been important status symbols. A large assemblage of pottery (almost 2000 sherds) was recovered. This was of post Deverel Rimbury plainware type, and included remains of over 250 vessels, some of unusual forms. Few were decorated. Many had a black-burnished finish giving an appearance similar to

bronze. The tempering used in the pottery suggests a local source. It is suggested that the pottery is associated with feasting and was deliberately deposited. A wooden bowl in a form similar to the pottery was also found.

Some disarticulated human bones were discovered,

> including part of the skull of a young woman. It seems likely that these represent some kind of ritual deposit. It seems likely that this site was an important gathering place, where people including high-status elite met for feasting and drinking, rituals, gift-exchange and trading. Metal working, which would have been an arcane process using rare materials, also took place. These events would have reinforced the status of the elite, and reinforced ideas of boundaries and territories. The location of the site in a marshy area by the river, a liminal space, would have made it particularly suitable for such activities.[40]

Runnymede Bridge Near Staines in Surrey

Another early feasting site is at Runnymede Bridge near Staines in Surrey, on the River Thames to the west of London. The Neolithic and Bronze Age site at Runnymede Bridge was excavated in the 1970s and 1980s, initially under rescue conditions during construction of the M25 motorway, and later as a research excavation by the British Museum. The site is now situated on the southern side of the River Thames, beneath and on either side of the present M25 bridge over the river—but in the Late Bronze Age it was on an island in the Thames. The Neolithic and later finds and features were contained within a complex sequence of river channel sediments and layers of alluvial deposition. The Neolithic finds are made up predominantly of pottery and stone artifacts plus human and animal remains. Also recorded were some in situ pile-driven uprights. The Late Bronze Age deposits, which date from the 9th or 8th century BC, "represent a remarkably complex, largely in situ, array of structures and artefacts, including a waterfront pile structure and an extremely rich accumulation of midden and other refuse deposits."[41] The archaeologist David Longley, who excavated the site in 1975–6, says of Runnymede Bridge[42]:

> It became apparent very early on in the course of excavation that two separate areas could be defined. A sticky black deposit containing large quantities of domestic refuse represented a midden overlying all features in the north-eastern half of the site, while a much lighter deposit containing pottery, bronze artefacts, bone and burnt flints defined the area of occupation over the south-western half.

We can get an idea of the size of the midden (the name that archaeologists give to a build-up of domestic rubbish and animal waste) from two of the British Museum excavators, Stuart Needham and Tony Spence. They say that in one area of the midden (42 square feet), as many as 17,500 finds were recovered weighing over 242 pounds. Burnt flint, pottery, fired clay and animal bone "were extremely abundant," with lesser quantities of charcoal, struck flint and metalwork, and occasional finds of antler, amber or coprolites; high phosphate levels "suggest a noteworthy organic component was originally present."[43]

The finds show that horses were used at Runnymede Bridge: a "circular bronze attachment with concentric ribbing" is similar to the "important hoard of harness fittings from Parc-y-meirch, Clwyd," and to examples from the hoard at Llangwylog, Anglesey (both in Wales). Two antler cheek-pieces from different bridle sets "attest further the use of horses either for traction or riding and at least two horses from the site had attained a considerable age (25–30 years) indicating that they were valued and well looked after." Among the personal items were a number of bronze artifacts, including vase-headed and nail-headed pins, rings and a possible wire bracelet. In addition, lignite bracelets and amber beads were found.[44] Certain bronzes at Runnymede Bridge were almost certainly imported from the Continent, including a vase-headed pin and a notched razor probably made in northern or central Europe.[45]

Longley also notes that a dog was present on the site and "may have been responsible for gnawing the ends of the human long bones which were found in that condition scattered over the site." The implications of this, he says, are that "the dead, or at least some dead people, were disposed of unceremoniously on the rubbish heap."[46] Ninety-three fragments of human bone were found scattered on the living floors at Runnymede Bridge.[47]

The British Museum excavation determined that a timber palisade was constructed between 930 BC and 870 BC in the northeast corner of the island, and renewed between 840 BC and 790 BC. A horse burial was associated with the secondary phase of palisade construction, when the rotting posts were renewed. The burial pit was dug through an earlier pit filled with midden deposits, and contained a partially articulated horse, along with other artifacts relating to the keeping of horses (for example, an antler cheek piece in an upper fill). An inverted hearth was placed directly on top of the horse, alongside several near-complete pots, including a large shouldered jar, possibly reflecting the occurrence of a contemporary feast and ceremony.[48]

Intriguingly, a Late Bronze Age hoard, dating to the 9th or early 8th century BC, was found a few hundred yards south of Runnymede Bridge. The hoard consisted of two caches of metalwork finds such as socketed axheads, sword, spearhead and knife fragments, casting jets and cake, and cauldron fragments. The caches may have originally been held in organic containers which did not survive.[49]

Celtic Feasting

We have no description of Celtic feasts in the Bronze Age, but we do have a description of Late Iron Age feasts in Gaul. The Greek writer Athenaeus, who flourished around AD 200, in his book *Deipnosophists* ("Dinner-Table Philosophers"), describes a feast, quoting the 1st century BC Greek philosopher Posidonius[50]:

> And Posidonius the Stoic, in the histories which be composed in a manner by no means inconsistent with the philosophy which he professed, writing of the laws that were established and the customs which prevailed in many nations, says: "The Celts place food before their guests, putting grass for their seats, and they serve it up on wooden tables raised a very little above the ground; and their food consists of a few loaves, and a good deal of meat brought up floating in water, and roasted on the coals or on spits. And they eat their meat in a cleanly manner enough, but like lions, taking up whole joints in both their hands and gnawing them; and if there is any which they cannot easily tear away, they cut it off with a small sword which they have in a sheath in a special box.... But when many of them sup together, they all sit in a circle; and the bravest sits in the middle, like the *coryphaeus* [= leader] of a chorus; because he is superior to the rest either in his military skill, or in birth, or in riches: and the man who gives the entertainment sits next to him; and then on each side the rest of the guests sit in regular order, according as each is eminent or distinguished for anything."

Clearly, Celtic feasts were hierarchical, with the bravest warrior seated in the center of the circle, and his bard seated next to him.

Athenaeus then gives an example of a particularly lavish feast thrown by Luernius, king of the Arverni tribe of the Auvergne in the 2nd century BC:

> And Poseidonius continuing, and relating the riches of Luernius the father of Bituitus, who was subdued by the Romans, says that "he, aiming at becoming a leader of the populace, used to drive in a chariot over the plains, and scatter gold and silver among the myriads of Celts who followed him; and that he enclosed a fenced space of twelve furlongs in length every way, square, in which he erected wine-presses, and filled them with expensive liquors; and that he prepared so vast a quantity of eatables that for very many days any one who chose was at liberty to go and enjoy what was there prepared, being waited on without interruption or cessation. And once, when he had issued beforehand invitations to a banquet, some poet from some barbarian tribe came too late and met him on the way, and sung a hymn in which he extolled his magnificence, and bewailed his own misfortune in having come too late: and Luernius was pleased with his ode, and called for a bag of gold, and threw it to him as he was running by the side of his chariot; and that he picked it up, and then went on singing, saying that his very footprints upon the earth over which be drove produced benefits to men."

The most striking feature of this passage is the description of the bard singing a praise poem in honor of the beneficent Luernius.

Feasting in the Late Bronze Age (2): Feasting in the Fens

Godwin Ridge is a Pleistocene sand ridge 628 yards in length, flanked on all sides by the channels of ancient streams, in the floodplain of the River Great Ouse, just above Earith, where the river debouches into the southwestern Cambridgeshire peat fens. The ridge, which lies to the east of the Neolithic enclosure at Godmanchester, was investigated in 2008-9 as part of the Over Narrows phase of Barleycroft/Over Quarry project.

The elevated western end of the ridges rises to 10 feet above sea level. Here the excavators found the remains of a Late Bronze Age midden in the soil beneath the sandy loam. The buried soil was between 10 inches and 2 feet thick; it was "distinctively coloured dark brown to black and its matrix included humified organic matter, with fine bone and charcoal fragments." In total, some 6,150 sherds of Late Bronze Age post–Deverel Rimbury plainware pottery were recovered.[51] The animal bone from the Late Bronze Age features is dominated by cattle, with pig coming a distant second. Only one Late Bronze Age feature yielded human bone: a pit containing the cremated fragments of an adult skull, tooth and long bone.[52]

Feasting in the Late Bronze Age (3): Sites on Dry Land

The Earth-Goddess

Feasting in the Late Bronze Age did not only take place in watery places. The god of fire and water was of course not the only god worshipped in the Late Bronze Age, and there is evidence for veneration of an earth goddess, later glossed by Julius Caesar as Dis Pater, the Roman god of the underworld.

To find a Late Bronze Age earth-goddess, we need to explore the Indo-European words for *earth*. The word *earth* in Indo-European is represented by Hittite *degan*, Greek *gaia*,

Greek *khamai* "on the earth," Phrygian *zemelo-* "earthling, human," Old Church Slavonic *zemlya*, Latin *humus*, Vedic *ksam-*, Greek *khthon*, Old Irish genitive *don* "place, ground earth."[53]

In Hittite the neuter *degan* is personalized as Daganzipa ("genie of the earth"). In the *Rigveda*, *ksam-* is normally used only for the physical earth, while the goddess is called Prthivi or Prthvi "The Broad One." In Greece the goddess Earth is usually Gaia or Ge. The Earth-goddess is also recognizable under the name of Plataia, the eponymous nymph of Plataiai in Boeotia, central Greece, and a consort of Zeus—she is also "The Broad One," like the Indian Prthivi. A better known consort of Zeus in Greek myth is Semele, mother of Dionysus. This seems to be a Thracian name of the Earth-goddess.[54]

So we know that the Bronze Age Hittites venerated an earth-goddess Daganzipa, and that the Greeks worshipped an earth-goddess Gaia from the time of the poet Hesiod, who flourished around 700 BC. Likewise, the Bronze Age people of India venerated an earth-goddess called Prthivi "the Broad One," while the people of Boeotia in central Greece worshipped a related goddess called Plataia. A goddess related to Prthivi, called Litavis, is known from a Latin inscription at Narbonne in the south of France.[55] Dedications to Litavis in Latin have also been found at Mâlain and Aignay-le-Duc near Dijon in the Côte d'Or department of eastern France.

There is no obvious evidence for Litavis in Britain, but looking at words related to *Prthivi* and *Litavis* pays some unexpected dividends. The Vedic *Prthivi* is related to Old Indian *prathati* "spreads out," Greek *platys* "broad, flat," Old English *folde* "earth, dry land" (poetic), Gaulish *Litavis* "earth-goddess," Gallo-Latin *Letavia* "Brittany," Old Irish *lethan*, Welsh *llydan* "broad," Welsh *llys* "castle, court." Welsh *llys* is related to Early Irish *liss/less* "enclosure, habitation."[56]

What stands out here is the Welsh word *llys*. In Welsh the word *llys* means "court, palace; courtyard, enclosed space," and Old Irish *les* means "the space about a dwelling-house or houses enclosed by a bank or rampart, farmyard, courtyard." The term *les* "is normally used in medieval Irish texts to refer to the enclosed space within the banks or ramparts that make up early medieval Irish 'ringforts'; that is, to embanked enclosures practically identical in form to the 'enclosed homesteads' of 1st millennium BC Britain." Interestingly, Welsh *llys* also means "court of law."[57]

In other words, a *llys* may originally have been an Iron Age enclosed settlement, and two examples can illustrate this. Castell Henllys ("Castle of the Old Court") at Nevern in Pembrokeshire, southwest Wales, is an Iron Age settlement enclosure, about 96 yards northwest to southeast by 80 yards, occupying an inland promontory, defined on the open, northwest side by a double rampart and ditch, with an annex beyond; occupation within the enclosure ceased around the end of the 1st century BC or the beginning of the 1st century AD. Castell Henllys was excavated over a period of more than thirty years from 1981 to 2008. These excavations showed that the main gateway was begun in the 5th century BC and started as a long stone-walled passageway flanked by pairs of massive timber posts supporting a large gate and, probably, a bridge or tower over the entrance. Two pairs of guard chambers, semi-circular rooms where the gatekeepers could shelter and inspect visitors, were recessed into the sides of the passage. The gateway was rebuilt several times during the occupation of the fort, and there were episodes when it was on the point of collapse, or even burnt down. Outside the main fort was a further set of defenses. Early on these included a chevaux-de-frise (a curtain of sharp, upright stones). It may originally have been far more extensive, but later, around 300 BC, the chevaux-de-frise was replaced by a substantial bank and ditch and only survives today where this later bank covered it. After the fort was abandoned in the Late Iron Age, a small but well-off Romano-British farmstead was established just outside.[58]

Helston is in southwest Cornwall, and was originally called *Henliston*, from Cornish *hen lis* "old court." To the southeast of Helston is Mawgan, and Halliggye Fogou. This is an Iron Age underground chamber that is believed to have been constructed in around the 4th and 5th century BC and been in use until at least the 2nd century AD. Fogous are found only in the far west of Cornwall, and their original function is unclear. They may have been used to store valuables, or as refuges; or they could have been places of ceremony and ritual. Halliggye Fogou is situated within an earthwork enclosing a settlement, possibly a defended Iron Age homestead on the Trelowarren Estate. It lies partly beneath a high plateau bounded by an embankment and runs beneath two enclosures (fields) at different levels. The fogou is a large complex example of its type constructed of drystone walling and capstones. It consists of a north to south orientated stone-lined chamber 65 feet 7 inches long, with a curvilinear passage, almost 92 feet long, branching westwards and culminating in a small side chamber. Both are over 6 feet high in places.[59]

All Cannings Cross, Wiltshire

While the feasting site at Washingborough was clearly focused on the River Witham, and Runnymede Bridge was on an island in the Thames, there are a number of feasting sites in Wiltshire and elsewhere that are very much on dry land. Three major feasting sites have been excavated in Wiltshire—at All Cannings Cross, Potterne and East Chisenbury. The first of these to be discovered was at All Cannings Cross, a farm near All Cannings to the east of Devizes. All Cannings Cross entered archaeological history when it was excavated by the pioneering archaeologist Maud Cunnington in 1911 and between 1920 and 1922[60]:

> Puzzled by the many hammerstones in a ploughed field, Cunnington excavated below the chalk scarp falling into the vale at All Cannings Cross Farm. A layer of dark earth, up to 55 cm [= 1 feet 10 inches] thick, was crammed with pieces of pottery and animal bones, and tools of bone, bronze and iron.
> It provoked immediate interest, not just because of the nature of the deposit ("quite out of proportion to the probable length of occupation") but also because of the date, which Cunnington estimated at 500 BC. Here, she said, was the first evidence for Britain's earliest users of iron, perhaps Celtic immigrants themselves.

The pottery that Cunnington found there, now known as All Cannings Cross pottery, dates from between 800 BC and 600 BC, and it does indeed seem to have come from abroad. The archaeologist and historian Nancy Sandars links the All Cannings Cross pottery to eastern France, in particular to the hillforts of Camp de Montmorot near Lons-le-Saunier, and Mont Guérin near Dôle, both in the Jura department of eastern France[61]; while the archaeologist Barry Cunliffe also links it to pottery found at Gundolsheim in Alsace, also in eastern France.[62]

The All Cannings Cross site covers an area of about 9 acres and "comprised a large quantity of artefactual material, including pottery, various bone tools and bronze items, animal and human remains, iron slag, crucible fragments, spindle whorls, loomweights and other items."[63] It was originally regarded as a large open settlement of Late Bronze Age/Early Iron Age date, but has recently been reinterpreted as a midden. The archaeologists John Barrett and David McOmish, who reinvestigated the site in 2003 and 2004, say that All Cannings Cross "is in a striking position at the foot of the Marlborough Downs escarpment, looking out across the low-lying Vale of Pewsey towards Salisbury Plain." It was clear from Cunnington's excavation, they say, that "occupation here was on the cusp of the dramatic changes that accompanied the shift from bronze- to iron-based technologies."[64] Bronze is represented at All Cannings Cross by the blade of a Late Bronze Age Armorican socketed ax, while iron is represented by a distinctive series of iron pins, also with Continental parallels.[65]

The site, say Barrett and McOmish,[66] "appears to comprise large midden deposits—made up of pottery fragments, large quantities of animal bone and other cultural deposits, along with buildings and pits." Cunnington, it seems

> had noted a somewhat enigmatic feature—"chalk floors"—in a variety of shapes and sizes. We were able to excavate one of these and, although damaged by ploughing and cut by Cunnington's trenches, it sealed extensive spreads of cultural material, including fragments of pottery and articulated animal bone.

Augering (the use of drills to take small samples of sub-surface deposits) "suggests that there may well be deep in situ deposits buried to a staggering depth of 2 meters (almost 7 feet) between plough-eroded spurs of chalk."

Among the broken pottery, animal bone, and other debris, Cunnington found more than 30 human cranial (skull) fragments, scattered and dispersed with no obvious pattern to their distribution; no other human remains were found. Some of the All Cannings Cross fragments had been deliberately modified, apparently to be "used for scraping or other purposes." One had been worked into a small circular roundel, "almost exactly the size of a penny-piece" and had a hole bored well off-center. Judging from the wear marks, it had apparently been carried or worn for some time, perhaps as a charm or amulet.[67]

Cunnington identified nine "chalk floors," or rectangular laid chalk surfaces. They appear to have been kept clean and some of them sealed thick dark humic soils containing concentrations of fragmented pottery and animal bone. These platforms were carefully constructed in a mixture of compacted chalk, flint and broken sarsen stones, forming a thickness of about 8 inches and encompassing relatively small areas, with the largest being roughly 29 feet by 19 feet. Some of the adjoining surfaces were burnt or fire-reddened, being constructed from compacted burnt clay, flints and chalk and containing reddened ash and charcoal fragments. It appears that some were related to consumption and depositional activities; for instance, Platform F sealed a large deposit of pottery, described by Cunnington as being "packed tightly together in a large dump." Platform E also produced an interesting assemblage of artifacts, incorporating a chalk loomweight within its surface, and 3 saddle querns and 14 hammerstones were discovered resting on the surface (hammerstones, as the name implies, are stone tools used as a hammer in, for example, chipping flint or breaking up bones). The other half of the platform had been burnt and this structure also sealed a pit (Pit 19), which contained four hammerstones, alongside worked clay, a serrated rib bone, and fragments of pottery and animal bones. The burnt platforms appeared to suffer very high temperatures and it may be possible in one sense to describe them as massive hearths where activities relating to food production and pottery and metalwork creation took place.[68]

The chalk platforms were originally thought to represent the floors of rectangular houses, which had been dismantled and sometimes burnt during abandonment. In the recent excavations at All Cannings Cross by Barrett and McOmish, a sequence of pits and two overlying chalk platforms were excavated on the southeast corner of the site amongst the deepest deposits of "dark humus," and some postholes were visibly associated with one of the structures. These were not interpreted as houses, but as feasting structures.[69]

All Cannings Cross is unenclosed, but nearby is Rybury Camp hillfort. This is described as a "probable Late Bronze Age or Iron Age univallate hillfort," 207 yards long north-south by about 164 yards, with an area of 4 acres.[70] The Iron Age hillfort overlies an Early Neolithic causewayed enclosure, which remains unexcavated save for a single trench cut by Desmond Bonney in 1963. The ditch was flat-bottomed and 6 feet 6 inches deep. Over 600 waste flint flakes were found throughout, but no worked implements. A few teeth and fragments of bone were also retrieved. Sherds from a single decorated Neolithic bowl which had eroded from above the inner edge of the southern section of the hillfort ditch were also found.[71]

It is intriguing that an Iron Age hillfort should have been built on the site of a Neolithic causewayed enclosure, but Rybury was not unique. The hillforts of Whitesheet Hill (Wiltshire), Maiden Hill and Hambledon Hill (Dorset), Hembury (Devon), and Crickley Hill (Gloucestershire) were all built on the site of causewayed enclosures. It is possible that some Iron Age Britons were attempting to return to some aspects of Neolithic life, including the Neolithic priesthood which supervised the building of monument with astronomical alignments.

Potterne, Wiltshire

Because All Cannings Cross was excavated when archaeology was in its infancy, relatively little is known about the site, and the best known midden in Wiltshire is the one excavated by Andrew Lawson at Potterne, southwest of Devizes, between 1982 and 1985. The midden there occupies an elevated position overlooking the Avon Vale (the valley of the Bristol Avon), and has uninterrupted views towards the west as far as the Mendips, some 30 miles away.[72] It came to light in 1982 when a gold bracelet was discovered during grave-digging in Blackberry Field, Potterne, the site of the civic graveyard.[73] The subsequent excavations revealed the presence of an extensive midden deposit at least 12 acres in extent and 3 to 6 feet deep. The midden "comprises pottery, animal bone, coprolites, worked bone and antler, bronze metalwork, human remains, flint, and numerous other artefact types overlying a surface containing numerous pits, post holes and other features. Almost all the artefactual material belongs to the early 1st millennium BC." The area excavated, in total 65 feet by 32 feet,

> yielded some 125,000 potsherds, plus 177 bronze artefacts including awls, tweezers and numerous sheet bronze fragments from vessels (mostly bowls). Worked bone and antler objects include pins, awls, combs, and a cheek-piece. Also present were amber and glass beads, plus fragments of shale bracelets and possibly cups. An archaeomagnetic date of 750 BC ... was obtained from material relating to the pre-midden occupation features, while the pottery assemblage probably spans the period c. 1000–700 BC.

The pottery was "typical All Cannings Cross decorated ware."[74] The antler cheek piece, says Lawson[75] "is evidence for the use of harnesses or bridles. The horse may have been a high status animal in the period, possibly only used by certain members of the community, or for some sort of light draught such as a travois type sledge." The site also produced "a small quantity of ferrous metal-working debris," probably of the 7th century

BC.⁷⁶ Artifact production is reflected by 15 crucible fragments, 4 mold fragments, 3 hearth/furnace lining fragments, 12 copper-alloy casting residues, and 14 ferrous slag residues, and bone, antler and shale roughouts.⁷⁷

Seventeen pieces of glass (glass beads) were found at the site—this glass was analyzed and found to be a high-magnesium high-potassium mixture, based on plant ash, comparable with glass manufactured in the Near East (Egypt and Mesopotamia) in the Bronze Age and up until around the 7th century BC—this may represent the actual import of glass beads, or their manufacture from imported raw glass.⁷⁸ This glass may have come to Britain by way of the Phoenicians, who had expanded from their home in Lebanon and by the 8th century BC had founded colonies in Sicily, Sardinia, North Africa (Carthage), and southern Iberia (Huelva).

Five amber beads were also found in the midden. All the beads are of simple subcircular form, one having a straight edge, forming sharp angles with upper and lower faces, the remainder having rounded edges. The four complete samples are of asymmetrical section. Amber beads are most commonly found in the Early Bronze Age, and only rarely in the Late Bronze Age, when beads of asymmetrical section are more frequent. Other amber beads of Late Bronze Age date come from Llangwyllog, Anglesey, north Wales, Carshalton and Runnymede Bridge in Surrey, and Lofts Farm, Essex. Three amber beads were recovered from different phases at Danebury hillfort in Hampshire, but amber beads are rare in Iron Age contexts.⁷⁹

As at All Cannings Cross, there is evidence that the midden was also a place of burial for the remains of a small number of people. At Potterne 134,000 animals bones were uncovered, and compared to this, "the human bone assemblage was tiny, with only 139 fragments recovered." Unlike the material from All Cannings Cross, the human bone at Potterne was not restricted to cranial fragments, though these did make up more than half the assemblage. The absence of jawbones and cervical vertebrae "suggests that it was defleshed crania, rather than heads, that were present on the site." Among the rest of the bones, thigh bones predominated; among the leg bones, "there was a marked preference for right over left limbs."⁸⁰ The very abraded condition of some of the bone fragments would suggest that "they might have been subject to various episodes of redeposition or disposal, probably of a not very reverential nature."⁸¹

Although the midden is classified as Late Bronze Age/Early Iron Age, Lawson's excavations showed that occupation of the site began in the 12th century BC. A complex sequence of postholes, stakeholes, pits and hearths, and a "concreted" surface, possibly a track-way, reveal evidence for a large Late Bronze Age settlement. Two areas of occupation activity were identified, separated by an area termed the "empty strip," which formed a concreted surface approximately 33 feet wide. This area was eroded down to the bedrock in places, suggesting a busy flow of traffic, such as people, animals and carts. To the south of this feature was a soil accumulation, approximately 1 feet 4 inches deep, which flanked the "empty strip" and appears to have been eroded by the traffic. This area was termed the "on-terrace" area and contained a sequence of occupation features such as hearths, 3 linear features and 65 postholes. A line of stakeholes and an alignment of four large greensand boulders were discovered running along the "terrace edge"; they have been interpreted as a fence-line, possibly to delineate the edge of the settlement area. In the northern "off-terrace" area, 39 postholes were recovered, 28 of which were sealed by overlying midden deposits.⁸²

As noted, a total of 139 fragments of human bone were recovered at Potterne. All the bones were fragmented, and some possess cut marks, and display evidence for burning, direct polishing and wear, and deliberate shaping. Most of the bones were found around the greensand boulders in phases 1 and 2 (greensand is a type of sandstone with a greenish color), and also along the terrace edge in the subsequent phases. The bones from this assemblage have been de-fleshed, modified through cutting and shaping, occasionally burnt, carried around or circulated, polished through wear or manipulation, possibly displayed on timber posts or used as vessels, and eventually deposited within the midden.[83]

A large number of the bone fragments at Potterne were "manipulated to make material statements, such as the angular, almost square skull fragments." A similar pattern is evident at All Cannings Cross, where four skull fragments had been carefully shaped and perforated. This suggests that skull bones "were modified into artefacts during performances which sought to forget or diminish the memory of the person," in order to reconceptualize the deceased "as part of the world of the dead." These artifacts may well have been regarded as powerful, being made up from the skull, and it is possible they were utilized in various contexts, such as to ward off ailments, to cause harm or to heal persons.[84]

East Chisenbury, Wiltshire

Another midden was discovered in 1992 at East Chisenbury, on the upper reaches of the River Avon. The excavator David McOmish says "the area of the midden, though not the presence of the midden mound itself, has been known to field-walkers since at least the Second World War, when personnel stationed at near-by Upavon aerodrome collected pottery and bone implements from local fields." It was not surprising, he says, "previous field-workers had failed to see the midden; it is so large that it has the appearance of being merely part of the natural hilltop." The midden is some 7 acres in area with deposits up to 6 feet 6 inches deep; it was placed on the western edge of a very prominent spur, and faced west, overlooking the valley of the River Avon and much of the central area of the Salisbury Plain.[85] The excavated midden material was dark and greasy in texture, and was dominated by a large ceramic component, including All Cannings Cross pottery. Other components of the artifactual assemblage include "spindle whorls, worked and decorated bone and fragments of stone, worked flint, shale and a glass bead." A large number of bones were found:

> Initial study of the well-preserved faunal assemblage points to disproportionately large numbers of foetal or neonatal sheep; other species such as cattle, pig and deer are well represented. Human remains, including two fragments of skull, were uncovered. One of these had apparently been placed deliberately within the mound, surrounded by sherds of pottery from the same vessel and a small block of sarsen stone.

Within the excavated layers of the midden were a "series of compacted chalk surfaces or platforms, free from artefactual debris."

Like all the Wiltshire middens, the East Chisenbury midden is unenclosed, but on its eastern side it overlies the bank of a circular enclosure, which was first noted by Colt Hoare in the early 19th century. The enclosure boundary, now a heavily plow-damaged bank around 3 feet high and 32 feet wide, "compares favourably in size with that of a hillfort and indeed invites comparison with this form of enclosure. The exact date of the enclosure and its relationship to the midden mound is unknown: field survey suggests that the enclosure underlies at least the later stages of the mound build-up."

Wittenham Clumps, Oxfordshire

Late Bronze Age middens have also been found outside Wiltshire. In 1947 a midden was identified by P.P. Rhodes at Wittenham Clumps, a group of small hills near Dorchester-on-Thames in Oxfordshire; the midden lay 200 yards to the west of the hillfort of Sinodun Camp, also known as Castle Hill. A black earth layer contained hematite coated sherds, which made up 9 percent of the pottery found there. Animal bones were also recovered, with sheep or goat and cattle bones most common; horse and dog teeth were also found.[86]

The site was again excavated between 2003 and 2006 by Oxford Archaeology, who also excavated the hillfort. Trench 14 was excavated to investigate the black earth layer found by Rhodes in 1947. Seven layers were found in Trench 14, of which the lowest three date to the Late Bronze Age. One of these layers contained a single Late Bronze Age pottery sherd, 47 fragments of animal bone, an iron swan's neck pin, and a piece of copper wire.[87] The iron swan's neck pin is a very early Iron Age type associated with imported Hallstatt material, and dates to between 800 BC and 650 BC; a similar pin was found at All Cannings Cross, while others have been found in north Germany and the Rhineland.[88] The layer above this was richer, containing 89 pottery sherds and 336 fragments of animal bone. The animal bone included a wolf bone which gave a radiocarbon date of 900 BC–790 BC.[89] Six small shallow features, possibly postholes, were cut into the lowest layer. They were filled by silt clay deposits, sometimes containing appreciable quantities of charcoal. The finds consist of a fragment of human skull and a small early Iron Age sherd in posthole 1444, four calcined bones in posthole 1439, three late Bronze Age sherds and a sheep/goat bone (astragalus or knuckle bone) in posthole 1450, and a further sheep/goat astragalus in posthole 1446.

A total of 29 Early Iron Age pits were found nearby. Pit 15010 contained 103 pottery sherds, animal bone including two horse mandibles, and a rich assemblage of charred plant remains and charcoal.[90] The lower fill of pit 15003 contained the crouched skeleton of a young adult male. Cut into the western edge of this pit was a smaller pit which contained the skeleton of a new-born baby. The animal bone assemblage (225 fragments) included cattle, horse, sheep, sheep or goat, pig, and frog or toad.[91]

The midden was unenclosed, but nearby Castle Hill may have been enclosed at the time when the midden was accumulating. A Late Bronze Age/Early Iron Age enclosure ditch was found during excavation of the hillfort. Late Bronze Age pottery was found at the bottom of the ditch, and Early Iron Age pottery was found in the middle and upper fills.[92]

Llanmaes, Vale of Glamorgan

In 2003 two metal detectorists working at Llanmaes in the Vale of Glamorgan, south Wales, discovered and reported a highly unusual metalwork assemblage of bronze cauldron fragments of the late Bronze Age (800–600 BC) and axes made in northwest France (Brittany and Normandy). Investigation of the site revealed the existence of the residues of a feasting site, within a rich cultural midden deposit. Subsequent excavations revealed a wealth of environmental evidence such as pig bones and plant remains, pottery, metalwork and human bone. Thirteen bronze cauldrons and bowls, 37 axes, imported metalwork and the "exceptional 79 percent pig bone (feasting meat) suggest that this was an exceptional gathering place with intensive feasting, exchanges and burial events taking place over many centuries (800–10 BC)."[93] A geophysical survey in 2005 revealed the existence of a sizeable univallate enclosure 270 yards from the midden; the enclosure was some 3 acres in area, with a bank and external ditch. Excavations in 2007 showed that the ditch had been cut in the Middle-Late Iron Age, then recut in the 2nd or 3rd century AD.

Looking for Druids in the Late Bronze

Julius Caesar said that the Druids were experts in "the stars and their motion," but there is very little sign of astronomically oriented monuments in the Late Bronze Age. However, David McOmish, in his paper on the East Chisenbury midden, makes an important point[94]:

> The midden at East Chisenbury, placed on the western edge of a very prominent spur, faces west overlooking the valley of the River Avon and much of the central area of the Salisbury Plain. This choice of orientation, repeated at a number of other transitional midden sites, is deliberate. Potterne faces west, as does the deposit at Bishops Cannings near Devizes; All Cannings Cross similarly is located on a steep west-facing slope.

This west-facing orientation may have something to do with the setting sun. We think of the sun as setting in the west, but the sun actually sets due west only on the equinoxes (March 20 or 21 for the spring equinox, September 22 or 23 for the autumn equinox). After the autumn equinox, the sun sets more to the south, and by the winter solstice (December 21 or 22), which was a significant time in the Neolithic and Early Bronze Age, the sun sets at its most southwesterly point. Halfway between the autumn equinox and

The Bog of Allen and Croghan Hill in the distance, May 4, 2007 (Sarah777).

the winter solstice is the Celtic festival of Samhain ("Assembly"), which is now celebrated as All Saints Day or Halloween. A photo taken by the archaeologist Kate Waddington of Potterne appears to show it directly facing the setting sun in November.[95]

All Saints Day and Halloween are associated with the dead, and it is possible that in the Iron Age Samhain was a time when the dead came back to life. In the 12th century Irish tale, *The Boyhood Deeds of Finn mac Cumhaill*, we learn that in Finn's day "there was a very beautiful maiden in Bri Eile, that is to say in the fairy-mound of Bri Eile, and the name of that maiden was Eile." The men of Ireland were apparently competing for the favors of this maiden, and one by one they went to woo her: "Every year on Samhain the wooing used to take place; for the fairy-mounds of Ireland were always open about Samhain; for on Samhain nothing could ever be hidden in the fairy-mounds."[96]

Bri Eile is also called Croghan Hill, and is in County Offaly, in the Irish Midlands. Eile was one of the *Aos Si* (Old Irish *Aes Sidhe*), or "People of the Mounds," who lived in fairy mounds, which are often in fact prehistoric burial mounds. Indeed, there is a large circular mound that occupies the summit of Croghan Hill; the mound has not been excavated, but it appears to be a Neolithic cairn that possibly covers a passage tomb and therefore dates from between 3500 BC and 2500 BC.[97]

Caesar also says that the Druids venerated the underworld god called Dis as the ancestor of the Gauls, and it is possible that the middens were dedicated to an earth goddess like the Vedic Prthivi or her Gaulish relative Litavis. Litavis may be associated with enclosed settlements, and although the middens were unenclosed, there is evidence of enclosures associated with most of the middens.

Koch says that the Druids belonged to the class of people called *aes dano*, or "people of the arts," which also included metalworkers and craftsmen of all kinds. Evidence for metalworking and a variety of manufacturing activities was found at Washingborough, and evidence for metalworking was found at All Cannings Cross and Potterne.

But perhaps the best evidence for priests and religious ceremonies are the chalk floors or platforms uncovered at All Cannings Cross and East Chisenbury. Kate Waddington says that "these hard, white, chalk surfaces created conspicuous spaces or "stages" which provided a vehicle for display and where a series of acts were performed."[98] Waddington goes on to say[99] that, for a time,

> the visual contrast between the clean white chalk and the surrounding deposits must have been incredibly striking. At East Chisenbury for example, the sequences of chalk layers suggest that large parts of the mound became covered in a patchy layer of chalk during specific periods of occupation. If this were the case, we may envisage substantial parts of the hilltop becoming illuminated in white on particular occasions in the agricultural cycle; the visual display, not only from the hilltop but further afield, must have been dramatic.

These highly visible white chalk surfaces "created a series of arenas where both intimate and communal performances took place," enhanced by the lighting of fires on or adjacent to the platforms, as demonstrated by All Cannings Cross. On the chalk platforms, says Waddington,[100]

> we can envisage people engaging in various activities, sometimes evoking the carnivalesque through colourful and debauched displays of singing, dancing, speaking and shouting. Food may have been prepared, animals killed for sacrifice and consumption, and then roasted on the fire-reddened surfaces. They may have provided necessary hard surfaces where cups and bowls and plates were smashed, artefacts destroyed, creating noise, disruption and affirmation. The structures may even have served a funerary role, where bodies of

the dead were laid out for funerary rites and where the belongings of the deceased were assembled and destroyed. At East Chisenbury, the fragmented and manipulated bones from at least ten people were recovered from the excavation trenches, and this suggests that hundreds, possibly thousands of human bones, were deposited within the mound. The incorporation of a human phalange within a chalk layer in Trench B may be an explicit indicator that human bodies were excarnated and fragmented here, as the small bones from hands and feet are rarely curated during such practices.

These events may have been located during specific times in the annual cycle, and perhaps during specific times of the day—death and regeneration ceremonies, for instance, are often linked with particular seasons and solar events, such as the rising and setting sun. The preferred westerly or easterly orientation of most of these sites is possibly significant in this respect.

In other words, the chalk surfaces hosted noisy ceremonies in which the social order was temporarily subverted ("the carnivalesque"), and the participants said farewell to deceased members of the community by placing their bones within the midden. It seems highly likely that these ceremonies were organized by priests, but were these priests called Druids? The word *druid* is often linked to the oak-tree, perhaps because of a remark by Pliny the Elder[101]:

> The Druids—for that is the name they give to their magicians—held nothing more sacred than the mistletoe and the tree that bears it, supposing always that tree to be the oak. Of itself the oak is selected by them to form whole groves, and they perform none of their religious rites without employing branches of it; so much so, that it is very probable that the priests themselves may have received their name from the Greek name for that tree.

In fact, the word *druid* is probably made up of two elements. The first is related to Old Indian *daru, dru-* "wood," Greek *doru* "wood; spear" (first attested in Homer), Greek *drys* "oak," Old Irish *derucc* "acorn," Old Irish *daur* "oak," Welsh *derwen* "oak"[102]; while the second is related to Old Indian *veda* "knows, understands," Greek *eido* "I see," Latin *video* "see," Old Irish *find* "white," Old Irish *fiss* "knowledge," Welsh *gwys* "summons."[103] If the Druids first emerged in the Late Bronze Age, then the name may well have meant "those who understand wood."

Wood was important in the Late Neolithic/Early Bronze Age, and again in the Late Bronze Age. Timber was used in the Late Neolithic/Early Bronze Age to construct timber circles at Durrington Walls and Marden, and the processional route at Thornborough henges. In the Late Bronze Age, timber was used to construct the post alignment and wooden platform at Flag Fen, the raised brushwood platforms at Washingborough, the palisade at Runnymede Bridge, and the "feasting structures" at All Cannings Cross.

Perhaps the most important Late Bronze Age site with a timber structure is the enclosure known as Paddock Hill, at Thwing in East Yorkshire, about 8 miles from North Sea coast at Bridlington. Excavation was undertaken between 1973 and 1987 by Terence Manby, initially under the assumption that the site was a henge. However, the excavations revealed a long and complex sequence of use of the site. The earliest activity was represented by some flints of Mesolithic date, including microliths, cores and flakes. Earlier Neolithic activity was also represented solely by artifacts, including flint arrowheads, scrapers and stone axes, plus some sherds of Peterborough Ware. The first major constructional phase occurred in the late Neolithic, when a henge comprising a circular ditch around 65 yards in diameter with external chalk bank was created. Grooved Ware and Beaker sherds are among the finds associated with the henge, which featured opposed northwest and southeast entrances. The earlier Bronze Age is represented primarily by artifacts, including some flint implements and Food Vessel sherds.

The site was extensively remodeled in the later Bronze Age. The silted-up henge ditch was recut, and a central post circle constructed, 56 feet in diameter and surrounding a central pit containing an urned cremation. Artifacts and other debris of mid-to-late Bronze Age were also present, including evidence for metalworking activity. Next, a more substantial enclosure was constructed comprising a ditch and internal rampart some 125 yards in diameter, completely enclosing the earlier enclosure. The rampart featured timber revetment and was retained at its rear by a double row of posts; a radiocarbon date of 1134–1006 BC was obtained for an unweathered occupation layer immediately beneath the rampart. This larger enclosure also featured opposed entrances on the same alignment as the earlier henge. Roughly contemporary is a ring slot around 82 feet in diameter, within and concentric to the earlier henge, and interpreted as a large timber building.[104] However, the structure was "so large that it is not certain that it could have been roofed." It seems likely that "large-scale food consumption" took place at Thwing—"this is shown by a considerable deposit of animal bones in the ditch terminals of the inner enclosure."[105]

The archaeologist Mike Parker Pearson, in a paper on Iron Age cosmology, discusses the orientation of roundhouses in the Iron Age, and links this to the site at Thwing. Throughout Britain, he says,[106]

> the roundhouses which characterize the Iron Age share a consistent set of orientations, with few exceptions, during the period from the Late Bronze Age after c. 900 BC until the

Butser Ancient Farm, near Petersfield in Hampshire, a reconstruction of an Iron Age village found on nearby Butser Hill, April 22, 2011 (Midnightblueowl).

first century AD. The majority of house entrances are orientated towards the east and southeast, not so as to provide optimal sunlight or shelter from the wind but so that their doorways might be aligned on sunrise at the equinoxes or at midwinter.

This orientation toward sunrise at the equinoxes or midwinter does not apply only to roundhouses[107]:

> This concern with the directionality of entrances is also found in the gateways to the settlement compounds and enclosures. The majority of these face broadly east or broadly west, or both. In southern Britain, the largest enclosures, "hillforts," usually have two entrances, one facing east and the other west. Most inhumation burials were laid out with the corpse facing east.

This is where Thwing enters the picture:

> The archaeological origins of this orientational concern with the east and southeast can be traced back to the Later Bronze Age. The large circular monument at Thwing on the Yorkshire Wolds contains, at its centre, a large circular post structure thought to be a roofed building but which might possibly be just a timber ring in association with a deposit of animal bones derived from feasting. The outer enclosure and the inner structure are both orientated on an axis facing towards the southeast. Associated metalwork apparently dates to the thirteenth-eleventh centuries BC, placing the construction of this remarkable building many centuries before the widespread adoption of the easterly/south-easterly axis in roundhouses.

Like Iron Age huts, the Late Bronze Age large circular post structure at Thwing was oriented toward the southeast. With its enclosure, feasting and timber structure oriented toward the sunrises at the equinoxes or midwinter, Thwing was surely a place where Druids—"those who understand wood"—played an important role.

As I said, All Cannings Cross is near a causewayed enclosure, suggesting that the Druids were the successors of the Neolithic priests who built great monuments like Stonehenge and Marden henge.

The End of the Bronze Age

In many ways, the Late Bronze Age seems to be a reaction against the Early Bronze Age. Burials with prestigious grave goods (amber, gold, bronze daggers) in round barrows that often made up large barrow cemeteries came to an end, and the dead, who had once imposed themselves on the landscape, became virtually invisible. What followed was almost a return to the Neolithic, with the feasting that characterized henges like Durrington Walls, and the resumption of excarnation as a burial rite. But while the de-fleshed dead of the Early Neolithic were buried in tombs like West Kennet Long Barrow, now the bones of the dead (especially skulls) were cast into watery places like rivers, lakes or fens, or buried in gigantic middens like All Cannings Cross, Potterne, East Chisenbury and Llanmaes.

The main gods were the god of fire and water, celebrated at the burnt mounds which sprang up all over Britain, and the earth goddess, venerated at the great middens in Wiltshire, Oxfordshire and the Vale of Glamorgan. The Late Bronze Age was not an age of monuments, but that was soon to change when Iron Age Britons began enclosing their hilltops and creating the first hillforts.

CHAPTER 4

The Age of Depositions (2): The Sky God and Iron Age Hillforts

The Sky God

The most spectacular monuments of the Iron Age are the hillforts, which are found throughout Britain, from Cornwall to the Scottish Highlands. As we saw, Late Bronze Age Britons set up burnt mounds to worship the god of fire and water, and established huge middens in honor of the earth-goddess, but the hillforts were almost certainly dedicated to the sky god.

The name of the Sky God can be traced across a vast area of the Indo-European world, from India to Italy. In India he is *Dyaus Pita* "Sky Father," while in Greece he is Zeus, the king of the gods. In Phrygian, a language spoken in Asia Minor (now Turkey), he is *Tiy-*, in Thracian *Zi-*, *Diu-* or *Dias-* (in personal names), in Messapian (a language spoken in southeastern Italy), he is *Zis* or *Dis*. In Latin, his name is preserved in *Jovis* (older *Diouis*), the genitive of *Jupiter* (*Diespiter* in old and poetic Latin), the Roman equivalent of Zeus.[1]

The name originated as one of a number of words built on the Indo-European root *dei-*, "give off light," and located in the semantic sphere "brightness of heaven, heaven, daylight. day." This root also gives Latin *dies* "day," Vedic *dive-dive* "day by day," and Old Irish *die* "day," as well as Latin *deus*, Old Irish *dia*, Welsh *duw* "god."

Strangely, there is no Celtic sky god related to Zeus, and instead there is a thunder god called *Taranis*, related to Old Irish *torann*, "thunder," Welsh *taran* "thunder." Taranis is only mentioned once in classical literature. In his poem *Civil War*, the poet Lucan (AD 39–AD 65)[2] speaks of

> those who pacify with blood accursed
> Savage Teutates, Hesus' horrid shrines,
> And Taranis' altars cruel as were those
> Loved by Diana, goddess of the north

Taranis is the equivalent of the Vedic god Indra, and the ancient Germanic god Donar (related to English *thunder*), also known as Thor, who gave his name to *Thursday*. He is also the equivalent of Tarhun ("Conqueror"), the god of sky and storm among the Bronze Age Luwian-speaking people of western Anatolia.

The oldest dedication to Taranis is in Gaulish (a Celtic language), written in the Greek alphabet, from the village of Orgon in the Bouches-du-Rhône department of southern France; here the name appears as the dative *Taranou* ("to Taranis"), which supposes a Gaulish form *Taranos*. At Amiens in northern France, an inscription bears the name

Taranuos, either a personal name or the name of the god. At Thauron in the Limousin region of central France, Jupiter is given the epithet *Taranuensis* "from the place of Taranis." In Germany and Croatia inscriptions give the name of a divinity *Taranucnus* "son of Taranis."[3] At the Romano-British site of Chester (*Deva*) in northwest England, there is an altar dedicated to *Jupiter Tanarus Optimus Maximus* "Jupiter Tanarus the Best and Greatest."[4]

Taranis is often linked to the Gaulish "wheel-god," found in numerous depictions in Gaul of *Jupiter Stator* holding a wheel in his hand, unlike the Roman *Jupiter Stator*, who holds a scepter. A figure wearing a bull-horned helmet and holding a wheel figures on the Gundestrup Cauldron, which was probably manufactured in Thrace (now Bulgaria) for Celtic clients, and dates from the Late Iron Age or Roman period. At Le Châtelet de Gourzon in the Haute-Marne department of northeastern France, there is a statuette depicting a Jupiter holding a wheel in the left hand and a thunderbolt in the right hand.[5]

The wheel probably represents the sun, and the symbol seems to date from the Late Bronze Age. In the Musée des Antiquités Nationales at St. Germain near Paris there is a hoard of bronzework from Réallons in southeastern France which dates to the period 950–750 BC; the hoard contains at least three bronze miniature wheel-pendants.[6] From the Late Iron Age defended settlement of Bibracte near Autun in Burgundy came a bronze five-spoked wheel about an inch in diameter; the same site also produced what is possibly a mold for a four-spoked wheel, made of stone.

There are no miniature wheels in Late Bronze Age/Early Iron Age Britain, and all we have to guide us are animal sacrifices, in particular cattle and horses. Cattle were sacrificed in Britain during the Neolithic, and this certainly continued into the Early Bronze Age. In Indo-European mythology, the bull is associated with the Anatolian sky and storm god Tarhun—in Anatolian iconography, the god is depicted driving a primitive kind of chariot drawn by bulls, and the bull is his sacred animal, sometimes standing alone on an altar as his cult-symbol. In Greek mythology, Zeus becomes a bull and carries off the Phoenician princess Europa—this myth is first found in the *Catalogue of Women*, attributed to Hesiod and dating from the 6th century BC. In the Indian *Rigveda*, Indra, the god of rain and thunderstorms, is repeatedly called a bull.[7] Bulls, of course have horns, which may explain the figure on the Gundestrup Cauldron.

Horses became important in sacrifice from the Late Bronze Age/Early Iron Age in Britain. Horses had great significance in early Indo-European religion: consider, for example, the Vedic Ashvins ("Possessors of Horses"), divine horsemen associated with the sun, and the Mycenaean *Iqeja*, which may be compared with Latin *equus*, Old Irish *ech* "horse." The name *Iqeja* appears on a Linear B tablet at Pylos in the Peloponnese, as *Potnia Iqeja* "Mistress of the Horses" (Linear B is a writing system based on the Minoan system of writing called Linear A; *Potnia* was used as a title for goddesses). In later Greek *Iqeja* became *Hippeia* "of the horses," and became an epithet of the goddess Athena, who supposedly taught mankind how to tame horses and was worshipped in Athens. The epithet *Hippeia* was also applied to the goddess Demeter in Arcadia, in the Peloponnese. The god Poseidon pursued Demeter when she was mourning the loss of her daughter Persephone. The goddess took the form of a horse and hid amongst the herds of Arkadian Onkios, where Poseidon found her and, assuming the form of a stallion, raped the goddess. She bore him two children—the horse Arion and the goddess Despoina.

Here we should also mention the Dioscuri ("Sons of Zeus"), Castor and Pollux (Polydeuces). From the earliest times they were associated with horses. The 7th century BC

Greek poet Alcman, says in a fragment of poetry: "Most worthy of reverence from all gods and men, they dwell in a god-built home beneath the earth always alive, Castor—tamer of swift steeds, skilled horseman—and glorious Polydeuces." Alcaeus (6th century BC), in his *Hymn to the Dioscuri*, writes[8]:

> Come hither, leaving the island of Pelops,
> strong sons of Zeus and leda;
> appear with kindly heart,
> Castor and Pollux,
>
> who go on swift horses
> over the broad earth and all the sea,
> and easily rescue men,
> from chilling death,
>
> leaping on the peaks of their well-benched ships,
> brilliant from afar as you run up the fore-stays,
> bringing light to the black ship
> in the night of trouble.

The 5th century BC Greek poet Pindar, in his *Olympian Ode* 3, refers to Castor and Pollux (Polydeuces) as having "fine horses," which is comparable to the description of the Ashvins in *Rigveda* Chapter 7, Hymn 68; and in his *Pythian Ode* 1, he says that Castor and Pollux have "bright horses."

Reaching for the Sky: Iron Age Hillforts

The sky god or the god of storm and thunder must have been important to Early Iron Age Britons because they began literally reaching for the sky, establishing settlements on hilltops known as hillforts. Hillforts can be defined as enclosed spaces "constructed in a highly-visible location to serve as a focus (if sporadic) for communal activity."[9] Hillforts are found throughout Britain, but the largest concentration is in in central southern England, in a broad band running from the south coast to north Wales. The first proper hillforts were built in the 6th or 5th century BC, and often had ramparts faced with timber or stone walling. In the 5th and 4th centuries BC, hillforts were built with a glacis rampart (a dump of loose soil that continued the slope of the ditch side up to the rampart top). In the 4th and 3rd centuries some hillforts became developed hillforts, "with enhanced entrances, sometimes with external hornworks added to create a more impressive approach."[10]

The traditional view is that hillforts were built to defend against enemy attacks, but as the archaeologist Barry Cunliffe observes, most early hillforts had two opposed entrances, which "are more appropriate to a society structuring its comings and goings and perhaps indulging in formal processions than one wishing to defend itself against aggression."[11] He points out that Neolithic henge monuments of the 3rd millennium BC, which are usually regarded as ritual spaces, also had opposed entrances. Even when the enclosures were reconfigured in the Middle Iron Age to have only a single gate, "that structure was usually greatly elaborated to make the liminal space much more extensive by creating a long passage formed by hornworks and inturns." This may have had a military function or served as a display of power, but it could just as well have had a ritual significance.

We don't know for certain what hillforts were called in prehistoric Britain, but in the Roman period a hillfort was a *dunum*, and names ending in *-dunum* attested in the ancient sources are concentrated in southern Gaul, with examples also in central and northern Gaul, in the Rhineland, in the lands south of the upper and middle Danube, and in Britain (for example *Camulodunum* at Colchester in Essex and *Sorviodunum* at Salisbury in Wiltshire). The etymology of *dunum* is obscure: Pokorny linked it to Latin *funus*, "funeral," perhaps originally meaning a "funeral mound"[12]; Watkins links it to Hittite *tuhhusta*, "it is finished," reconstructed from an Indo-European root *dheuh-* or *dhus-*, "to finish, come to an end, come full circle," and adds: "The closing enclosure of the circular ring fort, Celtic *duno-*, and the societal ceremony at the close of life, Latin *fu-nes-*, are both metaphorical extensions of this single basic notion."[13] Watkins notes that *tuhhusta* is "used very commonly in ritual texts from Old Hittite on to signal the end of an episode in the ritual."[14] This etymology of *dunum* seems to support Cunliffe's view that hillforts were primarily ritual spaces.

However, it is equally possible that the earliest name for a hillfort was something like Welsh *llys* or Irish *liss/less*, "enclosure," and that hillforts were dedicated to the earth-goddess Litavis, the god that Caesar calls Dis. Curiously, the Welsh *llys* survives in Liss, a village in Hampshire, far from the Celtic regions of Britain like Cornwall and Wales. Why this should be so is unclear, but early Anglo-Saxon settlement was in the Meon Valley to the southwest of Liss, and at Chalton to the south of Liss, so it is possible that Liss remained in British hands for some time after the departure of the Romans. It may be significant that a Roman villa was recently unearthed near Liss, together with an Iron Age roundhouse.[15]

The Earliest Hillforts

Palisaded Enclosures

The earliest hillforts, probably constructed in the Late Bronze Age or Early Iron Age, were palisaded enclosures: among these are Breiddin hillfort near Criggion in Powys, east Wales (10th/9th century BC); Moel y Gaer near Llantysilio in Denbighshire, northeast Wales (8th/7th century BC); Dinorben at Abergele in north Wales; and Blewburton Hill in Oxfordshire.[16]

Breiddin hillfort was excavated in the late 1960s and early 1970s in advance of quarrying. A sizeable area of the hillfort defenses was excavated, showing that the Iron Age rampart was a simple bank of stone partly quarried from rock outcrops on the uphill side. This helped to create a narrow, sheltered zone just behind the bank which revealed intensive signs of activity. Two quite different types of building structures—roundhouses and four-posters—had been crammed into this space. One of the most important results of the rampart excavations, however, was the discovery of a double row of postholes below the Iron Age rampart, representing a later Bronze Age line of defense. Finds associated with this period of occupation include various bronze tools and weapons such as a socketed ax, a socketed hammer, socketed spearhead, sword handle as well as ornaments such as dress pins. This period of occupation has been shown to date to between about 1000–800 BC.[17]

Moel y Gaer hillfort was extensively excavated in the 1970s, prior to the construction of a reservoir. The hillfort was occupied, perhaps discontinuously, between about the late 7th century BC until some time prior to the Roman conquest. In an earlier phase a settlement of substantial timber roundhouses was defended by a timber palisade. The defenses were subsequently replaced by a ditch and rampart of stone and earth, in this instance protecting a settlement of stake-walled roundhouses with numerous rectangular structures with four large posts, possibly representing raised buildings for storing grain.[18]

Dinorben hillfort was established in the 9th/8th century BC on a limestone promontory overlooking the Clwyd lowlands. Excavations were carried out by Willoughby Gardner from 1912 to 1922,[19] and by Hubert Savory, 1965-69. In 1977-78, excavations were undertaken on the last vestiges of the hillfort before it was finally quarried away. Earlier excavations had already shown that this important site had a long sequence of occupation from the Late Bronze Age through to the late Roman period. Excavations in 1977-78 focused on clarifying the dating of the defensive sequence and on recovering evidence of settlement in part of the interior. Radiocarbon dates indicate that the earliest rampart defending the settlement was built between the 7th-5th centuries BC.[20]

In 1868, well before the hillfort was excavated, a hoard of over 100 bronze horse harness fittings was discovered immediately below the western defenses of the hillfort. In the early excavations, fragments of human crania (skulls) were found in the floors of three houses, as well as in one of the guard chambers at the main entrance, all in the Early Iron Age levels of the hillfort. A further mandible (jaw) fragment, recovered from the ditch next to the entrance, was interpreted by the excavators as a fallen part of a decayed trophy head, formerly displayed over the gateway.[21]

The hillfort on Blewburton Hill near Didcot in Oxfordshire was first excavated in 1947-9 by A.E.P. Collins, who uncovered an Early Iron Age settlement, evidenced by much pottery, grain storage pits, post holes, and the trench of a timber palisade. It was again excavated in 1967 by D.W. Harding, who found that only half of the 10 acre hillfort had been occupied by the earlier Iron Age camp with its palisade trench. Finds included pottery, 2 shale pendants, fragments of shale bracelets and an iron currency bar. The settlement started as a palisaded enclosure, then was fortified with a box rampart and finally a dump rampart. Pottery suggests a Late Bronze Age occupation, transitional into the earliest Iron Age. Provisionally, therefore, the construction of the palisaded enclosure appears to have occurred in the 7th/6th century BC, with the first hillfort proper being constructed in the 6th/5th century BC.[22] When Collins was excavating Blewburton Hill, he found that a defensive ditch contained the skeleton of a man buried beside the skeleton of a horse—immediately in front of the stifle joint (the equivalent of the knee) of the right hind leg was an iron pin or rivet, and a few inches away were several sherds of a black burnished pot. After the removal of the horse's skeleton a very well preserved example of an iron adze was found lying on its side. Further clearing revealed the complete skeleton of a dog, and more sherds of the black burnished pot.[23] The finds suggest that the burial dates to the Middle Iron Age (400 BC-100 BC).

Some of the earliest hillforts were in Wales, and this suggests that the first hillforts may have developed along the Atlantic seaboard. In fact, one of the earliest hillforts in the British Isles is Mooghaun hillfort in County Clare in the west of Ireland. This site consists of a hill fully circumscribed by three concentric walls that "were most likely meant to define the hilltop as a sacred precinct."[24] The outer wall has a mean diameter of around 437 yards and defines an area of 27 acres in extent. It originally consisted of a bank that averages 36 feet in width and an outer ditch 19 feet wide. Ironworking, bronze-making and quern-making debris dating to the Iron Age was recovered from the summit. Two early medieval cashels (ringforts) had been built on top of the site's outer and middle enclosure walls. In and around the site are the numerous remains of other enclosures and *fulacht fiadh* (burnt mounds). The largest hoard of Late Bronze Age gold objects ever to be found in Ireland was discovered in 1854, 765 yards to the northeast of Mooghaun hillfort in what used to be a part of Mooghaun Loch. On the basis of several radiocarbon dates, including one from beneath the outer rampart wall, the excavator concluded that the enclosing walls were constructed in the final two decades of the 10th century BC.

Vitrified Hillforts

Vitrified hillforts, which are mostly found in Scotland, are hillforts that show evidence of having been subjected to such extreme heat that all, some or part of the structures were vitrified or calcined (vitrification is a chemical process by which silicate-based rocks are turned into a glass-like amorphous solid, while calcination is the loss of moisture, reduction or oxidation in carbonate rocks). These vitrified forts, says Cunliffe,[25] are a subset of Scottish hillforts with timber-laced ramparts the best known of which is Abernethy in Perth and Kinross, eastern Scotland, the type-site of the "Abernethy complex" of hillforts with timber-laced ramparts. In the hillforts of Scotland,

> the characteristic rampart structure consists of a rubble-and-earth core faced inside and out with dry-stone walling, the whole bonded by rows of horizontal timbers which project through the outer, and sometimes the inner, wall-face.... Half a dozen or so forts have produced direct evidence of timber-lacing but more than sixty of the Scottish sites belong to what is called the vitrified class, all examples showing signs of widespread burning of the timber-lacing causing the core material of the rampart to become discoloured and to fuse.

In other words, the timber lacing was set on fire, and the great heat caused the dry-stone walling to vitrify.

Cunliffe goes on to say[26] that for charred beams or planks from behind the wall at Finavon, Oathlaw, eastern Scotland, a 7th century BC radiocarbon date was obtained, with supporting dates spanning the 6th to 3rd centuries for subsequent levels. At Craigmarloch Wood, Renfrewshire, to the west of Glasgow, charcoal from beneath the wall provided a date in the 8th century BC. At Craig Phadrig, Inverness, dates spanning the 5th to 1st centuries BC were obtained for charcoal associated with the vitrified rampart of the fort. Cunliffe concludes that "many of the forts must originate in the seventh or even the eighth century"[27]:

> The Abernethy style forts originate, therefore, at the time when contacts between Scotland and the Hallstatt cultures of Europe were at their height. Similarities have been noted ... between the Scottish style of timber-lacing and the method employed on the Swiss site of Wittnauer Horn in both its Hallstatt B3 (Late Urnfield) and its Hallstatt C/D phases, and at Montlingerberg, another Late Urnfield fort in Switzerland.

Ritual in the Earliest Hillforts

There are some signs of ritual activity in the earliest hillforts. At Dinorben in north Wales, a hoard of horse harness fittings was buried beneath the western rampart, and human skulls and a mandible were found in the hillfort. At Blewburton Hill in Oxfordshire, a man was buried with a horse and dog, underlining the ritual importance of the horse in the Late Bronze Age and Iron Age.

The vitrified hillforts of Scotland underline the importance of fire in the Late Bronze Age and Iron Age. Fire obviously had ritual significance among early Indo-European peoples, but surprisingly, there is no universal fire-god. Agni was the god of fire in Bronze Age India, but the only related words are Latin *ignis*, Old Church Slavonic *ogni* and Lithuanian *ugnis* "fire." Vesta was the goddess of the hearth in Roman religion—her name is probably related to Old Indian *osati* "burns," Latin *uro* "to burn," Old Norse *ysja* "fire." English *fire* is related to Greek *pyr* and Umbrian *pir* "fire" (Umbrian is an extinct language spoken in Italy until the 1st century BC), which have no obvious connections with the sacred.

However, the Celtic words for "fire" come from a different family of words, which includes Old Indian *tapas* "heat, blaze, glow; spiritual heat," Latin *tepeo* "to be lukewarm," Umbrian *tefra* "burnt offerings," Old Irish *teine* "fire," Welsh *tân* "fire," Old Irish *tess* "heat."[28] The Old Indian word *tapas* has various meanings in the Bronze Age Vedic texts, all related to the central meaning of "heat" or "warmth." *Tapas* thus refers to "natural heat, such as that emitted by the sun or fire. It refers also to the natural heat associated with biological conception, embryonic "maturation," and birth. Thus the heat of sexual desire, the heat of sexual excitation, and the heat generated during sexual intercourse are all rendered by the noun *tapas*." *Tapas* also refers to "the heat of asceticism, to the heat generated by austerities, and thus to a voluntary and "nonnatural" heat."[29] In the *Atharva Veda*, all the gods are described as *tapas*-born (*tapojas*).

We get a clue about what fire may have meant to the prehistoric Celts in a story about the Irish mythological hero Cu Chulainn, who appears in the 11th/12th century *Tain Bo Cuailnge* ("Cattle Raid of Cooley"). Old Irish *tess* "heat" is the word used to reference the "heat" that was released from within the raging Cu Chulainn and so warmed the cold water vats in which he was immersed: "The vat burst around him. The second tub into which he was thrown boiled with fist-sized bubbles from that. The third vat into which he went afterwards, he heated it so that its heat and coldness were suitable for him."[30] Here heat is associated with the rage of the warrior Cu Chulainn, but in prehistoric times heat and fire may have well have been associated with the sun, creation and with the gods.

Hillforts in the Early-Middle Iron Age

Wiltshire

Evidence for ritual activity is relatively scarce in the earliest hillforts, but much more common in later hillforts. One of the earliest hillforts in Wiltshire was Lidbury Camp, near the East Chisenbury midden, excavated in 1913 by Maud Cunnington. She found pottery there similar to the pottery of All Cannings Cross, which she had excavated a few years earlier, with more coarse wares than fine wares.[31] In one pit she found "the jaw bones of two dogs, and of two ponies, and the hoof of a pony"[32]—these were probably ritual deposits. An arm bone (humerus) was found on the occupied floor of the outer ditch east of the entrance. Three separate fragments of skulls were found in different parts of the ditch, and one fragment in Pit 7; two vertebrae came from the ditch on the

Exmoor pony mare and foal on Porlock Common in Somerset, July 18, 2010. The Exmoor pony may be similar to horses used in the Iron Age (Nilfanion).

eastern side of the entrenchment; but "the most curious of these human relics was that of the upper part of an ulna [elbow bone] cut and shaped into a scoop-like implement."[33]

Another important hillfort in Wiltshire is Yarnbury Castle, a multivallate hillfort of 27 acres at Berwick St. James to the west of Amesbury. It began life as an Early Iron Age enclosure of 12 acres—sherds of cordoned and haematite coated bowls (5th century BC) were found near the bottom of the ditch when the hillfort was excavated in 1932.[34] The hillfort was constructed in the Middle Iron Age–Yarnbury-Highfield style saucepan pots have been found there, dating from the 4th to the 2nd centuries BC. The hillfort was intensively occupied—a survey found over 130 probable structures, presumably representing the sites of round houses as well as pits and other features.[35]

The excavator Maud Cunnington found numerous "detached fragments of humanity" in various ditches,[36] including the upper half of a femur (thigh bone), the upper half of a radius (one of the bones of the forearm), a lower jaw "with a fine set of teeth," the shaft of a femur (thigh bone), and the frontal bone of a skull. Cunnington notes that the "presence of burials close to the dwellings, often in pits not dug for the purpose, with evidence that the remains were deposited with little care, as in the case of Pit 2, as well as the frequent occurrence of detached and fragmentary human bones, is a persistent and interesting feature in connection with Iron Age sites." It has been suggested that the fragments of skulls bear witness to a head-hunting cult, says Cunnington, but this does not account for the limb bones:

> a more interesting suggestion has been made, that seems worthy of consideration, connected with the religious ideas of the people. The Druids taught that after death the soul

passed from one body to another.... A logical result of this teaching would be an indifference to to what becoomes of the body after death, and if this were indeed the case, it might to a great extent account for the remarkable rarity of rich and ceremonial burials of this period, and for the careless methods of burial within and about the settlements.

A third hillfort in Wiltshire is more significant for its location than for what is known about it. Around 500 BC a hillfort was built near Stonehenge, which is today known as Vespasian's Camp (the 16th century antiquarian William Camden gave the hillfort this name because he thought it had been built by the Roman general Vespasian). There was a period of intense occupation on the hillfort, represented by deposits of domestic waste over 3 feet thick that accumulated against the inner face of the ramparts; there is a lack of secondary occupation deposits, the pottery dating mainly to the 5th century BC, with Middle Iron Age types being almost entirely absent. The most diagnostic pottery was scratched cordoned bowls of the All Cannings Cross-Meon Hill type, dated to the 5th–4th century BC.[37]

No burials have been found at Vespasian's Camp, but to the west of Vespasian's Camp is Wilsford Shaft. Wilsford Shaft is a shaft 98 feet deep surrounded at the surface by an enclosing ditch bank some 39 feet in diameter, discovered during excavations in 1960–62; it may have been a well, a place for ritual deposition, or both. A range of deposits were recovered, the earliest being Bronze Age in date, comprising a shale ring, amber beads and bone pins, along with animal bone and organic materials, including wooden containers. The excavator Paul Ashbee argued that the ring, beads and pins should be interpreted as votive deposits, of a type similar to those found as grave furniture in Wessex in the Early Bronze Age. He stresses that there is a very strong possibility that many shafts may exist adjacent to the major round barrow cemeteries of Wessex and that the chthonic (underworld) "cult" of the Iron Age and Roman periods may well have a much earlier origin.[38] Radiocarbon dating of the lower organic remains gave a date for the shaft of 1470–1290 BC.[39]

In the Iron Age the shaft was used for deposition of human and animal bone. The human bone represents a minimum of five individuals (two infants, one juvenile and two adults); both adults were tentatively identified as male. The lowest bones are two adult left femurs (thigh bones), found at 8 feet 6 inches.[40] One femur was radiocarbon

Vespasian's Camp hillfort, Amesbury (north bank), April 5, 2008 (Psychostevouk).

dated to around 370 BC, while the other was dated to around 410 BC. Animal bone from a similar period was also found nearby. A horse calcaneum (also called hock, the equivalent of the ankle bone in humans), dated to around 500 BC, was found at 7 feet 8 inches, while a horse cuboid/tibia (the cuboid is part of the hock, the tibia connect the stifle, or knee joint, to the hock), dated to around 530 BC, was found at 9 feet 6 inches.[41]

Hampshire

The best known hillfort in Hampshire is Danebury at Nether Wallop near Andover, on the eastern edge of Salisbury Plain, excavated by Barry Cunliffe over a period of twenty years. Cunliffe says that the settlement started life in the Late Bronze Age as a hilltop enclosure, a ritual site crowned by a circle of tall posts set in ritual pits (one with the possible sacrifice of dog). The first hill-fort was built in 5th century BC, after the ritual posts had rotted and the pits silted up; circular huts were associated with this phase. About 400 BC, or perhaps a little earlier, there was a major change. In the interior regular rows of rectangular house structures were established along planned streets, while "an impressive entrance was built on the east side, and the defences were strengthened and remodelled. Danebury had become a major hill-town and the seat of considerable political authority." This condition continued for some 300 years with regular maintenance of the defenses and rebuilding of the houses. About 100 BC "the eastern gateway was completely rebuilt on a grand scale and with complex defensive hornworks." Soon after, however, "the gate was destroyed, and the fort abandoned." Between 1971 and 1975 a continuous strip 98 feet–131 feet wide extending across the center of Danebury from one side to the other was completely excavated revealing pits, gullies, circular stake-built houses, rectangular buildings and 2-, 4- and 6- post structures ranging in date from the 6th century BC to the ends of the second century BC. About 100 BC "rectangular buildings, possibly of a religious nature, were erected." Excavations from 1976–80 "located further pits, houses and buildings, as well as a main road crossing the fort from the east entrance." Three more rectangular "ritual" buildings were also found. A hoard of twelve bronze axes and other objects of the 7th century BC was discovered within the fort in 1974 and 1977, suggesting that occupation at Danebury may have begun as early as the 7th century BC.[42]

During his excavation of Danebury, Cunliffe uncovered a large number of storage pits or underground silos, and notes that they are common on all settlement sites. It had earlier been thought that they were constructed to protect the grain from raids, but Cunliffe believes they had a different function. In his view, the seed was placed in storage pits after harvesting and before sowing, so it would be protected by the "chthonic deities" (gods or goddesses of the underworld). Once the seed was sown, offerings were made to the chthonic deities in thanks for their protection of the grain.[43]

The nature of these offerings varied considerably. One offering at Danebury involved a dog and a horse which has been partially dismembered, its head and one foreleg being placed separately against the pit side.[44] In another pit were a pig and two calves.[45] Articulated horse legs were found six or seven times in a sample of 200 pits, indicating that this offering had some sort of religious significance.

But these offerings did not only involve animals. Some 300 depositions of human remains have been found at Danebury, including skulls. Fifteen complete or near complete skulls have been found in pits, together with about 30 skull fragments.[46] Two of the male skulls bear marks of sword wounds. Isolated skulls were placed in the middle or upper parts of pit fills (unlike complete bodies, which were placed towards the bottom of the pit). Humans were sometimes buried with animals. The pelvis of a young male aged between 18 and 25 was placed in the bottom, and in the center, of an elongated pit with a pig skull and the innominate (hip) bone of a child nearby. There was evidence that the legs had been hacked off and the pelvis violently severed from the trunk. Five sets of human remains were buried in pits along with a raven, a bird associated with death in Celtic mythology: there were a skull and disarticulated human bone in one pit, a female skull fragment and a male torso in another, a crouched skeleton in two further pits, and disarticulated human bone in a final pit.[47]

Dorset

Maiden Castle hillfort near Dorchester in Dorset was built on the site of an Early Neolithic causewayed enclosure. There are believed to be three main phases for the Iron Age occupation of the site. Initially, in the Early Iron Age, it was a univallate hillfort, defined by a single rampart enclosing only the eastern end of the hill. During the second half of the 3rd century BC the ramparts were extended to the west and during the mid–2nd century BC the ramparts were rebuilt on a larger scale. The ramparts of the later multivallate hillfort consisted of three banks and two ditches around the hilltop, with an extra bank and ditch to the south, and two complex entrances. The interior of the fort was intensively occupied. Excavation revealed traces of circular and rectangular huts evi-

Maiden Castle hillfort, Dorchester, Dorset, near the Western Entrance (author's photograph).

The view from Maiden Castle hillfort, looking over Dorchester (author's photograph).

One of the massive ditches of Maiden Castle, near the Western Entrance (author's photograph).

Maiden Castle seen from below (author's photograph)

dent from post holes, trenches and floor remains, as well as over 50 human burials, many within a cemetery at the eastern end of the site.[48] The excavation was carried out in the 1930s by Mortimer Wheeler, who divided the inhumation cemetery into "war" and "peace" components, and believed that the cemetery was proof that the Romans had stormed Maiden Castle after a bloody battle with its native inhabitants. However, Niaill Sharples, who carried out further excavations in 1985 and 1986, refuted this, pointing out that (1) there is no evidence indicating that the death of these individuals occurred at Maiden Castle; (2) they were buried in the traditional manner, and not inhumed in mass graves; (3) some individuals had wounds that had begun to heal, as indicated by bone regrowth; (4) the charcoal layer on which Wheeler based his statement that the settlement was partially burned probably resulted from iron-working; and (5) most of the projectiles recovered on the hilltop are of Late Iron Age, not Roman type. Sharples believed that the burials could well have been brought to the hillfort from elsewhere, implying that burial on the hillfort was reserved for honored members of the community.[49]

Somerset

Cadbury Castle, to the northeast of Yeovil in Somerset, was excavated by Alcock between 1966 and 1970. The Late Bronze Age and the initial Iron Age phases are believed to have been unenclosed, with enclosure and the long sequence of rampart building and extension beginning early in the Iron Age, and continuing at intervals throughout. Occupation evidence consists of numerous post holes and trenches representing four- and six-post structures as well as round houses. Numerous pits were also encountered, some containing objects that had clearly been deliberately placed rather than casually discarded, such as horse and cattle skulls. Among the artifacts recovered was a Late Iron Age hoard which featured, among other items, an ax, a saw blade, sickles and a currency bar.[50]

In 2000 a report was published by English Heritage reviewing Alcock's excavation. Here some clarification is given on the deposition of animal skulls. In pit C106 an ox skull lay on the initial layer of silt and rubble, and was then covered with burnt material. Pit C054.4 contained a thick band of charcoal and green clay approximately 10 inches from the bottom of the pit. Large slabs of stone were set into this layer, and two ox skulls were placed on these stones in the north part of the pit. The two ox skulls from pit C202 were from different layers; the first skull to be deposited was contained within a gravel layer above sticky silt, and the second skull lay above a yellow brown stony soil. The remainder of this pit was filled with an ashy dump. Pit C102 contained a horse skull lying upside down in a rubble dump that overlay a naturally infilled deposit of rubble and silt.[51]

Gloucestershire

Nottingham Hill at Gotherington to the north of Cheltenham in Gloucestershire is an Iron Age promontory fort consisting of a double bank with medial ditch and vestiges of an outer ditch cutting of around 120 acres of the hilltop. Two Ewart-Park type Late Bronze Age swords were ploughed up in the hillfort in 1972, which can be dated to between 800 BC and 700 BC. Subsequent excavation revealed an undisturbed Late Bronze Age hoard contained possibly in a box structure. It consisted of three leaf shaped swords, a looped palstave, socketed knife, bronze cylinder, cast conical headed rivets, cast bronze rings with bronze strap work, a tanged chisel, tanged "awl," a whetstone and a casting jet. The Cotswold Archaeological Research Group found a cup and ring marked stone during surface collection of occupation debris in October 1981. The stone was made of Oolitic limestone and had 2 cup marks and 3 channels two of which are rings.[52] It was found immediately to the rear of the inner rampart, and may have originally been built into the rampart.[53] Cup and ring marked stones belong to the Neolithic or Bronze Age, so Nottingham Hill was clearly a significant place over a very long period of time.

Oxfordshire

The hillfort near the midden at Wittenham Clumps in Oxfordshire was fortified in the Early Iron Age—the defenses consisted of a substantial ditch with a counterscarp bank on its outside edge and a rampart on the inner.[54] Pit 3152 within the hillfort contained a "remarkable sequence of human burials." At the base lay an adult male crouched on his right side with his head to the south. A patch of charred material lay close to the feet, and a sheep/goat humerus and a rib lay under the left arm. He has been dated to 370–160 BC. The burial was covered by a deposit of silty clay containing small amounts of pottery and animal bone. This was overlain by a further deposit of silty clay containing four partially articulated sections of an adult female skeleton: the left femur and pelvis, the left tibia (shinbone), the sacrum and lower spine and a medial section of the spine and ribs. Cut marks were present at the distal end of the femur and proximal end of the tibia, probably from the dismemberment or defleshing of the body. A cattle skull lay close to the skeleton, and a sheep/goat skull slightly higher in the backfill.[55]

Cambridgeshire

Stonea Camp in the Cambridgeshire Fens between Ely and Peterborough is the lowest hillfort in Britain, lying just 6 feet 6 inches above sea level. Situated at the southern end of an "island" of raised ground in the fens, the outermost earthworks enclose an area of 22 acres. It seems that the extant earthworks represent more than one phase of construction—three have been tentatively suggested, although excavations to date have been of limited use in establishing the correct sequence. No stratified, datable finds have come from any of the bank and ditch sections of the main earthworks, for example. Most artifacts have been recovered during fieldwalking and metal detecting, although some human remains turned up in the early 1990s trenches, including a child's skull bearing cut marks from a knife or sword, and a complete adult male skeleton in upper ditch fill. The camp overlies at least one and possibly 3 ring ditches of Early Bronze Age date, as well as indications of Neolithic activity (a flint handaxe). Jackson and Potter, who excavated Stonea in the 1980s, suggest an origin for the site in the Late Iron Age, possibly as an "infrequently visited centre of a ritual nature" (on the basis of the scarcity of finds and features indicative of any more intensive occupation), with the main period of activity falling in the period AD 40–60.[56]

Borough Fen enclosure on the River Welland, not far from the Neolithic causewayed enclosure at Maxey, is a well preserved Iron Age lowland fort on what would have once been a low, flat island in the Fens. The interior is entirely buried beneath clay and all its floors are still intact. The bank and ditch that surround it, too, are intact and the defensive ditch is waterlogged. In 1992–3, limited excavation was carried out along the sides of Redcow Drain, and sections through both ramparts were exposed. Organic material and Middle Iron Age pottery (3rd to 2nd century BC) were recovered from the water-logged primary fills of the main ditch.[57]

Northamptonshire

Hunsbury Hill is an Iron Age hillfort near Northampton occupied from the 4th century BC to the 1st century BC or AD. Excavations for ironstone at the end of the 19th century yielded great quantities of finds now in the Northampton and British Museums. Most of the interior was disturbed by this iron-working, but a small area to the southwest remains intact. In 1952 two trenches were excavated across the bank and ditch, revealing two phases of the rampart close to the eastern entrance. In 1988 the rampart was excavated in the northwest sector, and radiocarbon dates were obtained. The interior of the fort was riddled with 300 or more pits, of varying sizes—six or seven were walled and one possibly contained a crouched skeleton accompanied by an iron chariot tyre, bridle bit and other pieces of iron. Several unattached skulls were found, one with three holes bored in it, together with some 150 querns of the heavy bee-hive type. The quantity of iron objects and slag suggests early ironstone working.[58]

Well to the south of Hunsbury is Whittlebury, and here an Iron Age hillfort was discovered in 2000 in the vicinity of St. Mary's church and churchyard, which are sited on a prominent hill crest. As part of a broader program investigating the origins and development of the medieval settlement, a series of test pits was excavated across the modern village in 2001 and 2002. Test pits sunk 110 yards south-east of the church produced quantities of Iron Age pottery (in one instance over 50 sherds from a single 3 feet by 3 feet test pit) in association with features cut into the natural, together with evidence for a thick layer of redeposited clay interpreted as the degraded remains of a plowed out bank. In 2003, archaeological work was undertaken within the northern churchyard in advance of the sinking of a septic tank, together with the excavation of a number of further test pits along pipe trenches serving the new amenities within the church. These produced more Iron Age pottery, together with high quality late medieval wares. Over thirty individual skeletons were removed from the churchyard dating from the 11th to 14th century. Lying below these, and truncated by them, were the remains of three storage pits, containing large amounts of carbonized grain and the odd sherd of Iron Age pottery. One storage pit, however, remained largely intact, producing a classic Iron Age structured deposit. Four complete vessels had been placed on the base of the abandoned silo. These had been covered by an inert layer of soil, on top of which had been set part of a human skull, positioned perhaps to form a bowl. Another deposit of clean soil had been topped with a layer of animal bones, including an articulated horse leg, before the silo was capped with a thick layer of limestone cobbles. The presence of a hillfort was confirmed by a geophysical survey which located a ditch almost 20 feet in width and at least fourteen roundhouses ranging in size from 23 feet to 46 feet in diameter.[59]

Leicestershire

Burrough Hill, a univallate hillfort near Melton Mowbray in Leicestershire was first investigated in 1960 by Leicester University. Storage pits and a probable guard house at

Burrough Hill hillfort, Leicestershire, June 26, 2011—excavations in June 2011 just outside the entrance to the hillfort, with the earthworks in the background (Russ Hamer).

the southeast entrance, were excavated. Finds of pottery, Hunsbury type querns, a brooch and pin of iron were made. Further excavations in 1967–8 revealed storage pits containing animal bones and pottery dating from the 2nd century BC to mid–1st century AD. Since 2010 Leicester University have been again excavating the hillfort.

In 2011, a large pit was discovered beneath the cobbled road surface of the main hillfort entrance, and in the pit was a skeleton in a crouched position within a stone cairn. In 2012, a sub-rectangular pit within the hillfort interior was found to contain a skull in the center of the pit, with a quern stone placed on top of it. A tibia (shinbone) and a rib were also recovered. A horse skull was deposited in the upper backfill of a roundhouse gully.[60]

In 2014 the excavators discovered a hoard of bronze fittings from a 2nd or 3rd century BC chariot which appears to have been buried as a religious offering. The pieces appear to have been gathered in a box, before being planted in the ground upon a layer of cereal chaff and burnt as part of a religious ritual. The chaff might have doubled as a "cushion" for the box and also the fuel for the fire. After the burning, the entire deposit was covered by a layer of burnt cinder and slag.[61]

Shropshire

Old Oswestry hillfort in northwest Shropshire, near the border with Wales, is a site with a long history of use. The discovery of a stone ax and flint tools here suggests that the hill was first occupied in the Neolithic period. The first direct evidence of a settlement, however, dates to about 1000 BC, before the first ramparts were built.

The settlement appears to have been surrounded by some sort of palisade or fence.

Aerial view of Wrekin hillfort near Wroxeter in Shropshire (© 2011 Shropshire Council).

Each roundhouse was built using wooden posts with wattle-and-daub walls. A central post probably supported a thatched roof and inside was a hearth. A pottery crucible was discovered in one of the hearths, showing that light industrial activities such as bronze melting were taking place within the hillfort.

The first ramparts were built in the Early Iron Age. They enclosed the whole hilltop and consisted of a clay core, supported by timber and boulders and covered with earth, known as a box rampart. By the early Iron Age, when the first two ramparts were built, the settlement was formed of stone-kerbed roundhouses. Two houses found during excavations were 23 feet in diameter, and again had central hearths. Several sherds of early Iron Age (7th century BC) furrowed pottery had been imported from the Wiltshire area as well as salt containers from Cheshire, showing that the community had long-distance trading links at this time.[62]

The main hillfort in east Shropshire was the Wrekin near Telford. Excavation in 1939 revealed three phases of occupation. Firstly the multivallate fort, founded between the 7th and 5th centuries BC; this site had ceased to be intensively occupied by the 5th or 4th centuries BC and was succeeded by the univallate fort. Roughly 100 years after the construction of this fort the multivallate fort was reoccupied. It survived until about the middle of the 1st century AD, possibly being destroyed by the Romans in AD 48 or 50. A small-scale excavation of the interior of the fort in 1973 uncovered post-built structures and storage pits. Excavation also found pottery dating from the 9th to 8th centuries BC, suggesting that a settlement was established on the site in the Late Bronze Age.[63]

Other Early-Middle Iron Age Settlements

Wiltshire

Not all Iron Age Britons lived in hillforts, and in 1998–9 an unenclosed Iron Age settlement was excavated at Battlesbury Bowl outside Battlesbury Camp hillfort near Warminster in the west of Wiltshire. The Battlesbury Bowl settlement was founded towards the end of the Late Bronze Age in the 8th century BC and was occupied through the Early and Middle Iron Age until the 3rd century BC.[64] One of the most interesting features at Battlesbury Bowl was ditch 4043, a ditch at least 79 yards long. A deposit of seven cattle and three horse skulls was found in section 4105 of ditch 4043—at least some of the skulls had been carefully cleaned and possibly displayed before ending up in the ditch and it may be that it was the display, rather than any act of deposition, that was important.[65] One of the cattle skulls and the associated foreleg produced radiocarbon dates of between 790 BC and 420 BC.

The Early Iron Age inhabitants of Battlesbury Bowl buried the bones of their deceased relatives in pits and ditches. Human bone was recovered from 29 contexts within 21 features at the settlement. Disarticulated bones, or more commonly fragments of bones, were recovered from 25 contexts, mostly Late Bronze Age to early Middle Iron Age in date, predominantly pit fills and, less commonly, ditch and post-hole fills. The fragments mostly comprise elements of long bone and cranial vault (skullcap). Of the former, femur shaft predominate (the femur shaft is the body of the thigh bone). Not all fragments could be sided, but 60 percent of the assemblage comprises bone from the right (including 21 percent right femur and 12 percent right humerus) compared with only 21 percent from the left side. Canid gnawing (gnawing by dogs, foxes or wolves), evident from the crenulated (notched), worn ends of bone fragments and extant puncture marks, was observed in 28 percent of the disarticulated bone assemblage. The skeletal elements in which gnawing was observed are predominantly the larger long bones, like the thigh bone, shinbone or arm bone. A higher percentage of the material from the ditches compared with that from the pits show evidence for gnawing.[66] The bone specialist Jacqueline McKinley concludes[67] that the Late Bronze Age–early Middle Iron Age material "all comprises disarticulated bone fragments (representing the remains of a minimum of three individuals) with common evidence for canid gnawing and some weathering. The form and nature of the material is indicative of some level of exposure linked to deliberate human manipulation involving excarnation and possible "curation." In other words, the bones show evidence of having been gnawed by dogs, foxes or wolves, and of having been "curated"—in other words, kept as souvenirs of the deceased.

Towards the end of its life, burial practices changed at Battlesbury Bowl. Two later Middle Iron Age pits (350 BC–200 BC) contained inhumation burials. Pit 4223 contained two crouched inhumation burials. The body, of a man aged over 40 years, was laid on its right side with its head to the west. A horse lower mandible had been placed over the pelvis, and a fragment of bone from another adult (aged over 18 years) was also recovered from this level. Although a layer of soil was recorded between the two inhumations, it is possible that the two burials were not separated by any great length of time. The upper skeleton, of an adult female aged 35–55 years, was more tightly crouched, lying on its left side and with the head to the east, and further fragments of horse mandible were recovered from the surrounding soil. Pit 4332 contained a crouched inhumation, a juvenile aged about 10 years, possibly a male; associated with the burial were a Neolithic flint ax, part of a chalk loomweight, and three articulated sheep/goat vertebrae.[68] Both the burial and the animal bones produced radiocarbon dates in the range 410–190 BC.

Hampshire

A Middle Iron Age settlement at Weston Colley near Micheldever, to the north of Winchester in Hampshire, was excavated by Wessex Archaeology in advance of a gas pipeline. The settlement consisted of a large concentration of bell-shaped and other pits, associated with roundhouses, and a series of ditches, predominantly aligned northeast-southwest. Geophysical survey showed that the site formed part of an extensive Iron Age complex that included a D-shaped, banjo and rectangular enclosure with associated trackways and field systems. A horse mandible was discovered in Pit 5022, along with the articulated remains of a young dog.[69] In Pit 5069 the excavators found a partial female horse skeleton and an adult cattle hoof deposited together. The horse skeleton had been laid east-west on top of a raised chalk platform, with the head facing west. All four legs, tail and scapula had been carefully removed with a knife and were not in this pit. Surrounding the skeleton were large fragments of a semi-complete Middle Iron Age saucepan pot, as well as the rim sherd from a second pot.[70]

Dorset

Gussage All Saints is an Iron Age settlement in northeast Dorset which was excavated in 1972. The site was occupied throughout the second half of the 1st millennium BC and into the early decades of the Roman period. The enclosure ditch, irregular and asymmetrical, measured 130 yards north-south and 110 yards east-west internally. There appears to have been an external bank. The main entrance was to the east, and featured timber structures and was approached by "antennae" ditches which presented a funnel-like approach to the enclosure. Three main phases of occupation were identified. During the third phase, the ditch seems not to have been maintained as a physical barrier. Occupation in the first phase was represented largely by pits, post holes and some four-post structures. No round houses were identified. In the second phase, the pits and postholes were accompanied by one definite and one possible round house. The third phase saw the construction of several smaller enclosed areas, some of which may have contained timber buildings, though no clear patterning was visible among postholes and other features. The site produced a considerable assemblage of pottery from all 3 phases. Bronze and iron working occurred in all phases. The most notable metalwork deposit was from a single pit close to the site's main entrance, and dating to the 1st century BC. It consisted of a large assemblage of mold and metalworking debris arising from the production of harness and chariot fittings. Remains of over 50 individuals were found, mostly from the last phase.[71] Among the human remains was a tightly crouched male skeleton lying on its side with head to the north facing west. The arms and legs were flexed, with the arms drawn up in front of the chest. The skeleton was found in a deposit at the base of a cylindrical pit 6 feet 5 inches deep along with numerous animal bones and the articulated remains of dog and horse. Fragments of a right femur (thigh bone) and fibula (calf bone) were found in the same pit.[72] There were numerous remains of horses on the site, including 66 entire long bones.[73]

Somerset

Glastonbury Lake Village is a mile to the north of Glastonbury in Somerset and flourished between about 200 BC and 50 BC. It was built on an artificial island of timber, stone and clay which lay in a swampy area of open water, reeds and fenwood. In its early stages the site comprised five or six houses, one of which burnt down, and a series of clay spreads that provided bases for outdoor work. The island was later extended and more houses built. The site appears to have been permanently occupied even though its location in a swamp meant that everything had to be brought in by boat.

At its maximum Glastonbury Lake Village consisted of about 15 houses and had a population of, perhaps, 200. The houses were circular with walls of vertical posts infilled with wattle and daub; roofs were thatched with reeds or straw. Many of the clay floors were constructed for hearths, some for cooking and warmth, others for industrial purposes. The site was surrounded by an irregular palisade which was probably more structural than defensive and there was a landing stage on the eastern side.[74]

Glastonbury was excavated between 1892 and 1908 by Arthur Bulleid and Harold St. George Gray, who comment on one particular find[75]: "One of the most interesting objects of bone from the Village is the disc or roundel ... of human skull bone—part of the table of the of the occipital bone of an old person." This disc was "of concavo-convex section," measuring almost 3 inches in diameter and a third of an inch in thickness. It was "perforated centrally" by a hole a third of an inch in diameter on the external surface, but slightly larger on the inner side. Its precise use, they say, "is unknown, but it is generally regarded as an amulet or charm for superstious purposes, and may have been worn

Somerset Levels, seen from Glastonbury Tor, August 2, 2010 (Adrian Pingstone).

Somerset Levels Flood, February 26, 2014—confluence of the Rivers Parrett and Tone at Burrowbridge during flooding in February 2014 (Rodw).

on the person. The edges are very smooth." In addition to this disc, seven fragments of crania were found within the settlement, and nine outside the palisades, some with signs of violence.[76]

Cambridgeshire

Between June and December 2000 an archaeological excavation was carried out on land adjacent to Harston Mill, on the River Cam near Cambridge. In the Early to Middle Iron Age in the east of the site was a settlement of five post-ring structures, four-post granary structures and rubbish pits, set within a wider landscape divided by segmented ditches and fencelines. A structural posthole was dated to between 360 BC and 200 BC. Contemporary with this settlement were 189 grain storage pits, mostly located on the chalk belt in the west of the site, parallel to the River Cam.

Storage pit F3057 contained the articulated crouched burial of a child around 8 years of age, the partially articulated remains of a human infant aged around 9 months, a decorated pottery vessel containing goat bones and a goat skull with horns, all dated to between 410 BC and 370 BC. In all, the partially articulated carcasses of at least fifteen sheep or goats were found in the pit; signs of butchery were found on only 6 of the 716 bones, indicating that de-fleshing and skinning may have taken place before the deposition of some carcasses. The basal fill of storage pit F2645 contained three partial child skeletons together with a cattle skull; above the basal fill was the articulated skeleton of a female aged 15–25 years—the lower legs and arms and both hands and feet were missing, and the skull lay directly above a deposit of animal bone (sheep vertebra and cattle long bone). The lower fill of pit F3052 contained the left femur and tibia of a human infant, almost 7 pounds of Early Iron Age pottery including one complete vessel, and over 7 pounds of animal bone, including a charred, knife-cut mallard, wigeon and tufted duck legs; the upper fill contained the tightly flexed, possibly bound skeleton of an adult female aged 40 to 50 years, with a dog mandible and a sheep/goat mandible. The base of storage pit F4520 contained a dog skeleton and dog fetus, adult dog skulls (one male, one female), an inverted cattle skull on top of cattle long bone on a north-south axis, and a cattle skull with horncores on top of cattle long bone, again on a north-south axis.[77]

Godwin Ridge in the Cambridgeshire fens, which had been a feasting site in the Late Bronze Age, became a center of ritual activities in the Iron Age. These activities were focused at the western edge of the ridge, on the northern riverside and a dumped-soil platform 23 feet by 33 feet and between 6 inches and a foot thick. The platform's foundation layer contained the remains of four dismembered horses, and the disarticulated or partially articulated remains of a dog, two cows, a pig and 12 sheep, suggesting that it had a ritual purpose from the very beginning. Also associated with the platform "were the bones from at least fifteen different wild bird species, mostly coot, mallard, other ducks and great-crested grebe; swan, heron, bittern, crow and marsh harrier were also present, as was a Dalmatian pelican, a bird even larger than a swan that once bred in Britain.... The bones were disarticulated, while some were broken or displayed signs of butchery, suggesting that at least some of the birds had been eaten or otherwise utilised." Three copper-alloy brooches were found close to each other, including a Thistle and a Colchester brooch and a rare, near-complete Nauheim type of late 2nd or earlier 1st century BC date. Nearby, at the riverside, there was "an unequivocal 'ritual package,' a discrete group of three antler weaving combs."[78]

Eighty-nine skeletal elements were found across the western half of the ridge, with the majority (fifty-six) deriving from the northwestern end, where most (forty-eight) were spread across an area measuring 49 feet by 65 feet. The vast majority of the material "was loose and disarticulated. Altogether, portions of seven skulls were recovered from at least five adults, including a male and two females."[79] Canine gnawing was recorded on one tibia. There were also cut marks on a scapula and humerus, and a chop mark on a rib. These occurred "on fresh bone, with no evidence of healing, suggesting that they were made at around the time of death, arguably in relation to dismemberment. The most marked 'modification' involved a polished occipital portion of an adult's skull found along the northern channel side. Apart from shallow knife incisions, this included drilled holes arranged in a near-four-square pattern." The holes were drilled after death with a rotating blade.[80]

Based on the pottery and the radiocarbon dates recovered from the Godwin Ridge riverside platform area, the "human bone deposition would appear to have been a phenomenon of the Middle to Late Iron Age and into the third quarter of the first century AD."[81]

So to sum up. Godwin Ridge was an "island" in the Cambridgeshire fens where, during the Middle–Late Iron Age, excarnation was carried out and some of the bones (especially skulls) were buried, sometimes after they had been modified (like the skull with the four holes drilled into it). Other ritual activities were also carried out, like the burying of animals (most notably, horses), the deposition of precious objects such as brooches and antler combs, and, unusually, the burial of a large number of wild birds.

Facing the Sea: Coastal Promontory Forts

Iron Age coastal promontory forts (also known as cliff castles) are found along the Atlantic coasts of the British Isles in Cornwall, Wales and Ireland. One of the earliest coastal promontory forts is Dun Aonghasa on the island of Inis Mor off the west coast of Ireland, on the edge of a 330 feet high cliff. Dun Aonghasa was excavated between 1992 and 1995 as part of the Western Stone Forts Project. During excavation two main phases of prehistoric activity were revealed and some pre-enclosure activity was also detected by radiocarbon dating food remains from the inner enclosure to 1500 BC. Around 1100 BC the first enclosure was erected by piling rubble against large upright stones. A number of structures were detected and although poorly preserved it appeared they were constructed of timber with the main posts set on stone foundations. The best preserved structure uncovered was a roughly circular hut (Hut 1), 15 feet 9 inches in diameter the walls of which extended under the inner enclosure wall. The interior of the hut was filled with a midden type deposit including pottery, a clay mold fragment for a spearhead and a bone spindle whorl.

East of the hut a possibly contemporary stone-lined trough and stone hearth was cut into the midden layer and the hearth yielded a date of 752–392 BC. The foundations of a second hut and the remains of a stone lined pit were discovered to the east of Hut 1. Faunal remains recovered included sheep, cattle, fish, limpets and periwinkle shells. Some barley grains and a number of saddle querns were also uncovered along with large pottery vessels. Stone axes, hammers and whetstones, bone pins and needles and bone, stone, pumice, glass and amber beads were all retrieved. A number of clay molds used to cast bronze objects suggested on-site manufacturing and four perforated bronze rings found together near the cliff edge inside the fort may have been a deliberate deposit. A large fire and dense concentration of animal bone was detected in the inner enclosure and may have represented a feasting area. A large quarried hollow in the bedrock at the northeast corner contained an infant burial.[82]

Trevelgue Head at Newquay in Cornwall is a coastal promontory fort occupied from the 3rd century BC. The first Iron Age occupation was defended by an earth bank with palisade and ditch cutting off the promontory, the huts being wooden framed with wattle and daub walls. Later in the Iron Age two rows of substantial round houses were built across the headland inside the innermost rampart, two houses being fully excavated. Finds from these huts were of high quality, including Iron Age B Ware with curvilinear decoration, known as South Western Decorated Ware. Metal working was carried on early in the Iron Age and continued throughout the life of the settlement, possibly the reason for the long occupation. An iron mine was located under the cliff on the north side of the headland and there is also evidence for bronze smelting on the site. This was at a spot facing the sea where a cavity was found with signs of burning. The cavity was ovoid, 10 inches deep and 8 inches wide, with solid rock at the bottom and its sides lined with clay. At the bottom was a one inch thick layer of charcoal with the rest of the cavity filled up to ground level with slag and broken flints. Analysis showed the slag to be the result of the reducing of copper ore.[83]

In Wales, Pembrokeshire is the area with the greatest number of coastal promontory forts. Fifty-six promontory forts are found along the Pembrokeshire coast: some occupy fairly level ground using sheer cliffs on one side to enhance their defenses, while others employed massive banks and ditches to cut off entire promontories and enclose a settled area. Flimston Bay fort at Castlemartin in southwest Pembrokeshire "is one of the finest promontory forts of Pembrokeshire, with three lines of landward defence cutting off an eroding and collapsing limestone headland. Different phases of enlargement and reduction are suggested by the pair of close-set ramparts, with a third set some distance away. The interspace created could have functioned as a corralling space for stock, or as an annexe for trading, secure from the innermost enclosure. However, particular characteristics of its interior, including the precipitous cliff edges and the great blow hole known as "The Cauldron," probably formed long before the Iron Age and may have been part of the reason this headland was selected for enclosure."[84]

Barry Cunliffe says that the coastal promontory forts "show a remarkable similarity and it is difficult to resist the temptation to believe that the choice of location was to a large extent conditioned by a desire to control the interface between land and sea. In all probability these promontories were conceived of as liminal places and as such were endowed with particular power."[85]

The first Indo-Europeans seem to have come from a landlocked region, so there are many different Indo-European words for *sea*, and a variety of sea-gods. The oldest sea god we know of in Europe is Poseidon, who is mentioned in Bronze Age Mycenae, and has the attribute "earth-shaker," referring to earthquakes, and is from the earliest times referred to as "tamer of horses." There was a widespread cult of Poseidon Hippios ("Horse Poseidon") in classical Greece, with sanctuaries at Athens and Olympia. However, we know nothing about any prehistoric sea-god in Britain, and the closest we can get to a sea-god is an enigmatic passage from the Greek historian, biographer and essayist Plutarch. In his work *The Obsolescence of Oracles*, written perhaps in AD 83 or 84, Plutarch

Flimston Bay cliff castle, Pembrokeshire, Wales, seen from the ground (Janet Baxter Photography).

An aerial view of Flimston Bay cliff castle, with the blow hole clearly visible (© Crown copyright: Royal Commission on the Ancient and Historical Monuments of Wales; © Haulfraint y Goroni Comisiwn Brenhinol Henebion Cymru).

quotes a friend, Demetrius of Tarsus, lately returned from Britain after taking part in Agricola's educational drive or "cultural conquest" (his attempt to romanize Britain) in the late 1st century AD[86]:

> Demetrius said that among the islands lying near Britain were many isolated, having few or no inhabitants, some of which bore the names of divinities or heroes. He himself, by the emperor's order, had made a voyage for inquiry and observation to the nearest of these islands which had only a few inhabitants, holy men who were all held inviolate by the Britons. Shortly after his arrival there occurred a great tumult in the air and many portents; violent winds suddenly swept down and lightning-flashes darted to earth. When these abated, the people of the island said that the passing of someone of the mightier souls had befallen. "For," said they, "as a lamp when it is being lighted has no terrors, but when it goes out is distressing to many, so the great souls have a kindling into life that is gentle and inoffensive, but their passing and dissolution often, as at the present moment, fosters tempests and storms, and often infects the air with pestilential properties." Moreover, they said that in this part of the world there is one island where Cronus is confined, guarded while he sleeps by Briareus; for his sleep has been devised as a bondage for him, and round about him are many demigods as attendants and servants.

This fascinating passage tells us that in Iron Age Britain, isolated islands were inhabited by holy men, implies that the souls of the dead came to settle on isolated islands with few inhabitants, and says that a god Plutarch calls "Cronus" was imprisoned on one particular island.

Demetrius does not seem to be a figure that Plutarch invented. He has been identified with the Demetrius who offered two votive plaques in Greek at *Eboracum* (York): one to "the gods of the governor's headquarters, the other to the Titans Oceanus and Tethys, the god and goddess of the outer seas. Demetrius is a common name in Greek, but Greek inscriptions are very rare in Britain; and the gods to whom the vow is paid are highly appropriate for someone who has just travelled to distant islands, perhaps the Inner Hebrides.

In Greek mythology Cronus was a Titan, the son of Gaia ("Earth") and Uranus ("Sky"), known among the Romans as Saturn He overthrew his father and ruled during the mythological Golden Age until he was overthrown by his own son Zeus and imprisoned in Tartarus (the underworld). Briareus was another son of Gaia and Uranus, who helped Zeus to overthrow Cronus. The classicist A.R. Burn, in a discussion of "holy islands" in pre–Christian Britain, cannot find any equivalent to Cronus in Welsh or Irish mythology, but suggests that this "Saturn-like figure does resemble the Earth-Father (Dis Pater, not Dyaus Pater, the Sky-Father) from whom, according to Caesar the Gauls claimed to be descended."[87]

So when Iron Age Britons built coastal promontory forts facing the sea, they were perhaps paying homage to islands where the dead went after death and where an ancient god whom Plutarch calls "Cronus" was buried.

Ritual in Early-Middle Iron Age Britain

Burial Rites

It is clear that the Iron Age people of southern Britain practiced excarnation, like their Early Neolithic ancestors. The osteoarchaeologist Rebecca Redfern has studied human bone from the Iron Age sites of Gussage All Saints and Maiden Castle in Dorset. Gussage All Saints was excavated by Geoffrey Wainwright, who recorded six contexts of disarticulated human remains recovered from a ditch and proposed hut structure, all dating to the 3rd century BC. The human remains consisted of 11 pieces of cranium (skull) and one femur (thigh bone), all from adult individuals. The cranial material was dominated by parietal bones (the bones which form the sides and roof of the cranium), and the most frequently observed changes were cut marks and fractures that occurred around the time of death. The thigh bone shows signs of gnawing, most probably by a dog.[88]

Redfern also examined eight pieces of disarticulated human bone from Maiden Castle hillfort near Dorchester. These bones were recovered from trenches II and IV from pit, gully, or post-hole fills and soil layers, which had been created during the extended fort phase (phase 6), dating to the Early–Middle Iron Age. Three pieces were long bones, the remainder cranial (skull) material. The long bones had evidence for dry fractures, gnawing and fine cut marks. The cranial material appears to have been formed by radiating fractures produced by blunt-force trauma, and cut marks are also present. All this implies that bodies were allowed to decay, being gnawed by dogs, foxes or wolves, and the bones were then removed and buried in pits, post-holes or gullies.[89] Dogs, of course, also played an important part in excarnation during the Early Neolithic.

Why was excarnation so widely practiced in large parts of Britain during much of the Iron Age? One possible answer comes from the customs of the Celtiberians, the Celts who lived in parts of Spain and Portugal. The Roman politician and poet Silius Italicus (1st century AD) says that to the Celtiberians, "death in battle is glorious; and they consider it a crime to burn the body of such a warrior; for they believe that the soul goes up to the gods in heaven, if the body is devoured on the field by the hungry vulture."[90] The Roman writer Claudius Aelianus (2nd century AD) says that the Arevaci, a Celtic tribe who lived to the northeast of Madrid, "insult the corpses of such as die from disease as having died a cowardly and effeminate death, and dispose of them by burning; whereas those who laid down their lives in war they regard as noble, heroic and full of valour, and them they cast to the vultures, believing this bird to be sacred."[91]

These statements are supported by Celtiberian iconography. On two Numantian tomb paintings, a dead fighter, lying on the ground, is approached by a vulture which devours him. Pottery from Numantia in Soria province "shows scenes of warriors" corpses being devoured by birds under images of suns, and on a funeral urn from *Uxama* the human head is shown clearly inside the bird's body, represented by means of a rectangular container with talons and wings, almost certainly alluding to the ascension of the warrior's spirit mentioned in the literary texts."[92] Uxama is Osma in Soria province; the pottery from Numantia probably dates to the 1st century BC, while the funeral urn from Uxama probably dates to the 2nd century BC.[93] There are no vultures in Britain, but it may be that the raven played a similar role. Five sets of human remains at Danebury were buried with ravens, and in Irish mythology there is a war goddess called Badb who takes the form of a crow.

But there may be another reason. In the Neolithic and Early Bronze Age the sun played an important part in people's lives, and may have continued to do so in the Late Bronze Age and Iron Age. If a body is left in the open, it is exposed to the sun and sky, and of course to rain, sleet or snow. The common Indo-European word for *sun* is represented by the Indian sun god *Surya*, the Greek sun god *Helios*, and by the Latin *sol*. This common word is found in Welsh *haul* "sun," and in Irish *suil* "eye"[94] (the Irish word for *sun* is the unrelated *grian*). The Irish *suil* "eye" points to one attribute of the sun god, as all-seeing (this epithet was applied, for example, to the Greek Helios), and it is possible the sun was regarded as a protector.

The Welsh word for "sky" is *nef*, related directly to Old Irish *nem*, Old Indian *nabhas*, Hittite *nebis*, Greek *nephos*, and indirectly to Greek *nephele* "cloud," Old High German *nebul* "fog," Old Icelandic *nifl-heimr* "mist-home" (a realm of primordial ice and cold), Latin *nimbus* "cloud," and perhaps to *Neptunus* "Roman god of freshwater and sea."[95] The Welsh *nef* also means "heaven," suggesting that in prehistoric times the sky was associated with the Afterlife, as implied by the Old Icelandic *nifl-heimr*, the abode of the goddess Hel and of those who did not die a heroic death.

Reincarnation

Julius Caesar says that the Gauls believed in reincarnation, and Maud Cunnington suggested that the "careless" burial rites at Yarnbury Castle, with so many "detached fragments of humanity," may have been prompted by a belief in reincarnation. It is of course impossible to know whether Iron Age Britons believed in reincarnation, but there is a clue. Animals were given the same burial rites as humans, and even buried with humans, suggesting that the boundaries between animals and humans were fluid in Iron Age Britain. We can get some idea of what that could mean in practice by looking at the beliefs of the Nelson Island Eskimo (Yup'ik) of Alaska, who believe that both humans and animals have souls and can be reincarnated. The American anthropologist Ann Fienup-Riordan, in her discussion of "cosmological recycling"[96] refers to

> many tales in which "animals can be transformed into humans to meet men on their own grounds." Human-to-animal transformation tales deal with women and children who seek "freedom, safety or defense in their helpless condition" through animal transformations. Equally important are stories of men who see animals as humans; this permits humans to "see the world in a new way, from the animal's point of view." In one story "the shaman gives voice to the seals' opinions on their treatment during the past year when he returns at the end of his spiritual hunting."

In Yup'ik beliefs, "animals have *yua*, the spiritual entity that is contained in the bladder; in the elaborate Bladder Festival the hunters put the bladders of the seals they have killed back into the water to ensure the seals' reincarnation."[97] The Yup'ik understand the end of human and animal life as the departure from the body of its essential life force[98]:

> The seal's *yua* ("its person") retracted to its bladder when the seal was killed, where it remained until it was placed back in the water and reincarnated. The human life force likewise separated from the physical body at death and began a journey underground to the land of the dead, where it, too, awaited rebirth. Though some part of the human dead remained behind in the land of the dead, where it was maintained as a separate entity, an essential aspect was believed reborn in the namesake. Death was simultaneously an ending and a new beginning.

Human skulls received special treatment in some areas[99]:

> a few years after a human burial on Nunivak Island [in the Bering Sea off the coast of Alaska], people removed the skull when the next burial occurred. They set the skull on a mat on a high place facing east, and passersby placed grass over it. In the Bering Strait region, people arranged the skulls and scapulae [shoulder blades] of large game animals, including bear and caribou, atop the graves of accomplished hunters.

At Point Hope, Alaska, the American anthropologist Froelich Rainey "unearthed human skulls with carved and inlaid ivory eyes, ivory cup-shaped mouth covers, and, in one case, ivory nose plugs."

Fienup-Riordan adds[100]:

> the belief was widespread in many parts of the Arctic that spiritual entities animated the joints of both human and nonhuman bodies. People may have believed that these spirits animated body parts—the head in particular—once the joints had been severed. In fact, frequent references exist in Bering Sea mythology to the power of the part to call forth the whole. Although dismemberment and severing the head destroy life on one level, the potential for the regeneration of life continues to animate the body part ...
>
> The head, although severed from the body, still possessed the ability to observe human actions and to recount its experiences to its fellows.

Some of the Yup'ik practices seem to echo Iron Age practices in southern England and northern Scotland—the Yup'ik cast the seal's bladder into the sea, just as Iron Age Britons buried body parts in pits and ditches, and skulls were given special treatment.

Caesar also said that all Gauls believed they were descended from the underworld god that the Romans called Dis Pater, and it is quite possible that when Iron Age Britons placed human and animal remains in storage pits and ditches, they were returning them to the Celtic Dis, just as the Yup'ik returned the seal's bladder to the sea.

As I said, we will probably never know for certain whether Iron Age Britons believed in reincarnation, but in many cultures like the Yup'ik that hold this belief, it is thought that the soul of the deceased is reincarnated in a newly born member of the family—which might explain why selected bones were buried in or near settlements. If, as Caesar says, the Celts believed they were descended from the underworld deity that he calls Dis, then burial of bones in storage pits or ditches might be a form of thanks to the underworld god or goddess for the birth of a child and a newly reincarnated soul.

Horse Sacrifice

During the Iron Age horse sacrifice became very common in hillforts, settlements and other sites, from Dorset and Somerset in the west of England to Leicestershire in the Midlands. Horse sacrifice is first mentioned in the Bronze Age *Yajurveda* of India, which describes a ceremony called the *ashvamedha*, in which a king sacrifices a horse (a stallion) and his queen mimics copulation with the dead horse; the horse is then roasted and its flesh offered to various deities. This Vedic ceremony can be compared to a ritual described by the Welsh-Norman priest and traveller Gerald of Wales in his late 12th century work *Topography of Ireland*. He was travelling in the northwest of Ulster, in the area of Kenelcunill (Cenel Conaill), when he came across a people "accustomed to appoint its king with a rite altogether outlandish and abominable"[101]:

> When the whole people of that land has been gathered together in one place, a white mare is brought forward into the middle of the assembly. He who is to be inaugurated, not as a chief, but as a beast, not as a king, but as an outlaw, has bestial intercourse with her before all, professing himself to be a beast also. The mare is then killed immediately, cut up into pieces, and boiled in water. A bath is prepared for the man afterwards in the same water. He sits in the bath surrounded by all his people, and all, he and they, eat of the meat of the mare which is brought to them. He quaffs and drinks of the broth in which he is bathed,

not in any cup, or using his hand, but just dipping his mouth into it round about him. When this unrighteous rite has been carried out, his kingship and dominion have been conferred.

In the Late Bronze Age, horses were associated with the sun, for example in the Trundholm sun chariot, the Vedic Ashvins, divine twin horsemen who appear in the sky before dawn, and the Greek Dioscuri with their "bright horses." There are no divine twins in Irish mythology, but there is something similar. Navan Fort is a prehistoric site in County Armagh, Northern Ireland, traditionally associated with the kings of Ulster. Navan Fort is on a low hill about 1.6 miles west of Armagh. The site consists of a circular enclosure 820 feet in diameter, marked by a bank and ditch, with the ditch inside the bank, like a Neolithic henge. Inside the enclosure two monuments are visible. Off-center, to the northwest, is an earthen mound 130 feet in diameter and 20 feet high. Off-center, to the southeast is the circular impression of a ring-barrow about 100 feet in diameter.

Archaeological excavations have revealed that the construction of the earthen mound dates to 95 BC. A round-house like structure consisting of four concentric rings of posts around a central oak trunk was built, its entrance facing west, like the middens of Wiltshire and unlike Iron Age roundhouses, which tend to face east. The floor of the building was covered with stones arranged in radial segments, and the whole edifice was deliberately burnt down before being covered in a mound of earth and turf.[102]

Excavation of the ring-barrow revealed the remains of a figure-of-eight shaped wooden building underneath. This building was one of a number of very similar Early Iron Age structures that had been erected at this location, one on-top of the other. Indicative of continuous occupation, over a considerable period of time, it has been suggested that each of these structures represented a roundhouse with an attached circular yard. The larger yard was probably un-roofed, while the smaller roundhouse contained finds suggestive of domestic occupation. These included, amongst others, fragments of pottery, glass beads, shale armlets, animal bone, bronze artifacts and hearth waste. This range of artifacts may indicate that the buildings represented dwellings, possibly of high status individuals. During the excavations, archaeologists found the skull of a Barbary ape dated 390–20 BC, which must have come from North Africa.[103]

In Irish Navan Fort is called *Emain Macha*, or "Twins of Macha" (*emain* is related to Old Indian *Yama*, the god of death who was the son of the sun god Surya and a twin (his sister was Yami), and to Latin *geminus* "twin"). The *Metrical Dindshenchas* (which recount the origins of place-names) tell the story of the goddess Macha and how Emain Macha got its name[104]:

> Emain Macha is named from this event: Macha daughter of Sainrith mac Inboith came to race the two steeds of king Conchobar at the Fair, after Crunnchu had declared that his wife was swifter than the king's horses. The king told Crunnchu that he should die unless his wife came to the race. Then Macha came to save her husband, though pregnant, and raced the horses to the end of the green, and proved swifter than they. Then she was delivered of a boy and a girl at a birth, and the infants screamed, and the sound cast the Ulaid into their sickness, till each man was no stronger than a woman in childbed. And the sickness clave to them thenceforth. From this Macha and from the twins (*emon*) she bore come the names of Mag Macha [= "Plain of Macha"] and Emain Macha.

Macha is associated with horses and twins, and in the *Metrical Dindshenchas* she is called *grian banchuire*, or "sun of womankind."

It seems likely that there were numerous horse-gods in the Iron Age, but we know very little about them. However the *Iliad*, composed around 800 BC, does refer to a god-like figure connected with horses—in Book 10, Dolon, an ally of the Trojans, says to Odysseus[105]:

> If you're keen to infiltrate
> the Trojan army, over there are Thracians.
> fresh troops, new arrivals, furthest distant
> from the rest, among them their king Rhesus,
> son of Eioneus. His horses are the best.
> the finest and largest ones I've ever seen,
> whiter than snow, as fast as the winds.
> His chariot is finely built—with gold
> and silver. He came here with his armour—
> an amazing sight—huge and made of gold.
> It's not appropriate for mortal men
> to wear such armour, only deathless gods.

The god-like Rhesus with his snow-white horses possibly re-appears later under the guise of the so-called Thracian Horseman, known from the 4th century BC and into the Roman period. The Thracian Horseman, also known as *Heros* ("Hero"), is depicted on stelae found in all regions of Thrace (which includes Bulgaria, parts of Greece, and the European part of Turkey); the stelae are either funerary or dedicated to various deities. In these depictions, mostly from the time of the Roman Empire, the Thracian horseman

Thracian Horseman, Felix Romuliana Roman palace, eastern Serbia. The fragment depicts a rider wielding an ax and a shield-bearing soldier on foot (Anne Chen/Institute for the Study of the Ancient World, Creative Commons Attribution 2.0 Generic).

"advances, sometimes at a walk, sometimes at a gallop, towards an altar erected in front of a tree around which a snake is entwined." We also see him "leaping forward with a spear in his hand to hunt boar, or astride a lion. Sometimes he holds game—a doe or a hare, for instance—which he has flushed out and killed. A dog usually accompanies him."[106]

The Sacrifice of Sheep or Goats

The remains of sheep or goats accompanied human burials at Battlesbury Bowl in Wiltshire, Wittenham Clumps in Oxfordshire, and Harston Mill in Cambridgeshire. Irish and Welsh mythology have little to say about sheep or goats, and their significance may lie in shamanism. Shamanism is a practice that involves a practitioner reaching altered states of consciousness in order to interact with the spirit world and channel these transcendental energies into this world. The word *shaman* is probably borrowed from the Evenki language, spoken in Russia, Mongolia and China, and was first applied to the ancient religion of the Turks and Mongols living in the northern parts of Central Asia.

The Celtic scholar Ann Ross describes the druids as "priests who do not seem to have differed so very basically from the shamans of the Finno-Ugric peoples"[107] (the Finno-Ugric people include the Finns, Estonians, and a variety of peoples like the Khanty and the Mansi living in western Siberia). Later Ross refers to the description of the chief druid of the king of Ireland, Mogh Ruaith, in the 15th century *Siege of Drum Damhghaire* (also known as the *Siege of Knocklong*). Mogh Ruaith is said to ask for his "dark gray hornless bull hide" and to wear a "white speckled bird skin head dress of fluttering wings."[108]

A possible shamanistic trance is described in *The Wasting Sickness of Cu Chulainn*[109]:

> This is how that bull-feast used to be made: to kill a white bull, and for one man to eat his fill of its flesh and its broth, and to sleep after that meal; and for four druids to chant a

Shaman from Olkhon Island, Lake Baikal, Russia, August 1, 2009 (Arkady Zarubin).

spell of truth over him. And the form of the man to be made king used to be shown to him in a dream, his shape and his description, and the manner of work that he was doing.

It is possible that the bull was a spirit-guide in the shaman's quest for knowledge, and the same role may have been filled by sheep or goats. In the Great Basin of the western United States the bighorn sheep was the special spirit helper of the rain shaman among Native American tribes like the Paiute.[110] Among the Tuvinians, a Turkic ethnic group living in southern Siberia, shamans possess a striking ability to constantly change their inward and outward appearance[111]:

> During a ritual period with and without a mask, they talked and recitated musically, spoke their assistant's voice, conversed with him, imitated skillfully the voices and cries of animals and birds, their spirit-helpers—Siberian stag, ram, goat—and evil spirits—owl, crow, cuckoo.

So perhaps sheep or goats were buried with people because they were considered spirit-guides who could lead the deceased to the next world.

Other Places, Other Times

The burial rites practiced in southern England during the earlier Iron Age are difficult for us to understand, no matter how much we try to explain them. But they were not the only form of burial in the Iron Age: new forms of burial were imported from France in the Middle and Late Iron Age, and by the time the Romans invaded and conquered Britain AD 43, inhumation was widespread in East Yorkshire, and cremation was the preferred burial rite in large parts of southeast England.

CHAPTER 5

The Age of Depositions (3): Chariot Burials, Lunar Eclipses and Wooden Buckets in the Later Iron Age

The Arras Culture of East Yorkshire

Chariot Burials

Burial rites in East Yorkshire were very different from those of southern England, especially during the Middle Iron Age, at the time of the so-called Arras Culture. The Arras Culture, named after a cemetery at Arras near Market Weighton, is characterized by crouched inhumations in square barrows, sometimes with the remains of chariots or carts, either placed upright, or dismantled, the wheels being placed flat. Grave goods include cart- and harness-fittings such as iron cart-tires and three-link horse-bits, and personal ornaments and offerings. These burials were not a local innovation, but were inspired by burials in France, particularly in Burgundy and the Nanterre region of Paris.[1]

The earliest chariot burial in France is probably the one at Vix near Châtillon-sur-Seine, in the Côte d'Or region of eastern France. The so-called "Lady of Vix" was placed in a 13 feet by 13 feet rectangular wooden chamber underneath a mound of earth and stone which originally measured 138 feet in diameter and 16 feet in height. Her body was laid in the freestanding box of a cart, or chariot, the wheels of which had been detached and placed beside it. Only its metal parts have survived. Her jewelry included a 24-carat gold torc weighing almost 17 ounces, a bronze torc, six fibulae, six slate bracelets, plus a seventh bracelet made of amber beads. The grave also contained an assemblage of imported objects from Italy and the Greek world, all of them associated with the preparation of wine. They included the famous krater, a silver phiale (shallow bowl, sometimes seen as a local product), an Etruscan bronze oinochoe (wine jug), and several drinking cups from Etruria and Attica. One of the latter was dated to around 525 BC and represents the latest firmly dated find in the grave.[2] The Vix krater, used for mixing wine and water, is 5 feet 4 inches high, weighs 440 pounds, and is made of bronze. The three handles are supported by rampant lionesses, and each is decorated with a gorgon. A sculpted frieze depicting Greek hoplites circles around the lip of the krater. The striding soldiers are alternated with horse drawn chariots, and this pattern repeats throughout the band.[3] It was probably made in a Greek workshop in southern Italy at the end of the 6th century BC then dismantled for transportation by sea and up the River Rhone.[4]

From Vix the custom of cart burials spread via the River Seine to the Paris region and via the Seine and the Marne to the Champagne-Ardennes region. The best known burial in the Paris region is the one discovered in the late 19th century at Nanterre in the western suburbs of Paris, where a warrior was buried in the 3rd century BC with his cart and two horses.[5] Cart burials have also been found at Roissy in the northeastern suburbs of Paris, and at nearby Bouqueval and Plessis-Gassot. Numerous cart burials have been unearthed in the Champagne-Ardennes region: 14 have been found at Mairy (Ardennes), 8 at Recy (Marne), and 5 at Ecury-sur-Coole (Marne).[6] The graves are either large rectangular ditches, between 15 feet long, at La Cheppe (Marne) and 6 feet 10 inches long at Saint-Clément-sur-Arne (Ardennes), or simply chariot-shaped, as at Somme-Tourbe (Marne). In several cases, beside the main ditch is a small rectangular ditch containing the remains of a wild boar.[7] In addition to the cart, the deceased was usually buried with an iron sword, three lances, a knife, food offerings, and a helmet. Etruscan bronze wine jugs have also been found at Somme-Bionne (Marne) and La Gorge-Meillet, Somme-Tourbe (Marne) which date from the middle of the 5th century BC; in addition, the grave at Somme-Bionne had an Attic red-figure cup dating to around 420 BC.[8]

The Cemeteries of East Yorkshire

The cemetery at Arras to the east of Market Weighton contained at least 100 small barrows each covering a single contracted or extended inhumation. The majority of these barrows were excavated between 1815 and 1817 by the Reverend E.W. Stillingfleet and a chariot-burial was discovered in a chalk-pit here in 1876.[9] In the "King's Barrow" at Arras there was a single extended inhumation with the bodies of two horses, one laid on either side. The wheels from the vehicle had been removed and propped against each of the horses. Close to the head of the burial had been placed two pigs' heads.

A number of Arras culture cemeteries have been excavated since the 19th century. At Kirkburn to the southwest of Driffield, removal of surface soil prior to the construction of a hangar at Eastburn Aerodrome, exposed fifty graves, and a further twenty-five a short distance to the east, a year later. Each grave is 3–4 feet across and containing one, sometimes two inhumations, had a shallow encircling ditch. At the later site, these graves had an associated vessel each containing a small pig bone, and a decorated bronze bracelet was found on the arm of a female inhumation. Further finds include the lower portion of an Iron Age vessel, a leaf-shaped spearhead, two bronze tubes, and iron sword 28 inches long.[10] The sword, dating from between 300 BC and 200 BC, was found in Grave 3, buried with a man who was in his late 20s or early 30s when he died. After the dead man was placed in the grave, three spears were thrust into his chest as part of the funeral ritual. Another man, of similar age, was buried in the same cemetery, but with a chariot or cart. The handle of this sword is unusually elaborate, made of thirty-seven different pieces of iron, bronze and horn, and decorated with red glass. The sword was carried in a scabbard made from iron and bronze. The polished bronze front plate was decorated with a La Tène style scroll pattern, and with red glass studs and insets.[11]

To the west of Driffield are two adjacent cemeteries referred to as Garton Slack and Wetwang. Garton Slack was in use almost continually from the Neolithic to the Roman period. The Neolithic was represented by a cremation pit with traces of cremated bone and a crouched burial, and two pits containing Grooved Ware. The Bronze Age was represented by two barrow sites both with single cremations, one with a secondary (additional) burial and food vessel. A grave with a crouched burial, jet buttons, beads and bronze leaf beads was also found on the site. In the Iron Age there were six square ditched barrows, four containing crouched burials, and a square ditched barrow, 39 square feet with crouched inhumation and chariot burial.[12]

Excavation of Wetwang Slack has revealed several Bronze Age round barrows, part of a large Iron Age cemetery and a Romano-British farmstead. The section of the Iron Age cemetery contained over 250 burials, 150 of which were under square ditched barrows ranging in size from 29 feet 6 inches by 26 feet 3 inches to a few square feet in area. The primary burials were adult, contained mostly in planked coffins with food offerings and grave goods. Children were found as secondary burials or in flat graves. The cemetery is dated from the second half of the 2nd century to the first half of the 1st century BC.[13] There were three chariot burials in close proximity to each other. Burial 1, that of a young male, was accompanied by chariot- and harness-fittings, a long sword, seven spears, iron coverings for the spine of a wooden shield and the forequarters of a pig. In Burial 2, in addition to the vehicle and harness parts, there were personal possessions, including a mirror, a decorated bronze box of cylindrical form with a chain for suspension, and a gold and iron pin decorated with coral; two forequarters of pig were placed over the stomach of the dead person. The third burial, like the first, was accompanied by weaponry—a large iron sword, together with its suspension rings and iron fittings for the shield.[14]

Around 15 chalk figurines were found at Garton Slack, and altogether some forty or fifty figurines are now known from East Yorkshire, many representing a warrior carrying a sword on his back. Most of the figurines come from Iron Age or Roman sites, and all the swords are shown in scabbards suspended about their midpoint—a fashion known in northern Britain in the Iron Age. The warrior represented is presumably a god, mythical figure or ancestor, and the figurines may well have had a ritual or magical function.[15]

We might compare these chalk figurines with a short sword found at North Grimston, 4 miles southeast of Malton in North Yorkshire. Its owner had been buried with a second longer sword, rings from a sword belt, bindings from a shield and bones from a joint of pork. The hilt of the short sword, which dates from the late 2nd century or early 1st century BC is in the form of a man with arms and legs outstretched to form the grip, and is typical of a series of "anthropomorphic" swords found both in Britain and on the Continent.[16] Representations of the human form are rare in the Iron Age, and this man, like the chalk figurines, may represent a god or mythical ancestor.

A chariot burial dated to around 300 BC was found at Wetwang in 2001 during construction work and subsequently excavated. The grave was on the top of a hill, and contained the body of a woman lying in a crouched position, with an iron mirror propped against her legs. Her upper body was covered with joints of a pig. The dismantled pieces of a chariot were then placed around her, the box platform carefully positioned so that it covered her body. The wood of the chariot has rotted, leaving only the metal fittings from the chariot and the horse harness.[17]

Cowlam, to the north of Driffield, was excavated in 1867 and 1969. The excavations located contracted female inhumations with grave goods including brooches, necklaces and bracelets.[18] The assemblage, says Cunliffe,[19] dates to the early 4th century BC and "is clearly of direct Continental inspiration." It includes a brooch of Münsingen Ia type, and a necklace composed of seventy blue and white beads similar to necklaces found at Münsingen, a La Tène cemetery near Bern in Switzerland.

Not far from Cowlam is the cemetery known as Danes' Graves. It is said there were originally 500 barrows, 106 of which were excavated between 1721 and 1909. One grave, 9 inches long by 7½ inches wide contained a (dismantled) chariot burial. Grave goods (excluding the chariot burial) consisted of bronze, iron and jet bracelets, bronze and iron brooches and "objects," glass beads and hand-made clay pots used as food vessels.[20]

A square barrow cemetery at Rudston was excavated by Stead 1968–76. In the first modern excavation of an Arras culture cemetery 189 burials were excavated, most at the center of barrows with square-plan ditches. 135 graves orientated north-south were excavated along with 54 east-west orientated burials. The north-south burials were either crouched or contracted, and the east-west burials were normally extended or flexed. The type of grave goods varied between the two types of burial, though both groups contained male and female inhumations.[21] The grave goods of the north-south burials were modest, largely restricted to a brooch, a clay pot or a sheep's left humerus (front leg), while the east-west burials were more lavishly furnished, containing swords, spears, knives, sickles, ornaments and tools, as well as pig bones.[22]

It is not clear what the significance is of the different burial orientations; but east-west is a solar orientation, and east-west burials and pig meat seem to be reserved for the elite, judging from the grave goods that accompanied them to the next world. Elsewhere, in a discussion of the Iron Age broch (dry-stone tower) at Dun Vulan, South Uist, in the Outer Hebrides, Parker-Pearson notes that Dun Vulan's entrance faces east. A survey of 90 broch entrance orientations in Scotland showed that 41 face broadly east and 35 broadly west. The social significance of a western orientation is hinted at in Irish law codes of the 7th–8th century AD, in which the royal household faced to the west since the king sat in the propitious east end.[23] So perhaps the elite of East Yorkshire were buried with their heads to the east as a recognition of their higher status.

Chariot Burials Outside East Yorkshire

Most of the chariot burials are in East Yorkshire, but in 2003, a chariot burial was found at Ferry Fryston near Castleford in West Yorkshire during construction work on the A1 motorway. The chariot was found complete with its wheels upright in the ground, in contrast to the East Yorkshire burials, where the chariot is dismantled. Forensic analysis has established that the skeleton is that of a man aged 30–40, about 5 feet 9 inches in height in apparently good health and with an excellent set of teeth for the time—suggesting he enjoyed a more refined diet than most of his Iron Age contemporaries. Analysis of the radio-strontium from his tooth enamel indicates that his origins were not Yorkshire, but that he probably came from much further north, possibly either Scotland or even Scandinavia. The remains of what appeared to have been a brooch for fastening a cloak were found close to the man's left shoulder. Radiocarbon dating suggests that the man was buried some time in the 4th century BC.

Over 12,000 bone fragments from over 180 cattle were also discovered in burial pits around the chariot. At first, these were thought to be the remains of a large sacrificial feast indicating the high status of the man buried with the chariot. Subsequent tests have since shown that the bones date from the time of the initial Iron Age burial through to the 2nd century AD indicating repeated visits to the site over a period of up to five hundred years. Furthermore, they were from young cattle mostly 2–3 years old brought from different herds and outlying areas especially to the burial site.[24] Clearly this man was regarded as an important ancestor, and continued to be honored for several centuries, even into Roman times.

A chariot burial has also been found at Newbridge, Edinburgh, near the Bronze Age burial mound of Huly Hill. The chariot burial "is of exceptional interest," since it is the first example recorded in Scotland and the closest parallels are in northeastern France and Belgium where burials of complete carts are quite common. The Newbridge find contrasts with the only other known area of cart burials in the UK, in Yorkshire. Here, almost all burials are of dismantled carts. It has been dated to the 5th century BC, earlier than the Yorkshire examples.[25]

Ritual in Iron Age East Yorkshire

One of the most unusual features of the East Yorkshire burials is the use of spears. According to the archaeologists Ian Stead, it is clear that many of the spearheads found in graves were not buried as grave-goods but "as the remains of a ritual carried out during the burial ceremony." The best examples, says Stead,[26] are from Garton Station, a cemetery which lies to the south of Garton Slack:

> GS10 is an extreme case, with 14 spearheads in the grave: six of them had obviously been driven into the corpse, and the others were scattered around it. But they were not neatly grouped; it seemed that they had been hurled into the grave. There were 11 spearheads in comparable positions in GS7. Four had been driven into the waist and one into the chest, there were three around the skeleton, and three in the filling of the grave, grouped together and still standing vertically about 0.2m above the skeleton's waist.

This ritual was not confined to Garton Station. Grave R174 at Rudston had seven iron spearheads and two bone points scattered among and around the bones; at Wetwang Slack one of the cart-burials included a collection of seven spearheads scattered around the skeleton.

Toutatis finger ring from Eboracum (York), inscribed TOT (courtesy of York Museums Trust, http://york museumstrust.org.uk).

The spears thrust into bodies and the chalk figurines with swords must be related to the veneration of a particular deity, but the identity of this deity remains a mystery. One possibility is the deity mentioned by Lucan that he calls *Teutates*. The name is related to Oscan *touto*, Umbrian accusative *totam* "city," Irish *tuath*, Welsh *tud* "people," Old High German *diota* "people,"[27] and the etymology suggests that Teutates or was a tribal protector. Two dedications are known to Toutatis from Roman Britain: a silver plaque dedicated to Mars Toutatis in north Hertfordshire, and an altar dedicated to Riocalatis ("Hard King"), Toutatis and Mars Cocidius in Cumbria (Mars of course is the Roman god of war). In addition, a number of silver rings with the name TOT (Toutatis), have been found in eastern Britain, the vast majority in Lincolnshire, just to the south of East Yorkshire.

As for the pig meat, there is a Gaulish god called Mercury Moccus known from a single inscription at Langres (Haute-Marne) in northeastern France, the tribal capital of the Lingones–Moccus has been linked to Irish *mucc* and Welsh *moch* "pig."

Astronomy in Lincolnshire ... and in the Iron Age World

The Causeway at Fiskerton, Lincolnshire

The Iron Age is not known for monuments with astronomical alignments, but a recent discovery in Lincolnshire has shown that Iron Age priests had certainly not forgotten the astronomical knowledge accumulated by their Neolithic and Bronze Age ancestors. Fiskerton is on the River Witham near Lincoln and the Late Bronze Age feasting site at Washingborough, and in 1981 part of an Iron Age causeway roughly dated to 600 BC at its earliest, was excavated south of Fiskerton on the north bank of the river Witham. Posts were set vertically into the soft ground in clusters forming two roughly parallel lines, 13 feet apart, and perpendicular to the river. Lying between the posts were horizontal timbers which had been pegged into the ground forming a firm walkway over the boggy ground. There were two major phases of repair where vertical timbers had been replaced and when the horizontals rotted they had been consolidated with a layer of limestone chips. Finds include bone needles, pottery, and domestic and military metalwork, four axes and a hammer, a file with a decorated bone handle and a pruning hook. Four iron swords, two in scabbards, three socketed iron spear heads, and various items of horse furniture were also recovered.

Traditional excavation techniques indicated that the posts represented at most two phases of construction. Dendrochronology results from dating tree-rings, however, showed that the causeway had a long history of construction and repair. The exact date of construc-

Fiskerton Logboat from Fiskerton, Lincolnshire, which dates from the Late Bronze Age (courtesy of The Collection: Art and Archaeology in Lincolnshire).

tion cannot be determined, but the first felling event in the tree-ring record is 456 BC. Oak timbers were then felled every 16–18 years, and used in pairs to repair or consolidate the causeway at regular intervals along its length. Timbers were still being felled after 339 BC. The felling dates of many of the timbers of the causeway coincide with total lunar eclipses in the winter, and the periods between felling match the periods between eclipses, and it has been suggested that this activity was linked to prediction of the eclipses. Some of the metalwork items, including swords and a saw, have La Tene style decoration, and seem to be high status items deliberately deposited as votive offerings. This deposition appears to have occurred after the phases of construction or repair of the causeway itself had ceased, in the late 4th and 3rd centuries BC.[28] The metalwork deposited in the river at Fiskerton includes six swords, one with a coral-inlaid anthropomorphic hilt, and eleven spearheads, as well as an array of bronze fittings, many of which probably derive from scabbards or shields.[29] The anthropomorphic sword probably dates to the second half of the 4th century BC, and the coral inlays on the handles are ultimately of Mediterranean origin.[30]

The Timber Ramp at Caldicot, Southeast Wales

Fiskerton is not the only watery construction to be linked to lunar eclipses. Caldicot is in Monmouthshire, southeast Wales, near the Severn Estuary and the Early Bronze Age Crick barrow. In 1988 during the construction of an artificial lake at Caldicot Castle, Bronze Age structures and artifacts were encountered in a former course of the Nedern Brook, less than a mile north-northwest of where this stream now flows into the River Severn. Excavations uncovered a timber "hard" (ramp) on which people could walk to load and unload boats moored in the stream, and a wooden causeway or trackway.[31] Two dates for the felling of the timbers correspond to the year before and the year after two lunar eclipses (987 and 989 BC).[32]

Timber Trackways in Ireland and Continental Europe

Fiskerton and Caldicot are not unique, for watery constructions are also linked to lunar eclipses outside Britain. At Derrynaskea, Co. Longford in Ireland the felling of timbers took place in the same year as a lunar eclipse (974 BC). At Corlea, also in Co. Longford, the felling of timbers for the trackway known as Corlea 5 (in 560 BC) also corresponds to a lunar eclipse. The first dates of the Roman bridge at Le Rondet, Haut-Vully, Switzerland (6 BC and AD 31), coincide with a lunar eclipse. At Biesheim in Alsace, France, timbers from a Roman bridge on the Rhine were dated to 3/4 BC, close to the time of a lunar eclipse on October 28, 3 BC. Finally, at the lake called Dümmer See in southern Lower Saxony, Germany, the felling of timbers for *Bohlenweg* ("Timber Trackway") VI occurred in the same year as the lunar eclipse in AD 43.[33] The area around Haut-Vully in Switzerland was inhabited in the Iron Age by the Helvetii, and was conquered by Julius Caesar in 58 BC—so it may well have been the astronomical knowledge of the Helvetii that prompted Caesar to say that the Druids were experts in "the stars and their motion."

The Iron Age Hillfort of Glauberg, Western Germany

Judging from the chronology of these sites, the practice of felling timbers at the time of lunar eclipses started in Ireland, spread to Wales and eastern England, then crossed the Channel to continental Europe. In fact, the moon seems to have played a more significant role in Iron Age continental Europe than it did in Britain. Early Iron Age Europe is associated with the Hallstatt culture, named after a site in Austria, and best known for its *oppida* (defended settlements) and richly furnished graves. One well known example is Glauberg, a fortified ridge near Glauburg in Hesse, not far from Frankfurt. The site became a fortified oppidum in the 6th or 5th century BC, and was occupied until the 2nd or 1st century BC. Glauberg is perhaps best known for its burial mound 328 yards from the oppidum. Tomb 1 contained a bronze flagon, dating from the late 5th century BC, and a gold torc, and in a wide trench to the west of the tomb was a life-sized sandstone statue, also dated to the 5th century BC. Around the burial mound was a ditch system, part of the large system of ditches all around the Glauberg hill and especially the mound, which has recently been called a *Prozessionsstrasse* ("Processional Road"). According to the astrophysicist Bruno Deiss, all these ditches have an astronomical meaning, with the great *Prozessionsstrasse* "aiming at the point of the Southern Major Standstill of the moon's 18.61-year precession (maximum extreme of the moon setting), and other ditches aiming at the dates of the solstices."[34]

The Coligny Calendar

The moon also plays a role in the famous Coligny calendar, a large bronze calendar found at Coligny in the Ain departement of eastern France near the border with Switzerland. The calendar, dating to the late 2nd or early 1st century BC, had been broken up and buried in a Gallo-Roman temple. It records 62 months of a 5-year cycle displayed in 16 columns each of 4 consecutive months, except for columns 1 and 9, each of which comprises 2 normal months and 1 intercalary month. Each month was of 29 or 30 days, and each was identified with the name followed by MAT(U) for the 30-day months and ANMAT(U) for the 29-day months. Since *matu* means "complete," while *anmatu* means "incomplete," the word presumably relates to the length of each month; but the words can also mean "good" and "bad," and might also indicate whether the months are propitious or not.[35] Each month is divided into two parts after the 15th day with the word ATENOUX ("renewal"), which signifies the end of the light half (the waxing moon) and the beginning of the dark period (the waning moon). Within each month, certain days are labeled as "inharmonious."

Iron Age Druids

The Druids may have been "those who understand wood," and the priests who supervised the building of timber causeways, ramps, trackways and bridges in Ireland, southeast Wales, Lincolnshire and on the Continent were almost certainly Druids who not only understood wood but were also experts in "the stars and their motion," clearly placing great value on lunar eclipses. Druids must also have supervised the construction of the "Processional Street" at Glauberg, and the making of the Coligny Calendar.

The archaeological evidence suggests that Druidism started in Ireland in the late Bronze Age and soon spread to Wales. By the Early Iron Age it had reached Lincolnshire, and by the Middle Iron Age it had reached Continental Europe. The evidence also suggests that by the time of the Roman Conquest of Gaul in the 1st century BC, Druidism

Dolmen de la Grenouille near Saint-Piat, Eure-et-Loire, northern France, August 9, 2014 (Dumuids).

was thriving on the Continent, but was marginalized in Britain, surviving in places like Anglesey, north Wales, where Llyn Cerrig Bach was an important depositional site until the Roman invasion, probably every bit as important to the local Celts as La Tène in Switzerland; and possibly at Fiskerton in Lincolnshire, where weapons were cast in the River Witham after the causeway was no longer maintained.

Caesar says that the Druids of Gaul assembled frequently in the territory of the Carnutes, who lived around Chartres, Orléans and Blois, in the departments of Eure-et-Loire, Loiret and Loir-et-Cher. The origin of the name Carnutes is unclear, but one possibility is that it is related to Irish *carn*, "cairn," referring to the Neolithic dolmens and menhirs found in the region—for example, at Changé, Saint-Piat in Eure-et-Loire. This would clearly be an appropriate place to assemble if the roots of Druidism lay in the Neolithic.

The Carnutes resisted the Roman conquest of Gaul: two men called Gutuater and Conconnetodumnus attacked the new Roman city of Cenabum (Orléans), killed a number of Romans and plundered their property.[36] It seems that *Gutuater* was actually the title of a priest rather than a name. Two inscriptions are known from Autun in eastern France, both set up by men described as *gutuater*; a third inscription is known from Mâcon, also in eastern France, set up by a man described as a *gutuater* of Mars; and a fourth inscription at Le Puy in south-central France was set up by a man who describes himself as *gutuater*.[37] The first part of *gutuater* is related to Old Irish *guth* "voice," and to Old Indian *puruhuta*, "much invoked" (an epithet of the god Indra),[38] which may be the origin of the English word *god* (literally "that which is invoked").

Metalwork was cast into the River Witham at Fiskerton, and a number of watery

Lamarche bridge at the source of the River Seine (Source-Seine) in eastern France, May 18, 2015 (Michel Foucher).

places in Switzerland and France also received offerings to the gods. The most famous is La Tène, an archaeological site at the northeastern end of Lake Neuchâtel in Switzerland, near the point where the River Thielle flows out of the lake. It was first discovered in 1857, when unusually low water levels revealed a series of wooden piles. Iron objects, mainly weapons, were dredged up from the bottom of the lake. Excavations carried out from 1880 to 1885 produced more finds and human skeletons, as well as evidence for timber structures interpreted as buildings along the bank of the river and two bridges or causeways across it about 361 feet apart. Most of the finds date from the 3rd and 2nd centuries BC, but there are also significant quantities from the 1st century BC. The vast majority are of iron, though there are also bronze, wooden and bone items. Among the weapons are 166 swords, 269 spearheads and 29 shields; there are also personal ornaments, including 382 brooches and 158 belt clasps.[39]

Two notable watery sites in France are Sources de la Seine in the Côte-d'Or department of eastern France, and Source des Roches at Chamalières in the Puy-de-Dôme department of central France, which were active in the second half of the 1st century AD. As the name suggests Sources de la Seine is the region where the River Seine rises, while Sources des Roches is a mineral spring. Some 3000 wood carvings were found at in the spring at Chamalières, while some 350 were found in the streams of Sources de la Seine. The carvings represent whole people, or body parts like heads, trunks, pelvises, arms and legs. At Sources de la Seine there were also votive offering made of stone or bronze.[40] Excavators also found in the spring at Chamalières a Gaulish inscription on a lead tablet invoking the Celtic god Maponos ("Divine Son"), which probably dates to the 1st century AD.

Late Iron Age Cremation Cemeteries in Southeast England

Many hillforts went out of use in the first half of the 1st century BC, at a time of "massive social and economic change."[41] During this period, a new form of burial rite emerged in Kent, Essex and Hertfordshire which involved cremation and the placing of the remains in a ceramic pot or wooden bucket, or in a simple pit. This new rite was influenced by burial practices in northern France, among the people that Julius Caesar called the Belgae. Among the Belgae were the Remi, who lived in the Champagne-Ardennes area of northeastern France—their name may mean "The First," related to Old Irish *riam*, "in front of him," *remi*, "in front of her," and to Latin *primus*, "first."[42] In the territory of the Remi is the village of Acy-Romance, and here an Iron Age settlement and cemetery was excavated between 1983 and 2003. From the 5th century BC, inhumation was practiced: the dead were buried in square ditches, the men with weapons, the women with jewels, the chiefs with their chariots (as in the Iron Age cemeteries of East Yorkshire). In the middle of the 3rd century BC, cremation became the normal burial rite. The ashes of the dead were placed in ceramic urns or directly into the earth. According to the status of the individual, up to twenty pottery vessels were also placed in the grave as well as quarters of meat, often pig.[43] No wooden buckets were found at Acy-Romance—indeed, wooden buckets are only known on the Continents from burials at Goeblingen-Nospelt in Luxembourg, which was probably in the territory of a Belgic tribe called the Treveri.

The Belgic burial rite of Acy-Romance and Goeblingen-Nospelt is associated with the so-called Aylesford-Swarling culture of southeast England, named after two cremation cemeteries in Kent, Aylesford near Maidstone and Swarling near Canterbury. The largest cemetery of this period is the one uncovered at King Harry Lane, St. Albans, with 463 burials (cremation and inhumation). Rich burials have been found at Lexden Tumulus near Colchester in Essex, and at Baldock and Welwyn Garden City in Hertfordshire.

The cremation cemetery at Swarling was excavated in 1921, when about 19 graves were found. Each grave contained 4 to 6 urns and a wooden bucket with iron hoops and handles. Grave goods included La Tene III brooches with early Roman influence and dated the cemetery from 1st century BC to the early years of the Roman occupation.[44] The Aylesford cemetery dates from the same period, with similar cremations in urns, and with the famous Aylesford Bucket. This wooden bucket wrapped in bronze contained cremated human bones. It was found in a grave with a bronze jug, a pan as well as three bronze brooches and four pots. The pan and jug, which may have been used for preparing wine, are from southern Gaul or Italy. Similar examples have been discovered across Europe and are often found together in graves from this period. The phaleras (bucket mounts) for the handle of the bucket are in the form of helmeted heads.[45]

Lexden Tumulus is an Iron Age barrow located in a prominent location overlooking the valley of the River Colne to the north. It is situated inside an extensive Late Iron Age settlement surrounding modern Colchester, known in Late Iron Age and Roman times as *Camulodunum*. The barrow is circular in plan and is about 5 feet high and 124 feet by 114 feet wide, and the most probable date of the burial, based on analysis of the grave goods is around 15–10 BC. The barrow was excavated in 1924 by P.G. and H.E. Laver, who revealed one of the richest Iron Age burials ever discovered in Britain. The main burial was positioned in a central pit which may have contained a timber chamber. The deceased's remains had been cremated and were buried with a large number of rich grave goods including domestic and personal goods. These included a number of imported objects from the Mediterranean including amphorae and figurines. A Bronze Age axhead was found, which may have been an heirloom or cult object. One of the most important finds in terms of dating was a silver medallion, created from a cast of a coin of the Emperor Augustus, which can be dated to the period 18–16 BC.[46] Camulodunum was the capital of the *Trinovantes* ("Newcomers"), who were closely related to the Catuvellauni of Hertfordshire.

At Baldock in North Hertfordshire a roughly circular pit 5 feet 3 inches in diameter was dug down into the solid chalk to a depth of a foot. In it were placed "a large bronze cauldron, two bronze dishes, two bronze mounted wooden buckets, two iron firedogs, an Italian Dressel 1A amphora and part of a pig. The cremated body, much of which was recovered from the cauldron, had been wrapped in the skin of a brown bear since phalange bones of the beast were found mixed with those of the human occupant."[47] And at Welwyn Garden City, the cremated body of a man aged about thirty-five was wrapped in a bear skin—the grave also included five wine amphorae, a bronze Campanian pan, a silver cup of Italian origin, colored glass gaming beads, and an iron object which may have been the boss of a shield.[48]

The practice of burying cremated remains in a bucket also spread to Wiltshire and Hampshire. A Late Iron Age cremation in a wooden bucket was found near Marlborough in Wiltshire in 1807. The bucket is of fir wood, with triple iron hoops and drop handles embossed with human and animal forms. The bucket is "elaborately decorated with repoussé male and female heads, both facing and in profile, and with pairs of horses. It was probably made in north Gaul in the first century BC and was certainly a prestigious object in its own time and an indication of the wealth and status of its owner."[49] In 1905 a barrow was excavated at Hurstbourne Tarrant to the north of Andover in Hampshire, revealing a rich primary Belgic bucket cremation burial.[50]

Cremation cemeteries have also been found in West Sussex and Hampshire that differ from the Aylesford-Swarling cemeteries. Excavations in 1992 in advance of the A27 Westhampnett Bypass to the northeast of Chichester, West Sussex, discovered a Late Iron Age religious site. Two, or perhaps four shrines were discovered with a range of pyre sites and related features, and 161 unurned cremation burials. The cremations are arranged around an open circular space with the shrines to the east. One grave was marked by a funerary monument.[51]

At Owslebury, south of Winchester, Hampshire, there was an Iron Age settlement where 18 Belgic cremations and one "warrior" inhumation were found lying within a rectangular enclosure[52]—the "warrior" was accompanied by his sword and shield.[53] A similar "warrior" burial was found at Adanac Park, Nursling, Hampshire, in an Iron Age inhumation cemetery dating to the 1st century BC or the 1st century AD.[54]

A Late Iron Age Shrine in Hampshire

With the new burial rites came a new form of shrine. The Late Iron Age shrine on Hayling Island near Portsmouth in Hampshire is one of the best authenticated examples of a Late Iron Age shrine in North-west Europe. The archaeologists who excavated the shrine identified two phases of use in the Late Iron Age. Three main elements formed the focus of the ritual ensemble in Phase I: an enclosure measuring some 82 feet by 82 feet "with its entrance aligned to the east, an inner enclosure, also with an eastern entrance, and a pit set on the western margin of the inner enclosure." The coins associated with Phase I can all be dated to the early-mid 1st century BC, up to around 30 BC. In Phase II, the elements that replaced Phase I "used the same outer enclosure, but the inner enclosure was demolished to make way for the circular structure built around the central pit." The circular structure is made up of an inner gully, 30 feet in diameter, "with postholes within it, presumably forming the foundation of the walling, and an outer gully of variable depth that appears to have served to drain water away from the structure's foundations."

The objects deposited include a large number of coins, mainly coins of the immediate area, but also those of the peoples to the west and a significant number from Gaul, primarily from Armorica (Brittany) and central/northern Gaul, and some Roman republican coins. Analysis of the coins shows that they are relatively early in date, the majority being of the mid/late 1st century BC, and that there may have been a gap in the practice of coin deposition in the early 1st century AD. Other votive material from the site includes two fragmentary "currency bars," fibulae (brooches), shield binding, iron spearheads, vehicle fittings and some fragmentary human remains. The "horse and vehicle equipment from phases I and II includes a three-link bridle-bit of cast bronze with bronze-cased iron rein rings, datable to the 1st century BC." One of the "more remarkable objects found was a bronze yoke-terminal with inlaid red enamel decoration on its terminal knob. It is without parallel in Britain, but is almost identical to examples from Mont-Beuvray," an oppidum (defended settlement) near Autun (Saône-et-Loire) in the Burgundy region of eastern France.[55]

The shrine on Hayling Island may have been inspired by religious sanctuaries among the Belgae of northern France, such as the sanctuary at Gournay-sur-Aronde near Compiègne in the Oise department of northeastern France, in the territory of the Bellovaci. The meaning of *Bellovaci* is uncertain, but it may be related to Old Indian *bhasah* "barking, baying," Old Icelandic *belja* "roar, bellow," Old English *bellan*, "roar, bellow."[56] If *Bellovaci* means "The Roarers," then it comes from the same root as *Belgae*, which is related to Irish *bolgaim* "swell," Old English *belgan* "be angry." Gournay began life as an oppidum in the shape of a quadrilateral, with an area of 29 acres. In the southwest corner of this large quadrilateral was a small trapezoid enclosure with an area of 7 acres, which was strongly defended with an earth rampart around 32 feet wide topped by a narrower rampart of earth and dry stones. The sanctuary is inside the oppidum, 110 yards east of the small defended enclosure, and was in use between the beginning of the 3rd century BC to the middle of the 2nd century BC. This sanctuary is a square enclosure about 49 yards in length, surrounded by a ditch in which sacrifices were placed. This ditch filled up and was surrounded by a palisade—a new ditch was then built outside the palisade opposite the entrance to the enclosure.

The original ditch. which the excavators called the "show pit," was in use for two centuries, during which time it was enlarged and lined with timbers. In it were deposited weapons and skeletal remains, following a particular plan—for example, in the area around the entrance, the deposits consisted of the skulls of cattle. In all 2800 human or animal bones and 2200 metallic objects or fragments were found in the "show pit." The metallic objects included 100 swords, 150 scabbards, 220 shield bosses, 70 spearheads, and 80 brooches, all of which were folded, broken or cut.

In the center of the sanctuary were ten pits, nine grouped in a circle around a central pit. Only the central pit survived—the nine others were filled with postholes to build a sub-oval temple facing the east which enclosed the central pit. This was followed by a square temple, also facing the east, which was destroyed by a fire. Following the Roman Conquest a third temple was built with a dry stone *cella* (inner chamber) surrounded by a wooden gallery. This went out of use in the middle of the 1st century AD, and it was not until the late 3rd century that a Roman temple was built on the same place as the earlier Gaulish temples.

Three types of sacrifices were found in the Gaulish sanctuary. There were at least 11 human sacrifices, as shown by severed vertebrae; animals sacrifices included cattle, horses, sheep, pigs, and dogs; and there were numerous swords, scabbards, spearheads, shield bosses and brooches. The analysis of the sacrifices permitted the excavators to outline the stages of the sacrificial process. First the victim was killed (or destroyed in the case of objects), and placed in one or more of the central pits; the victim or object was left in the central pit for several months, then carefully exhumed, and either placed in the "show pit," exhibited inside the sanctuary, or subjected to further ritual acts such as the removal of the skull. Among the animals sacrificed, there were 100 sheep, 42 cattle, 40 pigs and 8 horses; most of the cattle were about 9 years old, the horses about 10 years old, while the pigs were 12–24 months old, and the sheep less than four months old.[57]

Middle/Late Iron Age Settlements

Hampshire

In the Late Iron Age, a new form of settlement developed in southern England, inspired by developments in Gaul. Between 58 and 51 BC, the Roman general Julius Caesar conquered Gaul and turned it into a Roman colony. After the Roman conquest of Gaul, Commius, a Gaulish ally of Caesar belonging to the Atrebates tribe of northeastern France who later fell out with the Romans, established a settlement at Silchester in northern Hampshire. This was an enclosed oppidum—that is, "a nucleated settlement of the Later Iron Age, covering an area in excess of 24 acres, whose boundaries are marked by large earthworks comprising bank and outer ditch, which are generally taken to be of a defensive nature." They occur "on earlier, redefended hill-tops, on the sides of valleys, and immediately adjacent to rivers in southern, central and eastern England."[58]

Within a generation of its foundation in the second half of the 1st century BC, Silchester was a "populous settlement, its core occupying an area of over 100 acres." The archaeological record "shows evidence of wide-ranging contacts with Britain—as well as across the Channel to to France and south to Italy, Spain and the Mediterranean" by the early 1st century AD. Excavations in the 1980s on the site of the basilica (the great public hall that occupied one side of the forum) uncovered the Late Iron Age settlement "with evidence of of some regular planning, the traces of circular and rectangular timber buildings," and abundant evidence of metalworking. Many elements of this early settlement "were different from what is found in contemporary settlements in southern England, including evidence for diet. Quantities of oysters, on the one hand, and containers of wine, olive oil and fish sauce, on the other, pointed to a highly Romanized community."[59]

In the south of Hampshire, an oppidum was established at Oram's Arbour in Winchester. Oram's Arbour is on high ground to the west of the River Itchen, and Barry

The remains of the Late Iron Age oppidum of Oram's Arbour, on high ground to the west of Winchester, now a park. Winchester is visible in the distance (author's photograph).

Cunliffe says that intensive occupation of the valley-side began "in the second to first century BC during the currency of saucepan pots. At this time a bank and ditch were constructed to enclose on the north, west and south sides an area in excess of 34 acres.... Occupation within the enclosure was probably continuous but by the first half of the first century AD the nucleus had moved further towards the river where fragments of coin moulds and quantities of Gallo-Belgic pottery suggest a settlement of some importance."[60]

However, not all parts of Hampshire were affected by the new ways. At Viables Farm on the southern fringes of Basingstoke, an Iron Age and Romano-British enclosed farmstead was partially excavated in 1974–76 by the Basingstoke Archaeological and Historical Society. The enclosure had an entrance in the southwest corner and many internal features including post holes, pits and gullies were noted. The site may have been enclosed in the Late Iron Age (1st century BC) and this main phase of activity continued into the 1st century AD. After this the ditch gradually silted up, but in the 4th century AD, timber-built structures were erected. The early excavations identified a large pit (6 feet 6 inches diameter) within the enclosure, which contained two adult females associated with a number of animal burials. Beneath all of these was a "cist" (a small dug pit chamber) containing carved antler weaving combs and toggles, an antler terret ring (horse harness) and a silvered-bronze terret ring. The two females were buried close together in an unusual way. Inhumation 2 was a young female, aged 25–30 years, lying face upward, with her right arm extended over a horse skull. Her head was resting on the neck of a sheep. Burial

1 was an older female, 35–40 years, placed in a crouched position with her head resting on the pelvis of Burial 2. Immediately beneath them were two complete sheep, parts of two horses and parts of two cattle.[61]

Dorset

Before Caesar conquered the whole of Gaul, the Romans had established a colony in the south of France, in Languedoc and Provence, which came under Roman rule around 120 BC. Around this time, Hengistbury Head, at the entrance to Christchurch Harbour in Dorset, became a port, with a range of industrial activities and trade links with southwest Britain, Spain and France. Two distinct phases of Late Iron Age settlement have been identified at Hengistbury Head. Late Iron Age 1 (100–50 BC) consisted of timber buildings and a trackway along the coastal strip, with concentrations around the two inlets of Barnfield and Rushy Piece. Rushy Piece also has evidence of a possible harbor. Industrial activities within the settlement included bronze working, glass working, shale working, iron working, extraction of silver and possible salt production.

The presence of copper and silver alloy from Callington on the Devon-Cornwall border, cassiterite from Cornwall, silver rich lead from the Mendips and pottery from Cornwall, Devon and the Mendips demonstrate trade between Hengistbury Head and western Britain. Overseas trade is also present with Italian Dressel 1A amphorae, wheel thrown pottery from Armorica and coins of Armorica and northwest Gaul up to the Caesarian campaign. There is evidence that Hengistbury Head was importing wine, figs and glass, and exporting metals, corn, hides and cattle, and probably slaves.

The Late Iron Age 2 phase (50 BC–AD 43) developed without any noticeable dislocation from Late Iron Age 1. The settlement, now more extensive, had developed into a series of palisaded enclosures fronting onto the old shoreline road. Industrial activities included iron working, bronze working and shale working. Long distance trade had been maintained, but had been much reduced and included imports of Catalan wine, olive oil, fish based products from southern Spain and finewares from Aquitania. Hengistbury Head's role as a production and distribution center was maintained, coins were minted here to allow small-scale local exchange. The coin distribution shows its sphere of influence was now restricted to the lower reaches of the Stour Valley.[62]

Wiltshire

In 2004 a metal detectorist discovered a hoard of cauldrons at Chiseldon near Swindon in Wiltshire. A local historical society conducted a small excavation and uncovered a vessel made from copper-alloy and iron, as well as copper-alloy from a second vessel. In 2005 a team from the British Museum found a minimum of 12 fragmentary Iron Age metal cauldrons deliberately buried together in a pit with two cow skulls. The cauldrons were stacked or placed in the pit whole and roughly half were upside down. The others were either the right way up or on their sides. The cauldrons are globular in shape and vary in size between approximately 2 feet and 2 feet 8 inches wide at the rim. They are made from bands of iron and sheet copper-alloy with iron handles. They probably date to between 200 BC and AD 100. The site is overlooked by two hillforts—Barbury Castle, which was intensively occupied in the Middle Iron Age, and Liddington Castle, which was probably constructed in the 7th/6th century BC and occupied until the 5th century

BC. The site is also located along the Ridgeway, a prehistoric route linking a number of hillforts in the region.[63]

The Ridgeway is an ancient trackway that extends from Avebury in Wiltshire along the chalk ridge of the Berkshire Downs to the Goring Gap on the River Thames, 8 miles upstream from Reading. The Ridgeway near Chiseldon consists of "dendritic paths and trackways cut into the ridge/hillside" which extend for over a mile in a southwest to northeast direction. In places parallel trackways cover an area up to 32 yards wide with individual tracks measuring up to 7 yards wide. For a 328 yard section at the foot of the escarpment to the north of Barbury Castle hillfort the trackway "divides into a number of branches which lie on banks/lynchets and which also cut through a possible Medieval or Post Medieval boundary bank." To the northwest of Barbury Castle the Ridgeway "meets up with a number of other trackways running north south and up into and around the hillfort." The date of origin of the Ridgeway is "open to debate but may have been in use as a drove way from the Bronze Age."[64]

Gloucestershire

In 1998 and 2004, a Middle/Late Iron Age settlement was excavated at Bishop's Cleeve near Cheltenham, not far from the hillfort of Nottingham Hill. The earliest phase of occupation consists of a number of roundhouses, with associated pits, postholes and spreads of material, concentrated in the northwest of the site. A total of 169 sherds (4 pounds 12 ounces) of pottery from these (and later) features date to the Middle and Late Iron Age. Seven pits could be dated to this phase of activity. They were generally sub-circular or oval in plan, with steep or vertical sides and flat or slightly concave bases, and up to 5 feet 3 inches in diameter and 2 feet 8 inches deep. Among the smaller pits, 2119 (2 feet 2 inches in diameter) contained a deposit of burnt objects associated with weaving—part of an antler comb, up to three antler needles, a triangular clay loomweight and a spindle whorl fashioned from a fossilized fish vertebra.[65]

There was a Late Iron Age oppidum at Perrott's Brook near Bagendon, to the north of Cirencester. Here a large dyke system, constructed perhaps in the early 1st century AD, encompassed an area of between 197 and 494 acres. Nearby at North Cerney is an Iron Age enclosure known as The Ditches, which was constructed in the 2nd or 1st century BC, and formed part of the same complex. Excavation at the Perrott's Brook oppidum revealed an industrial area at the entrance including coin minting. Both sites have evidence of high-status occupation in the early 1st century AD, with imported Gallo-Belgic pottery from around Reims in northeastern Gaul and Samian ware, possibly from La Graufenesque in the Toulouse area of southern Gaul. The subsequent building of an exceptionally early villa at Ditches in the late 1st century AD further indicates the inhabitants' high status and rapid adoption of Romanized lifestyles.[66]

Worcestershire

At Holt near the River Severn to the north of Worcester, a settlement pattern of cropmarks of single-ditched fields enclosing or connecting subrectangular enclosures was seen on air photographs. Small enclosures, possibly those of dwellings, and the eastern segment of a ring ditch are also visible. Rescue excavations in 1974–5 revealed the ploughed out remains of a Bronze Age barrow, the ditch about 66 feet in diameter and a central burial area virtually intact containing several cremations set in and around a mound of soil. Five of these were accompanied by flint knives. The ring ditch was cut by the shallow south ditch of an Iron Age enclosure within which were the remains of a large square timber structure, the walls set in trenches which contained stone-packed post holes. Domestic debris—potsherds, bone and charcoal—suggest this structure may have been a dwelling. Remains of a further structure of post hole construction, possibly a barn, were found between the dwelling and the south ditch. Other finds included Iron Age pottery and metalwork.[67] This site is of particular interest because an Iron Age enclosure was built close to a Bronze Age barrow.

Shropshire

A multi-period site was excavated at Sharpstones Hill, Shrewsbury. Three Middle Bronze Age barrows were found with evidence of cremation burials in each. Two of the barrows were probably disc or saucer barrows, the third has been almost entirely destroyed by building operations. Several pits and postholes of Late Bronze Age/ Early Iron Age date were uncovered—a quantity of plain, heavily-gritted cooking wares were found in some of the pits, and a cremation containing a bronze awl. A Middle Iron Age univallate enclosure roughly 45 yards square was also excavated. The main entrance, 5 feet 6 inches wide, was situated on the east side, with a smaller causewayed entrance only 27 yards away at the north-east corner. A circular, trench built hut, 30 feet in diameter and other Iron Age structures were found within the enclosure.[68] As at Holt in Worcestershire, the Iron Age enclosure on Sharpstones Hill was built near Bronze Age barrows.

One of the most intriguing prehistoric sites in Shropshire is not a settlement but a trackway. The Clun-Clee Ridgeway is a trackway that runs across south Shropshire from the Rhuddwr Brook at Anchor in southwest Shropshire near the border with Wales to Bewdley on the River Severn in Worcestershire by way of Titterstone Clee Hill and the valley of the River Clun. The outstanding archaeological interest of the ridgeway lies in the huge number of flint implements and manufacturing debris found along the route, indicating a local flint industry. This is remarkable in that Shropshire has no native flint and the material must have been imported, the nearest source being the Marlborough Downs, eighty miles distant.[69]

In 1991 a Bronze Age barrow at Bromfield near the confluence of the rivers Onny and Terne was excavated, revealing an Iron Age inhumation burial associated with the barrow. The burial, identified from a soil stain, was associated with fragments of a La Tene I iron brooch and a pennanular iron bracelet with adhering textiles, and a bronze pendant, suggesting a date in the 5th–4th century BC.[70] Nearby are two Middle Bronze Age cemeteries excavated in 1966-7. The northern cemetery was a large cremation pit with two inurned burials and two other pits containing burnt bones; and about 130 pits disposed in a semi-circle containing charcoal, bones and broken pots from which twenty vessels were reconstructed, most of which have affinities with Wessex biconical urns, possibly dated to around 1400 BC. The southern cemetery contained a number of cremations in upright urns near a barrow and a ditch 32 feet in diameter with one central cremation. Surrounding the remains of a barrow B7, which contained an un-urned cremation, were a number of satellite cremation burials, some accompanied with urns, others without. The burials are all thought to be of earlier Bronze Age date. Fifty-four yards to the south-west of this barrow a second, but larger cremation cemetery was discovered consisting of 140 cremations, many yielding Deverel-Rimbury pottery. Radiocarbon dates indicate the use of this cemetery between 1556 BC and 762 BC.[71] This type of cemetery is most common in Wessex, in particular Hampshire, Dorset and Wiltshire.

Leicestershire

In 2000, Ken Wallace, a member of the Hallaton Fieldwork Group, discovered some Late Iron Age coins scattered across a field on a hilltop in Hallaton, Leicestershire. After finding more than 200 coins, he realized their importance and reported the find, "instigating what became one of the most important Iron Age excavations and community archaeology projects in the country." The resulting finds, now known as the Hallaton Treasure, include 5,294 Iron Age coins, a silver bowl, a crescent-shaped silver ingot, and a silver decorated Roman parade helmet, all dating to the 1st century AD—roughly AD 30–60. The site has been interpreted as a shrine. The hilltop was enclosed by a ditch which stretched across the east-facing side of the hilltop. The boundary ditch was the focus of the excavations and the majority of the coins were discovered in the entranceway, in 14 separate hoards. The excavators also found 6,901 bone fragments, almost exclusively from pigs (97 percent). Pig meat was reserved for feasting, and it is likely that around 300 pigs were buried at the site. Many of the bones were anatomically attached to each other, which suggests that large joints of meat were buried as offerings to the gods.[72] At least three dogs were buried in the entranceway and boundary ditch. Two of the burials were disturbed by later re-modeling, but the third was still partially articulated—the body "had been carefully positioned with its neck stretched unnaturally backwards, and it may have been placed to guard the entrance to the shrine."[73]

Cambridgeshire

Coveney is near Ely in Cambridgeshire, and in the Iron Age a small ringwork known as Wardy Hill lay on the edge of the fen, between 8 feet 10 inches and 9 feet 10 inches above sea level, surrounded by fen on all sides except the west. Owing to severe plough damage, the ringwork was excavated in 1991–2. The main entrance was defended by a "remarkable series of ditches and ramparts, similar to Wessex forts." In the interior were four "huts" with circular eavesdrip gullies, associated in two pairs. They were "not contemporary and probably represent successive stages of paired dwellings. The density of finds was very high, at 28,000 artefacts recovered, even though the site had a short life in during the first century BC and a little later." Much of the pottery had Middle Iron Age affinities, but was intermixed with Late Iron Age wheel-made material. High status pottery of "samian and La Tène-style vessels" came from the buildings. The ringwork "was perhaps the most important of the many Iron Age sites in the Isle of Ely."[74]

Norfolk

Excavations at Thetford in the south of Norfolk between 1981 and 1982 revealed an Iron Age to early 1st century AD complex of rectangular enclosures, hut sites (possibly shrines) and burials. The earliest phase, around 200 BC to early 1st century AD, was a complex ditched enclosure of one acre. This was replaced in phase 2 by an enclosure of over 3 acres containing double- ring round houses, and 2 smaller round houses, of the early 1st century AD to around AD 50. Outside the enclosure, 5 ring ditches of 16 feet–32 feet in diameter surrounded unfinished graves. This enclosure was later replaced in phase 3 by a triple ditched enclosure covering an area of almost 9 acres, and enclosing a central area of 1.2 acres, produced when the inner ditch of phase 2 was filled and the outer ditch was extended to the east. Outside this, a new outer ditch was added, being separated from the original outer ditch of phase 2 by 7 or 8 parallel palisade-trenches. An entrance was defined by a pair of east-west fences leading to a gateway at the inner causeway, which consisted of 2 or more massive timbers set in large sub-rectangular post-pits. The end of this phase was marked by demolition of the fences and of the gateway some time in the 3rd quarter of the 1st century, probably after about AD 60. Finds include a complete Gallo-Belgic platter, 3 Late Iron Age local coins, a number of early brooches of the Colchester type, and several copies of Claudian asses (low value Roman coins made of copper).[75] Although the site has been interpreted as "Boudica's Palace," Martin Henig points to the fact that the discovered huts have 2 opposed entrances, which suggests that they were not dwellings, but possibly Iron Age shrines.[76]

A number of rich Late Iron Age finds have been uncovered in Norfolk over the years. The most famous is the Snettisham Treasure, first discovered at Snettisham in north Norfolk in 1948. Excavations were carried out, and further finds were made in 1950, 1964, 1968, 1973 and 1990. The hoard was found in a number of pits, three of which were double pits with two compartments, one on top of the other. The most spectacular part of the hoard is Hoard L—the upper compartment consisted of a small nest of 7 silver and bronze torcs. Then in a corner of the shallow pit, there was an opening to a larger pit which had the richest treasure of all. There were 2 bronze bracelets at the top, then two silver torcs and finally ten gold torcs. In 1991 a great deposit of iron slag was found in the filling of a ditch. A magnetometer survey set up to trace the ditch, and it is now apparent that it forms an enclosure, 20 acres in extent. Coins found in the hoard (234 in all) indicated that the hoard was buried around 70 BC. Most of the coins are Gallo-Belgic coins also found in France, which pre-date Julius Caesar's conquest of Gaul.[77]

In 1982, at Crownthorpe in the parish of Wicklewood, southwest of Norwich, a metal detectorist uncovered a large bowl-like vessel. Careful excavation "revealed a hoard of six more vessels buried tightly together inside the first bowl. Subsequent study showed that some of them had originated in Southern Italy, while others exhibit native Celtic-style decoration. Together they make up a complete Roman-type drinking set, but exhibiting a fusion of Roman and Celtic forms." The assemblage dates from the mid–1st century AD, and had been deliberately hidden in the ground at about this time, either for safekeeping or as an offering to the gods.

In 1992, another metal-detectorist was walking a field at Saham Toney, to the west of Norwich, when he unearthed a series of small decorated bronzes, later identified as a group of Late Iron Age horse-harness fittings, consisting of harness rings, worn horse-bits, and a complete set of five terret-rings. This "exceptional group of objects was accompanied by some beautifully enamelled harness decorations, all of the early 1st century AD."

In 2000, a Late Iron Age bridle-bit came to light at a farm to the north of East Dereham, not far from Saham Toney. Its appearance "was so perfect that it was initially thought to be modern, if not brand new. But its end loops betray its antiquity. They are decorated with elaborate but asymmetrical Celtic-style enamelled moldings, which make this an exceptionally rare piece, again dating to the final decades of the Iron Age."[78]

Lincolnshire

One of the most important Late Iron Age sites in Lincolnshire is Sleaford on the River Slea, a tributary of the Witham. The later Iron Age occupation of Sleaford is represented by large numbers of ditches, gullies, pits, postholes and stake holes. The site appears to have consisted of at least five enclosures and three structures. One of the structures "was probably rectangular in shape, consisting of fourteen stake holes in a ditch along one side of the structure. These are thought to be supports for wattle work which would have been daubed to form a wall: a large amount of daub was recovered from this area which would support this theory." The structure is thought to be approximately 16 feet in length. A second structure was measured at 39 feet by 23 ft. In addition to the enclosures and structures a large complex of pits, intersecting gullies, and ditches suggest a concentration of occupation in this area. An unmetaled trackway runs across the site in a northwest to southeast direction. A large quantity of finds were recovered including late Iron Age fine wares, coin pellet mold fragments and crucible. The center of the mint on the site has not yet been found, but a large assemblage of fragmentary coin pellet molds were recovered. The pellet molds are in trays and the apertures for the pellets came in three different sizes, probably relating to different denominations. It has been speculated "that this may have been a major mint and could have produced as many as 18,000 pellets." The trays or molds themselves only appear to have been used for the production of silver pellets and were used only once. They appear to have been deliberately broken to remove each pellet and then discarded.[79]

South Yorkshire

Sutton Common is the name used by the Ordnance Survey for three fields approximately 550 yards to the south of Askern Town, 5 miles north of Doncaster in South Yorkshire. The name has also been used for an Iron Age period site consisting of two multivallate enclosures located on a pair of sand islands in a small floodplain and separated by a palaeochannel named the Hampole Beck. The site was first excavated between 1933 and 1935, and large-scale excavations were undertaken on the larger enclosure between 1998 and 2003. The earliest activity on the site was a small mortuary enclosure: a single burial of pyre debris was dated to the Early Bronze Age. The main part of the fort comprised a D-shaped enclosure occupying the whole of the main island, surrounded by a box rampart, inner ditch, palisaded bank, outer ditch, and further elaborations of the defenses. Two gatehouses, one facing east and the other west, provided the only access. The western gateway could only be reached by a causeway across the wetlands; a cross-bank and additional bank-and-ditch arrangements controlled access to the causeway. The integrated dendrochronological and radiocarbon analysis dated the onset of construction of the defenses to 372 BC. The limited items of material culture associated with the marsh-fort were all recovered from the ditch terminals of the east-facing entrance; these were accompanied by animal bones, two human crania and the only samples of yew wood found on site. These are interpreted as forming part of a structured deposition. The interior of the fort was dominated by four-post structures; some 150 granaries, ordered in rows of up to eight structures, occupied the site. In several instances charred grain was found in the postholes, and is interpreted as evidence of structured deposition during construction. No other structures were identified, and palaeoenvironmental studies indicate that the site was never inhabited. A second phase of activity within the interior was identified and dated provisionally to the 4th to 2nd century BC. This phase comprises twelve enclosures of basic geometric shape, between 10 feet and 20 feet across, defined by narrow, steep ditches. It is suggested that these acted as "temenos" or sacred places where the ashes or pyre debris were scattered as part of mortuary rituals.[80]

North Yorkshire

Nosterfield Quarry, which lies a short distance from the Neolithic Thornborough henges, was excavated between 1991 and 2008. Late Neolithic Grooved Ware pottery was found in 38 pits, mostly on the Ladybridge Farm spur to the east of the main site. The Grooved Ware ceramic assemblage weighed 6 pounds 3 ounces and represented a minimum number of fourteen Woodlands vessels, twelve Durrington Walls and four Clacton (Woodlands is a site in Amesbury, Wiltshire, while Clacton is a site in Essex). Burnt material from the pottery was dated to between 2800 BC and 2200 BC.

Evidence for Middle Bronze Age occupation is characterized exclusively by funerary activity. This consisted of an inhumation burial and a small cremation cemetery made up of five urned, one possible urned and four unurned cremations. The skeleton in the inhumation burial was in a poor state of preservation, compounded by the fact that it had apparently been weathered prior to burial and therefore probably represented a secondary interment. The skeletal material had been arranged in the pit without any anatomical ordering, with the long bones laid out next to each other, and the skull placed on top. Various parts of the skeleton were missing, including the vertebrae and long bone joints. A sample of bone from the skeleton was radiocarbon dated to 1530–1380 BC.

There was no activity at Nosterfield from the Middle Bronze Age to the later Iron Age, when two square enclosures were constructed. Enclosure (feature nos050304) measured approximately 32 feet by 32 feet and enclosed an area of almost 550 square feet. No internal burial was evident, but it is assumed to represent either the truncated remains of a square barrow or of a ritual enclosure. Approximately 28 feet to the east of this enclosure was a large pit containing four equid burials, three of which appear to be of horses and the fourth possibly a mule. A multiple burial of this kind is a very rare discovery, and a radiocarbon date from a femur of one of the burials returned a date of between 100 BC and AD 90.[81]

Innovation and Tradition in the Middle/Late Iron Age

In the Middle/Late Iron Age, parts of Britain came under the influence of new ideas from across the Channel in northern France, with the Middle Iron Age inhumation cemeteries of East Yorkshire, and the Late Iron Age cremation cemeteries of southeast England. Late Iron Age oppida like Silchester and Oram's Arbour in Hampshire, Bagendon in Gloucestershire, St. Albans in Hertfordshire, Colchester in Essex and Sleaford in Lincolnshire show unmistakable Continental influences, as do shrines like Hayling Island in Hampshire, and Hallaton in Leicestershire, and depositions of metalwork like those found at Snettisham in Norfolk.

However, in parts of Britain life went on as before. At Holt on the River Severn in

Worcestershire, an Iron Age enclosure was built close to a Bronze Age barrow, and at Sharpstones Hill, Shrewsbury in Shropshire an Iron Age enclosure was built close to several Bronze Age barrows. At Sutton Common in South Yorkshire a multivallate enclosure apparently used for ritual purposes was built on the site of an Early Bronze Age mortuary enclosure; and at Nosterfield Quarry in North Yorkshire, four horses (or three horses and a mule) were buried in the late Iron Age on a site that had been active in the Late Neolithic and Bronze Age.

Despite the continuity, much was changing in Late Iron Age Britain, and this process of change was to be accelerated when the Romans invaded and occupied Britain for almost four centuries.

CHAPTER 6

The Romans in Britain: Roman Gods and British Gods, Roman Burial Rites and Decapitated Burials

The Romans in Britain

The Romans invaded Britain in AD 43 and occupied it until around AD 410 when the last legions departed. The invasion met with some opposition: Caratacus, a chief from the Cauvellauni tribe of Hertfordshire, resisted the Romans until AD 51, with the help of the Silures of southeast Wales and the Ordovices of north Wales. The Romans eventually defeated Caratacus somewhere in the territory of the Ordovices—Caratacus escaped and sought refuge with Cartimandua in the north of England, but she surrendered him to the Romans.

The Romans also faced a revolt from Boudica (also known as Boadicea) in AD 60 or 61. Boudica's husband Prasutagus was ruler of a tribe in Norfolk called the Iceni, and a nominally independent ally of Rome. When he died, he left his kingdom jointly to his daughters and the Roman Emperor in his will. However, his will was ignored—the kingdom was annexed as if conquered, Boudica was flogged, and her daughters were raped. During the course of her revolt, Boudica destroyed Roman Camulodunum (Colchester), Londinium (London), and Verulamium (St. Albans), before being eventually defeated by the Romans.

After the Romans occupied Britain, they set up a system of towns and tribal territories (Latin *civitates*, singular *civitas*) ruled over from a tribal capital, and for the first time we can give names to some of the people who built the hillforts, enclosures and other settlements of Iron Age Britain.

The Tribal Capitals of Roman Britain

Exeter (Devon)

The most westerly tribal capital in England was *Isca Dumnoniorum* (Exeter), the tribal capital of the Dumnonii. *Isca* is Celtic, related to Latin *piscis*, "fish," and Irish *esc*, "water." The name *Dumnonii* is identical to the (Fir) Domnann of Connacht in the west of Ireland, and the word is related to Welsh *dwfn*, "deep," Irish *domhain*, "deep," Gaulish *Dubno-rix/Dumno-rix*, "World-King," Brittonic *Dubno-vellaunus*, "World-Leader." Dumnonii may mean "worshippers of (the god) *Dumnonos*"—perhaps he is "The Mysterious One."[1] The name *Dumnonii* survives in the post–Roman kingdom of Dumnonia, first mentioned in the 6th century, and in the modern county of Devon. The name *Isca* survives in the River Exe, which flows through Exeter, and in the River Usk in south Wales, which flows through Newport.

Dorchester, Dorset

The main Roman settlement in Dorset was *Durnovaria* (Dorchester), not far from the Iron Age hillfort of Maiden Castle. The first element is found in Welsh *dwrn*, "fist," but also in Old Greek *doron*, "palm, span of the hand," Albanian *dorë*, "hand," Latvian *dure/duris*, "fist," while the second element, found in the tribal name *Treveri*, is related to Old Indian *var, vari*, "water," Old Norse *vari*, "liquid, water," Latin *urinor*, "to plunge under water, dive"[2] (the Treveri lived in the lower valley of the Moselle, around the German city of Trier). Durnovaria was associated with the *Durotriges*, whose name has defied interpretation. All we can say for certain is that the *var* element in Durnovaria is very old, belonging to the Indo-European language that preceded Celtic.

Ilchester, Somerset

The Durotriges were also associated with *Lindinis* (Ilchester in Somerset), on the River Yeo (also known as the Ivel). *Lindinis* appears to be Celtic, related to Welsh *llyn*, "pond, pool." Rivet and Smith, in *The Place Names of Roman Britain*, say that *in-* "suggests a wet place," citing Welsh *gwernin* "alder-swamp" (from *gwern* "alder"), but a diminutive is possible also; however, *-ina* is a recognized Celtic suffix, perhaps as in British *Sabrina*, here in plural form (*Sabrina* = the River Severn).[3]

Winchester, Hampshire

There were two tribal capitals in Hampshire, *Venta Belgarum* and *Calleva Atrebatum*. Venta Belgarum (Winchester), built near the Late Iron Age oppidum of Oram's Arbour,

The church of St. John the Baptist (12th century), which stand on the site of a late Roman cemetery to the east of the River Itchen, and outside the Roman city (author's photograph).

was the capital of the *Belgae*, who left traces of their Late Iron Age presence at Owslebury near Winchester, at Nursling near Southampton, and Hayling Island near Portsmouth. The meaning of the word *Venta* is much debated. Venta is usually treated as Latin, somehow related to Latin *vendo*, "sell," or as Celtic, but in fact it is probably neither. In classical antiquity there was an Illyrian town called *Vendum*, belonging to the Iapydes, who lived in what is now Croatia. In Albanian, which may be related to Illyrian, there is a word *vend*, "place, country," suggesting that *Venta* meant something like "homeland."[4] *Venta* may be a very ancient word, related to *Veneti*, the name of two Iron Age tribes, the Veneti who lived around Venice in northeast Italy, and the Veneti who lived in the Vannetais region of southern Brittany. It may also be related to an obscure Iron Age tribe called the *Venedi*, who are first mentioned by Pliny the Elder in the 1st century AD and apparently lived on the Baltic in what is now Poland; by the 7th century the Venedi had become the Slavic Wends, whose name survives in the district known as Hannoverian Wendland in Lower Saxony, eastern Germany.

The Church of St. Mary the Virgin, Silchester (12th century), which stands behind the Roman wall (clearly visible in the foreground). The plan, siting and orientation of the church strongly suggest that it was built on the site of a small, square Romano-British temple (author's photograph).

Standing on top of the Roman wall at Silchester (author's photograph).

Silchester, Hampshire

Calleva Atrebatum (Silchester) was the capital of the Belgic Atrebates, built on or near the site of the Iron Age oppidum. Calleva probably means "Settlement in the Woods," related to Welsh *celli*, "wood."[5] The Atrebates originally lived around Arras in the Artois region; their name is related to Oscan *triibum*, "house," Old Welsh *treb* "dwelling," Old Frisian *therp/thorp*, "village."[6]

Chichester, West Sussex

It is likely that the Belgae of northern France also had a strong influence on Sussex, Kent, Essex and Hertfordshire. The main town in Sussex was *Noviomagus Reginorum* (Chichester in West Sussex), the capital of the Regini ("Stiff Ones" or "Proud Ones").[7] Noviomagus means "New Field," and the *-magus* element is related to Old Indian *mahi*, "earth," Latin *magnus*, "big," Welsh *maes*, "field."[8] The tribal name Regini is related to Latin *rego*, "to rule," *rex*, "king," *rigeo*, "be stiff," Old Irish *reg-/rig-*, "to stretch out (the hand), Old Irish *ri/rig*, "king."[9] The town is close to the Late Iron Age shrines where 161 unurned cremation burials were found, probably inspired by burial practices in Belgic Gaul.

Canterbury, Kent

The main Roman town in Kent was *Durovernum Cantiacorum* (Canterbury), the capital of the Cantiaci. The first element of Durovernum means "fort, market," related to the English word *door*, and the equivalent of the Latin *forum*, while the second element

-verno means "alder, alder-swamp, marsh," and is related to Welsh *gwern*.[10] The origin of the name *Cantiaci* is unclear, but it may be related to the word *canton*, "administrative division of a country," which is derived from Gaulish *cantos*, "circle (of a wheel)"; or to Welsh *cant*, "troop, multitude, crowd," Irish *cete*, "meeting."[11] Canterbury is not far from the Late Iron Age cremation cemetery at Swarling.

Colchester, Essex

The main Roman town in Essex was *Camulodunum* (Colchester), near the Late Iron Age settlement and Lexden Tumulus—this was a *colonia*, a town reserved for Roman citizens, usually retired soldiers. Camulodunum is named after the war god Camulos, best known from a dedication to Mars Camulos in Rindern (North Rhine Westphalia)—here the stone is decorated with a tree on either side and a coronet of oak leaves.

St. Albans, Hertfordshire

The final Belgic town is Verulamium (St. Albans), capital of the Catuvellauni. There was an oppidum at St. Albans in the Late Iron Age, and the name *Catuvellauni* is close to *Catalauni*, a tribe who lived around Châlons-en-Champagne in the Marne region of northeastern France. The first element of their name is related to Gaulish *catu-*, "fight, struggle," found in *Caturix*, a god worshipped in Switzerland and Germany, Old Irish

The foundations of a Roman town house at Verulamium (St. Albans) (photograph by Diana Gardner).

A fragment of Roman wall at Verulamium (St. Albans) (photograph by Diana Gardner).

A length of Roman wall at Verulamium (St. Albans) (photograph by Diana Gardner).

cath, "fight, struggle," while the second element is Gaulish *uellaunos*, "chief, commander,"[12] related to Latin *valeo*, "to be strong," Old Irish *falhn-, folhn-*, "to rule, reign," *flaith*, "prince, lord." The first element of *Verulamium* may be related to Greek *eurys*, "broad, wide" and Old Indian *uru*, "broad, wide," while the second element is related to Old Breton *lom*, Welsh *llaw* and Old Irish *lam*, "hand," implying that Verulamium was the town of a leader with "wide hands," that is, a generous leader.[13]

London

London was established as a commercial center by the time of Boudica's revolt. The name *Londinium* first appears at that time in connection with its destruction by fire. Evidence for the fire has been found on a number of sites, in the form of a layer of ash one foot thick. The buildings at that time were mainly of wattle and daub, but there had been a planned development of more permanent buildings dated AD 44–50, with a reconstruction dated AD 50–60, on the site of the forum. The first forum and basilica is dated mid-Flavian (AD 69–96), the final forum being not earlier than Hadrian (AD 117–138). A second major conflagration, not connected with any known historical event, took place in the early 2nd century. Other important buildings, all of the 2nd century include the governor's palace, the fort and bath houses. The city wall was probably built in the late 2nd century and certainly before AD 225, but the riverside wall is 3rd century.[14]

In the Late Bronze Age skulls were deposited in the Thames, and the practice continued in the Roman period. Walbrook in the City of London was once part of Roman Londinium, and over one hundred human skulls have been found in the Upper Walbrook Valley in Moorgate since the 19th century. These skulls were once believed to represent victims of Boudica's revolt against Rome, but it is now thought that they were possibly the product of "native ritual practices, in which the heads of deceased persons were deposited into the sacred Walbrook stream as part of a votive religious rite." A research study has suggested that the skulls "had been deliberately deposited without their lower jaws and that the discolouration of the bone suggested that they had been exposed for some time after death."[15]

Cirencester, Gloucestershire

To the west of Verulamium was *Corinium Dobunnorum* (Cirencester in Gloucestershire), the capital of the Dobunni and successor to the Late Iron Age oppidum at Perrott's Brook. The origin of the tribal name *Dobunni* has resisted interpretation, while the origin of *Corinium* is obscure. Around 30 BC, a tribal leader called *Corio* issued coins in Somerset and southern Gloucestershire, and *Corinium* may be linked to his name, and to *Corinium* in Liburnia, a coastal region of what is now Croatia). Alternatively, it is possible that the first element of *Corinium* represents the tribal name *Cornovii*, of which more shortly. The Cornovii may have worshipped a horned god, and there is archaeological evidence for horned figures in the territory of the Dobunni. A small bronze ox-head was found near Shepton Mallet in Somerset, which was probably in the territory of the Dobunni. On the top of the head, which is probably a mount for the handle of a vessel, is a loop; from the forehead two horns project horizontally and curve to meet each other.[16] A bronze bull's head was also found at Wolverley in north Worcestershire, possibly just outside the territory of the Dobunni, dated, like the example from Shepton Mallet, to the 1st century

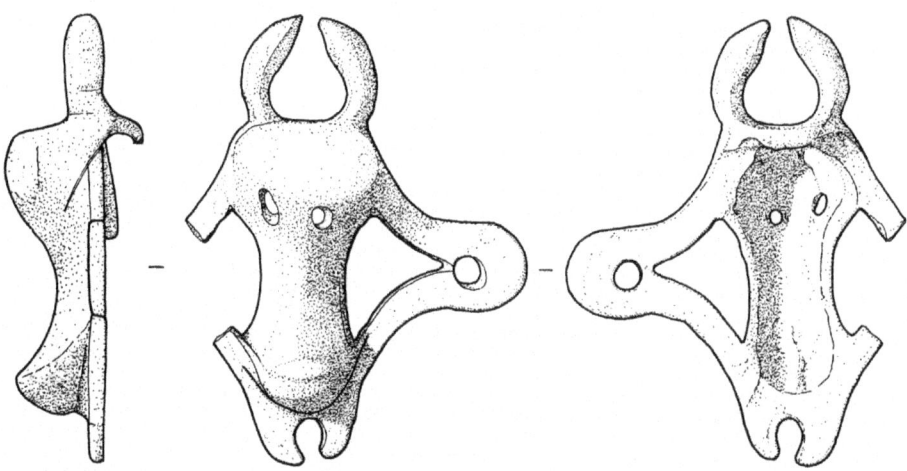

Bull's head bucket mount from Wolverley and Cookley, Worcestershire (Portable Antiquities Scheme).

AD. The head is very simple in style: the forehead is bulbous, and the horns may be depicted by a slight bump.[17] At Cirenceser, a ram-horned snake appears in company with a stag-horned god.[18]

Gloucester

The other important town in Gloucestershire was the *colonia* of *Glevum* (Gloucester). The name *Glevum* derives from a word related to the Welsh *gloyw* "bright, shining,"[19] perhaps referring to a river. Gloucester is on the River Severn, which in Roman times was called *Sabrina*. The name is connected to other river names such as the Sambre in northern France and Belgium, the Sèvre in western France, and the Sabrann in Ireland (the old name for the River Lee in Cork). It may be related to Latin *sapa* "must, grape juice," Illyrian *sabaium* "beer," English *sap*.[20]

An interesting relief has been found at Gloucester in the New Inn, Northgate Street. The relief shows Mercury with his caduceus, cockerel and purse, while his consort has an axe, patera (libation bowl), and wooden bucket.[21] This bucket may well be a reference to the bucket in which the ashes of many Britons were buried in Late Iron Age Kent, Essex and Hertfordshire.

Wroxeter, Shropshire

North of Glevum was *Viroconium* (Wroxeter in Shropshire), the tribal capital of the *Cornovii*, and successor to the Wrekin hillfort. The meaning *Viroconium* is uncertain, but the early scholar of Celtic John Rhys, in a 1908 paper,[22] suggested that *Viroconium* derives from a mythical founder *Guricon* or *Gurcon*, whose name could be translated literally as "Man-Hound," and figuratively as "Man-Protector"; and the French scholar Xavier Delamarre has come to a similar conclusion: *Viroconium*, he says, is the "establishment of the Man-Wolves," founded perhaps by a warrior group, since the dog in Celtic could also designate a warrior belonging to a war-band.[23]

Aerial view of Wroxeter Roman Town, Shropshire, the successor to the Wrekin hillfort, with the north wall of the Roman baths (the Old Work) clearly visible (© 2009 Shropshire Council).

The Cornovii, whose territory includes Shropshire and Cheshire, are something of an enigma. A tribe with an identical or similar name was also located in Cornwall, where the Cornovii formed a kingdom after Dumnonia/Devon became part of Anglo-Saxon England. The name *Cornovii* appears to be related to Latin *cornu*, "horn," Breton *kern*, "crown of the head," Irish *cern*, "angle, corner; excrescence, swelling," Gaulish *carnyx*, "trumpet," and Welsh *karn*, "hoof."[24] It is possible that the Cornovii were "worshippers of a horned deity of the *Cernunnos* (stag-god) type."[25] (Incidentally, if *Corinium* (Cirencester) had a link with the *Cornovii*, the Breton *kern* and Irish *cern* might explain why *Corinium* became *Ciren*cester.

Whether the Cornovii worshipped a horned god is unknown, but recently a cast copper alloy bulls head vessel or bucket mount, dated to the Late Iron Age/Early Roman period (100 BC–AD 200), has been found in south Cheshire, which was part of the territory of the Cornovii. The mount is realized in three dimensions; being an irregular triangular shape in plan and sub-rectangular (broadly D-shaped) in cross section. The front face of the bulls is most elaborately decorated. The top edge of the bulls head is horizontal (being relatively flat) and is sub-oval in shape. The sides of the mount then taper along their lengths, terminating at a slightly flared snout; both sides of the mount are symmetrical. At the widest point of the head before the edges start to taper are located two (one each side of the head) projecting horns.[26] A bronze ox-head bucket mount was also found in a grave at Welshpool in Powys, Wales, close to the border with Shropshire, which has been dated to between AD 150 and AD 200[27]; another was found in the district of Telford and Wrekin, Shropshire, dating to the Late Iron Age or early Roman period.[28]

There is considerable evidence for the worship of a horned god in Roman Britain, especially along Hadrian's Wall in the north of England. At Netherby Roman fort at Arthuret near Carlisle in Cumbria, a head made from sandstone has two ramhorns which curve round and down towards the ears. At Carvoran Roman Fort near Hexham in Northumberland a head fashioned from yellow sandstone has horns that grow from the top of the head. At Lanchester Roman Fort in County Durham a small figure has a horned head, and is bearded; Alnwick Castle in Northumberland also has a horned, bearded head; Chesters Roman fort near Hexham in Northumberland has a horned head fashioned from a block of stone. At Moresby Roman fort on the coast of Cumbria a god wears a pleated cape and has two long horns on the top of his head. A spear-wielding naked horned god was found at Maryport Roman fort on the Cumbrian coast to the north of Moresby.[29]

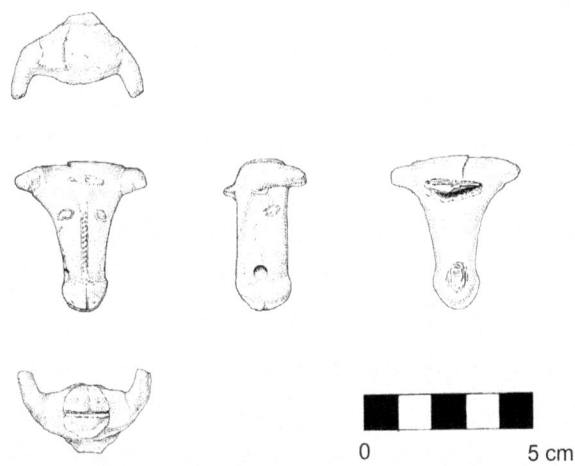

Bull's head bucket mount from South Cheshire (Portable Antiquities Scheme).

Outside Britain we have the Tanderagee (or Tandragee) idol, so-called because it once stood in the grounds of Ballymore Rectory, Tanderagee, Co. Armagh, Northern Island. This figure, perhaps dating from the Iron Age, "consists of a large head superimposed on a small, badly-proportioned body. The mouth is wide and grotesque, the moustache boldly drawn. A line which may to indicate the edge of a helmet comes well down over the brow. From this helmet, or from the actual head project two horns."[30] But the most famous horned god is Cernunnos, found on the so-called Pillar of the Boatmen, a monument in the Gallo-Roman city of Lutetia (Paris), which dates to the early 1st century AD and depicts a god with antlers which have torcs hanging from them.

To all these horned deities we should add the horned helmet dredged from the River Thames at Waterloo Bridge in London, and dated to between 150–50 BC. The helmet is made from sheet bronze pieces held together with many carefully placed bronze rivets. It is decorated with the style of La Tène art used in Britain between 250 and 50 BC.[31]

Horns clearly had a religious significance in Roman Britain, and may explain the burials of cattle skulls and the sheep or goats accompanying the dead at a number

Bull's head bucket mount from Telford and Wrekin, Shropshire (Portable Antiquities Scheme).

The ruins of the soldiers' barracks Chesters Roman Fort, October 27, 2007 (Steven Fruitsmaak).

of Iron Age sites including Battlesbury Bowl in Wiltshire, Viables Farm at Basingstoke in Hampshire, Harston Mill in Cambridgeshire, and Rudston in East Yorkshire.

Leicester

East of Viroconium is *Ratae* (Leicester), the tribal capital of the *Corieltauvi*. *Ratae* is related to Irish *raith*, "earthen rampart, fort,"[32] while *Corieltauvi* may signify "army of Litavis,"[33] the earth goddess known from inscriptions at Narbonne in the south of France and near Dijon in eastern France. The Corieltauvi probably occupied a large territory that included Lincolnshire, Leicestershire, Nottinghamshire, Derbyshire and Northamptonshire. Most of the coins discovered at Hallaton in Leicestershire were probably minted by the Corieltauvi. In 2012 a silver ring inscribed TOT (the Celtic god Toutatis) was found in a field near Hallaton—the ring probably dates to the 2nd or 3rd century AD. Sleaford in Lincolnshire seems to have been an important center of the Corieltauvi which minted coins, and Corieltauvian coins have been found as far north as Ferriby South on the banks of the Humber in Lincolnshire. It is likely that the Late Bronze Age feasting site at Washingborough and the Iron Age causeway at Fiskerton were in the territory of the Corieltauvi, and that this "Army of the Earth Goddess" was a very ancient tribe which came into being alongside the first Celts in the Late Bronze Age.

Caistor St. Edmund, Norfolk

East of Leicester is *Venta Icenorum* (Caistor St. Edmund in Norfolk), the tribal capital of the Iceni (literally, perhaps, "Homeland of the Iceni"). The name *Iceni* appears to be related to Itchen, the river that runs past what used to be the eastern gate of Roman Winchester. The origins of the name Iceni are obscure. There is an *Iciniaco*, now Theilenhofen in Bavaria, and a river *Icauna*, now the Yonne in northern France[34]—these names may be linked to the Indo-European root *iek-*, "to heal," which gives Old Irish *hicc*, "healing," Welsh *iach*, "fit, healthy," Greek *akos* "remedy," *Akestor*, "epithet of Apollo the Healer."[35] This root may be also the origin of the name Jeker, a river in Belgium which flows into the Meuse at Maastricht.

The name *Venta* and the possible link between *Iceni* and Itchen suggests a prehistoric link between Hampshire and Norfolk. One of the earliest Iron Age sites in Norfolk is the one at West Harling near Thetford. This is an Early Iron Age settlement consisting of two earthworks found and partly excavated in 1932. The eastern enclosure consisted of a C-shaped bank 1–2 feet high, 20 feet wide and 70 feet diameter, with an opening towards the west. The only trace of the western camp is a shallow ditch with a slight external bank. Pottery finds over the whole site date it to Early Iron Age. The settlement stands on the crest of a hill surrounded by former wetland.[36] The pottery found on the site is known as West Harling-Fengate pottery (8th/7th–5th century BC), which is similar to Kimmeridge-Caburn pottery found on the south coast, and named after Mount Caburn hillfort in East Sussex and Kimmeridge on the Isle of Purbeck in Dorset. As Barry Cunliffe says[37]: "This may hint at a degree of contact through longshore maritime contacts, in support of which it is worth noting the presence of large decorated jars of Early All Cannings Cross at Minnis Bay, Kent and Darmsden, Suffolk" (Minnis Bay is near Margate, Darmsden is on the River Gipping near Ipswich).

Lincoln

North of Venta Icenorum, and close to the Late Bronze Age site at Washingborough and the Iron Age causeway at Fiskerton, was the Roman *colonia* of *Lindum* (Lincoln), probably derived from the same Celtic root as Lindinis. Late Iron Age occupation has been found near Brayford Pool,[38] a natural lake formed by the widening of the River Witham, and presumably the pool suggested by the name *Lindum*.

Brough-on-Humber, East Yorkshire

North of Lincoln is the territory of the *Parisii* in East Yorkshire, who buried their elite in carts in square barrow cemeteries during the Middle Iron Age. They have the same name as the *Parisii* of France who gave their name to the French capital Paris. In Roman times the capital of the French Parisii was Lutetia, in what is now the Latin Quarter of Paris on the left bank of the Seine, but in the Iron Age the capital was at Nanterre to the west of Paris, In the late 19th century a cart burial was found at Nanterre, and between 1993 and 2005 excavators uncovered a number of cemeteries near the cart burial dating to the 4th and 3rd centuries BC, with about 30 tombs. Grave goods included swords and decorated scabbards. Nearby was a settlement dating to between the 3rd and 1st centuries BC, with a port on the Seine; the settlement covered at least 20–25 ha and was divided into different quarters (residential, manufacturing, storage, meetings, religion).[39]

The origin of the name *Parisii* is uncertain, and there are three possible interpretations of the name. Koch links it to Welsh *paraf* from *peri*, "to make, to produce, to command to be done," hence Welsh *peryf*, "lord, commander"[40]; while Xavier Delamarre believes the name is related to Old Breton and Old Cornish *per*, Welsh *pair*, Old Irish *coire*, "cauldron," and that the *Parisii* are related to the *Quariates*, who lived around *Queyras* in the Hautes-Alpes, southeastern France[41]; and Pierre-Yves Lambert links it to Old Irish *carr*, Welsh *pâr* "spear"[42] (which would certainly explain the spears thrust into bodies during Iron Age funerals).

The main town of the Parisii was *Petuaria*, which means "The Fourth Part" (Welsh *pedwar*, "four"). A town with a similar name (*Pedeverius*) is found in Gaul—it is now Pithiviers in the Loiret region of north-central France, but in the 1st century BC it was in the territory of the Carnutes, where the Druids apparently assembled before they were suppressed by the Romans. Petuaria has traditionally been identified with the walled town of Brough-on-Humber, since a 2nd century AD dedication slab, reused in a 4th-century AD building at Brough, recorded the dedication of a new proscenium (stage) in the theater at Petuaria. However, excavations in 1933–37 and 1959–61 revealed a chronology of military rather than civil fortification.[43]

We get a few insights into the religious life of East Yorkshire during the Roman period. At Shiptonthorpe Romano-British settlement near Market Weighton (2nd–4th century AD), a waterhole contained partially articulated animal remains and skulls, quern fragments, most of the decorated samian sherds found at the site, leather shoes, metal objects, plants including holly and mistletoe (which is associated with the Druids), and the remains of wooden writing tablets that may originally have had votive dedications.[44]

There is also an intriguing burial from close to the Roman road north of Brough. Dating from the first century AD, it lay under thin limestone slabs and the only remaining traces of the coffin were iron nails. The grave goods included iron hoops, about 5 inches in diameter, which would have held together the wooden staves of a bucket. Decorating the bucket was a small bronze human bust around half an inch across the shoulders with swept back hair, a drooping moustache and prominent eyes, very "Celtic" in appearance, not dissimilar to the pommel of the anthropomorphic hilt of the short sword from North Grimston. The two iron scepters topped with crested helmeted heads also buried in the grave were in contrast classical in feel. The person buried there may have been an aristocrat of the Parisi tribe, but the scepters could also be the regalia of a priest.[45]

York

The most important town in the region was the Roman legionary fortress and *colonia* of *Eboracum* (York). The name is related to Gallo-Roman *eburos* and Old Irish *ibar*, "yew." The legionary fortress at York was built on the northeast bank of the River Ouse in AD 71 to house the 9th Legion. It occupied an area of 50 acres and included barracks and other buildings including a bathhouse and principia. The fortress was rebuilt in stone in AD 107–8. In the early 3rd century York was the headquarters of the Emperor Severus in his unsuccessful campaign to conquer Scotland. In the 4th century York became the military base of the Dux Brittaniarum, the headquarters of the northern region.

Aldborough, North Yorkshire

Further north was *Isurium*, the tribal capital of the *Brigantes*, now Aldborough near Boroughbridge in North Yorkshire. The name *Isurium* may be compared to the *Isara* in Gaul, the old name for the River Isère in France. This may be derived from the Indo-

European root *eis-1*, "to move rapidly," which gives Old Indian *isira*, "strong, active," Latin *ira*, "anger."[46] The Brigantes have the same name as a tribe in Co. Wexford, southeast Ireland, and both tribes venerated the same goddess, called Brigantia in Britain and Brigid in Ireland.[47] The name means "Elevated Ones," and the root survives in Welsh *bre*, "hill."

During the Late Iron Age the main settlement of the Brigantes was at Stanwick Camp near Richmond in North Yorkshire, a univallate hillfort with some 4 miles of ramparts enclosing an area of 766 acres. It was first excavated in 1951–2 by Mortimer Wheeler, then re-examined in the 1980s. Wheeler considered the site to be the center of Brigantian resistance under Venutius following a schism with his wife Queen Cartimandua—loyal to the Romans—around AD 51. He proposed an initial defended settlement at the Tofts—an enclosure of 17 acres—dated to AD 47–8. He suggested that the settlement was subsequently enlarged first by the addition of a northern enclosure and finally a still larger one to the south. Wheeler thought the site was destroyed by Petillius Cerialis and the Ninth legion in AD 71–2.

The more recent work also proposes an initial settlement at the Tofts, but significantly pre-dating the rampart construction. A date in the 2nd or 1st centuries BC is proposed for this occupation. In all 5 main structural periods were recognized. Roman imports of Tiberio-Claudian date appear at the end of Period 3, whilst during the Claudian Period 4, two successive circular buildings of monumental proportions were erected. Period 5 is characterized by stone buildings and an abundance of Neronian imports, especially south Gaulish samian, Gallo-Belgic wares, glass and amphorae. The construction of the ramparts is now considered to have been a secondary and single event, the whole complex established according to a single plan in the mid–1st century AD (Period 4). The site is not now thought to have been a center of resistance, but instead the center of the Brigantian client kingdom in alliance with Rome until AD 69 when Cartimandua's rule collapsed.[48] During the later excavations, five Iron Age burials were found, one accompanied by a horse's head, another by a baby.[49]

In 1845 a hoard was discovered at nearby Melsonby, dating to between AD 40–80: most of the hoard consisted of parts from horse harnesses and carts or wagons made from brass, which was introduced by the Romans; there was also a small bronze model of a horse's head, which was made to be nailed to a wooden object, possibly a bucket.[50]

Carlisle, Cumbria

The most northerly town in Roman Britain was *Luguvalium* (Carlisle in Cumbria), the capital of the *Carvetii*. The name of the *Carvetii* is related to Welsh *carw* and Latin *cervus*, and means the "Deer People," presumably referring to the emblem of their tribe. Luguvalium means "Town of Luguvalos"—*Luguvalos* is a personal name meaning "as strong as Lugus" (the name of an important Celtic god).

Caerwent, Monmouthshire

There were two tribal capitals in Wales, Caerwent and Carmarthen. Caerwent, or *Venta Silurum*, was the capital of the *Silures* (literally, perhaps, "Homeland of the Silures"). The origin of the name *Silures* is uncertain: the only comparable name is *Silurus Mons* to the north of Malaga in southern Spain, which was mentioned by the Latin writer Avienus in his *Ora maritima* (4th century AD). It may be derived from *silo-riks*, "indicating an agricultural population group "rich" (Celt. *-rix*) in seeds or crops (Celt. *silo-*)."[51] The Silures joined Caratacus in around AD 48 in resisting the Roman invasion of Britain, and even after the capture of Caratacus in AD 51 continued to wage a guerrilla war against the Romans—they were not finally subdued until about AD 78.

The presence of the *Venta* element suggests a prehistoric link between Monmouthshire and Hampshire. As in Hampshire, the people of Middle Iron Age Monmouthshire made use of saucepan pots (they were found at Llanmelin hillfort near Caerwent). In fact, saucepan pots are found over a wide area of southern Britain, from Dorset in the west to Sussex in the east, stretching north through Wiltshire to Gloucestershire, Herefordshire and Worcestershire, and west into Monmouthshire, southeast Wales.

Carmarthen

The other tribal capital was *Moridunum* (Carmarthen) in southwest Wales, the capital of the *Demetae*. *Moridunum* is Celtic, meaning "Sea Fort," while the origins of the name *Demetae* are obscure—Koch suggests it could be linked to *dafad* "sheep," in the sense of "tame, domestic."[52] The word *dafad* is from the Indo-European root *deme-*, *dome-* "to tame," which also gives Old Indian *damyati* "is tamed," *damita-* "tamer," Latin *domitum* "tamed," *domitor* "tamer," Old Irish *damnaim* "tame," *damnad* "taming," Gothic *ga-tamjan*, "tame"[53]—which suggests that *Demetae* could mean "tamers" as well as "tame."

The Small Towns of Roman Britain

Tintagel, Cornwall

There were a number of small towns in Roman Britain, and one of the most westerly of these was probably Tintagel Island in northeast Cornwall. The *Ravenna Cosmography* (7th century AD) refers to a town called *Purocoronavis*, almost certainly a corruption of *Durocornovium*, "Fort of the Cornovii."[54] The Cornovii may have worshipped a horned deity, and recently a copper alloy zoomorphic mount or escutcheon in the form of a bull or ox head, with elongated flared snout and short horns, has been found in St. Kew, northeast Cornwall, not far from Tintagel. The mount is probably made of bronze rather than brass, so it is more likely to date from the Iron Age than the Romano-British period.[55]

In the *Ravenna Cosmography*, which dates from around AD 700, *Durocornovium* is named in a route sequence going west from Exeter[56]:

> As Professors Leo Rivet and Colin Smith have suggested, with the exception of Exeter, all the places named in it must have been minor in Roman times. It is possible that they were derived from some earlier list kept for adminstrative purposes. If a recognised route ended here it would explain why, of the five Roman milestones found in Cornwall, one was discovered in 1889 in the entrance to the churchyard [of Tintagel], and a second came from within a mile. The excavated finds include both post–Roman imports, locally made pottery of the 3rd and 4th century, coarse wares and a fourth century Oxford ware bowl. Thomas had noted that Tintagel was the site of a defended-promontory settlement, known in the area as "the fort (duro) of the Cornovii" which became in the later Roman period an administrative post for the enforced gathering of taxes in the long north Cornish farming belt and for other duties ie. customs due to its coastal location.

The ruins of Tintagel Castle, Cornwall, November 2005 (Maniple).

Church of St. Materiana, Tintagel, Cornwall (late 11th century), March 29, 2009 (Herbthyme).

In the 6th–7th centuries Tintagel Island was a high-status site, possibly a stronghold of the post–Roman kingdom of Dumnonia. Large quantities of imported Mediterranean pottery and glass dating from the 5th and 6th centuries have been found there, as well as a large and elaborate building.[57] Near the parish church of Tintagel, dedicated to St. Materiana, is an earthwork enclosure, and excavations in 1991 showed that the enclosure is an early Christian churchyard dating back to the 6th century. Many of the graves of the inhumation cemetery were cist graves.[58]

Wareham, Dorset

In Roman times the pottery known as black burnished ware was made in the Wareham-Poole Harbour region of Dorset. At Swineham Point, to the east of Wareham and near the Bronze Age settlement and burnt mound at Bestwall Quarry, Romano-British pottery has been found extensively over a wide area. Evaluation of the area in 1989–90 included test-pitting and geophysical survey over an area of 136 acres, and confirmed the presence of a substantial Roman industrial settlement over 5 acres. There are a number of enclosures in the settled area and a field system to the west. The site was inhabited from the Late Iron Age to the 4th century and can be seen as part of a wider network of such sites in Purbeck and around Poole Harbour, probably centered on trade through Hengistbury.[59]

Salisbury, Wiltshire

There was no tribal capital in Wiltshire, and we don't know the name of the Iron Age tribe there—although the territory of the Durotriges may have extended into Wiltshire as far as the River Wylye, which flows through southwest Wiltshire before it joins the River Nadder at Wilton near Salisbury; while the territory of the Dobunni may have extended into northwest Wiltshire. However, there were several small towns, including *Sorviodunum* and *Cunetio*. *Sorviodunum* was established at the foot of the Iron Age hillfort known as Old Sarum, to the north of Salisbury, about which little is known (much of the archaeology was probably destroyed by the 11th century Norman castle and cathedral). Sorviodunum bears a name which is similar to *Sorviodurum*, near the city of Straubing in Bavaria. The origin of the first element *Sorvio-* is unclear. Perhaps the most popular explanation is that it is derived from the Indo-European root *ser-1*, "to flow,"[60] found in Latin *serum*, "the watery part of curdled milk, whey," *Saravus*, "a river in Gaul" (now called the Saar): Sorviodunum is close to the Salisbury Avon, and *Sorvio-* may represent the old name for the River Avon near Salisbury. The Anglo-Saxons probably thought that it was derived from the Indo-European root *ser-4*, "to put together, bind together," which gives Gothic *sarwa*, "armor," Anglo-Saxon *searu*, "armor."[61] Finally it could be derived from the Indo-European root *ser-2*, "to guard, watch over, support,"[62] which gives Avestan (Old Iranian) *haurvaiti*, "he guards," *pasus-haurvo*, "cattle-guardian," Latin *servo*, "to watch, keep safe." It is possible that this final root is the origin of the name *Serbi* or *Serboi*, known to early Roman and Greek geographers as an Iranian tribe living on the River Don in what is now Russia; they later became the Serbs of Serbia, and the Slavic Sorbs of Germany and Poland, who are the same as the Wends and therefore the Baltic Venedi.

Mildenhall, Wiltshire

Cunetio is at Mildenhall on the River Kennet near Marlborough. John Koch links *Cunetio* to the *Cynetes* of the Algarve, southern Portugal, and the *Kynwydion*, the war band of Dark Age Strathclyde. The name *Kynwydion*, which is derived from Celtic *cwn*, literally "dogs" but metaphorically "warriors," appears in a Middle Welsh text entitled *The Descent of the Men of the North*, in this brief entry: "And from Cynwyd Cynwydion there came the Three Hundred Shields of Cynwydion"[63]; and in Triad 6 of the medieval *Welsh Triads*, in the entry "Cynfawr Host-Protector, son of Cynwyd Cynwydion."[64] As *Cunetio* was probably a town belonging to the Atrebates of Silchester, the "Town of the Warriors/War-Bands" does seem plausible.

Sandy Lane, Wiltshire

There were two other small towns in Wiltshire, *Verlucio* and *Durocornovium*. *Verlucio* lies to the north of Devizes, situated near Bell Farm, less than a mile southeast of the village of Sandy Lane, in the parish of Calne Without. *Verlucio* means "Very Bright Place": the first element *uer-* is related to Celtiberian *ueramos* and the Welsh prefix *gor-*, "extremely"; while the second element is related to Latin *lux*, "light," Welsh *llug*, "shimmer, radiance."

Wanborough, Wiltshire

Durocornovium, or "Fort of the Cornovii"—with the same name as the probable settlement at Tintagel Island in Cornwall—was at Wanborough, on the eastern edge of modern day Swindon. The town lies on the line of the Roman Ermin Street (the road from Cirencester to Silchester), at the junction with the road from the Roman town at Mildenhall/*Cunetio*. The site was occupied from the mid–1st century, though the coin evidence suggests that the period AD 244–367 was the main period for occupation. Courtyard buildings, strip buildings and part of Ermin Street have been uncovered.[65] There is no way of knowing whether Wiltshire was once occupied by people called *Cornovii*, but Durocornovium is not far from Chiseldon, where at least 12 cauldrons were buried in a pit with two cow skulls.

Bath, Somerset

In Roman times Bath—*Aquae Sulis* ("Waters of Sulis")—was famous for its hot springs and temple of Sulis Minerva, dedicated to the Roman goddess Minerva and the Celtic Goddess Sulis. *Sulis* is probably derived from the Indo-European root *suel* "sun" (related to English *solar*). Ranko Matasovic notes that in Old Irish the word derived from *suel* is *suil*, meaning "eye," and that the goddess Sulis "seems to have been venerated near hot springs and wells. The connection between the concepts of "sun," "the eye" and "the spring" also belongs to the realm of mythology"—the sun is the "eye of the sky" and a well is the "eye of the earth."[66] Sulis has the reputation of a healer-goddess, but the only real evidence for this is her association with a thermal spring. However, 130 lead and pewter curses (called in Latin *defixiones*) have been found in the reservoir at Bath[67]:

> Sulis was clearly perceived as an avenger of wrongs. Water and curses have a well-established link; as late as the nineteenth century in Wales, a man was imprisoned for inscribing a curse on a lead sheet and throwing it into a well. In a sense the named or

The Roman Baths in Bath Spa, Somerset, July 2, 2006; everything above the level of the pillar bases is of a later date (photograph by David Iliff).

unnamed malefactor was being symbolically sacrificed to the goddess. The "fixing" was an important element of the *defixio*, so that the curse would not rebound on the curser [...] The curses are very harsh, associated with fertility, sleep, blood and internal disorders.

Little is known about Iron Age Bath, but a pair of Late Iron Age bronze spoons were found in 1866 when opening a quarry for road metal at Weston, now a suburb of Bath. The spoons were found at a depth of 7 feet in an old course of a stream.[68] Bronze spoons are usually found in pairs and one spoon always has a small hole on the right side. The other spoon does not have a hole, but is always decorated with a cross with a circle in the middle which divides the bowl into four quarters. It has been suggested that something, perhaps water, blood or beer, might have been allowed to drip through the hole in one spoon onto the other spoon during attempts see into the future.[69] Interestingly, the cross with four equal arms recalls the Early Bronze Age gold sun discs, like the ones found at in a barrow at Mere in Wiltshire and at Jug's Grave near Bradford on Avon, which is not far from Bath.

Cambridge

In the Roman period there was a defended settlement at Cambridge known as *Duroliponte*, centered on what is now Castle Hill, which was founded in the 2nd century

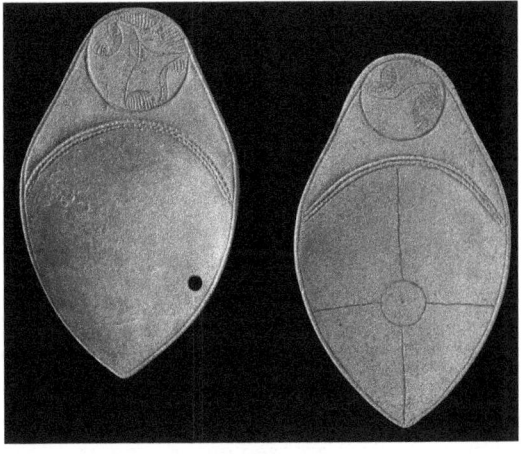

Iron Age bronze spoons from Crosby Ravensworth, Cumbria, similar to the spoons found in Bath (© The Trustees of the British Museum. All rights reserved).

and continued into the 5th century. The first element of the name is *Duro-* "fort," while the second element may be related to Welsh *gwlyb*, "wet," Latin *liquidus*, "flowing, fluid, liquid," referring perhaps to the River Cam.

Stonea, Cambridgeshire

There was a Roman settlement on an island in the fens of Cambridgeshire at Stonea, not far from the Iron Age Stonea Camp. A substantial building, discovered during a survey at Stonea Grange Farm, Wimblington, was probably the most important Roman site in the whole of the southern Fenland. When first identified, it appeared as a raised mound of building stone with debris of ceramic tile and plaster, about 79 yards in diameter, standing 1 feet 8 inches above the field surface. Excavations by Potter and Jackson for the British Museum showed that the first phase was a large stone building, 52 feet by 52 feet, with an apse on the west side, erected on a stone platform. Stone is not locally available and probably originated from the Peterborough region, about 18 miles away. The building was heated with a hypocaust system and had plaster painted like marble and glazed windows. The massive footings suggest that it was two or three stories high, and would have appeared as a tower dominating the fens. It was constructed in the first part of the second century AD and a corridor and hall were added soon afterwards.

The site was laid out with a grid of gravel roads forming *insulae* of urban character, with wooden buildings, wells, and clusters of pits. Both the stone tower and many of the wooden buildings were demolished in the early 3rd century, but parts of the site were occupied during the 3rd and 4th centuries. A large pit, filled in the Antonine period (2nd century AD), contained much organic material including wooden artifacts. Near the main site was a probable Romano-Celtic temple of square plan. Several cult objects have been looted from the site in recent years, the most striking being a gold votive tablet dedicated to Minerva. These objects presumably came from the temple.[70] Pottery finds suggest a main period of construction and use for the temple of mid–2nd to early 3rd centuries AD. Finds associated with the temple site included a clay figurine of a horse, while surface finds included various copper alloy items possibly linked to Mercury, Minerva and others.[71]

Burial in Roman Britain

During the Roman period, burial was strictly controlled by the state, so that everyone was either cremated or buried. Early Roman cemeteries in Britain tend to be cremation cemeteries, and it was only from the later 2nd century that cremation was gradually replaced by inhumation as the preferred rite.[72]

The inhabitants of Roman Britain no longer deposited body parts in pits and ditches, as their earlier Iron Age ancestors had done, but they practiced a form of burial which recalls earlier customs: the so-called "decapitated burial," which is most commonly found in the 4th century, when the power of the Roman Empire was declining, and Christianity had not yet become established. In decapitated burials, the head is detached, presumably after death and before interment. If the head is in the coffin, it may be placed between the knees, the upper legs, or the feet, outside the knees or feet, or on the pelvis.[73]

Cemeteries with decapitated burials are found throughout Roman Britain. In 2007 Wessex Archaeology excavated a Roman cemetery at Little Keep, Dorchester (the Roman town of *Durnovaria*), 87 yards from the Roman cemetery at Poundbury, and 306 yards west of the Roman town walls. A total of 29 graves of late Romano-British date were excavated together with the remains of five truncated graves and a disturbed grave. There was clear archaeological evidence for the decapitation of five individuals, that is 17 percent of the burials; all were adults over 35 years of age, three were over 50, two were females and three were males. In each case, the skull and neck vertebrae above the point of severance had been placed at the far end of the grave adjacent to or over the leg/ankle, though space for the head in the correct anatomical position was maintained within the grave.[74] Later the bone specialist Jacqueline McKinley says that the "occurrence of so large a number of decapitations in one cemetery is rendered even more intriguing at Little Keep in that the practice is seen as a predominantly rural one, rarely seen and certainly far less common in large urban centres such as Roman Dorchester."

Another town where decapitated burials are found is Winchester (Roman *Venta Belgarum*) in Hampshire, at the Lankhills cemetery, just to the north of the Roman town, which dates mainly to the 4th century. In seven graves the head had been severed from the body and the skull, mandible, and uppermost vertebrae were discovered still articulated lying by the legs or feet.[75] Of the seven decapitated skeletons, three belonged to men, two to women, and one to a child.[76] The heads seem to have been severed from the front, between the third and fourth vertebrae, probably with a knife. Bone damage was minimal, suggesting a degree of precision perhaps possible only if the deceased was already dead when decapitated.[77]

One rural example of decapitated burials is the cemetery at Winterbourne Down, Pitton, to the east of the Roman town of Old Sarum (*Sorviodunum*) near Salisbury in Wiltshire. This was a 4th century Romano-British cemetery that contained 36 cremations and 14 inhumations. Of the 14 inhumations, three contained infant skeletons and one of these was accompanied by a pot containing an iron pin. Of the adults, five had been buried in coffins; two with coins, one of Constantine II (337–340), the other of Valentinian I (364–375). There were cleats and hobnails in five of the graves. Three adults had been decapitated.[78]

In 2008, human remains were recovered at Swanpool Walk, St. Johns, Worcester (Roman *Vertis*) during excavations ahead of proposed development of the land. Five grave cuts were discovered containing human skeletal remains, each representing an individual inhumation grave. Skeleton 1447 from the land off Swanpool Walk was found to have been decapitated, with the head having been placed in the grave by the feet; this burial contained the remains of a young adult, probably female.[79]

Excavations at the Roman town of Towcester in Northamptonshire (Roman *Lacto-*

durum) revealed the remains of two decapitated young adult males dating from the 2nd to 4th centuries. In one case, the skull had been placed over the lower legs, while in the other the skull was in its correct anatomical position. Both males have evidence of perimortem trauma—trauma around the time of death—to the bones. The bodies were found in an urban Roman cemetery among the other burials, and the decapitation was not the cause of death. The cutmarks show that the decapitation took place around the time of the death, but the clumsy manner of cutting and burial within the community cemetery suggest this was ritual rather than punishment.[80]

A Romano-British cemetery was excavated at Stanton Harcourt, Oxfordshire in 1978. Thirty-four graves were identified, of which 33 were excavated. Thirty four skeletons were recovered, two, an infant and an adult, from Grave 60. The graves were oriented north-south, and the majority of skeletons lay with the head to the north. Most of the skeletons were supine, but three lay face down. Three skeletons were found, each with a group of three coins from the middle of the 4th century; a further three had the head cut off and placed near the feet.[81]

In 1999 a small Romano-British cemetery and midden was excavated at Wayside Farm on the southeastern outskirts of Devizes in Wiltshire. There were three closely spaced graves, all aligned approximately east-west. According to the archaeologists John Valentin and Stephen Robinson, two of the individuals in the graves had been buried in coffins; two had been buried with hobnail boots; and complete pottery vessels were found in two graves.[82] In one grave, the head was removed and placed toward the foot end of the grave, with a complete pottery vessel next to it.[83]

The midden was on a broadly north-south alignment, covering an area of 1,255 square yards, with a depth varying between a foot towards the center and 4 inches at its fringes. It is likely that the midden was formed as a result of a single episode of dumping. Most of the artifacts in the midden are Late Romano-British in date, including all of the coins but one. The heart of the midden was Pit F4225 which contained large quantities of pottery and animal bone (including complete ox skulls), and human bone fragments, including a femur (thigh bone) or humerus (upper arm bone) and a tibia (shinbone).[84] The most important part of the Wayside Farm pottery assemblage is Late Roman Oxfordshire color coated fine ware, which dates from after AD 350.[85] Three thousand, two hundred and thirty fragments of animal bone were found on the site—83 percent cattle, 8 percent sheep/goat, 7 percent pig. Cattle remains are dominated by mandibles (jaw bones), loose teeth and numerous fragments from the skull.[86]

Valentin and Robinson conclude[87] that the midden artifacts appear to constitute votive offerings. The high proportion of pottery fine wares and animal bone butchery waste, including skulls, may be indicator of non-domestic (ritual) activity. A bronze garment collar found on the site (in Pit F4225) may have belonged to a priest,[88] and was deliberately crumpled before being buried. They imply that the midden may be a successor to the nearby Early Iron Age sites of Potterne and All Cannings Cross.

Not far from Wayside Farm, either 19 or 21 bronze statuettes were found near a ruined house at The Green, Southbroom, Devizes in 1714. They were enclosed in an urn, probably an amphora, which was covered with tiles or bricks secured with cement. The urn contained coins one of which is said to have been of Severus (AD 193–211).[89] Among these statuettes is a figure of Mars holding two ram-headed snakes.

Romano-British Temples and Shrines

Nettleton, Wiltshire

The Romans of course built numerous temples and shrines, and some of these were dedicated to local gods rather than the official gods of the Roman Empire. At Nettleton near Chippenham in northwest Wiltshire, there was a temple dedicated to Apollo, but a peculiarly British Apollo. The earliest features recorded on the site comprise a number of Late Iron Age ditches, suggesting there was a settlement in this area prior to the Roman occupation. The temple was built soon after AD 69 and consisted of a simple circular shrine. Around 230, the shrine was surrounded by an octagonal podium and precinct wall with a gatehouse, but around 250 the whole structure was burnt. It was replaced with an octagonal temple incorporating the remains of the podium and consisting of an inner chamber surrounded by eight chambers and enclosed by a covered walkway. The temple was adapted in the early 4th century with the blocking of alternate chambers, giving the building a cruciform plan. This may reflect the conversion of Rome to Christianity but soon after the building was altered again and was once more being used for pagan worship. After AD 370 layers of straw, manure and household rubbish suggests that the building was being used as a domestic dwelling or animal barn. One of the altars at Nettleton was dedicated to Apollo Cunomaglus ("Apollo the Hound-Lord") by a lady called Corotica,[90] a Celtic name, possibly meaning "Beloved." The Hound-Lord may be a reference to the dogs who played such an important role in Iron Age burial rites in Wessex. Apollo is often associated with healing; however, Diana and Silvanus were also worshipped at the temple, suggesting that Cunomaglus could have been a god of hunting.

Ashwell, Hertfordshire

In 2002 a hoard of Romano-British temple treasure was discovered at Ashwell in Hertfordshire, not far from the rich Late Iron Age burial at Baldock. The hoard consists of some 27 gold and silver objects and was buried in the later 3rd or 4th century AD, evidently in a structured deposit, concealed in a small hole in the ground in a compact and ordered manner. Objects include a silver figurine, a suite of gold jewelry and at least 20 votive "leaf" plaques of gold and silver. Of the plaques, 10 are inscribed, the majority with votive dedications to the hitherto unknown goddess Senuna. The results of geophysical survey have clarified the distribution of Iron Age and Roman surface finds by revealing rectilinear (Romano-British) and curvilinear (Iron Age) settlement complexes linked by a road. The hoard had been concealed immediately outside an isolated sub-circular enclosure midway between the settlements. Excavations between 2003 and 2006 demonstrated that the enclosure was not the shrine of Senuna—which must lie elsewhere, perhaps within one of the settlement complexes—but a ritual site used for feasting and other activity associated with funerary practice from at least the early first century AD to at least the third century AD.[91] *Senuna* may mean "The Old One," and be linked to a river *Senua* mentioned in the *Ravenna Cosmography* and located somewhere in southern Britain.

Barkway, Hertfordshire

In 1743 a temple hoard was found at Barkway in northeast Hertfordshire, not far from the border with Cambridgeshire. The temple was probably dedicated to Mars: a very large silver votive leaf is inscribed with a dedication to Mars Toutatis by a man called Tiberius Claudius Primus. Vulcan, the Roman god of fire and craftsmanship, identifiable by his blacksmith's hammer and tongs, is also depicted on other silver leaves.[92]

Lydney Park, Gloucesteshire

Lydney Camp is a Late Iron Age promontory fort on the west bank of the Severn close to the Welsh border, established in or just before the 1st century BC. In the 2nd and 3rd centuries AD the Romano-British population there were engaged in iron-mining, and in the late 3rd or early 4th century the hillfort became the site of a Romano-British temple. The presiding deity at Lydney "is named as Nodens on the single curse tablet from the site and on two other metal plaques from the site as Mars Nodons and Nudens Mars." Among the votive objects (ritual deposits) found at the site are dog figurines—some are "highly schematic," but one figurine, possibly of an Irish wolfhound, is "amongst the most accomplished pieces of bronze sculpture from Roman Britain." Other ritual offerings include "the bone representation of a woman and a hollow bronze arm." The "discovery of an oculist's stamp (to be stamped into cakes of eye medicine)" suggests the presence of a healer at the temple.[93] Given the fact that the temple was built on an iron mine, it seems possible that Nodens was an underworld deity connected with mining.

Haddenham, Cambridgeshire

At Haddenham in the Cambridgeshire fens, not far from the Iron Age ritual site at Godwin Ridge, a Romano-Celtic shrine was placed on top of a Bronze Age barrow. The barrow had been deturfed in the mid 2nd century, and a masonry-footed octagonal cell constructed on its southern edge, placed directly over a cluster of secondary cremations in the barrow ditch. In the floor of the octagon were many sheep mandibles with hooves laid out on either side, and in two cases a coin had been placed in the mandibles. The shrine entrance was at the southeast, marked by a graveled and ditched track; the whole was enclosed by a rectangular ditch. In the northwest corner of the compound a series of intercutting pits contained four complete sheep skeletons, each accompanied by a pot. A boar burial was found at the south-east of the compound. In the late 3rd century the shrine was rebuilt as a square-post structure on the crown of the barrow mound and surrounded by a ring of posts partially encircling the barrow. Two more sheep mandibles were placed in the structure. Flooding in the later fourth century caused the site to be abandoned and the timber structure was dismantled.[94]

I said earlier that sheep may have been spirit-guides in Iron Age Britain, and this shrine seems to support that idea. Coins were placed in two sheep mandibles, and in Greco-Roman mythology a coin was given to Charon, the ferryman of Hades, to carry souls across the River Styx.

As well as the sheep, some 2,600 bird specimens were found among its 33,000 animal bones, The birds were predominantly domestic fowl, but "the assemblage also included such wild birds as pelican, coot, duck and geese," together with buzzard, cormorant, heron and crow or rook. All were thought to have been sacrificed, "with the wild birds perhaps performing a role as winged messengers."[95] The sacrifice of wild birds links Haddenham to the nearby ritual site at Godwin Ridge.

Cambridge

In the late 2nd century, a timber shrine was constructed in Ridgeons Gardens just off Castle Street in Cambridge. It consisted of a subterranean cellar 26 feet long, 13 feet wide and 11 feet deep, with an apsidal end with a niche; several post-holes at the edges supported a substantial timber superstructure. Its religious associations are suggested by various finds in the immediate vicinity, including the burial of two dogs and a bull's head in the gravel flooring and an unusual sequence of animal burials in the ash layers derived from the building's early 3rd century destruction: they included a sacrificed horse surrounded by seven complete pottery vessels, a bull and a sheep, and three dogs arranged in a triangular formation around a pot. Immediately above the ash layer a large quantity of pottery was found, including samian and color-coated wares, at least 256 flagons and a quantity of glass vessels, all suggesting some specific event such as a great feast. This was all sealed with clay and subsequent rubbish dumping. Northwest of the shrine lay some 13 later 3rd and 4th century shafts. Each contained a mature dog and one or two infant burials in a wicker-work basket or on a rush mat, together with a pair of child's shoes.[96]

Stanwick, Northamptonshire

In the Roman period there was a villa and associated settlement at Stanwick, close to the Early Bronze Age barrow at Irthlingborough where the skulls of at least 184 cattle were discovered. Early Bronze Age Barrow 5, at the edge of the Roman settlement, became a shrine and remained one into the 4th century, with periodic remodelings. including the construction of a surrounding wall. Roman pottery from the 1st to the 4th century may reflect the insertion and removal of a column or post. The wall was surrounded by a mass of oyster shell probably discarded by those visiting the site. Votive deposits included coins, a bronze frog and a set of bronze leaves that may have formed a wreath.[97]

Wroxeter, Shropshire

At Wroxeter, to the south of the forum, a major classical temple building, perhaps built in the 2nd century, has been excavated, "with a four column façade and a clay and cobble podium faced with large sandstone blocks. Fragments of sculpture, among them a life-sized horse's head and a relief depicting Venus looking into a mirror with an attendant beside her, suggest that the deity in the temple might have been either Venus or Epona, the Celtic horse goddess, or conceivably both together."[98]

Heslington East, York

Heslington East lies roughly 2 miles southeast of the city of York, and there was a Romano-British settlement here in the 3rd and 4th centuries. The area was terraced and divided up by ditches and cobbled trackways. Stone and timber buildings, one of the former including a hypocaust system, and several kilns were incorporated with these new arrangements, and a probable masonry mausoleum was set up at the point where the main track entered the largest enclosure. In the second half of the 4th century, a stone-lined well was dug, which was in use until the late 4th or early 5th century. A total of 1045 sherds of Romano-British coarseware pottery were found in the well, including a virtually complete Huntscliff-type jar, possibly manufactured in East Yorkshire. A total of 1067 animal bone fragments were also recovered from the well, A high proportion were butchered bones, including 14 of the 39 horse bones. The lowest fill in the well contained few bones, while the second fill contained two adult female pig skulls. The third fill contained a horse skull and two horned cattle skulls. The fourth fill contained most of the bones from a red deer skeleton, and two further skeletons, a dog and a calf, together with a large, complete red deer antler from an "impressively large and mature stag."[99] The horned cattle skulls and red deer antler suggest that the horned god was venerated at Heslington East.

Newcastle upon Tyne

The temple of Antenociticus at Benwell in Newcastle upon Tyne may have been built soon after the construction of the nearby Roman fort (AD 122–124) and possibly as late as AD 180. It is of simple apsidal type comprising a small rectangle in plan with a south apse. The walls still stand to 1 feet 8 inches in height and are constructed of sandstone rubble with ashlar facing. The doorway to the temple was situated in the east wall. The apse contains the base of a cult statue, the head of which is now in Museum of Antiquities, Newcastle. Antenociticus was a native god clearly revered by the Romans. The head of the statue shows the deity with curling hair, two locks of which curve around the crown of the head and possibly depict two stag antlers. There is a torc around the neck.[100]

Carrawburgh Roman Fort, Northumberland

Carrawburgh Roman fort near Hexham in Northumberland was probably constructed around AD 130 and remained in use until the 4th century. The most interesting part of the fort is Coventina's well (actually a spring or reservoir), which was excavated in 1876. The excavation revealed a spring encased in a rectangular basin, about 8 feet 6 inches by 7 feet 10 inches, which lay at the center of a walled enclosure or temple, measuring 40 feet north/south by 38 feet transversely within a wall 2 feet 11 inches thick. The contents of the well included at least 13,487 coins, from Mark Antony (44–33 BC) to Gratian (AD 375–383), a relief of three water nymphs, the head of a male statue, two dedication slabs to the goddess Coventina, ten altars to Coventina and Minerva, two clay incense burners, and a wide range of votive objects.[101] Also found in the well were jewelry, bones, and many other objects.[102] On one incense burner she is referred to as "Augusta," the only non-Roman goddess in Britain to receive this designation.[103] The well was packed with objects of bronze, bone, potter, glass, lead, leather, jet and shale, as well as the thousands of coins.

Maintaining the Old Ways in Roman Britain

The Cornovii

The Cornovii were the main tribe of Shropshire and Cheshire, and possibly also inhabited northern Wiltshire and Cornwall. They may have worshipped a horned god, but what this means is most unclear. In the Neolithic red deer antler picks were used for constructing sites like Silbury Hill and Stonehenge in Wiltshire, and for mining flint at Grime's Graves in Suffolk. After use the antler picks were often carefully deposited at the base of ditches and pits. At Stonehenge half of all the 90 picks excavated from the ditch were broken or worn beyond the point where they could still be used, but half had only slight or medium wear: they could have been used again but instead were deliberately left with the ditch.[104] A cluster of antler fragments was placed alongside some sarsen boulders at the summit of Silbury Hill. At Durrington Walls near Stonehenge, 57 antlers were found together in a large pit.[105] At the Grime's Graves mine one of the pits contained two antler picks, a Cornish greenstone axe, and the skull of a phalarope, a rare shorebird or wader.

In the Late Bronze Age/Early Iron Age antler was used to make cheek-pieces for horses (for example, at Runnymede and Potterne), and in the Iron Age it was used to make weaving combs, like ones found at Danebury hillfort in Hampshire and at the hillfort of Ham Hill near Yeovil in Somerset. As the burials from Viables Farm, Basingstoke and the pit from Bishop's Cleeve, Gloucestershire demonstrate, antler objects like weaving combs were placed in ritual deposits during the Iron Age, and as the antler from Heslington East, York shows, red deer antlers were being deposited in wells as late as the 4th century AD.

The horns of the Cornovii could of course refer to cattle horns. Cattle and in particular cattle skulls played a significant role in British religion from the Neolithic to the Roman period throughout a wide area of Britain from Dorset and Somerset in the south and west of England to Yorkshire in the north of England. Finally, the horns could refer to the horns of sheep or goats, which played a significant role in Iron Age religion, and continued to do so at the Romano-Celtic shrine at Haddenham.

What is the connection if any between Cornwall, Wiltshire and Shropshire? In the Bronze Age Cornwall was a source of tin which was combined with copper to make bronze. So there must have been strong links between Wessex and Cornwall in the Early Bronze Age, when the Wessex culture flourished, with its rich burials—such as the ones near Stonehenge—which often included bronze daggers among the objects that accompanied the dead into the next world. The links between Wiltshire and Shropshire are more specific: flint implements from Wiltshire are found along the Clun-Clee Ridgeway, and the cremation cemetery at Bromfield is influenced by similar cremation cemeteries in Wessex, and pottery from Wiltshire was found at Old Oswestry hillfort So the Cornovii may well date from the Late Bronze Age when the first Celts were emerging along the Atlantic coasts.

Temples and Shrines

Roman gods were worshipped at most temples and shrines, but this still left room for British religious practices. At Wayside Farm near Devizes, there was a small cemetery with one decapitated burial and a midden containing high-status pottery and a large number of cattle mandibles. The temple at Barkway, Hertfordshire was dedicated to the Romano-British god Mars Toutatis. At Haddenham in Cambridgeshire a Romano-British shrine was built on a Bronze Age barrow: many sheep mandibles were found in the shrine with hooves and coins in two mandibles, alongside a boar burial. At Cambridge, two dogs were buried with a bull's head; and a horse was buried with seven complete pottery vessels, a bull and a sheep; and a mature dog was buried with infants in baskets. At Heslington East in York, a 4th century well contained large amounts of pottery, adult female pig skulls, a horse skull, two horned cattle skulls, the skeleton of a red deer, a dog, a calf, and a complete red deer antler.

The End of Paganism

During the 4th century a new religion, Christianity, swept through the Roman Empire and by the late 4th century it was the state religion of Rome. Around AD 410 the last Roman legions left Britain, and with Britons pitted against Anglo-Saxons in large parts of England and southern Scotland, the Age of Arthur was about to begin.

CHAPTER 7

The Beginnings of the Age of Arthur: Arthur the Bear-Man

Paganism in Christian Britain

By the early Middle Ages all the inhabitants of Britain were Christians, and their pagan past was beginning to fade from memory. However, as Christianity took hold, British writers—usually Welsh—began writing about Britain's pagan past, often in Welsh but occasionally in Latin. Many of the pagan figures they wrote about are Welsh, and are scarcely known outside Wales, but one figure was known throughout a wide area of Britain, and that is Arthur. The origins of Arthur and his link to the pagan past are complex, and in this and the following chapters I hope to unravel his pagan beginnings. But first I need to begin by explaining the political situation of Britain just after the departure of the Romans, the time when Arthur supposedly flourished.

Britain After the Romans

The last Roman legions left Britain in around AD 410, and Roman Britain began to fragment. We have few sources for this period of British history, and one of the most quoted is a long sermon entitled *On the ruin and conquest of Britain*, written in Latin by the British cleric Gildas in the first half of the 6th century.

According to Gildas, after the last Roman legions left, Britain was attacked by Picts and Scots (Irish), who occupied the north of Britain as far as Hadrian's Wall. Hoping for help from Rome, the inhabitants of Britain sent a letter (known as the "Groans of the Britons"), some time between AD 446 and AD 454, to Aetius, a Roman general who was fighting insurgents in Gaul at the time. This help was not forthcoming, so a council was held "to deliberate what means ought to be determined upon, as the best and safest to repel such fatal and frequent irruptions and plunderings by the nations mentioned above." The council along with the "proud tyrant" decided that "those wild Saxons, of accursed name, hated by God and men, should be admitted into the island, like wolves into folds, in order to repel the northern nations."[1]

After the "proud tyrant" invited the Saxons to settle in England, says Gildas, they arrived in three "keels" and settled in the "eastern part of the island," to be later joined by more of their countrymen. In inviting the Saxons to settle in Britain, the council and the "proud tyrant" were merely following the Roman practice of employing groups of "barbarians" to fight in their army in return for money, food and land.[2] A treaty was signed with these "barbarians," but the Saxons were not satisfied with the terms of the treaty, and "devastated all the neighbouring cities and lands."[3] There was constant conflict until the British united under a leader called Ambrosius Aurelianus, who defeated the Saxons at the Siege of Mons Badonicus (Mount Badon), whose location is unknown but much debated.

Gildas says that the Saxons settled in the "eastern part of the island," and the cemetery evidence supports this. The first Anglo-Saxon settlers practiced cremation, and there are early cremation cemeteries from East Yorkshire to Suffolk: at Sancton in East Yorkshire; at Cleatham and Loveden Hill in Lincolnshire; at North Elmham in Norfolk; at Caistor St. Edmund in Norfolk (the old Roman town of *Venta Icenorum*); and at Eye in Suffolk. South of Eye there are mixed inhumation and cremation cemeteries: at West Stow in Suffolk; Mucking on the Thames Estuary in Essex; Ringlemere Farm, Woodnesborough near Sandwich in Kent; Bishopstone near Seaford in East Sussex; Highdown Hill near Worthing in West Sussex; Boscombe Down and Chessell Down on the Isle of Wight; and Winchester in Hampshire.

By the late 6th/early 7th century, there were Anglo-Saxon kingdoms in Kent, Essex, East Anglia, and Northumbria (eastern England from the Humber to the Scottish border, and southeast Scotland as far north as the Firth of Forth); by the late 7th century there was an Anglo-Saxon kingdom in the Midlands called Mercia, centered on Tamworth and Lichfield in Staffordshire, and a kingdom called Wessex which included the modern counties of Hampshire, Wiltshire, Dorset and Somerset.

Outside the Anglo-Saxon areas, a kingdom was formed in Devon and Cornwall called Dumnonia, which survived until the 9th century. Wales was largely unaffected by the Anglo-Saxon settlement of England, and several Welsh kingdoms are known from the early Middle Ages, including Gwent in southeast Wales, which took its name from *Venta* (*Silurum*); Dyfed in southwest Wales, named after the *Demetae*; and Gwynedd in north Wales. In Scotland several kingdoms are known from this period, including a British kingdom at Dumbarton Rock on the bank of the River Clyde downstream from Glasgow; Dal Riata, which was probably based at Dunadd in Argyll on the west coast of Scotland; and the kingdom of the Picts, which was probably based at Inverness or along the Moray Firth on the east coast of Scotland.

What's in a Name?

Arthur the Bear-Man

Arthur is one of the most fascinating and enigmatic figures of the early medieval period, known over a wide area of Britain, from Cornwall and Somerset in the west of England, through Wales to the Midlands, the north of England and the Central Lowlands of Scotland. He was a figure of Welsh mythology before the Norman Conquest, but in 1136 the Norman cleric Geoffrey of Monmouth published his *History of the Kings of Britain*, and turned Arthur into a historical figure, a great British warrior and king fighting against the Anglo-Saxons in the 5th century.

There are several theories about the origin of the name Arthur. It may be derived from the Roman family name *Artorius*, but the most likely derivations are either from Brittonic (proto-Welsh) *Arto-uiros*, "Bear-Man," or from *Arcturus*, the brightest star in the constellation Boötes.

Arthur was above all a legendary hero, but the name *Arthur* also is attested in Britain as early as the 6th century, attached to ordinary mortal beings. A certain *Artur* or *Artuir*, son of Aedan mac Gabran, king of Dal Riata is mentioned in three medieval documents. In Adomnan's *Life of St. Columba* (AD 700), Aedan asks Columba which of his three sons—Artur, Eochaid Find or Domangart—will succeed him; Artur is also mentioned in the genealogical section of the *History of the Men of Scotland* (650–700); and Artur's death is recorded in the *Annals of Tigernach* (AD 1088), in around AD 590. Artur is a British name, and it is possible his mother was British.

Arthur and other similar *Art-* and *Arth-* names were very popular in Scotland in the 6th and 7th centuries. Artur mac Conaing, from the *History of the Men of Scotland*, may have been named after his uncle Artur mac Aedan. The *Annals of Tigernach* list an Artuir son of Bicoir Britone, who slew Morgan mac Fiachna of Ulster in 620/625 in Kintyre, southwest Scotland. A Feradach, grandson of Artur, was a signatory at the synod that enacted the Law of Adomnan in 697. Other similar names include Artur's own nephew (or brother) Artán mac Conaing and a cousin Artán mac Conall.

Similar names are occasionally found further south. Athrwys ap Meurig lived in Gwent, and Arthur ap Pedr was a prince in Dyfed, born around 570–580.[4] A slate with the name *Artognou* etched on its was found in a 6th century context at Tintagel in Cornwall, the "capital" of the early medieval kingdom of Dumnonia (Devon and Cornwall). The name *Artognou* means "Bear-Knowing,"[5] and the relative popularity of names involving *Art-* or *Arth-* suggests that prehistoric Britons regarded bears as in some way significant—though the evidence for this is very sketchy.

It is unclear how long bears survived in the wild in southern Britain, but it seems there were still bears in Wiltshire and Dorset in the Late Neolithic (3rd millennium BC). In the 1930s John Stone excavated a pit at Ratfyn, to the north of Amesbury in Wiltshire, and found a scallop shell, charcoal, 519 flints (he refers to a "flint industry"), the scapula (shoulder blade) of a brown bear, and 15 very small fragments of Late Neolithic Grooved Ware, as well as a number of ox bones, including five scapulae.[6] Martin Green, while excavating at Down Farm, Gussage St. Michael, Dorset in the late 1970s, found a group of Neolithic ritual pits. One pit contained a group 7 stone ax from North Wales, a large flint scraper and a boar's tusk. Another pit contained a complete cow skull with a bone from a brown bear (this was an ulna, or elbow bone). Several of the pits contained Grooved Ware, and radiocarbon dates center around 2200 BC.[7]

Bears certainly survived in the wild in Scotland into the Bronze Age and even Iron Age. The canine tooth of a brown bear has been found in High Pasture Cave, Skye, along with a fragment of Bronze Age pottery dating to the late 2nd or early 1st millennium BC.[8] A single canine tooth of a brown bear was found at the Iron Age "Road" Broch in Keiss on the east coast of Caithness in northeast Scotland.[9] The broch (drystone roundhouse) dates from the 1st century BC/1st century AD, but was reused in the 2nd/3rd centuries AD.[10]

Bears may have survived even longer in parts of North Yorkshire. Kinsey Cave near Giggleswick in North Yorkshire, on the edge of the Yorkshire Dales, was first excavated by Jackson and Mattinson between 1925 and 1931, and again by English Heritage in 2005. A carved reindeer antler tang and five chipped stone tools were recovered from the cave environs. In addition, significant quantities of Roman artifacts "of cultic appearance" were recovered from the upper layers of the cave, including perforated bone spoons and round pieces of perforated pottery, as well as items of dress jewelry. Recent radiocarbon dating of material from the cave has shown that the cave was in use over a long period of time. A brown bear specimen was dated to 12,500 BC. A carved reindeer antler tang dated to 11,400 BC. Human bone was dated to between 3960 and 3790 BC, in the Early Neolithic. Wild lynx bone was dated to between AD 425 and 600—the latest recorded date for wild lynx in the British Isles.[11] And a brown bear vertebra found during the recent English Heritage excavation of the cave was dated to the 5th/early 6th century,[12] showing that bears survived in the wilds of North Yorkshire well into the early medieval period.

As I mentioned earlier, the cremated remains of two men were buried in bear skins at Late Iron Age sites at Baldock and Welwyn Garden City (Hertfordshire). Burial with bear skins first began in Germany, mostly in male graves, in an area associated with the Germanic Jastorf culture (6th–1st century BC). The oldest burial is one at Döhren in Saxony-Anhalt, northern Germany, which is dated to the second half of the 5th or to the 4th century BC, but most belong to the 1st century BC. They are found as far south as Tisice in the north of the Czech Republic, but are concentrated in central Germany (Thuringia and Hesse), and in northern Germany (Saxony-Anhalt, Mecklenburg-West Pomerania and Lower Saxony).[13] However, two burials with bear-claws are also found further west, at Clemency in Luxembourg, in what later became part of the Roman province of Belgic Gaul, and at Neuwied/ Heimbach-Weis near Koblenz in the Rhineland-Palatinate, in what later became part of the Roman province of Upper Germany. Given that the burial in bear skins was a Germanic custom, then the Hertfordshire burials don't prove that there were still bears in southern Britain—the skins may have been imported from Germany or elsewhere, along with the rich grave goods.

What bears meant to those whose cremated remains were wrapped in the bear-skins will never be known, and the only clue we have in the British Isles comes from Armagh in Northern Ireland. At Armagh, "stone animals, including two bears, were recovered during the rebuilding of the Protestant Cathedral in 1840. Under the Cathedral was a pre–Christian Iron Age burial ground and the statues were clearly connected with these burials."[14] This find

> suggests that images of bears, together with images of other animals, were used as some kind of votives for gods or ancestors in burial rituals. It might even suggest that individuals of a certain totemic affinity were buried with an idol marking his or her totemic relationship. Such idols could be thought to function as guides for the deceased on their journey to the other world.

Armagh was originally called *Ard Macha* ("High Place of Macha"), after the horse goddess Macha, who also gave her name to *Emain Macha*, or Navan Fort, an Iron Age enclosure near Armagh. The bears were found on Cathedral Hill, an important pagan cult center of the Ulaid, who had their royal residence at Navan Fort. There is an enclosure around the top of Cathedral Hill which had been radiocarbon dated to around AD 290. According to tradition, Cathedral Hill was chosen by St. Patrick as the site of his principal church.[15] The smallest bear can be compared to one found in Limoges in west-central France. The space between the legs of all three bears is left uncut, though recessed, and on either side of the largest bear, carved in relief between the legs and facing towards the rear, is the head of a large dog or wolf. It is unclear how long bears survived in the wild in Ireland, but brown bear bones have been found in Neolithic-Early Bronze Age contexts at the house Site C and stone circle Site K at Lough Gur, Co. Limerick; and a single bear metacarpal was found in an Early Bronze Age Beaker context at Newgrange, Co. Meath.[16]

Hill of Tara, Ireland, the Banqueting Hall, possibly a ceremonial avenue, May 2, 2007 (Brholden).

There is no Irish Arthur, but there is an early legendary king of Ireland with a bear name, Art mac Cuinn, who is supposed to have reigned in Tara in the 2nd century AD. Art Mac Cuinn, also known as Art Oenfher (*oenfher* = "the lone one, the lonely," literally "one-man"), was the son of Conn Cetchathach ("Conn of the Hundred Battles").[17] In the 15th century tale called *The Adventures of Art Son of Conn and the Courtship of Debchaem*, Art visits an otherworldly island in order to win the hand of the fairy Delbchaem ("Fair Shape"). Art's son was Cormac mac Airt, perhaps the most famous of the legendary kings, who also visited the Otherworld. In a 12th century tale called *Cormac's Adventure in the Land of Promise*, Cormac is walking on the rampart of Tara one day at dawn when he sees a warrior approaching who carries a branch with three golden apples. When Cormac learns that the branch, when shaken, will produce a marvelous music that casts sleep upon all who hear it, he asks to have it. The warrior gives him the branch, but says that Cormac must grant him three wishes. A year later, the warrior asks for Cormac's daughter, and Cormac agrees; a month later, the warrior asks for Cormac's son, and Cormac again agrees. Finally the warrior asks for Eithne, Cormac's wife; Cormac refuses, but the warrior takes his wife. Cormac pursues the warrior and his captives, and finally comes to a castle where he is entertained by a handsome warrior. A pig is put on the spit for roasting, and Cormac is told that the pig cannot be cooked until a truth is told for each quarter. Cormac must tell the fourth story, and he relates how his daughter, son and wife have been taken from him—after this the pig is ready. The warrior sings a lullaby which puts Cormac to sleep. When he awakes, he finds 50 warriors around him, as well as his daughter, son and wife. The handsome host is given a golden cup, a cup of truth, as he demonstrates. He tells three lies and the cup breaks into three parts; he then tells Cormac that neither his wife nor daughter have slept with any man since they left Tara, nor has his son slept with any woman, and the cup is once more fused together. The host then reveals his true iden-

Hill of Tara, Stone of Destiny, where the High Kings of Ireland were crowned (Germán Póo-Caamaño).

tity—he is Manannan mac Lir, the sea god and chief of the Otherworld. He allows Cormac to keep the magical branch and the cup for his lifetime—at the death of Cormac they vanish, presumably returning to the Otherworld.[18]

It is not clear whether bears were venerated in Britain during the Iron Age or Roman period, but a bear goddess was worshipped in Switzerland. Dea Artio is a goddess best known from an inscription and a bronze sculpture at Muri near Bern. The sculpture shows a large bear facing a woman seated in a chair, with a small tree behind the bear. The woman seems to hold fruit in her lap, perhaps feeding the bear.[19]

It is possible that bears had a religious significance, but it is equally possible that bears were valued because of their strength and fierceness. Trajan's Column in Rome was completed in AD 113 to commemorate the Emperor Trajan's victory in the Dacian Wars, and the historian Michael Speidel says that scene 36 on Trajan's Column depicts Germanic warriors[20] (the Batavi were a Germanic tribe from the Netherlands):

> On the relief, eight soldiers of the emperor's strike force wear Roman auxiliary uniforms: knee-breeches, tunics, mailshirts, and neckerchiefs. Their weapon of attack is the sword, with which Batavi tribesmen were wont to fight and with which, when they closed in for the shock attack, they stabbed their foes. Unlike other regular auxiliaries on the Column, however, these men sport strange headgear: four wear openwork crossband helmets, two

wear broad-pawed bearskins, two others narrow-pawed wolfskins. Most of them are bearded, while most regular soldiers on the Column are clean-shaven.

The wolfskins and bearskins seen here cover head and shoulders, leaving the arms free.... Like Herakles, the warriors on the Column fasten their skins over the chest by crossing and knotting the animal's forelegs.

Speidel goes on to say[21] that in the mid 1st century AD bear-hoods came into use among regular non-Germanic Roman auxiliaries, worn by eagle-bearers, standard-bearers and musicians. P. Coussin, he says, believed that "Rome adopted bear-hoods from from her northern neighbours. Roman soldiers who killed Germanic bear-warriors may have stripped off their hoods as trophies and worn them as badges of bravery." The earliest known bear-hooded Roman standard-bearer is Pintaius of cohors V Asturum, whose gravestone at Bonn dates to the reign of Claudius (AD 41–54). The next one is Genialis, image-bearer of cohors VII Raetorum, whose gravestone at Mainz dates to the time of Nero (AD 54–68).

The importance of the bear in northern Europe is underlined by a set of folktales known as the Bear's Son tales, in which a bear and his human wife have a

The Bear Goddess Artio from Bern, Switzerland, dating from the Roman period (Bernisches Historisches Museum, Berne, photograph by S. Rebsamen).

Germanic soldiers wearing bearskin hoods, as depicted on Trajan's Column in Rome (© Roger B. Ulrich, by permission).

male child. There are two groups of folktales, one from Europe and Asia, the other from British Columbia (Canada) and the adjacent Yukon and southern Alaska. In the Eurasian type, the child is a strong man who becomes a dragon slayer. With his companions, or brothers, he descends to a lower world where he overcomes monsters, devils or a dragon, rescuing three princesses.[22] These folktales find echoes in Germanic literature. In the 13th century Icelandic *Saga of King Hrolf Kraki*, Bodvar Bjarki, "Battle Bear" is "the son of bears and is able to take on the form of the bear in battle, where he is a ferocious and nearly unassailable opponent."[23] They have also been linked to the Old English epic poem *Beowulf*: the name *Beowulf* probably means "bee-wolf," referring to a bear, and Beowulf has the grip of thirty men and in the rage of battle slays his foes with a "bear hug" ("the sword did not kill him, no, my fighting grasp crushed his bone-house and the surges of his heart").[24]

Arthur and the Star Arcturus

Arthur may be the Bear-Man, but the name could also be derived from Arcturus ("Bear-Guardian"), the brightest star in the constellation Boötes, which was associated with savage and tempestuous weather. Richard Hinckley Allen[25] points out that Pliny called it a *horridum sidus* ("horrible star"), and that Demosthenes, in his action against Lacritus in 341 BC, tells us of a bottomry bond (money borrowed with a ship as collateral), made in Athens on a vessel going to the Dnieper River and the Crimea and back, that stipulated for a rate of 22½ percent interest if she arrived within the Bosphorus "before Arcturus," *i.e.* before its heliacal (dawn) rising about mid–September; after which it was to be 30 percent. The play *Rudens*, written around 211 BC by the Roman dramatist Plautus, is introduced by a Prologue spoken by Arcturus, who sinks a ship in which the villain is abducting the heroine: "I roared a wintry blast and roiled the waves./For I'm Arcturus, a ferocious star:/Fierce when I rise; while setting, fiercer far."[26] In this he was probably inspired by the 3rd century BC *Phaenomena* of Aratus, who wrote: "many a sailor has marked the coming of the stormy tempest, remembering either dread Arcturus or other stars that draw from ocean in the morning twilight or at the first fall of night."[27]

Some idea of what Arcturus may have meant to early medieval Britons can be found in the *Egloga Moralium Gregorii in Job* by the 7th century Irish monk Lathcen mac Baith. This is a very abbreviated version of Gregory the Great's *Commentary on Job*, completed in 595. According to Lathcen, quoting Gregory, Arcturus is not a star but a group of seven stars made up of groups of four and three stars[28]:

> ... made up of seven stars, it shines in the expanse of the sky.... It revolves with seven stars, and at one time raises up three of them and depresses the other four downward, while at another time it raises up four and lowers down three.

This Arcturus rotates continually in the same place, and never sets:

> Arcturus always turns about and never sinks.... Arcturus however illuminates the periods of night in such a way that, located in the expanse of the sky, it turns about but never sets. It revolves without ever moving about, but always remaining in the same place, it inclines towards all parts of the world, without ever falling.... In Arcturus, which illuminates the night sky with its turning without ever setting.

So it is likely that Arcturus in early medieval Ireland was not perceived as a single star, but as a group of stars, most likely the constellation Ursa Major, or the Big Dipper, which is visible throughout the year.

There is no evidence that Arcturus was ever important in Britain, but the Neolithic Thornborough Monument Complex in North Yorkshire was aligned on Orion's Belt, and the Hurlers in Cornwall may be laid out to resemble Orion's Belt—and Orion, like Arcturus, was associated with stormy weather.

Early References to Arthur

The Death-Song of Cynddylan

However, if there is a connection between Arthur and his name, it is not a straightforward one. In his earliest manifestation, Arthur was not obviously a bear, but a warrior and wonder-worker. Probably the earliest reference to Arthur is in the poem *Marwnad Cynddylan* ("The Death-song of Cynddylan"). Cynddylan was a prince of Powys who was killed at the Battle of the Winwaed in AD 655—this was a battle probably fought somewhere in the vicinity of Leeds, in which King Oswiu of Northumbria defeated and killed Penda of Mercia. The poem was probably composed soon after Cynddylan's death, and implies that the military deeds of Cynddylan and his brothers are of such great valor that these warriors might be seen as "whelps of great Arthur, a mighty fortress."[29]

In the 7th century, the kingdom of Powys probably included parts of Shropshire. In the Roman period Viroconium (Wroxeter), the capital of the Cornovii, was the fourth largest settlement in Roman Britain, with a population of about 7000—the baths had a capacity of about 1000, and the city also had a *macellum* (indoor market), one of only two in the country. After the Roman legions withdrew from Britain, Wroxeter seems to have flourished. A large timber-framed villa-type building was erected on the baths basilica site which faced south towards the remains of the baths complex—it was constructed within the remains of the villa as though in a courtyard. Many small ancillary buildings

Letocetum Roman town, Wall, Staffordshire, March 2011 (Bs0u10e01).

lay to the west, south and east, some of which appeared to be storage facilities. The north wall of the *frigidarium* (cold pool) of the baths still survives today (the Old Work), and it is thought that in the post–Roman period the *frigidarium* was converted into a church, since there are burials located outside the west end within the hypocausts and courtyards of the bath.[30]

The poem does not mention Wroxeter, but it does mention Tern (the River Tern, which flows into the Severn near Wroxeter), and Lichfield (probably the Roman town of *Letocetum* in Staffordshire).

Y Gododdin

There is a similar reference in another Welsh poem *Y Gododdin*. This tells of a battle between the Votadini (*Gododdin* in Welsh), a tribe living in northeast England and southeast Scotland, and a force of Anglo-Saxons, fought at Catterick in North Yorkshire some time in the early 7th century. There is no agreement on the date of the poem, in which it is said that the warrior Gwawddur "fed black ravens on the rampart of a fort, though he was no Arthur."[31]

Catterick was originally a Roman town, probably known as *Cataractonium*, which began life as a fort in the late 1st century, but soon became a civilian settlement. Timber buildings, probably shops and workshops, were erected on the main east-west road in the 2nd century. Further north, a more complex building with stone foundations covered nearly an acre and probably included a bath house. In the first half of the 3rd century some shops were rebuilt in stone, one being used as a temple podium. The late 3rd century town wall destroyed many existing buildings and the whole layout of the town was radically altered in the early 4th century. Later the temple was pulled down and the podium used for shop stalls. Building continued to the last half of the 4th century, a flourishing community still existing at the end of the century. Anglo-Saxon brooches were also found at Catterick, with occupation continuing into the 6th century.[32] Timber buildings were

Edinburgh Castle (*Eidyn* in early Welsh poetry), August 10, 2012 (Kim Traynor).

constructed on the site of Roman buildings, probably in the 5th century.[33] An early cemetery comprising 44 Anglian inhumations has been discovered outside the town—it is dated to the period AD 450–550 from the brooches associated with the inhumations.[34]

The poem refers to the "fortress of Eidyn," that is, Edinburgh, which may have been a stronghold of the early medieval Votadini. The "fortress of Eidyn" was probably on the site where Edinburgh Castle now stands. The area of Edinburgh Castle known as Mill's Mount produced the earliest finds and occupation features (cobbled surfaces and hearths) dated to the early centuries AD, providing tentative evidence for the existence of native Iron Age and Dark Age forts. The principal finds were Roman and native pottery and a fibula brooch dated to the 1st–2nd centuries, sealed by layers which produced a comb dated 7th–10th centuries AD.[35]

History of the Britons

Another early text which mention Arthur is the *History of the Britons*, written in Latin in AD 829 and attributed to the Welsh monk Nennius. In a section on the "wonders of Britain" (Chapter 73), Nennius tells us[36]:

> There is another marvel in the region which is called Buelt. There is a mound of stones there and one stone placed above the pile with the pawprint of a dog in it. When Cabal, who was the dog of Arthur the soldier, was hunting the boar Troynt, he impressed his print in the stone, and afterwards Arthur assembled a stone mound under the stone with the print of his dog, and it is called the Carn Cabal. And men come and remove the stone in their hands for the length of a day and a night; and on the next day it is found on top of its mound.

Builth or Builth Wells is in Powys, mid–Wales, not far from the border with Herefordshire in England; Cabal is from Vulgar Latin *caballus*, "nag, pack-horse," or possibly from Old Irish *capall*, "draught-horse"—the word is probably not Indo-European, and is also found in Greek, Old Turkish and Persian.[37] Here Arthur is seen as a hunter rather than a warrior, and is associated with a dog rather puzzlingly called Horse, and with the "swine Troynt," of which more shortly. Interestingly, *Carn Caball* can also mean "horse's hoof," suggesting that originally there was no dog involved in the story.

A second wonder also features Arthur, this time in Ercing (now Archenfield in western Herefordshire)[38]:

> There is another wonder in the region which is called Ercing. A tomb is located there next to a spring which is called Licat Amr; and the name of the man who is buried in the tomb was called thus: Amr. He was the son of Arthur the soldier, and Arthur himself killed and buried him in that very place. And men come to measure the grave and find it sometimes six feet in length, sometimes nine, sometimes twelve, sometimes fifteen.

If Arthur's dog is called "Horse," it may imply that the dog was of gigantic size, and if the grave of Arthur's son Amr varies between six and fifteen feet, it may suggests that Amr was also gigantic. All of which hints at the possibility that Arthur was originally regarded as a giant—which may explain why in the *Marwnat Cynddylan*, Arthur is referred to as a "mighty fortress."

In Chapter 56 of the *History of the Britons*, we also read the following account of a series of battles that Arthur is supposed to have fought.[39] (Hengest or Hengist is the mythical founder of the Anglo-Saxon kingdom of Kent):

the Saxons increased their numbers and grew in Britain. On Hengest's death, his son Octha came down from the north of Britain to the kingdom of the Kentishmen, and from him are sprung the kings of the Kentishmen. Then Arthur fought against them in those days, together with the kings of the British, but he was the *dux bellorum* ["leader in battles"]. The first battle was at the mouth of the river called *Glein*. The second, the third, the fourth and the fifth were on another river, called the *Dubglas*, which is in the country of *Linnuis*. The sixth battle was on the river called *Bassas*. The seventh battle was in Celyddon Forest, that is *Cat Coit Celidon*. The eighth battle was in *Guinnion* Fort, and in it Arthur carried the image of the holy Mary, the everlasting Virgin, on his shoulders, and the heathen were put to flight this day, and there was a great slaughter upon them, through the power of Our Lord Jesus Christ and the power of the holy Virgin Mary, his mother. The ninth battle was fought in the city of the Legions. The tenth battle was fought on the bank of the river called *Tribruit*. The eleventh battle was on the hill called *Agned*. The twelfth battle was on *Badon* hill and in it nine hundred and sixty men fell in one day, from a single charge of Arthur's, and no one laid them low save he alone, and he was victorious in all his campaigns.

The location of many of these battles is disputed, but we can make educated guesses about most of them. The "river called Glein" may be the River Glen in Northumberland, which flows past Yeavering, where Edwin, king of Northumbria, had a royal palace in the early 7th century. The Dubglas is probably the River Witham in Lincolnshire, and the "country of Linnuis" is the territory of Lindum, the Roman city now called Lincoln, which may have survived as a British kingdom into the first half of the 6th century.[40]

The battle on the "river called *Bassas*" may refer to Baschurch in Shropshire, which is mentioned in a 9th/10th century poem *Canu Heledd* ("Song of Heledd") in relation to the Powys prince Cynddylan, and is near the River Perry, a tributary of the Severn. Near

The Berth Hillfort, Baschurch, Shropshire with an area of marsh visible at one end of the hillfort (© 2007 Shropshire Council).

Baschurch is The Berth, two large glacial mounds, surrounded by water and marsh and fortified with stone and earth ramparts. They are linked together by a gravel causeway 150 yds long and connected with the rising ground towards the south by an extension 250 yds in length. Excavations at The Berth in 1962 by Mr. P.S. Gelling, have revealed traces of both Iron Age and late Roman occupation. One sherd of later Iron Age duck-stamped pottery was found, and a few other Iron Age sherds had irregular scored decoration. Metal finds included some iron knives and daggers and a La Tene III brooch. In 1963 traces were found of two distinct timber buildings in an area about 50 yds northwest of the main entrance. The floors of both were on much the same level; one appears to be Iron Age, and the other which is represented by large post-holes set in line 15 feet to 16 feet apart, probably belongs to the 4th century AD. Other finds in the area include a bronze cauldron of Roman or sub-Roman date, formerly identified as a waterclock, and a Roman blue glass bead found in 1976 on the top of the larger mound.[41] It is possible that The Berth was occupied by Cynddylan or another Powys prince in the period after the Roman legions departed.

The *Cat Coit Celidon*, or Battle of the Caledonian Forest, may not be a real battle but a mythical one, which forms the subject of a poem attributed to the Welsh bard Taliesin called *The Battle of the Trees*.[42] *Guinnion* Fort may be the Roman fort of *Vinovia* or *Vinovium* (Binchester) in County Durham. Binchester Roman fort was first excavated in the 19th century, and relatively little was known about it, until excavations resumed in 2007. Three masonry structures, probably mausolea, were excavated by Wessex Archaeology in 2007 as part of a *Time Team* investigation of the Roman fort.[43] Roman cemeteries were usually located along the sides of roads, and the Binchester cemetery was on Dere Street, the Roman road from York to Corbridge. One mausoleum contained the poorly preserved skeleton of an adult male aged between 22 and 30 years, in a supine, extended position with the head towards the southwest. Large numbers of iron nails with the back-fill indicate that the body was originally deposited in a coffin. Human remains from a large robust male aged between 20 and 40 years were also recovered from another mausoleum. The associated grave goods suggest a 2nd century AD date for the mausolea.

After the departure of the legions, Binchester Roman fort continued to be a focus of activity. Inserted into the debris filling the western furnace-chamber of the commanding officer's baths-suite was an adult female burial. The body had been laid on its back in a crouched position and was accompanied by grave-goods. These included a string of twenty-six beads, a very coarse handmade bowl, and a reversed S-shaped copper-alloy brooch with birds' head terminals of a type broadly dated to the late 5th and early 6th centuries AD—which suggests the burial occurred around AD 550. This discovery prompted the radiocarbon dating of approximately fifty burials, none with grave goods, found during excavations carried out in 1971 ahead of the extension of what was then the Binchester Hall Hotel. These were all thought to be post-medieval in date but the radiocarbon dating showed they spanned the period from around AD 600 to 1000. These burials indicate the presence of an extensive Anglo-Saxon cemetery, and by implication a settlement, within the confines of the former Roman fort. It is possible that the early female burial here was of someone of high status or reputation whose grave became the focus for the location of a later cemetery.[44]

The city of the Legions is probably Chester, where Aethelfrith of Northumbria defeated and killed the king of Powys in AD 615. Chester (Roman *Deva*) was a Roman legionary fortress of 59.3 acres built between AD 78 and 86 on a sandstone plateau enclosed by two arms of the River Dee. The defenses consisted of a turf rampart, but throughout the 2nd century the defences and internal buildings were replaced with stone. Early in the 3rd century the defences were refurbished—the ramparts and interval towers were heightened and widened—and this was followed by a reconstruction of the fort's internal buildings.[45] Chester's amphitheater was the largest in Roman Britain. The first amphitheater was built between AD 80 and 90 and "had a stone outer wall, a central arena and a seating bank supporting timber seats." Possibly in the late 2nd century, the amphitheater "was extended and enlarged. A new outer wall was built and seats in the upper tiers were now accessed by vomitoria (vaulted stairways situated behind the seating)."[46]

After the Romans left Britain, the amphitheater may have been used from the 5th century on as a "fortified settlement for occupation or as a refuge"—the building of the church of St. John immediately outside the east entrance in the 7th century "may be further evidence for the existence of a settlement at the amphitheatre." At this time Chester may have been part of the Welsh kingdom of Powys, and perhaps the seat of the Cadelling dynasty, and an important ecclesiastical center—"the city was probably a scene of a synod of the British church shortly after 600, and just to the south there seems to have been an early mother church at Eccleston."[47]

Tribruit seems to be the same as *Tryfrwyd*, mentioned in the Welsh poem *Pa gur yv y porthaur?* ("What man is the gatekeeper/porter?"), which I'll be discussing shortly. *Agned* is sometimes called *Bregouin*, and may be the Roman fort of *Bremenium* at Rochester in Northumberland—in a poem written by the 6th century Welsh bard Taliesin, the northern British ruler Urien Rheged is said to have fought a battle there.[48] *Badon* is the battle fought by Ambrosius Aurelianus in the 5th century and first mentioned by Gildas. Of the battles Arthur supposedly fought, some are apparently mythical, some were fought by other people, and the rest are unknown.

Arthur's appearances in the *History of the Britons* suggests that by the early 9th century, he was regarded as an historical figure, but as a historical figure with a strong presence in the world of the supernatural. But in the first work in which Arthur plays a recognizable role, *The Spoils of Annwn*, Arthur seems to be much less a historical figure and more a pagan god.

Chapter 8

Arthur in the Underworld

The Many Forts of Arthur

The Old Welsh poem *The Spoils of Annwn* is attributed to the 6th century bard Taliesin, and may have been composed as early as AD 800. The poem concerns a voyage to Annwn, the Welsh Otherworld, in Arthur's ship *Prydwen*. Annwn seems to consists of a series of fortresses, and Arthur is mentioned in connection with several of them[1] (lines 21–2, 29–30, 33–4, 41–2, 47–8):

> And when we went with Arthur, brilliant difficulty,
> except seven none rose up from the Fortress of Mead-Drunkenness
> I merit not the Lord's little men of letters.
> Beyond the Glass Fortress they did not see the valor of Arthur.
> Three fullnesses of Prydwen went with Arthur.
> Except seven none rose up from the Fortress of Guts (Hindrance?)
> And when we went with Arthur, dolorous visit,
> except seven none rose up from the fortress of God's Peak
> When we went with Arthur, sorrowful strife,
> except seven none rose up from the Fortress of Enclosedness

The Mound Fortress

The Prison in the Mound Fortress

This poem is difficult, and at times impenetrable, but it does give us some idea of the world in which Arthur moved, especially in the first twenty or thirty lines. Eight fortresses are mentioned in *The Spoils of Annwn*, and the poem begins with a description of the first fortress, the Mound Fortress (lines 3–10):

> Equipped was the prison of Gweir in the Mound Fortress,
> throughout the account(?) of Pwyll and Pryderi.
> No one before him went into it,
> into the heavy blue/gray chain; a faithful servant it held.
> And before the spoils of Annwfyn bitterly he sang.
> And until Judgment shall last our bardic invocation.
> Three fullnesses of Prydwen we went into it.
> Except seven none rose up from the Fortress of the Mound.

The first questions to ask are: where are we? and who are our companions in this journey? Firstly, we are in the in "Mound Fortress," in Welsh *Caer Sidi*. The word *sidi* is related to the Irish *sid* or *sidh*, which refers to "hills or mounds (often in reality containing prehistoric burials) conceived of as hollow and the residence of supernatural beings."[2] The Welsh word *caer* can mean "hillfort," so the Mound Fortress may be on one level a Bronze Age barrow inside a hillfort.

Pwyll and Pryderi

Our first companions are Pwyll and Pryderi, and their story is told in the First Branch of the *Mabinogion*, a collection of Welsh mythological tales written between 1060 and 1200. The First Branch, entitled *Pwyll Prince of Dyfed*, is set in Dyfed, a kingdom in southwest Wales which included Pembrokeshire and parts of Carmarthenshire, and a good part of the action takes place in Arberth, which is usually assumed to be Narberth in Pembrokeshire. The First Branch starts with Pwyll setting off from Arberth to hunt in Glyn Cuch, the valley of the River Cych, in the north of Pembrokeshire. When Pwyll reaches the valley of the Cych, he lets his dogs loose and chases after them. He hears the sound of another pack of dogs, and reaches them just as they are bringing down a stag. Then, in the translation by Will Parker[3]:

> he caught sight of the colour of the pack, barely noticing the stag itself. Of all the hunting dogs he had seen in this world, he had never seen dogs the same colour as those. The colouring they had was a dazzling bright white and with red ears.

Pwyll drives off the pack that has killed the stag, and lets his own dogs feed on the stag instead. The owner of the pack that has killed the stag then approaches, dressed in a brownish-grey hunting smock, and it turns out that he is Arawn, king of Annwn, the Welsh Otherworld. Arawn reproaches Pwyll for his "rudeness and discourtesy" in letting his dogs feed on the stag that Arawn's dogs had brought down, and Pwyll offers to make amends, whereupon Arawn asks him for a favor. He is at war with a neighboring king called Hafgan (either "Summer-Song" or "Summer-White") and asks Pwyll to fight Hafgan. To do this, he and Pwyll will change places for a year and a day, and Arawn will give him "the most beautiful woman you have ever seen to sleep with every night, and my form and appearance will be upon you so that neither the chamber-boy nor the steward nor anybody else that has ever served me will know that you are not I." In a year and a day Pwyll will meet Hafgan at the ford in the guise of Arawn, and will fight him in a very particular way: "a single blow you must give him: he will not survive it. And even if he asks you to give him another, you mustn't. For despite any more [blows] I [ever] gave him, he was always able to fight back just as well the next day."

Pwyll then went to Arawn's court and was greeted by everyone as if he were Arawn. The queen was indeed beautiful, and he conversed with her familiarly and affectionately during the day—but as soon as they went to bed, he turned his face to the side with his back to her, and didn't say a word until the next day. After a year and a day, he met Hafgan at the ford, dealt him a single blow, and despite Hafgan's pleas, did not strike him again. Pwyll then met Arawn in the valley of the Cych, and they resumed their old roles. From that day, Pwyll and Arawn were firm friends, and Pwyll was no longer known as "Prince of Dyfed," but "Chief of Annwn."

After his year in Annwn, Pwyll returned to Dyfed. One evening, he was at Arberth enjoying a feast, when after the first course he decided to go for a walk, and made for the top of the mound called Gorsedd Arberth. The word *gorsedd* is a compound of *sedd* "seat" and *gor-* "over,"[4] and is related to the Irish *sid* or *sidh*, as in *Caer Sidi* or "Mound Fortress." Gorsedd Arberth was clearly a special place: "'Lord,' said one of the court 'it is a peculiarity of the mound that whatever high-born man might sit upon it, he will not go away without one of two things: either wounds or blows, or his witnessing a marvel.'" Sure enough, while they were sitting there, they did witness a marvel:

> As they were seated, they could see a woman on a large stately pale-white horse, a garment of shining gold brocaded silk about her, making her way along the track which went past the mound. The horse had an even, leisurely pace; and she was drawing level with the mound it seemed to all those who were watching her.

Pwyll asked who she was, but nobody recognized her, so Pwyll asked one of his courtiers to go up to her to find out who she was. The courtier tried to catch up with her, but "the greater was his speed, the further away from him she became." So the courtier fetched a horse, and followed her, but "the more he struck the horse, the further away she became. Yet she still had the same pace with which she had begun." The next day they went up to the mound at the same time, woman appeared once more, and Pwyll asked a boy to follow her, with the same result. The next day they went again to the mound at the same time, and the lady appeared as before. This time Pwyll pursued her, but unable to catch up with her, he addressed the mysterious rider:

> "Maiden," he said "for the sake of the man you love the best, wait for me!"
> "Gladly I'll wait" said she "but it might have been better for the horse if you had asked me a good while before."

It turned out that the mysterious horse-lady was Rhiannon, that she was the daughter of Hyfaidd the Old, that she was being given to a man against her will, but that she wanted to marry Pwyll. Eventually, after Pwyll made one unsuccessful attempt to win her hand, they did in fact marry, and Rhiannon gave birth to a baby boy. On the night of his birth some women were brought in to watch over him—they fell asleep, and when they awoke the next morning the boy was gone. The women killed a puppy, smeared its blood on Rhiannon, and accused Rhiannon of killing the baby. As a result Rhiannon was required to do a penance:

> she was to stay at the court of Arbeth for the duration of seven years. There was a mounting-block by the gate. She had to sit beside it every day telling anyone coming by the whole story (of those she supposed did not know it) and offering whichever guest and stranger would allow themselves to carried, to be carried on her back to the court. But only rarely did anyone allow the carrying. In this way she passed the next part of the year.

Meanwhile Teyrnon Twryf Liant, ruler of Gwent-Ys-Coed ("Gwent Below the Wood"), at the other end of Wales, was watching over his prize mare. His mare would give birth every night at the Calends of May (May 1st or Beltane, the great Celtic festival at the beginning of summer), but "no-one ever knew what became of her foals." This time he brought the mare into his house, and watched as she gave birth to a foal. There was a great commotion outside, an enormous claw reached through the window to seize the foal, Teyrnon drew his sword and severed the arm from the elbow down. He heard a commotion and scream and rushed outside to investigate. When he returned, there was a "small child in swaddling clothes, wrapped in a sheet of brocaded silk" by the door. They named the child Gwri Golden-Hair, and brought him up as their own. As time passed, they heard stories of Rhiannon and her penance, and realized that Gwri looked exactly like Pwyll. So they took the boy to Narberth, where he was reunited with his parents, and renamed Pryderi ("Care, Anxiety").

The First Branch starts with an encounter between Pwyll and the chief of the Otherworld, and is dominated by the Otherworld. The chief of the Otherworld is accompanied by dogs that were "dazzling bright white and with red ears," no doubt a reference to the dogs that played such an important part in excarnation from the Neolithic to the Iron Age. Once Pwyll has returned from the Otherworld, the story is dominated by Rhiannon ("Great Queen"). Rhiannon is usually identified with the Celtic horse-goddess Epona ("Great Mare"), whose cult was widespread in the Roman Empire between the 1st and the 3rd centuries. Depictions of Epona and dedications to the goddess are concentrated in three regions: the terri-

Epona and her horses, from Köngen, Germany, dating from around AD 200 (P. Frankenstein / H. Zwietasch; Landesmuseum Württemberg, Stuttgart).

The ruins of the Roman Amphitheatre at Caerleon near Newport, South Wales (Greenshed).

tory of the Aedui, who lived around Autun (Saône-et-Loire) in Burgundy; the valley of the Moselle and the territory of the Treveri, which covers parts of France, Belgium, Luxembourg and Germany; and territory along the Roman *limes* (frontier) in Germany, which stretched from the northwest of the country to the Danube in the southeast.[5] Epona is usually shown riding a horse or accompanied by a horse and foal or by two or more horses. She is "most often shown riding side-saddle, with the horse moving at a leisurely pace towards the right, although sometimes she rides astride."[6] Epona was also connected with fertility—"she may carry a sheaf of corn or large circular emblems of fruit or bread,"[7] or a cornucopia.[8] There is general agreement[9] that Epona "helped the dead in their journey to the Otherworld"—on some monuments she "is depicted leading a walking figure, who appears to represent the dead."

However, horses played an important part in religious life from the Late Bronze Age/Early Iron Age, well before Epona came to prominence in the Roman Empire. It is perhaps significant that the infant Pryderi is found in Gwent, in an area where there is much evidence for horses in the Iron Age. Horse fittings were found at the Early Iron Age feasting site at Llanmaes in the Vale of Glamorgan; a Late Iron Age copper alloy horse figurine has been found near Abercarn, not far from Caerleon; and horse trappings have been found at a number of sites, including a decorated terret from the Lesser Garth in Cardiff, similar decorated terrets from the hoard found at Seven Sisters near Neath, and an enameled bronze harness mount from Chepstow.[10]

Clearly there is a connection between Pwyll and the Welsh Otherworld, and between the Mound Fortress and Gorsedd Arberth, the mound where Pwyll first saw the horse-goddess Rhiannon.

The Four-Peaked Fortress

The Cauldron of Annwn

The otherworldly journey continues with stops at two more fortresses, the first of which contains a cauldron (lines 11–24):

> I am honored in praise. Song was heard
> in the Four-Peaked Fortress, four its revolutions.
> My poetry, from the cauldron it was uttered.
> From the breath of nine maidens it was kindled.
> The cauldron of the chief of Annwfyn: what is its fashion?
> A dark ridge around its border and pearls.
> It does not boil the food of a coward; it has not been destined.
> The flashing sword of Lleawch has been lifted to it.
> And in the hand of Lleminawc it was left.
> And before the door of hell lamps burned.
> And when we went with Arthur, brilliant difficulty,
> except seven none rose up from the Fortress of Mead-Drunkenness.
> I am honored in praise; song is heard
> in the Fortress of Four-Peaks, isle of the strong door.

Before I try to answer the question: where are we?, first a note on the nine maidens. The poet implies that the nine maidens are the Muses, but their origins are not necessarily to be found in classical Greece. The Roman geographer Pomponius Mela, writing around AD 43, says in his *Description of the World*[11]:

In the Britannic Sea, opposite the coast of the Osismii, the isle of Sena [Sein] belongs to a Gallic divinity and is famous for its oracle, whose priestesses, sanctified by their perpetual divinity, are reportedly nine in number. They call the priestesses Gallizenae and think that because they have been endowed with unique powers, they stir up the seas and winds by their magic charms, that they turn into whatever animals they want, that they cure what it incurable among other peoples, that they know and predict the future, but that it is not revealed except to sea-voyagers and then only to those traveling to consult them.

This island is thought to be the Île de Sein, 5 miles from the Pointe du Raz in western Brittany. The significance of the number nine is unknown, but it is worth pointing out that the Bush Barrow lozenge had nine smaller lozenges at its center, indicating that the number nine was important in Britain from the Early Bronze Age.

The Isle of the Strong Door

So where are we? The key to the Four-Peaked Fortress, "isle of the strong door," with it cauldron kindled by the breath of nine maidens, may lie in the Second Branch of the *Mabinogion*, entitled *Branwen Daughter of Llyr*. The main characters in the Second Branch are Bran the Blessed, "the crowned king of this Island, and exalted with the crown of London," his sister Branwen, and their half-brother Efnisien. As the story opens, Bran ("Raven") was at Harlech in northwest Wales when Matholwch king of Ireland came to ask for Branwen's hand in marriage. A feast was held in Aberffraw on Anglesey (the medieval capital of the kingdom of Gwynedd) to celebrate the wedding, and Matholwch slept with Branwen. The next morning Efnisien, the half-brother of Bran and Branwen, saw Matholwch's horses and asked who they belonged to. When told that they belonged to Matholwch, who had just slept with his half-sister, he became enraged[12]:

"So this is what they have done with a girl as good as her, my own sister—giving her away without my consent! They could not have insulted me more!"
With that he [started] striking up at the horses. He sliced their lips back to their teeth, and their ears back to their heads, and their tails to their backs—and wherever he could get a grip on their eyelids, he would cut these back to the bone. And the horses were mutilated thus, to the extent that no further use could be got from the horses.

On hearing this, Matholwch and his followers returned to their ships. Bran, unaware of what had happened, sent two of his courtiers to find out why Matholwch had left without taking his leave. On discovering the reason, he offered Matholwch a healthy horse for each one mutilated, together with a "silver rod as thick [as his little finger] and as tall as himself and a gold plate as broad as his face." Matholwch then came back to Bran's court, but was still out of sorts, so Bran offered him further compensation:

"I will give you this cauldron, and the peculiarity of the cauldron is this: a man who is killed today and thrown in the cauldron, by the next day he will be as good as he was at his best, except he will not be able to talk."

Matholwch and Branwen returned to Ireland, and within a year Branwen gave birth to a boy called Gwern ("Alder"). In the second year, people began mocking Matholwch for the humiliation he had suffered at the hands of Efnisien, and in revenge, Matholwch drove Branwen out of the room they shared, forced her to bake bread in the court, and had the butcher box her ears every day. During the next three years, Branwen raised a bird, and sent the bird with a message to Bran. The bird delivered the message to Bran when he was at Caer Seint (the Roman fort of Segontium, now Caernarfon). Bran then decided to attack Ireland, and to "leave seven men as elders here: with Cradawg son of Bran as their chief, with his seven riders." When the Irish saw Bran and his army approaching, they offered to give the sovereignty of Ireland to Gwern, Bran's nephew, and to build a house large enough to contain Bran (he was a giant). But the Irish laid a trap—they "put a hook on each side of every one of the hundred columns that were in the house, and put a crane skin-bag on each peg, and an armed fighting man in every one of those." Efnisien came in ahead of the others, and caught sight of the bags:

> "What is in this bag?" he demanded to one of the Irish
> "Flour, friend" he replied
> What he did was this, feeling around till he found the [the hiding warrior's] head, and squeezing his head until he could feel his fingers sink into the brain through the bone.

Efnisien then proceeded to kill the other 99 men in the same way. After this Bran and his retinue arrived, and sovereignty was bestowed on Bran's nephew Gwern. Bran called the boy over to him, and from there the boy went over to Bran's brother Manawydan then Nisien. Finally Efnisien spoke:

> "Why doesn't my nephew—my sister's son—come to me?" asked Efnisien "Even if he weren't the king of Ireland I would still like to show affection to the boy."
> "Let him go, gladly," said Bendigeidfran. And the boy went to him gladly.

Efnisien then threw the boy into the fire, and pandemonium followed as everyone reached for his weapons. Branwen tried to save her son, but Bran held Branwen between his shield and his shoulder, while the Irish began to kindle a fire under the cauldron of rebirth:

> (And then) the dead were thrown into the cauldron, until it was full. They would rise up the next day—fighting men as good as before, except they would not be able to talk.

Efnisien, seeing this, crawled into the cauldron and stretched himself out until the cauldron broke into four pieces, dying in the process.

In the end the British were victorious, but only seven survived, along with Bran, wounded in his foot with a poisoned spear. Then, because of his poisoned foot, Bran ordered the survivors to sever his head:

> "Take the head" said he "and bring it to the White Hill in London, and bury it with its face towards France. And you will be on the road a long time. In Harlech you will be seven years in feasting, the birds of Rhiannon singing to you. The head will be as good company to you as it was at its best when it was ever on me. And you will be at Gwales in Penfro for eighty years. Until you open the door facing Aber Henvelen on the side facing Cornwall, you will be able to abide there, along with the head with you uncorrupted. But when you open that door, you will not be able to remain there. You will make for London and bury the head."

The survivors duly cut off Bran's head, and set off with the head, landing at Aber Alaw in Anglesey. There Branwen died of a broken heart and was buried in a "four-sided grave," popularly believed to be the Bronze Age funerary mound known as Bedd Branwen. The men then set off for Harlech, and learned that Caswallwn son of Beli had overrun the island and was now the crowned king in London. They reached Harlech and

> began a feast, and the indulgence in food and drink was begun. And [as soon as] they began to eat and drink there came three birds, which began to sing a kind of song to them;

and when they heard that song, every other [tune] seemed unlovely beside it. It seemed a distant sight, what they could see far above the ocean yet it was as clear as if they had been right next to them. And they were at that feast for seven years.

The significance of the birds of Rhiannon is unknown, but wild birds were clearly important to the religious rituals of the Iron Age site of Godwin Ridge and the Roman shrine of Haddenham, both in the Cambridgeshire fens.

At the end of the seven years they moved to Gwales in Penfro (possibly the island of Grassholm, off the coast of Pembrokeshire) and a "beautiful kingly place high above the ocean," with two open door and one closed one, the one they must not open. There they "were completely free of care. Of all the grief that they had witnessed or experienced themselves—there was no longer any memory, or any of the sorrow in the world." At the end of eighty years, one of the seven survivors, Heilyn son of Gwyn, became curious and opened the door and looked out to Cornwall:

And when he looked, suddenly everything they had ever lost—loved ones and companions, and all the bad things that had ever happened to them; and most of all the loss of their king—became as clear as if it had been rushing in towards them.

Grassholm is a small island 8 miles from the coast of Pembrokeshire, best known for its huge colony of gannets. Investigations of Grassholm in 1972 and 2012 revealed a small Iron Age settlement with two roundhouses in the center of the island, and a medieval settlement of conjoined rectangular buildings on the western side of the island.[13]

After Heilyn opened the door, the seven survivors, who included Pryderi and Bran's brother Manawydan, left Gwales and made for London, where they buried Bran's head at White Hill, thought to be the site of the Tower of London.

As in *the Spoils of Annwn*, there are seven survivors, and Gwales in Penfro is clearly "the isle of the strong door." Cauldrons are usually associated with feasting, but the caul-

Grassholm Island, Pembrokeshire, Wales ("Gwales" in the Second Branch of the *Mabinogion*), showing one of the few areas free of birds (Janet Baxter Photography).

dron of regeneration is likely to refer to the cauldrons or buckets used in the Late Iron Age to hold the cremated ashes of elite members of the community.

Bran, as I said, means "Raven," and five sets of human remains were buried with a raven at Danebury hillfort in Hampshire. Ravens have also been found at Owslebury near Winchester, Wittenham Clumps in Oxfordshire, Winklebury hillfort in Basingstoke (Hampshire), and Rooksdown in Basingstoke. The raven on the base of a pit at Rooksdown was associated with three horse skulls placed "upright" on the base and a puppy skeleton. A raven at Owslebury was associated with a buzzard and a crow or a rook with the skeletal remains of a chicken (an unusual bird in Britain at the time).[14]

Ravens or crows have also been found on Romano-British sites. The largest number of raven burials was found in Roman Dorchester, where at least 14 skeletons were identified from seven shafts or pits. Ravens or crows have been found alongside dogs and puppies in 15 burials: in shaft 6 at Dorchester, all but one of the dog burials were associated with ravens; seven adult dogs and 87 puppy ABGs (articulated bone groups) were found in a shaft at Oakridge, Basingstoke, along with a crow. Three cattle skeletons were found with a raven in the well at Stanion Roman villa in Northamptonshire. It is clear that in the later Iron Age and Romano-British period ravens were associated with death, as dogs were in the Neolithic and earlier Iron Age.

The Four-Peaked Fortress

The most challenging part of this section is identifying the meaning of the Four-Peaked Fortress with its four revolutions. This is pure speculation of course, but I think the number *four* was significant in British prehistory. The Early Bronze Age gold discs often had crosses on them with four equal arms, and for the Late Iron Age bronze spoons, one of the pairs was divided into four quarters by a similar equal-armed cross. Whether the cross with four equal arms represented the sun, the sky or something else entirely will probably be never known, but it clearly had great significance for prehistoric Britons over a very long period.

The Fortress of Mead-Drunkenness

After stopping at the Four-Peaked Fortress, Arthur and his men visit the Fortress of Mead-Drunkenness. The role of mead in early British societies is underlined in the poem *Y Gododdin*, in which the warrior Gwawddur "fed black ravens on the rampart of a fort, though he was no Arthur." Mead is mentioned forty-three times—here are some examples[15]:

> Men went to Catraeth, keen their war-band.
> Pale mead their portion, it was poison.
>
> Men went to Catraeth at dawn:
> Their high spirits lessened their life-spans.
>
> They drank mead, gold and sweet, ensnaring;
> For a year the minstrels were merry.
>
> Men launched the assault, nourished as one
> A year over mead, grand their design.
> How sad their tale, insatiable longing,
> Bitter their home, no child to cherish it.

> Because of wine-feast and mead-feast they charged,
> Men famed in fighting, heedless of life.
> Bright ranks around cups, they joined to feast.
> Wine and mead and bragget, these were theirs.

Mead is described as "poison," as "ensnaring," which makes men "heedless of life" and "lessened their life-spans."

The Glass Fortress

After the Fortress of Mead-Drunkenness, Arthur and his men visit the Fortress of Hardness, then proceed to the Glass Fortress (lines 29–32):

> I merit not the Lord's little men of letters.
> Beyond the Glass Fortress they did not see the valor of Arthur.
> Six thousand men stood upon the wall.
> It was difficult to speak with their sentinel.

Something similar to the Glass Fortress is mentioned in the *History of the Britons* (Chapter 13).[16] As the Milesians (the final inhabitants of Ireland, according to Irish mythology) were voyaging towards Ireland, "there appeared to them, in the middle of the sea, a tower of glass, the summit of which seemed covered with men, to whom they often spoke, but received no answer." The unspeaking men of the Glass Fortress and the tower of glass recall those regenerated by the magic cauldron. who can perform as well as they did before they died but cannot speak.

The Brindled Ox

After line 32 the poem becomes virtually incomprehensible, but there is one section that stands out (line 35, lines 39–40):

> I do not merit little men,
> slack their shield straps.
> They do not know the brindled ox,
> thick his headband.
> Seven score links
> on his collar.

Cattle played an important part in British religion from the Neolithic to the Roman period, so it must be significant that there is a brindled ox in the Otherworld associated with Arthur, even if we have no idea why the ox has a collar with seven score links.

Arthur as a Real Character

Arthur is a rather anonymous character in *The Spoils of Annwn*, and he only began to emerge as a real character in the poem *Pa gur yv y porthaur?* ("What man is the gatekeeper/porter?"), in the prose tale *Culhwch and Olwen*, and in Geoffrey of Monmouth's *History of the Kings of Britain*—but the supernatural elements were never far away.

Chapter 9

Arthur the Witch-Slayer, Warrior and King

Arthur the Witch-Slayer

"What man is the gatekeeper?"

Arthur first emerges as a witch-slayer in the poem *Pa gur yv y porthaur?* ("What man is the gatekeeper/porter?"), which may have been composed as early as the 9th or even 8th century AD. In this poem,[1] Arthur is interrogated by a gatekeeper or porter who will not let him in unless he vouches for those travelling with him. His companions include Cei and Bedwyr, Arthur's most important warriors in the early Welsh tales. In *Pa gur?* Arthur is depicted as the slayer of witches and monsters (lines 37–44):

> Though Arthur was playing [or laughing]
> He caused blood to flow
> In the hall of Wrnach [or Afarnach]
> Fighting with a witch.
> He slew Pen-Palach [Cudgel-Head]
> in the hall of Dissetach.
> On the heights of Eidyn
> He fought with champions [or dog-heads].

The only name that can be identified here is *Eidyn*, "Edinburgh," the stronghold of the Votadini in the Dark Ages.

Although Arthur plays a recognizable role in *Pa gur?*, he is overshadowed by Cei and Bedwyr, who are both depicted as formidable warriors. Here is the description of Cei (lines 31–36, 65–74):

> Cei pleaded with them
> While he slew them three by three.
> When Celli was lost
> There was savagery.
> Cei pleaded with them
> While he hewed them down.

> Prince of the plunder,
> The unrelenting warrior to his enemy;
> Heavy was he in his vengeance;
> Terrible was his fighting.
> When he would drink from a horn,
> He would drink as much as four;
> When into battle he came

> He slew as would a hundred.
> Unless God should accomplish it,
> Cei's death would be unattainable.

Celli may be *Celliwig* in Cornwall, Arthur's earliest court, or it may be *Calleva*, the Roman capital of the Atrebates (now Silchester in Hampshire), which probably remained in British hands until the 6th century or later.

And here is the description of Bedwyr (lines 45–50):

> By the hundreds they fell
> To Bedwyr's four-pronged spear [or Bedwyr the Perfect],
> On the shores of Tryfrwyd,
> Combating with Garwlwyd
> Furious was his nature
> Both with sword and shield

Garwlwyd ("Rough-Grey") sounds like a character in the medieval *Welsh Triads* (Triad 32) called Gwrgi ("Man-Dog") Garwlwyd, who "used to make a corpse of one of the Cymry every day, and two on each Saturday so as not to slay on Sunday."[2] *Tryfrwyd* is the same as the *Tribruit* mentioned in the *History of the Britons* as being one of Arthur's battles.

Culhwch and Olwen

Arthur's role as a slayer of witches continued in *Culhwch and Olwen*, one of the so-called native tales of the *Mabinogion*, which was probably composed in the late 11th century. As the story opens, Cilydd son of Cyleddon Wledig or Celyddon Wledig (possibly "lord of the Caledonian forest" in Scotland) takes as his wife Goleuddydd, daughter of Amlawdd Wledig.[3] Goleuddydd became pregnant, but

> from the time she grew with child, she went mad, without coming near a dwelling. When her time came upon her, her right sense came back to her; it came in a place where a swineherd was keeping a herd of swine, and through terror of the swine the queen was delivered. And the swineherd took the boy until he came to the court. And the boy was baptized, and the name Culhwch given to him because he was found in a pig-run.

This story is no doubt linked to the fact that the second element of Culhwch's name, *hwch* meant "pig, swine" (in modern Welsh it means "sow"). However, the story-teller reassures us, "the boy was of gentle lineage: he was first cousin to Arthur"—Arthur's mother was Eigyr or Igraine, another daughter of Amlawdd Wledig.

Not long after this, Goleuddydd grew sick and died. Some years later, Cilydd decided to remarry, and was advised to choose the wife of King Doged. So they killed the king and carried off his wife and daughter. When the new queen was introduced to Culhwch, she suggested that Culhwch marry her daughter, but Culhwch said he was too young to wed. So the queen swore a destiny on him—that he would not find a wife until he won the hand of Olwen, the daughter of Ysbaddaden the Chief of Giants. Culhwch immediately fell in love with Olwen on hearing her name, and his father advised him to seek help from his cousin Arthur.

So Culhwch journeyed to Arthur's court, where he immediately was confronted by a surly gatekeeper, like the one in *Pa gur?*, who refused to admit him. Culhwch threatened him, and the gatekeeper consulted Arthur, who agreed that Culhwch could be admitted. Culhwch then asked Arthur to trim his hair—a sign that they were kinsmen—and Arthur agreed. Once this was done, Culhwch asked Arthur for a favor, in the name of a long list of warriors in Arthur's court: Cai and Bedwyr; Gwyn son of Nudd (Nudd is the god Nodens of Lydney Park); Gwalchmei son of Gwyar, who is the Sir Gawain of later literature; Gwenhwyvar Chief of Queens, the Guinevere of later tradition, whose name is usually translated as "White Phantom" or "White Fairy"; and Lludd Llaw Eraint ("Lludd Silver-Hand"), the god Nodens, and the Welsh equivalent of the Irish Nuada, the first king of the Tuatha De Danann ("Peoples of the Goddess Danu").

Arthur sent out messengers to find Olwen, but after a year had passed, they had still not found her. So Cei said that he and Culhwch would go in search of her:

> Cei had this peculiarity, nine nights and nine days his breath lasted under water, nine nights and nine days would he be without sleep. A wound from Cei's sword no physician might heal. A wondrous gift had Cei: when it pleased him he would be as tall as the tallest tree in the forest. Another peculiarity had he: when the rain was heaviest, a handbreadth before his hand and another behind his hand what would be in his hand would be dry, by reason of the greatness of his heat; and when the cold was hardest on his comrades, that would be to them kindling to light a fire.

Cei's heat is similar to the heat of the Irish mythological hero Cu Chulainn, who could boil cold water in a vat when he was in a rage.

So Culhwch, Cei, Bedwyr and a number of other men set out in search of Olwen. eventually they found the fort where Olwen lived with her father Ysbaddaden Chief of Giants. Culhwch and his five companions then presented themselves before the Giant, and Culhwch told him he wished to marry his daughter. The giant told them to come back the next day:

> They rose, and Ysbaddaden Chief Giant snatched at one of the three poisoned stone-spears which were by his hand and hurled it after them. And Bedwyr caught it and hurled it back at him, and pierced Ysbaddaden Chief Giant right through the ball of his knee. Quoth he, "Thou cursed savage son-in-law! I shall walk the worse up a slope. Like the sting of a gadfly the poisoned iron has pained me. Cursed be the smith who fashioned it, and the anvil on which it was wrought, so painful it is!"

The six companions returned the next day and once more asked for the giant's daughter Olwen. The giant said he needed consult Olwen's great-grand-parents, and the six stood up:

> As they arose he took hold of the second stone-spear which was by his hand and hurled it after them. And Menw son of Teirgwaedd caught it and hurled it back at him, and pierced him in the middle of his breast, so that it came out in the small of his back. "Thou cursed savage son-in-law! Like the bite of a big-headed leech the hard iron has pained me. Cursed be the forge wherein it was heated. When I go uphill, I shall have tightness of chest, and belly-ache, and a frequent loathing of meat." They went to their meat.

The men returned once more the next day and again asked for Olwen. Ysbaddaden asked them to raise up the forks—his eyelids had fallen over the balls of his eyes—so he could look at his future son-in-law:

> They arose, and as they arose he took the third poisoned stone-spear and hurled it after them. And Culhwch caught it and hurled it back, even as he wished, and pierced him through the ball of the eye, so that it came out through the nape of the neck. "Thou cursed savage son- in-law! So long as I am left alive, the sight of my eyes will be the worse. When I go against the wind they will water, a headache I shall have, and a giddiness each new moon. Cursed be the forge wherein it was heated. Like the bite of a mad dog to me the way the poisoned iron has pierced me."

This episode is similar to an episode in which Lugh, the Irish version of the Celtic god Lugus, kills the giant Balor by casting a spear through his eye. The fact that Ysbaddaden uses stone spears suggests that he belongs to the Neolithic, and to the time of Neolithic monuments like Stonehenge, which early medieval Britons may have thought were the works of giants.

The giant finally agrees that Culhwch can marry Olwen, but only if he completes a series of impossible-sounding tasks. Many of these tasks are carried out by Cei and Bedwyr, and I'll only focus on those that involve Arthur.

The list of tasks is long, and many of them relate to the hunt for the boar Twrch Trwyth (the "swine Troynt" in *History of the Britons*)—Culhwch must get the comb and scissors that are between the ears of Twrch Trwyth, for only with these will the giant be able to brush his hair. Only the dog called Drudwyn can hunt the boar Twrch Trwyth, and the only huntsman that can manage Drudwyn is "Mabon son of Modron, who was taken away when three nights old from his mother." The name Modron is derived from Matrona, the Latin name for the River Marne in France first mentioned by Julius Caesar in his *Gallic War*.[4] Mabon is the Welsh version of the god Maponos ("Divine Boy" or "Divine Son"), from Gaulish *mapos* "young boy, son." Maponos is mentioned in inscriptions from Gaul (Bourbonne-les-Bains in Haute-Marne, northeastern France, and Chamalières in central France), but is mainly attested along Hadrian's Wall, at Brampton in Cumbria, at Corbridge in Northumberland, at Ribchester in Lancashire, and at Vindolanda in Northumberland. In France the most interesting inscription is the Gaulish inscription from Chamalières, which requests help from Maponos in a military revolt.[5] In Britain the most interesting artifact is a silver crescent found at Vindolanda Roman

The River Marne (home to the goddess Matrona) at Chelles, a commune in the eastern suburbs of Paris. September 27, 2009 (Myrabella).

The bathhouse of Vindolanda Roman fort near Bardon Mill, Northumberland, May 19, 2007 (Optimist on the run).

fort near Hexham in Northumberland, with the inscription *Deo Mapono*, "to the god Maponos."[6]

Eventually Cei and Bedwyr found Mabon son of Modron, who was in a prison in Gloucester. When they reached the prison, they heard "a great wailing and lamenting from the dungeon," and when they called out to the prisoner, Mabon son of Modron replied: "Alas, there is reason enough for whoever is here to lament. It is Mabon the son of Modron who is here imprisoned; and no imprisonment was ever so grievous as mine" (shades of Gweir imprisoned in the Mound Fortress in *The Spoils of Annwn!*). They then returned to Arthur, who raised an army, and went to Gloucester—while Arthur's warriors assaulted the fort, Cei broke into the fort and escaped with Mabon on his back.

The story of the accomplishment of the tasks is halted for a short time by a dispute between two of Arthur's men:

> A short while before this Creiddylad daughter of Lludd Silver-hand went with Gwythyr son of Greidawl; and before he had slept with her there came Gwyn son of Nudd and carried her off by force. Gwythyr son of Greidawl gathered a host, and he came to fight with Gwyn son of Nudd. And Gwyn prevailed, and he took prisoner Greid son of Eri, Glinneu son of Taran, and Gwrgwst the Half-naked and Dyfnarth his son. And he took prisoner Pen son of Nethawg, and Nwython, and Cyledyr the Wild his son, and he slew Nwython and took out his heart, and compelled Cyledyr to eat his father's heart; and because of this Cyledyr went mad. Arthur heard tell of this, and he came into the North and summoned to him Gwyn son of Nudd and set free his noblemen from his prison, and peace was made

between Gwyn son of Nudd and Gwythyr son of Greidawl. This is the peace that was made: the maiden should remain in her father's house, unmolested by either side, and there should be battle between Gwyn and Gwythyr each May-calends for ever and ever, from that day till doomsday; and the one of them that should be victor on doomsday, let him have the maiden.

Curiously, both Creiddylad and Gwyn are children of Nodens, called Lludd Silver-hand in the case of Creiddylad and Nudd in the case of Gwyn.

One of Culhwch's tasks was to get the cauldron of Diwrnach the Irishman, the steward of Odgar, the son of Aedd, king of Ireland, to boil the meat of his marriage feast. So Arthur sent a messenger to Odgar son of Aedd to ask for the cauldron of Diwrnach the Irishman, but received a negative answer. He then sailed for Ireland with a small force in his ship Prydwen, and made for the house of Diwrnach the Irishman. He asked Diwrnach for the cauldron, and when Diwrnach refused, Bedwyr stood up, seized the cauldron, and put it on the back of Arthur's servant Hygwydd. Llenlleawg the Irishman seized Arthur's sword Caledfwlch and killed Diwrnach. A battle ensued, the Irish were routed, and Arthur and his men boarded Prydwen with all the treasures of Ireland in the cauldron. This episode recalls the cauldron of Annwn: in *The Spoils of Annwn* the poet says that "The flashing sword of Lleawch has been lifted to it," and clearly Lleawch and Llenlleawg are two versions of the same name.

Once this was accomplished, Arthur and his men set out on the hunt for the boar Twrch Trwyth—this was an epic event:

> Then Arthur summoned unto him all the warriors that were in the three Islands of Britain, and in the three Islands adjacent, and all that were in France and in Armorica, in Normandy and in the Summer Country, and all that were chosen footmen and valiant horse-

Wild boar and piglets, New Forest Wildlife Park, Hampshire, June 26, 2007 (Dave Pape).

men. And with all these he went into Ireland. And in Ireland there was great fear and terror concerning him. And when Arthur had landed in the country, there came unto him the saints of Ireland and besought his protection. And he granted his protection unto them, and they gave him their blessing. Then the men of Ireland came unto Arthur, and brought him provisions.

After this Arthur went to Esgeir Oerfel where the boar lived with his seven piglets. The Irish fought the boar, but he laid waste a fifth of Ireland; Arthur's men fought with him, but could not get the better of him; then Arthur fought him for nine days and nights without killing even one piglet. The warriors asked Arthur who he was, and he told them that Twrch Trwyth "was once a king, and that God had transformed him into a swine for his sins":

Then Arthur sent Gwrhyr Gwalstawt Ieithoedd, to endeavour to speak with him. And Gwrhyr assumed the form of a bird, and alighted upon the top of the lair, where he was with the seven young pigs. And Gwrhyr Gwalstawt Ieithoedd asked him, "By him who turned you into this form, if you can speak, let some one of you, I beseech you, come and talk with Arthur." Grugyn Gwrych Ereint made answer to him. (Now his bristles were like silver wire, and whether he went through the wood or through the plain, he was to be traced by the glittering of his bristles.) And this was the answer that Grugyn made, "By him who turned us into this form, we will not do so, and we will not speak with Arthur. That we have been transformed thus is enough for us to suffer, without your coming here to fight with us." "I will tell you. Arthur comes but to fight for the comb, and the razor, and the scissors, which are between the two ears of Twrch Trwyth."

Said Grugyn, "Except he first take his life, he will never have those precious things. And to-morrow morning we will rise up hence, and we will go into Arthur's country, and there will we do all the mischief that we can.

The boar and his seven young pigs then swam to Wales and fought against Arthur and his men for many days, causing great slaughter. Finally Arthur and his men managed to force Twrch Trwyth into the Severn, and Mabon son of Modron snatched his razor from him, while Cynedyr the Wild took his scissors. The Great Boar clambered out of the river and headed for Cornwall, where they finally succeeded in getting the comb. Twrch Trwyth was driven into the deep sea, and was never seen again.

After this epic battle, Arthur returned to Celliwig to bathe and rest, then prepared himself for the last task, getting the blood of the Very Black Witch from the head of the Valley of Grief in the uplands of Hell (the giant Ysbadadden needs this to prepare his beard for shaving):

Arthur set out for the North and came to where the hag's cave was. And it was the counsel of Gwyn son of Nudd and Gwythyr son of Greidawl that Cacamwri and Hygwydd his brother be sent to fight with the hag. And as they came inside the cave the hag grabbed at them, and caught Hygwydd by the hair of his head and flung him to the floor beneath her. And Cacamwri seized her by the hair of her head, and dragged her to the ground off Hygwydd, but she then turned on Cacamwri and dressed them down both and disarmed them, and drove them out squealing and squalling. And Arthur was angered to see his two servants well nigh slain, and he sought to seize the cave. And then Gwyn and Gwythyr told him, "It is neither seemly nor pleasant for us to see thee scuffing with a hag. Send Long Amren and Long Eiddil into the cave." And they went. But if ill was the plight of the first two, the plight of those two was worse, so that God knows not one of the whole four could have stirred from the place, but for the way they were all four loaded on Llamrei, Arthur's mare. And then Arthur seized the entrance to the cave. and from the entrance he took aim at the hag with Carnwennan his knife, and struck her across the middle until she was as two tubs. And Cadw of Prydein took the witch's blood and kept it with him.

This is a very untypical Arthurian story, and may well be a reference to earlier Iron Age burial practices in which the parts of the deceased such as the head and long bones were removed for burial in a storage pit or ditch.

All the tasks that involve Arthur are somehow linked to the Otherworld: Mabon is a god imprisoned in an otherworldly dungeon; Gwyn son of Nudd is expressly linked to the underworld when Ysbaddaden says that "God has placed [him] over the brood of devils in Annwn, lest they should destroy the present race"; Twrch Trwyth is a king transformed into a boar for his sins; and the Very Black Witch lives in the uplands of Hell.

Arthur, King of Britain

Culhwch and Olwen implies that Arthur is king of Britain, and this is also implied in the *Welsh Triads*, which were compiled in the 13th century and preserve fragments of Welsh folklore, mythology and traditional history in groups of three. According to Triad 1,[7] "The Tribal Thrones of the Island of Britain," Arthur is Chief Prince throughout Britain:

> Arthur as Chief Prince in Mynyw (= St. David's), and Dewi as Chief Bishop, and Maelgwn Gwynedd as Chief Elder;
> Arthur as Chief Prince in Celliwig in Cornwall, and Bishop Bytwini as Chief Bishop, and Caradawg Strong-Arm as Chief Elder;
> Arthur as Chief Prince in Pen Rhionydd in the North, and Gerthmwl Wledig as Chief Elder, and Cyndeyrn Garthwys as Chief Bishop.

The cathedral at St. David's, Pembrokeshire, April 19, 2006 (Chrisrivers).

St. David's in Pembrokeshire, west Wales, is the final resting place of St. David, the patron saint of Wales; Dewi is the Welsh form of David; and Maelgwn is a 6th century king of Gwynedd in north Wales mentioned in Gildas's long sermon *On the Ruin and Conquest of Britain*. Celliwig is Arthur's court in Cornwall; Bishop Bytwini is unknown, though *Culhwch and Olwen* mentions "Bedwini the Bishop (who blessed Arthur's meat and drink)"; Caradawg Strong-Arm, or Caradoc Freichfras in Welsh, was a semi-legendary ancestor of the kings of Gwent, who may have become confused with the Caratacus who resisted the Roman invasion between AD 43 and 51. Gerthmwl Wledig is unknown, though the title *Wledig* ("Land-Holder") implies he was an early leader of some importance; Cyndeyrn Garthwys is St. Kentigern, the late 6th century apostle of the kingdom of Strathclyde; Rachel Bromwich, who translated the *Welsh Triads* believes that *Pen Rhionydd* refers to the Rhinns of Galloway[8] (the Rhinns of Galloway in the west of Dumfries and Galloway, southwest Scotland, is a hammerhead peninsula which includes the town of Stranraer and the village of Portpatrick).

Pen Rhionydd has been linked to *Rerigonium* ("Very Royal Place"), a Roman fort mentioned by Ptolemy in the 2nd century. The fort has never been located, but there is general agreement that it was close to Loch Ryan, perhaps in the vicinity of Innermessan farm,[9] which is not far from Stranraer. We can say nothing about Innermessan in the Roman period or the Dark Ages, but it may well have been a significant place, for in the 12th century King David I of Scotland (1124–1153) granted land to an unknown Anglo-Norman lord who built a motte and a wooden castle there. This mound is still 42 feet high with a summit diameter of over 95 ft. A town developed around the castle, and reached its peak in the 1400s and 1500s, when Innermessan was the largest town in the Rhinns district, with many stone-built houses, some with slate roofs. By 1684 it was being described as a little hamlet or village, and today nothing remains of Innermessan but the motte.[10]

To the south of Loch Ryan is Kirkmadrine church in the parish of Stoneykirk. The present Kirkmadrine church was built in the 1800s, but three of the oldest Christian memorials surviving in Scotland have been found in or around the churchyard. The three memorials (known as Kirkmadrine 1, 2 and 3) may date from the mid-to-late 6th century AD. They have incised Latin inscriptions, and bear Greek *chi-rho* crosses (so called because of the first two letters in the Greek spelling of Christ). They commemorate priests or bishops. Kirkmadrine 1 reads: HIC IACENT S(AN)C(T)I ET PRAECIPUI SACER DOTES IDES VIVENTIUS ET MAVORIUS ("Here lie the holy and distinguished priests/bishops, namely Viventius and Mavorius"). Kirkmadrine 2 commemorates someone called Florentius. Kirkmadrine 3 has an allusion to a passage from the Book of Revelation: "The beginning and the end." It may not have been a burial marker and may, instead, have been located in an appropriate liturgical context at the church.[11] There was almost certainly a very early monastery at Kirkmadrine, underlining the importance of the Rhinns of Galloway in the Dark Ages.

Arthur in Geoffrey of Monmouth's *History of the Kings of Britain*

Arthur remained a figure of Welsh mythology until 1136, when the Norman cleric Geoffrey of Monmouth published his Latin *History of the Kings of Britain*, and turned

Arthur into a European celebrity fighting against the invading Saxons. Although Geoffrey treats Arthur as a historical figure, he does draw on two elements that are part of the mythological Arthur. The first of these is the figure of Uther Pendragon. Uther is mentioned in passing in *Pa gur?* when Arthur identifies one of his companions as "Mabon son of Modron,/Uther Pendragon's man." He is also the subject of a poem, *The Deathsong of Uther Pendragon*—in the poem the deceased Uther claims that his "champion's feats partook in a ninth part of Arthur's valour."[12]

Geoffrey tells an intriguing story of how Uther got his name *Pendragon*. According to Geoffrey, the British king Aurelius Ambrosius (Geoffrey's version of Gildas's Ambrosius Aurelianus) was ill and a Saxon called Eopa, disguised as a monk, gave the king a medicine that was actually a poison. As Aurelius lay dying, says Geoffrey[13]:

> there appeared a star of wonderful magnitude and brightness, darting forth a ray, at the end of which was a globe of fire in form of a dragon, out of whose mouth issued forth two rays; one of which seemed to stretch out itself beyond the extent of Gaul, the other towards the Irish Sea, and ended in seven lesser rays.

Troubled by the star, Uther ordered his magician Merlin to be called, and Merlin explained the star in these terms[14]:

> the star, and the fiery dragon under it, signifies yourself, and the ray extending towards the Gallic coast portends that you shall have a most potent son, to whose power all those kingdoms shall be subject over which the ray reaches. But the other ray signifies a daughter, whose sons and grandsons shall successively enjoy the kingdom of Britain.

When Uther became king, he remembered Merlin's explanation of the star and

> commanded two dragons to be made of gold, in likeness of the dragon which he had seen at the ray of the star. As soon as they were finished, which was done with a wonderful nicety of worskmanship, he made a present of one the cathedral church of Winchester, but reserved the other for himself, to be carried along with him to his wars. From this time, therefore, he was called Uther Pendragon, which in the British tongue signifies the dragon's head; the occasion of this appellation being Merlin's predicting, from the appearance of a dragon, that he should be king.

Geoffrey's explanation of the meaning of Pendragon is not correct—it actually means "Chief Dragon"—but it does not detract from what is a great story. But is it only a story? Edward Gibbon, in *The History of the Decline and Fall of the Roman Empire*, records[15] that in the fifth year of the reign of the Eastern Roman Emperor Justinian (AD 527–565), in the month of September

> a comet was seen during twenty days in the western quarter of the heavens, and which shot its rays into the north (AD 531). Eight years afterwards (AD 539), while the sun was in Capricorn, another comet appeared to follow in the sagittary; the size was gradually increasing; the head was in the east, the tail in the west, and it remained visible above forty days. The nations, who gazed with astonishment, expected wars and calamities from their baleful influence; and these expectations were abundantly fulfilled.

Abundantly fulfilled because in AD 542 an outbreak of plague reached Constantinople from Egypt—the so-called Plague of Justinian, which may have killed up to a 100 million people across the world, and reduced the population of the eastern Mediterranean by a quarter.

Comets have of course long been associated with important events, and it may be that Geoffrey is simply drawing on a familiar literary device to signal the future greatness

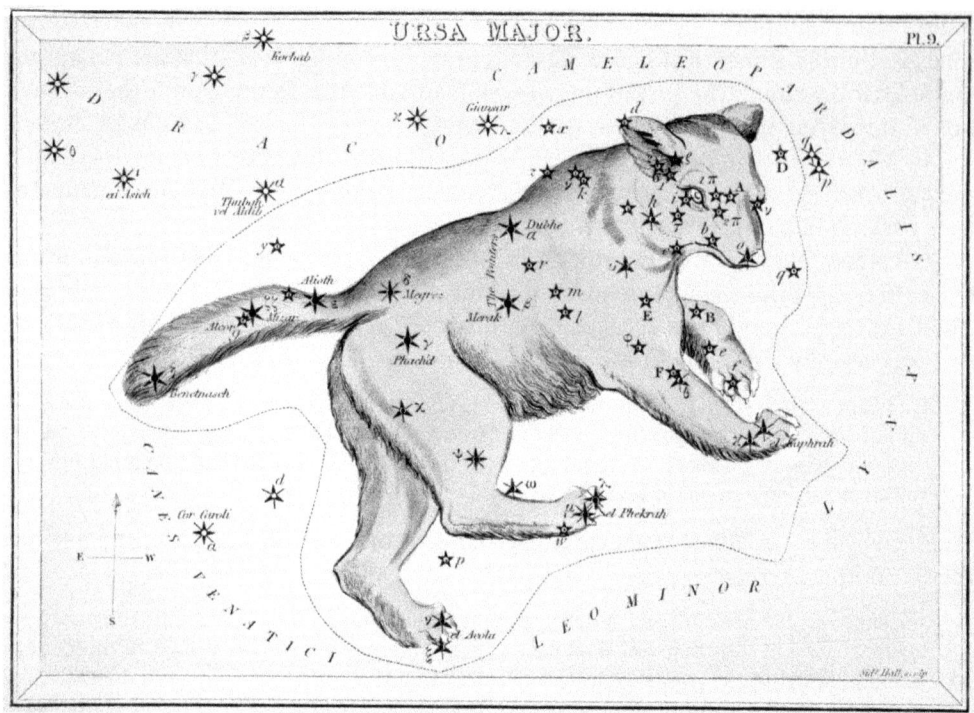

Ursa Major: plate 9 in *Urania's Mirror* by Sidney Hall (1825) (Library of Congress, restoration by Adam Cuerden).

of Arthur. But it is equally possible that there was already an astronomical dimension to the story of Arthur, especially if Arthur is derived from Arcturus. Thomas Green speculates in *Concepts of Arthur* that the "seven lesser rays" of the dragon-star may originally have signified the seven stars of the Plough (Ursa Major, the Great Bear), which is known in British folklore as Arthur's Wain.[16]

After the death of Aurelius Ambrosius, Uther became king and subsequently won a great victory over the Saxons. He then held a celebration in London, attended by, among others, Gorlois duke of Cornwall and his wife Igerna, the greatest beauty in all Britain. Uther, in *The Death-song of Uther Pendragon*, says that "he is the one called *gorlassar*, possibly connected with Geoffrey's Duke Gorlois"; *gorlassar* is derived from Welsh *gorlas* "bright blue,"[17] and would be an appropriate name for a celestial figure. As soon as Uther saw Igerna, he "fell passionately in love with her." She was "the only lady that he continually served with fresh dishes, and to whom he sent golden cups by his confidants; on her he bestowed all his smiles, and to her he addressed all his discourse."[18] Gorlois noticed this and "fell into a great rage, and retired from the court without taking leave." Incensed by this, Uther ordered him to return to court, but Gorlois refused, whereupon Uther marched into Cornwall and set fire to the main cities and towns. Gorlois then put Igerna in the town of Tintagel, which "he looked upon as a place of great safety" (Tintagel was a high-status place in the 5th and 6th century, probably the capital of the kingdom of Dumnonia, which at the time included Devon and Cornwall).

After Gorlois had put Igerna in Tintagel, he himself went to his castle at *Dimilioc*, possibly Domellick farm near St. Dennis, 5 miles northwest of St. Austell. The parish church at St. Dennis stands on a hill, and a single trench cut in 1962 revealed the bank of an outer rampart but no ditch or finds to provide dating evidence[19]; perhaps this was Gorlois' "castle at *Dimilioc*." Uther then sent for Merlin who, with the help of his "medicines," transformed Uther into the exact likeness of Gorlois (shades of Pwyll in the First Branch when he assumed the form of Arawn chief of Annwn!). Uther then proceeded to Tintagel in the guise of Gorlois, was admitted without any problems, and "stayed the night with Igerna and had the full enjoyment of her, for she was deceived with the false disguise which he had put on, and the artful and amorous discourses wherewith he entertained her." That same night Igerna "conceived of the most renowned Arthur."

The second mythological element that Geoffrey draws on is Guinevere, whom he calls Guanhumara. Guinevere is mentioned in *Culhwch and Olwen* as "Gwenhwyvar Chief of Queens," and also appears in the *Welsh Triads*, Triad 56, "Arthur's Three Great Queens"[20]:

> Gwenhwyfar daughter of (Cywryd) Gwent, and Gwenhwyfar daughter of (Gwythyr) son of Greidiawl, and Gwenhwyfar daughter of (G)ogfran the Giant.

Gwenhwyfar appears to be a triple goddess, reminiscent of the Matres or Matronae ("Mothers" or "Matrons"), who always appear in groups of three, and were venerated in eastern Gaul and Germany. The identity of Cywryd is uncertain, but Gwythyr son of Greidawl was the character in *Culhwch and Olwen* who must fight Gwyn son of Nudd every May Day for the maiden Creiddylad; and (G)ogfran the Giant may derive from the Irish Gabruan, the mother of Findabair, who is the Irish equivalent of Gwenhwyfar.[21]

In the *History of the Kings of Britain*, the story of Guinevere begins when Arthur marries Guanhumara, "descended from a noble family of Romans, who was educated under duke Cador, and in beauty surpassed all the women of the island." Guinevere plays no part in the story until Arthur receives a letter from the (fictional) Roman general Lucius Tiberius, demanding that he pay tribute to Rome. Arthur consulted his advisers, and it was agreed they should go to war with Rome. Before setting out for Rome, he entrusted the government of the kingdom to his nephew Modred (Mordred). Geoffrey has borrowed this name from earlier Welsh tradition—Modred appears in the *Annales Cambriae* ("Annals of Wales"), which probably date from the mid 10th century, in this entry for 537 or 539: "The Battle of Camlann, in which Arthur and Medraut fell."[22] The Arthurian scholar Caitlin R. Green says: "Geoffrey's form of the name, *Mordredus*, was derived from a Cornish or Breton source and the name is known from Cornish *Domesday* returns and the Bodmin manumissions of AD 960–1000."[23] Green is presumably referring to Tre-Modret (Tremodrett) near Roche in Cornwall, and Carveddras (Carvedras) near Truro in Cornwall, which is derived from *Kaervodred* "Fortress of Modred."

Arthur set off for France, and defeated Lucius in a battle in a valley called Suesia, perhaps the valley of the Suize, not far from Langres in the Champagne-Ardennes region of France. Arthur was on his way to Rome and beginning to pass the Alps, when he received news that "his nephew Modred, to whose care he had entrusted Britain, had by tyrannical and treasonable practices set the crown upon his own head; and that queen Guanhumara, in violation of her first marriage, had wickedly married him."[24]

Geoffrey did not invent this particular story, in the sense that there was a tradition involving Gwenhwyfar and another man. In the *Dialogue of Melwas and Gwenhwyfar*, which dates from the early to mid 12th century, Guinevere is talking first[25]:

> "Who is the man who sits in the common part of the feast,
> without for him either its beginning or end,
> sitting down there below the dais?"
>
> "The Melwas from Ynys Wydrin (Isle of Glass);
> you, with the golden, gilded vessels,
> I have drunk none of your wine."
>
> "Wait a little...
> I do not pour out my wine
> for a man who cannot hold out and would not stand in battle
> [and] would not stand up to Cai in his wine."

In the following verses "Gwenhwyfar continues to taunt Melwas, while he proclaims his valor versus that of Cai. In the poem

> there is a reference to Gwenhwyfar and Melwas having met at a court in *Dyfneint*, "Devon," but the nature of this meeting isn't clear. The background to this poem is a pre-Galfridian Welsh story concerned with the rescue of Gwenhwyfar ("white fairy/enchantress") by Arthur from an Otherworld Island of Glass controlled by Melwas ("honey youth")—who appears in other works as a magician who was a "thief that by magic and enchantment took a girl [presumably Gwenhwyfar] to the end of the world."

The story of Arthur's rescue of Guinevere is told in Caradoc of Llancarfan's *Life of Gildas*, which dates from the 1120s or 1130s. In this story, the saint went to *Glastonia* "at the time when king Melwas was reigning in the summer country." Caradoc goes on to say[26]:

> Glastonia, that is, the glassy city, which took its name from glass, is a city that had its name originally in the British tongue. It was besieged by the tyrant Arthur with a countless multitude on account of his wife Gwenhwyfar, whom the aforesaid wicked king had violated and carried off, and brought there for protection, owing to the asylum afforded by the invulnerable position due to the fortifications of thickets of reed, river, and marsh. The rebellious king had searched for the queen throughout the course of one year, and at last heard that she remained there. When he saw this, the abbot of Glastonia, attended by the clergy and Gildas the Wise, stepped in between the contending armies, and in a peaceable manner advised his king, Melvas, to restore the ravished lady. Accordingly, she who was to be restored, was restored in peace and good will.

After learning of Modred's treachery, Arthur returned to Britain and pursued Modred to the river Cambula in Cornwall (possibly the River Camel), and in the battle that followed, Modred was killed and Arthur was mortally wounded. He was then taken to the island of Avalon to be cured of his wounds, and gave up his crown to his kinsman Constantine, son of Cador duke of Cornwall.

Geoffrey does not describe Avalon is his *History*, but he does in a subsequent work, the *Life of Merlin*[27]:

> The island of apples which men call "The Fortunate Isle" gets its name from the fact that it produces all things of itself; the fields there have no need of the ploughs of the farmers and all cultivation is lacking except what nature provides. Of its own accord it produces grain and grapes, and apple trees grow in its woods from the close-clipped grass. The ground of its own accord produces everything instead of merely grass, and people live there a hundred years or more. There nine sisters rule by a pleasing set of laws those who come to them from our country. She who is first of them is more skilled in the healing art, and excels her sisters in the beauty of her person. Morgen is her name, and she has learned what useful properties all the herbs contain, so that she can cure sick bodies. She also

knows an art by which to change her shape, and to cleave the air on new wings like Daedalus [...] Thither after the battle of Camlan we took the wounded Arthur.

The "nine sisters" sound like the nine priestesses on the isle of Sena and the nine maidens who kindled the cauldron in *The Spoils of Annwn*. Avalon and the island of apples may be inspired by *Emain Ablach*, "Emain of the Apples," a name applied to the Isle of Man in its role as the blessed and otherwordly domain of the Irish sea-god Manannan mac Lir.

Arthur and the Saints

Arthur is portrayed in several saints' lives other than the *Life of Gildas*, always in an unfavorable light. In the *Life of St. Carantoc*, written around AD 1100,[28] Arthur cannot subdue a dragon without the help of the saint. In this passage, Carantoc has just returned from Ireland[29]:

> And afterwards he came again to his own country, Ceredigion, to his cave, with many clergymen, and there performed many miracles.... And Christ gave him an honourable altar from on high, the colour of which no person could comprehend; and afterwards when he came to the Severn to sail over it, he cast the altar into the sea, and it went before him where God wished him to go. In those times, Cato and Arthur lived in that country, dwelling in Dindrarthou.

At the time a terrible dragon was laying waste the countryside, and Arthur was trying to catch this dragon. When Carantoc arrived, he asked Arthur if he knew where his altar had landed, and Arthur replied: "If I shall be paid for it, I will tell thee," and asked the saint to catch the dragon for him. Carantoc prayed, and the dragon "came with a great noise, running as a calf to its dam." He then brought the dragon to Cato in his castle in *Carrum*, where people tried to kill the dragon—but the saint set the dragon free, "which injured none as God had commanded." By now Carantoc had recovered his altar—"Arthur intended to make it a table, but whatsoever was put thereon, was thrown off to some distance. And the king requested that he would receive Carrum for ever by a written deed, and afterwards he built there a church." *Carrum* is thought to be Carhampton in west Somerset, site of an early Christian settlement and cemetery, and a church dedicated to St. Carantoc: this was recorded in the Norman period and may have survived into the 16th century.[30]

In another saint's life, Arthur is shown as arrogant and petty-minded. According to the 11th century *Life* of St. Cadoc, who is associated with Llancarfan in the Vale of Glamorgan, south Wales, Ligessawc son of Eliman had killed three of Arthur's soldiers, and Arthur was demanding compensation, A council of judges and priests met and decided that 100 cows should be given to Arthur for every soldier killed. The *Life* continues: "This being accepted, Arthur, in an insolent manner, refused cows of one colour, but would have those of two colours, viz:—with the fore part red, and the hind part white, and required those so distinguished by colour, with much wrangling." Cadoc then ordered the young men of the company to bring him the requisite number of heifers of any color, and the saint changed them into the colors Arthur desired.[31]

The most negative portrait of Arthur is found in the early 12th century *Life* of St. Padarn, a saint associated with Llanbadarn Fawr on the outskirts of Aberystwyth in west Wales. In this episode,[32] Padarn is resting in a church when a certain tyrant whose name was Arthur ... came on a certain day to the cell of St. Padarn the bishop; and while he spoke to Padarn, he looked at his coat, and being seized with the affection of avarice, asked if he could have it; and the Saint answering, said, "This coat is not suitable for the wearing of any malicious person, but for a clerical habit." He went out of the Monastery in a rage, and again returned in a state of anger that he might take away the coat against the wishes of the attendant saints. One of the disciples of Padarn seeing him returning in a rage, ran to St. Padarn, and said, "The tyrant who was here before is returning in an insulting manner, and treading the ground levels it with his feet." Padarn answered, "Yes, may the earth swallow him." With the word, the earth opened its bosom to some depth, and swallowed Arthur as far as his chin, who immediately acknowledged himself guilty, and he began to praise both God and Padarn; until by asking pardon, the earth delivered him up.

Arthur's punishment here suggests that he may have originally been an underworld deity.

The Once and Future King

At the end of *The History of the Kings of Britain*, Arthur was taken to the island of Avalon to be cured of his wounds. Geoffrey does not say whether Arthur died of these wounds, but in 1191 the supposed tomb of Arthur and Guinevere was discovered at Glas-

Arthur's Tomb at Glastonbury Abbey, summer 1984 (Tom Ordelman).

tonbury close to the Old Church, which had been destroyed by fire several years earlier. This discovery was witnessed by the Norman-Welsh priest and historian Gerald of Wales, who writes in his work *On the Instruction of Princes*[33]:

> Although legends had fabricated something fantastical about his demise (that he had not suffered death, and was conveyed, as if by a spirit, to a distant place), his body was discovered at Glastonbury, in our own times, hidden very deep in the earth in an oak-hollow, between two stone pyramids that were erected long ago in that holy place. The tomb was sealed up with astonishing tokens, like some sort of miracle. The body was then conveyed into the church with honor, and properly committed to a marble tomb. A lead cross was placed under the stone, not above as is usual in our times, but instead fastened to the underside. I have seen this cross, and have traced the engraved letters—not visible and facing outward, but rather turned inwardly toward the stone. It read: "Here lies entombed King Arthur, with Guenevere his second wife, on the Isle of Avalon."

The legends that Gerald refers to are touched on in the *Chronicle of the Kings of England*, a work by the Anglo-Norman priest and historian, William of Malmesbury, first published in 1125[34]:

> At that time, in a province of Wales, called Ros, was found the sepulchre of Walwin, the noble nephew of Arthur; he reigned, a most renowned knight, in that part of Britain which is still named Walwerth; but was driven from his kingdom by the brother and nephew of Hengist…, though not without first making them pay dearly for his expulsion. He deservedly shared, with his uncle, the praise of retarding, for many years, the calamity of his falling country. The sepulchre of Arthur is nowhere to be seen, whence ancient ballads fable that he is still to come. But the tomb of the other, as I have suggested, was found in the time of King William, on the sea-coast, fourteen feet long.

William is here referring to Arthur's nephew Gawain, who is said to be buried at Walwyn's Castle in the cantref (hundred) of Rhos in Pembrokeshire, southwest Wales. The key phrase here is that "he is still to come," which is contradicted by Gerald of Wales' later assertion that he saw the tomb of Arthur and Guinevere at Glastonbury.

Not surprisingly, it was William of Malmesbury's version of Arthur that survived into the Middle Ages. Sir Thomas Malory, in *Le Morte d'Arthur*, first published in 1485, says (Book 21, Chapter 7)[35]:

> Yet some men say in many parts of England that King Arthur is not dead, but had by the will of our Lord Jesu into another place; and men say that he shall come again, and he shall win the holy cross. I will not say it shall be so, but rather I will say: here in this world he changed his life. But many men say that there is written upon his tomb this verse: *Hic iacet Arthurus, Rex quondam, Rexque futurus.*

Hic iacet Arthurus, rex quondam, rexque futurus is in English "Here lies Arthur, king once, and king to be," which of course provided T.H. White with the title of his Arthurian fantasy novel *The Once and Future King*.

William of Malmesbury was not the first to report such beliefs about Arthur. In 1112 the city of Laon in northeastern France was burnt in a popular insurrection against the bishop. The clerks of the cathedral set out on a pilgrimage with the shrine of the Blessed Virgin to collect money for rebuilding. In the following year they crossed the Channel, and visited Canterbury and many other places in the south of England. According to Herman of Tournai, in his *Miracles of St. Mary of Laon*, on their way from Exeter in Devon to Bodmin in Cornwall, they were shown the Seat and Oven of King Arthur[36]; and at Bodmin a man with a withered hand, who was hoping to be cured by the shrine began to contend with one of our attendants named Haganel…, saying that Arthur was still alive. Whence no small tumult arose, many rushed into the church with arms, and unless the aforesaid clerk Algardus had intervened the matter would have almost come to the shedding of blood.

The Oven of King Arthur is probably the King's Oven, an ancient tin smelting furnace used as a marker in the bounds of the royal forest of Dartmoor in 1240.[37] This is not the only early Arthurian place-name: Lambert of Saint-Omer, in his *Liber Floridus* of 1120 refers to an "Arthur's Palace" in Pictland (Scotland), thought to be an old Roman temple at Stenhousemuir near Falkirk now known as Arthur's O'on (Oven), which was demolished in 1743.

Perhaps the earliest work to imply that Arthur was still alive was a Welsh work called the *Stanzas of the Graves*, which may date to the 9th century. According to stanza 44[38]:

> [There is] a grave for March, a grave for Gwythur,
> a grave for Gwgawn Red-sword;
> the world's wonder (*anoeth*) [is] a grave for Arthur.

The Arthurian scholar Thomas Green notes: "The poet's implication is that the graves of these Arthurian heroes are known but that of Arthur himself is *anoeth*, impossible to find/achieve, probably because he was rumoured not to be dead."

This is perhaps the key to Arthur—he was originally a god connected with rebirth or reincarnation, dwelling on a sacred island, perhaps associated with the sun, the moon or another heavenly body, who, like the Greek god Cronus, once presided over a mythological golden age.

The End of the Welsh Arthur

Geoffrey of Monmouth's *History of the Kings of Britain* virtually signaled the end of Arthur as a Welsh hero, and ushered in the great French Arthurian romances of the 12th and 13th century. The Age of Arthur had ended in Britain, and it was not until the end of the 15th century that Arthur was to return to Britain in Thomas Malory's *Le Morte d'Arthur*, this time not in Welsh or Latin, but in English.

CHAPTER 10

Arthur and the Early Medieval World: Holy Islands and the Arthurian Cycle in Cornwall

The Evolution of Arthur in Early Medieval Britain

So what do we know about Arthur. The name is probably related to Irish *art*, Welsh *arth* "bear," and *Art-* or *Arth-* names were popular in Scotland in the 6th and 7th centuries, but also known in Wales and Cornwall. There is no record of bears in southern Britain after the Late Neolithic; but they certainly survived in western Scotland until the Bronze Age, and in northern Scotland until the Iron Age; and in parts of North Yorkshire until the 5th or 6th century AD. Late Iron Age bearskin burials have been found in Baldock and Welwyn Garden City (Hertfordshire), but this type of burial was a Germanic custom, so the bearskins may have been imported. In the 1st century AD, Germanic soldiers in the Roman army wore bearskins, and other Roman soldiers wore bear-hoods.

By the 4th century there were Germanic soldiers serving in Roman Britain, as indicated by late 4th century metal buckles from leather belts with distinctive Germanic designs. Buckles of this kind have been found at Richborough Roman fort near Sandwich in Kent, where a full burial of a German soldier has been discovered; at the Roman fort of Bradwell-on-Sea in Essex; and also in several of the Roman towns, including London, Leicester and Winchester.[1] The Roman authorities may also have recruited Germanic warriors, not organized in regular military units, to reinforce the defenses of some Romano-British settlements. Roman pottery decorated to suit Germanic taste has been found at Caister Roman fort near Yarmouth in Norfolk, and at Colchester in Essex, Richborough, Aldborough in North Yorkshire, York, Ancaster in Lincolnshire, Brancaster in Norfolk and Leicester. It is perfectly possible that the Germanic soldiers brought with them versions of the Bear's Son tale that informed the Icelandic *Saga of King Hrolf Kaki* with Bodvar Bjarki ("Battle Bear"), and the Old English epic poem *Beowulf*.

Initially, at least, Arthur was linked to the Midlands and northern England. In Powys, near the border with Herefordshire we have *Carn Caball*, or "horse's hoof," said to be the burial place of Arthur's dog *Cavall* ("Horse"). We have one of Arthur's battles at Baschurch in Shropshire, possibly linked to The Berth, which is more a "marsh-fort"— like Sutton Common in South Yorkshire—than a hillfort. Two of Arthur's battles are in Northumberland, one in County Durham, and four are in Lincolnshire. Interestingly, it is in Lincolnshire that silver rings dedicated to TOT (Mars Toutatis) have been found— for example, at Scopwick, 6 miles south of Lincoln, at Horncastle, between Lincoln

Richborough Roman fort near sandwich in Kent, October 6, 2008 (Midnightblueowl).

and the coastal town of Skegness, and at Kirton in Lindsey, between Lincoln and the Humber, all within the territory of Lincoln (Lindsey) where the battles were supposedly fought.

In one of the earliest Arthurian works, *The Spoils of Annwn*, Arthur is linked to the Welsh Otherworld, which is apparently an island since Arthur and his men travel there in Arthur's ship *Prydwen* ("Fair Form"). Annwn contains a Mound Fortress (perhaps a Neolithic or Bronze Age burial mound), a Four-Peaked Fortress, "isle of the strong door," and a "brindled ox" with a special collar. Arthur is indirectly linked to Pwyll and Pryderi, husband and son of the horse-goddess Rhiannon. Arthur is also linked fairly directly to Bran in the Second Branch, whose decapitated head leads the survivors of the battle with the Irish to an otherwordly island, Gwales (possibly Grassholm of the coast of Pembrokeshire, southwest Wales). *Bran* means "Raven," and later legends record that Arthur was transformed into a crow or raven. A Spanish chronicle of 1582 asserts that it was "common talk" that Arthur "had been enchanted to the form of a crow and that many penalties were inflicted on anyone who killed one of these birds." This theme is taken up in the Spanish novel *Don Quixote* (1605–1615)[2]:

> "Have you not read, sir," answered Don Quixote, "the annals and histories of England, wherein are recorded the famous exploits of King Arthur…; of whom there goes an old tradition, and a common, all over the kingdom of Great Britain, that this king did not die, but that, by magic art, he was turned into a raven; and that, in process of time, he shall reign again and recover his kingdom and sceptre, for which reason it cannot be proved that, from that time to this, any Englishman has killed a raven?"

In a later work, *Culhwch and Olwen* (11th century), Arthur's sphere of influence widened. Arthur helps rescue Mabon son of Modron (Maponos son of the River Marne) from his dungeon in Gloucester (though Maponos is usually associated with northern England). In this tale, Cornwall enters the Arthurian story for the first time: the hunt for the boar Twrch Trwyth takes place in Ireland, Wales, along the River Severn, and in Cornwall; and Arthur's court is identified as Celliwig in Cornwall (*Celliwig* = "settlement in the wood").

In Geoffrey of Monmouth's *History of the Kings of Britain*, written in the 12th century after the Norman Conquest, Arthur's father is Uther (from Welsh *uthr* "fearful, dreadful, awful, terrible"), who is associated with a "star of wonderful magnitude" in the form of a dragon, possibly a comet, or possibly the constellation Ursa Major (the Great Bear). Cornwall plays a considerable part in Geoffrey's story: Arthur is conceived at Tintagel in Cornwall, and Modred, who seizes the throne and marries Guinevere, may have Cornish origins. At this point other regions also became associated with Arthur: for example, Guinevere is abducted by Melwas and taken to the Isle of Glass, identified as Glastonbury in Caradoc of Llancarfan's *Life of Gildas*. Most significantly, after Arthur is wounded, he is taken to the island of Avalon, which can be compared to *Emain Ablach*, "Emain of the Apples," a name applied to the Isle of Man in its role as the blessed and otherwordly domain of the Irish sea-god Manannan mac Lir.

William of Malmesbury says in his *Chronicle of the Kings of England* that the "sepulchre of Arthur is nowhere to be seen, whence ancient ballads fable that he is still to come." In the *Miracles of St. Mary of Laon*, at Bodmin in Corwall a man with a withered hand "began to contend with one of our attendants named Haganel…, saying that Arthur was still alive."

Who Was Arthur?

The obvious conclusion is that Arthur was bear-warrior brought to Britain by Germanic troops in the Roman army some time between the 1st and 4th centuries AD. The concept of a bear warrior may have appealed to prehistoric Scots, since bears still roamed the wilds of Iron Age Scotland, and to those living in the north of England where bears survived until the 5th or 6th century. However, bears may have had less appeal in southern Britain, and the bear warrior Arthur may have replaced an earlier figure associated with cattle (in the Neolithic and Early Bronze Age), horses (in the Late Bronze Age and Iron Age), and ravens (in the Iron Age and Roman period).

Arthur is associated with horses at Carn Cabal, which is actually a mountain near Builth Wells called Carn Gafallt, where four Middle Bronze Age gold torcs were found hidden under a small heap of stones. He is also associated indirectly with horses in *The Spoils of Annwn*, in the sense that Annwn is linked to Pwyll and Pryderi, husband and son of the horse-goddess Rhiannon. Horses were venerated in Britain throughout the Iron Age and Roman period, from Dorset in the south and west of England to North Yorkshire in northern England, and were perhaps associated with the sun and rebirth. Here we shouldn't discount the possible influence of the Thracian Horseman. We know that Thracian troops were stationed in Britain: a military diploma found at Malpas near Cheshire, issued during the reign of the Emperor Trajan (AD 98–117) mentions Thracian units[3]; a 1st century tombstone from Cirencester mentions a Frisian called Sextus Valerius Genialis who served in a Thracian unit[4]; and a 1st century tombstone from Colchester mentions a Longinus Sdapeze, an officer of the 1st squadron of the Thracian cavalry unit.[5]

Arthur is associated with a brindled ox in *The Spoils of Annwn*, and with cows in the *Life* of St. Cadoc. Cattle were venerated for at least 4000 years from the Neolithic to the late Roman period, and there is ample evidence for a horned god in the Roman period. Horned bulls have been found at St. Kew in northeast Cornwall, at Shepton Mallet in Somerset, at Wolverley in north Worcestershire, at Whitchurch in Shropshire, in the west of Cheshire, and at Welshpool in Powys, east Wales. Representations of a horned god have been found in the north of England, at Netherby Roman fort in Cumbria, Carvoran Roman fort near Hexham, Chesters Roman fort near Hexham, Lanchester Roman fort in County Durham, Alnwick Castle in Northumberland, and at Moresby and Maryport Roman forts in Cumbria.

Then again, Arthur may simply have been a tribal protector like Toutatis or Mars Toutatis, known from Hertfordshire, Leicestershire, Lincolnshire and Cumbria—a fair chunk of central and northern England—and perhaps venerated throughout Britain.

However, the most likely explanation of Arthur is that he was a god connected with water, which played such an important role in British religion from the Late Bronze Age to the Roman period, with deposition in rivers, lakes, fens, marshes and (in the Roman period) wells, and coastal promontory forts facing the sea in Cornwall, southwest Wales and Ireland. This would link Arthur to Cronus, confined on an island off the coast of Britain in the 1st century AD in Plutarch's *The Obsolescence of Oracles*—and perhaps comparable to Julius Caesar's Dis Pater, ancestor of the Gauls.

From the earliest times (*The Spoils of Annwn*) Arthur had a ship called Prydwen in which he sailed to the Otherword, and he was associated with the "isle of the strong door"; in later writings (*History of the Kings of Britain*), he was taken to the island of Avalon to be cured of his wounds. His role in *The Spoils of Annwn* is similar to that of the raven Bran, who ended up on Gwales with his seven companions, and can be compared to the Irish war goddess Badb who takes the form of a crow.

If Arthur was a god, did he date from the Iron Age, or from an earlier period? Arthur was never a well-defined figure, so he is unlikely to have been a Late Iron Age god. There are hints that Arthur may originally have been considered a giant: he is a "mighty fortress" in the *Marwnat Cynddylan*, and his son Amr has a grave which varies in size but is sometimes suitable for a giant. What's more, Bran the Blessed, who shares some of the characteristics of Arthur in *The Spoils of Annwn*, is a giant who can walk across the Irish Sea from Wales to Ireland. Judging from the giant Ysbaddaden's stone-spears, giants are associated with the Neolithic and the Age of Megaliths, so Arthur may be a very ancient god.

Holy Islands in Early Medieval Britain

Wales

Islands were always part of the story of Arthur, and they also played an important role in early medieval religious life. In the early Christian period, a number of monasteries were founded on islands that may well have been sacred in pagan times. For example, Caldey Island is off the coast of Pembrokeshire in southwest Wales, some 2.5 miles from Tenby, and a priory was founded there in 1113 as a daughter house of the Tironensian St. Dogmael's Abbey. In the sanctuary of the old priory church there is a 5th or 6th century inscribed stone, 5 feet 7 inches tall, known as The Caldey Stone (ogham is an early Irish

Caldey Island Priory, Pembrokeshire, April 30, 2009 (JohnArmagh).

form of writing). At the top right and left edges are incomplete notched inscriptions in memory of MAGLIA DUBRACUNAS—"[The stone] of Maglia–Dubracunas, son of ..." Dubracunas was associated with St. Illtud and St. Samson, and is said to have consecrated Samson as abbot of Caldey in succession to Piro. The Latin inscription, carved in the 9th century, is on the front face and is taken to be ET SIGNO CRUCIS IN ILLAM FINGSI ROGO OMNIBUS AMMULANTIBUS IBI EXORENT PRO ANIMAE CATUOCONI—"And by the sign of the cross which I have provided upon that stone, I ask all who walk there that they pray for the soul of Catuocunus."[6] Caldey Island is mentioned in the *Life* of Samson, who visited the monastery when it was ruled by a priest called Piro.[7]

It is clear that Caldey was an important place in the prehistoric period, judging from the evidence found in a number of caves on the island. In the cave known as Daylight Rock, excavators found a "prolific assemblage of flint and flaked stone" dating to the Early Mesolithic, as well as the (undated) bones of a child and an adult together with a perforated bead. In Potter's Cave, excavation of the east entrance uncovered Late Bronze Age-Iron Age pottery, Early Bronze Age Beaker pottery and Neolithic pottery in mixed upper layers, whilst some small Mesolithic implements were recovered from the basal layer. Cemented within and beneath stalagmite were flint and human bone. Later excavations of the cave interior recovered the bones of two individuals, many animal bones, four pieces of copper or bronze wire and flat pot sherds without markings, which may be of a Romano-British date. Continued excavations in the west entrance and passageway recovered forty eight blue glass beads of an Iron Age (1st or 2nd century BC) date and two human burials. In Nanna's Cave, excavators found "the imperfect skull of an adult female and various bones

Nanna's Cave, Caldey Island, Pembrokeshire, which, like other caves on the island, was used for human burial (© Crown copyright: Royal Commission on the Ancient and Historical Monuments of Wales; © Hawlfraint y Goron: Comisiun Brerhinol Henebion Cymru).

of two individuals, the whole cemented together by stalagmite." Round bottomed Neolithic bowls were also recovered together with pottery from the Bronze Age and Bronze Age/Iron Age tradition. The Romano-British period was also represented by pottery of the 3rd–4th centuries AD, and two spindle whorls.[8] Excavation of Ogof yr Ychen cave found the remains of three human adults, and a child's bones from a much later date (they were found in Romano-British deposits).[9] Clearly the caves of Caldey Island were inhabited in the Mesolithic, and were regarded as sacred from the Neolithic to the Iron Age and Roman period, particularly suitable for the secondary burial of bones after excarnation.

Holy Island is an island on the western side of Anglesey—from which it is separated by a narrow winding channel—not far from the Iron Age site of Llyn Cerrig Bach. In the 3rd/4th century AD the Romans built a fort on a low cliff overlooking Holyhead harbor. The 6th century Cornish saint Cybi established a monastery in the fort (now called Caer Gybi), which is first mentioned in 1282 as a *clas* (monastic community).[10] Nothing remains of Cybi's monastery (it was attacked by the Vikings in the 10th century), but recently a cemetery of long-cist graves, dating to the 6th–8th century AD, was discovered during the construction of the A55 dual carriageway, to the north-west of Ty Mawr Farm near Holyhead At this site the graves were located around, and cut into, the remains of a Bronze Age barrow.[11]

Scotland

Early Christianity in Scotland is inextricably linked to the Irish monk St. Columba, who founded a monastery on the island of Iona, off the west coast of Scotland, in AD 563. The monastery existed until about the turn of the 8th–9th centuries when the wooden complex was destroyed by Norse raiders. Nothing remains above ground of the original monastery except possibly the vallum, the bank and ditch that enclosed the monastery, and the cell on Tor Abb said to have been used by St. Columba. Excavations have shown that the Columban monastery, which consisted of about a dozen huts and a small church, lay in the vicinity of the early 13th century abbey. A few grave-slabs of the 7th and 8th centuries, generally simple incised or outline crosses, still survive from the early monastery.[12] Columba died in 597, and by 700 he was being venerated as a saint. Recently evidence has been found that the island was inhabited in the Late Bronze Age. National Trust for Scotland archaeologist Derek Alexander spotted a dark band of organic material in a collapsed bank on the side of a burn (stream). It turned out to be a rubbish pit which he suspected dated back to the Bronze or Iron Age. Fragments of limpet and whelk shells, burnt and unburned animal bones and sherds of pottery and a flint and a large cobble stone tool were among the things found. Recent results of radiocarbon testing from the Scottish Universities Environmental Research Centre in East Kilbride has confirmed a 95 percent chance that the midden dates from between 930 and 810 BC.[13]

Recently an early monastic site has been identified on Inchmarnock, a small island off the west coast of Scotland, not far from the Firth of Clyde. Excavations were carried out near the remains of the 12th century chapel of St. Marnock which uncovered a probable earlier stone church and also a much earlier monastic settlement, specifically the detritus associated with a schoolhouse where novices were taught to read and write, as well as compasswork and instruction in elementary design and decoration. A number of inscriptions were found, dating to the 7th and 8th centuries. One of the earliest pieces, recovered from the monastic enclosure ditch, is a rough water-worn slate cobble, possibly a prayer-stone, on which the name Ernan has been written no less than three times. Ernan is the saint's name which is commemorated in the name Marnock, from the Gaelic familiar form of Mo-Ernan. Meanwhile, from the metal-working area near the church came a fragment of an incised slate board datable to around 750. On one side was a curvilinear cross-motif, set beside an ogham alphabet; on the other were two lines of almost identical Latin text, identifiable as a line of octosyllabic Hiberno-Latin verse: *adeptus sanctum praemium* ("having reached the holy reward"). This is a unique survival, a line of verse

St. Martin's Cross, Iona (8th century), July 10, 2014 (NickGibson3900).

from a hymn that formed part of the *Antiphonary of Bangor*, a late-7th century liturgical commonplace book. Another important find was the so-called "Hostage Stone" which appears to depict three armored warriors leading an ecclesiastical figure off to their boat.[14]

Inchmarnock was clearly inhabited in the Bronze Age, judging from a rich burial found there. A cist was discovered in 1960 and found to contain the skeleton of a woman, accompanied by a flint knife and a lignite collar of 135 beads. The cist was re-excavated in 2006, and the excavators confirm that the young woman had been buried wearing a spacer-plate necklace. Analysis of the necklace in advance of restringing by the excavator and colleagues at National Museums Scotland revealed that it was mostly of Whitby jet, and had been put together from parts of at least five necklaces. During the excavation the researchers found four jet fusiform beads, bringing the necklace's total to 139: the largest number of any jet or jet-like spacer plate necklace in Britain.[15] A fragment of bone from the skeleton was radiocarbon dated to 2133–1902 BC, in the Early Bronze Age.[16]

With its high-status Bronze Age burial, Inchmarnock may well have been regarded as a holy island in the Iron Age, the home of a revered ancestor. It may even have been the island where, according to Plutarch, "Cronus" was confined. Demetrius may well have gone to the Clyde: there was a Roman fort at Old Kilpatrick on the Clyde, downstream from Glasgow, which was certainly in existence by the 2nd century but may have been established earlier. According to Barrett's *Calendar of Scottish Saints*, the head of St. Marnock "was frequently borne in procession to obtain fair weather"[17]—a hint perhaps that Marnock took over the functions of an Iron Age god or goddess.

England

Lundy Island lies off the coast of north Devon, and Brychan, king of Brycheiniog (Brecon) in south Wales, is said to have retired to Lundy Island with a number of his followers and founded a monastery there. One of the oldest sites on Lundy is Beacon Hill cemetery, which lies on the highest point of the island and is still occasionally used. As well as the more recent graves there are indications that the site has been used for at least 1500 years. Towards the north are the remains of a 12th or 13th century chapel which has been ruined for many centuries. Further south can be seen the excavated remains of several stone-lined and covered cist burials. Also within the cemetery have been found four early Christian grave markers. Two of the stones, inscribed OPTIMI ("the memorial of Optimus") and RESTEUTA (a Celtic name) date from around AD 500, and "are almost certainly, at this date, for memorials of clerics, priests or members of religious communities who avoid mention of earthly parentage."[18] The third stone, POTITI, "of Potitus," with an encircled cross, is later 6th century. The fourth stone dates to between AD 600 and 650, and is inscribed IGERNI [FIL]I TIGERNI, and probably marks the grave of a prominent layman. The cemetery lay on top of an Iron Age settlement. Excavations uncovered one large circular hut in association with pottery and salt-making debris, thought to date from the 1st century BC to 2nd century AD. It had an entrance on the south-east and a drainage gully with a quern stone left lying on the cover slabs. It measured at least 20 feet in diameter and although by then deserted, it was probably still visible in part when the site was reused by the 5th century for the cemetery. At this time most of the double walling was dismantled, and the largest slabs used to make a rectangular space for a burial.[19] Lundy may well have been regarded as a sacred island—there is a Neolithic chambered

Modern statue of St. Aidan beside the ruins of Lindisfarne Priory, June 20, 2014 (Kim Traynor).

tomb in the south of the island, evidence of Bronze Age settlement in the north of the island, and Bronze Age barrows in the center of the island.

Lindisfarne is a tidal island off the coast of Northumberland, and in 634 a monastery was established there by Aidan, an Irish monk from Iona. Not a great deal is known about prehistoric Lindisfarne. There was a prehistoric flint and stone tool production site at Ness End quarry, and a possible hearth at the Snook. A Neolithic whinstone adze was found in the Bishop's Palace Garden in 1926. In 1986 a sherd of prehistoric pottery and two sherds of Roman pottery were discovered in a medieval midden near Jenny Bell's Well. The most significant archaeological evidence found so far on the island was recorded in 1996 at Marygate in the Castle Hotel Gardens. Gullies and slots, a post pit and postholes cut the natural sandy clay and, although no datable artifacts were recovered, charcoal from a posthole produced a radiocarbon date from the Neolithic period with a range of 3365 to 3685 BC.[20]

We think of islands as areas of dry land in the middle of the sea, but in prehistoric Britain there were also islands in the Fens, like Whittlesey Island near Peterborough (Bronze Age), Stonea Camp in Cambridgeshire (Iron Age), and Stonea Roman settlement, and Iron Age marsh-forts like Sutton Common in South Yorkshire and The Berth in Shropshire. So it is not surprising that monasteries should have been established on inland "islands."

Glastonbury Tor is a 518 feet high hill near Glastonbury, which was a virtual island in the Somerset Levels until the Levels were drained in the Middle Ages. There was probably an early monastery or hermitage on Glastonbury Tor. Excavations in 1964–6 uncovered timber buildings, evidence of bronze-working, evidence of much meat-eating (food

Terraces on Glastonbury Tor, Somerset, and the tower of the Church of St. Michael (14th century) May 19, 2014 (Rodw).

bones), and 14 sherds of imported Mediterranean pottery dating to the 6th century.[21] Given its isolated position, it is more likely to have been a hermitage—Aldhelm, the Anglo-Saxon abbot of Malmesbury, writing in the late 7th century, refers to British monasticism disparagingly as "a life of contemplative retirement away in some squalid wilderness,"[22] and Glastonbury Tor would certainly have qualified as a wilderness in the 6th century. By the 13th century there was a church of St. Michael on Glastonbury Tor; this was destroyed by an earthquake in 1275, and replaced in the 14th century.

The early history of Glastonbury Tor is uncertain. There are earthworks on the Tor which have been interpreted as medieval lynchets (banks of earth that build up after ploughing). However, it has been pointed out that the top of the Tor is too steep for effective cultivation, with or without animals. One possibility is that the terraces originated in the Neolithic period, which was a time of great earthworks like causewayed enclosures and henges. The Tor is highly visible from anywhere in the landscape and as such would have been a significant landmark. It is possible that the Neolithic modifications were later reworked into lynchets as and when they were needed, although the upper levels were too steep for such use.[23]

Other islands in the Somerset Levels also became religious sites. In the 7th century Aethelwine, brother of king Cenwalh of Wessex, is said to have retired to Athelney, then an island in the Somerset Levels, to live as a hermit; he was later venerated as a saint under the name Egelwine.[24] In the late 9th century, Alfred king of Wessex, established a monastery there dedicated to our Blessed Savior, St. Peter, St. Paul and St. Egelwine. In the 8th century king Cynewulf of Wessex established a monastery at Muchelney, also an island in the Somerset Levels.[25]

Ely in Cambridgeshire, near the Iron Age ringwork called Wardy Hill, is an island in the fens, which at 85 feet is the highest land in the Fens. A double religious house (a

The gatehouse of Ramsey Abbey in Cambridgeshire, February 14, 2009 (Thorvaldsson).

mixed community of men and women) was founded at Ely in 673 by Etheldreda, daughter of Anna, the king of East Anglia. The monastery was laid waste by the Danes in 870, but 8 monks are said to have returned and founded a secular college. It was refounded by Ethelwold, Bishop of Winchester, as a Benedictine abbey in 970, and dedicated to St. Peter and the Blessed Virgin by Archbishop Dunstan in 974.[26]

Ramsey in Cambridgeshire was also an island in the Fens known as Bodsey Island, and a monastery dedicated to Saints Mary and Benedict was founded there in 969 when the site was offered by Ailwine (Aethelwine) to St. Oswald, Bishop of Worcester.[27]

Crowland in Lincolnshire, near the Iron Age Borough Fen enclosure, was another island in the Fens, and in 714 a monastery was founded there by king Ethelbald of Mercia. Crowland is closely associated with St. Guthlac (673–714). Guthlac was born into the Mercian nobility and became a soldier at the age of 15. After nine successful years, he rejected the warrior life and became a monk at the important royal monastery of Repton in Derbyshire. After living under monastic rule for several years, he withdrew to Crowland, a secluded, desolate, elevated spot in the midst of the wild fens of East Anglia, to pursue the life of the religious hermit. For about thirteen years, he lived under a harsh, self-imposed ascetic rule, having St. Bartholomew as his guide and comfort. During his time at Crowland, Guthlac, as *miles Christi* ("soldier of Christ"), became known throughout the region for his holiness. At Crowland he was ordained as a priest by Haedda, Bishop of Lichfield, and gathered a few disciples, including his sister, Pega, before his death in 714. Guthlac quickly came to be revered as a saint. According to his hagiographer, Felix, a monk of Crowland, the saint's body was found incorrupt in 715, one year after his death. About 740, scarcely twenty-five years after the saint's death, Ælfwald, King of the East Angles (713–749), commissioned Felix to write Guthlac's *Life*. Oral tradition suggests that the saint's tomb was popular with pilgrims from as early as the 9th century. By about 900, his cult had spread to Westminster, St. Albans and Durham.[28]

The parish church of Crowland in Lincolnshire, and the west front of the ruined nave of Crowland Abbey, May 17, 2009 (Thorvaldsson).

Bardney Abbey, on a slight island in marshy ground around the River Witham in Lincolnshire, was founded in 697 by Ethelred, king of Mercia and his wife Osthryd. It housed a shrine to Osthryd's uncle, St. Oswald, who was king of Northumbria until he was killed in battle in 642. After his death, Oswald's head went to Lindisfarne Abbey, and his arms to the Northumbrian stronghold of Bamburgh in Northumberland, but his body ended up in Bardney.[29] Bardney is downstream from Lincoln, and not far from the Iron Age causeway at Fiskerton.

Hillforts in Early Medieval Britain

In *The Death-Song of Cynddylan* Arthur is compared to a "mighty fortress," and in *Y Gododdin* he is linked to "the rampart of a fort," so it is likely that Arthur was originally connected to Iron Age hillforts, which sometimes became fortified strongholds in the early medieval period, after the departure of the last Roman legions.

Castle Killibury is near Wadebridge and the River Camel in north Cornwall. Excavations of 250 square yards adjacent to the plowed down southern inner rampart revealed evidence of a long sequence of timber buildings, including four-post structures and a seven post frame for the ring-beam of a round house 30 feet in diameter. Cornish La Tene decorated pottery (Glastonbury Ware) was associated with all structural phases, with a little Cordoned Ware from the later levels. All the material for the pottery originated from the Lizard. Radiocarbon dates suggest occupation of the hillfort from the 3rd century BC. Radiocarbon dates of 930 and 840 BC together with a lugged sherd suggest some occupation, possibly with an enclosure, during the Late Bronze Age. Two small sherds of 5th/6th century AD Bi amphora, found at the plowsoil base indicated post–Roman activity.[30] The Bi amphora probably came from the eastern Mediterranean, brought by traders from the Eastern Roman (Byzantine) Empire. The River Camel, of course, may be the *Cambula* where, according to Geoffrey of Monmouth, Arthur fought Modred and was mortally wounded.

Dinas Powys is a hillfort in the Vale of Glamorgan to the southwest of Cardiff, 1.5 miles from the sea, with a view across the Bristol Channel reaching as far as Glastonbury Tor in Somerset. It was excavated between 1954 and 1958 by Leslie Alcock, who found much early medieval pottery dating from the 5th to 7th century, including "Phocaean slipwares from Asia Minor" (Phocaea, now Foça, is on the west coast of what is now Turkey) and "southern Mediterranean examples which were produced near Carthage" in North Africa.[31] He also found a 7th century Kentish blue glass squat beaker similar to examples from princely Anglo-Saxon burials found at Sutton Hoo in Suffolk and Prittlewell (Southend) in Essex.[32] Alcock also found evidence for industrial activity, such as bronze and iron metalwork and tools for jewelry making, together with twelve thousand animal bones (sheep cattle and pigs) which indicated that animals were entering the settlement at Dinas Powys and being butchered there.[33] Dinas Powys is not far from Llancarfan, which is associated with Arthur in the *Life* of St. Cadoc.

Trusty's Hill is a hillfort at Anwoth near Gatehouse of Fleet, on the south coast of Galloway in southwest Scotland. Excavations carried out in 1960 revealed occupation relating to two periods. In the Iron Age, an area 50 feet by 80 feet on the summit was enclosed by a 4 feet wide timber-laced stone wall. An oval stone guard-hut built in a natural hollow outside the entrance on the southeast and a massive rock-cut ditch across the neck of the promontory to the northeast also belong to this period. In the 6th–7th centuries AD, additional ramparts of poorer type with external revetment only were constructed outside the entrance, and possibly timber huts inside. A group of class I Pictish symbols are cut on a rock outcrop at the fort entrance, and now protected by an iron grille. The symbols are deeply incised, and are as follows: in the upper left-hand corner the double-disc ornament traversed by the Z-shaped floriated rod (usually called the double-disc and Z-rod); to the right, and separated by a natural fissure, a marine monster (possibly the so-called Pictish beast); and immediately below it a heart-shaped figure with incurvation terminating in spirals and surmounted with a conical spike; at the left-hand lower corner a human mask with two horns ending in spiral curves on the top of it.[34] Pictish symbols are usually found in eastern Scotland, and one of the only other sites in western Scotland with a Pictish symbol is the hillfort of Dunadd in Argyll and Bute, thought to be the stronghold of the Dark Age kingdom of Dal Riata. Recently the Galloway Picts Project and GUARD Archaeology excavated Trusty's Hill and found that it was a high-status site[35]:

> An abundance of domestic rubbish, including animal bones, a rotary quern, tools and a spindle whorl demonstrate that Trusty's Hill was once the home of a small community. There was also clear evidence, in the form of crucibles, a clay mould and iron slag, that metalworking and the production of high status jewellery was being carried out in part of the site. But the clincher for the Galloway Picts Team was the discovery of high status jewellery itself and even rarer pottery sherds from France. The pottery sherds not only date to the seventh century AD, exactly the right time when Pictish Symbols were being carved in Scotland, but are so rare from this period that only people of the highest status—kings, princes, lords and bishops—acquired this pottery.

To the west of Trusty's Hill is the Rhinns of Galloway, which may be the *Pen Rhionydd* mentioned in Triad 1 as being one of Arthur's courts.

Cornwall and the Arthurian Legend

Tristan and Isolt

Cornwall does not figure in the Arthurian story until *Culhwch and Olwen* (11th century), and the *History of the Kings of Britain* (12th century), and there seems to be no strong link between Arthur and Cornwall. However, in the 12th century there arose a series of tales concerning Tristan and Isolt, and they seem to be strongly rooted in Cornwall. There are a number of medieval versions of the tale which differ in various respects, and I would like to offer a summary of the Tristan tale provided by the authority on Arthurian matters, Caitlin R. Green (also known as Thomas Green). The Tristan tale recounts the adventures of a prince named Tristan, the nephew of King Mark of Cornwall, who finds his way to his uncle's court at Tintagel. He has various adventures (including the killing of a dragon), then ends up by being responsible for transporting the beautiful Isolt from Ireland to Cornwall to marry his uncle Mark. Isolt is carrying with her a love potion provided by her mother, and Tristan and Isolt mistakenly drink the potion and immediately fall in love with each other[36]:

> The tale then becomes one of deception through a variety of episodes. Thus Isolt substitutes her maid for herself on her wedding night, though Mark knows nothing of this and is

simply grateful to his nephew for bringing his wonderful new wife to him. Similarly, in the summer Mark's court moves to Lancien, supposedly in south Cornwall. The two continue their illicit relations, using the king's chamber when he is out hunting, until one day Mark discovers them and exiles Tristan from his court. Not discouraged, the obsessed pair contrive new ways to meet, Tristan throwing twigs into the stream that runs beneath Isolt's window to tell her to hasten to an apple orchard to meet him. Unfortunately for them, an evil dwarf discovers them via magic and informs Mark. Mark spies on them from the branches of a tree, trying to find proof of their guilt, though he leaves convinced of their innocence when he is unknowingly revealed to Tristan and Isolt by the light of the moon, allowing them to make a play of the meeting.

Although this falsified innocence of their meetings allows Tristan's reinstatement to court, Mark's conviction does not last. Tristan is given a favoured retainer's sleeping position, next to the king's bed, whilst the dwarf, angry at his mistreatment after his supposed lies about the orchard, sets a trap so that Tristan is caught visiting Isolt whilst Mark is away from his bed by flour on the floor. Tristan and Isolt are sentenced to be burnt, though Tristan escapes by jumping from a chapel—known as "Tristan's Leap"—over a cliff to safety. Isolt is then sentenced to be ravished by lepers, a fate she is rescued from by her lover, who takes her into hiding in the forest of Morrois.

After further adventures, Isolt and Mark are reconciled at the ford of Mal Pas as the potion-inspired obsession begins to wane (though her and Tristan's love remains), and Tristan is once more banished, though he actually goes again into hiding. Meanwhile, Isolt is required by unfriendly lords to prove her innocence of adultery by a public Trial by Ordeal—she agrees on the condition that King Arthur is present and it should take place at Blancheland, Mark's high hunting ground. On the appointed day she proves her innocence through trickery with the help of Tristan, with whom she then consents to continue cuckolding Mark with!

This does not last long, and Isolt eventually persuades Tristan to go far away for the sake of them both. He ends his life in Brittany, married to another Isolt. On his death-bed Tristan asks for the original Isolt to come to him. Isolt agrees, but the second Isolt, seized by jealousy, tells him that the other Isolt is not coming. Tristan dies, and when the original Isolt arrives, she lies down in his arms and dies too.

As it turns out, all of the place-names in the tale are Cornish, particularly in the version of the story by the Norman poet Béroul. Tintagel, of course, is the high-status 5th/6th century site in north Cornwall which may have been the "capital" of the kingdom of Dumnonia. The ford of *Mal Pas* ("Evil Crossing") is an early medieval ferry crossing on the Truro River south of Truro; *Blanche Lande* is in the parish of Kea, to the west of *Mal Pas*; and Mark's court at *Lancien* has been identified as Lantyan near Fowey, well to the east of Truro. The forest of *Morrois* is woodland attached to the manor of Moresk outside Truro—Moresk Castle at St. Clement to the north of *Mal Pas* is mentioned in a 15th century document as having been destroyed around 1104. An Anglo-Saxon charter-boundary dated 967 names a *hryt eselt*, "Isolts's Ford" in Cornish, with the stream crossed by this emerging at Porthallow on the Lizard peninsula to the south of *Blanche Lande*. What's more, there is a 6th century memorial stone from Castle Dore near Fowey (and therefore near Mark's court at Lancien) inscribed in Latin DRUSTANUS HIC IACIT CUNOMORI FILIUS, "here lies Drystan, son of Cunomorus." In Béroul's version, the hermit in the story "goes off to the Mount, for the fineries that are there," referring no doubt to the fact that two markets were held in the 12th century opposite St. Michael's Mount, a tidal island near Marazion in southwest Cornwall.

All these sites have some connection with the history of Cornwall in the Iron Age

St. Michael's Mount and Causeway at low tide, Cornwall (Whitelined).

Doniert's Stone, a 9th century memorial stone near St. Cleer, Cornwall, September 26, 2007 (Tinwidget).

or early medieval period. For example, there was probably an early monastery at Old Kea near *Mal Pas*. At the time of the Domesday Book (1086) Old Kea church is identified as a place, *Landighe* (literally, "church-site of thy Kea"), and by the name of its saint, Latinized as *Cheus*. Such a reference in Domesday normally denotes a religious community dedicated to the saint.[37]

No Cornish royal court is known at Lantyan near Fowey—the nearest possible royal site is Liskeard (about 19 miles north of Fowey), recorded in Domesday as *Liscarret*, implying that it was a *lis* or royal court. The first mention of Liskeard is in a manumission (a document freeing a slave) of around AD 1000.[38] At St. Cleer, to the north of Liskeard, is a site known as "King Doniert's Stone." This consists of two late 9th century granite cross-shaft fragments and an underground passage and chamber. The fragments stand in an enclosure on the south side of the road from St. Cleer to Redgate, and are the only surviving examples of 9th century stone crosses in Cornwall. The northern cross, termed the "Doniert Stone" is 4 feet 6 inches high with panels of interlace decoration on three sides and a Latin inscription in lower case cursive script on the east face DONIERT ROGAVIT PRO ANIMA ("Doniert ordered (this cross) for (the good of) his soul"). Doniert is mentioned in the early Welsh chronicle *Annales Cambriae*, as the king of Dumnonia called Dumgarth (or Dwingarth) who is recorded as having drowned in the sea in about 875.[39]

Castle Dore near Fowey is a multivallate Iron Age hillfort that was in use from the 5th to the 2nd centuries BC. Two glass bracelets recovered during the original excavations can be dated from the mid 3rd or the later 2nd centuries BC. Both are thought to be imports of middle La Tene dates.[40]

Porthallow on the Lizard peninsula is near Helston—this was originally *Henliston*, from Cornish *hen lis* "old court," suggesting that the kings of Cornwall had a court there;

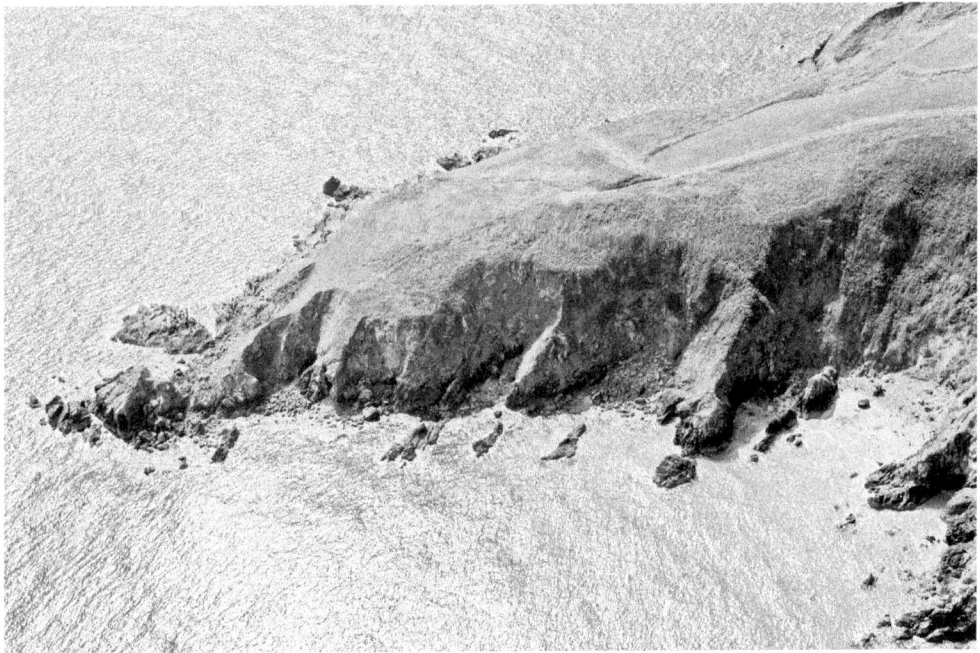

Lankidden cliff castle, Lizard Peninsula, Cornwall, not far from "Isolt's Ford" (© Cornwall & Scilly Historic Environment Record).

it was taken over by the Anglo-Saxons in 930 and became the center of a royal manor.[41] Not far from Porthallow is Lankidden, a univallate cliff castle of about three acres. The rampart, 110 yards long, ends in the east on the edge of steep cliffs, but in the west the terminal has been destroyed by cliff erosion.[42]

In the 12th century there was a monastery on St. Michael's Mount, a tidal island in Mount's Bay near Penzance. The monastery was supposedly given by Edward the Confessor (the last Anglo-Saxon king) to the Abbey of Mont Saint-Michel in Normandy as an alien Benedictine cell. In 1135 the Norman abbot was present at the consecration of the church which had been built together with conventual accommodation for a prior and twelve monks from the parent house.[43] Recently a Late Bronze Age hoard has been discovered at St. Michael's Mount—it consisted of 49 artifacts, including five socketed axes, tucked under a rock in a cavity.[44] Perhaps St. Michael's Mount was a sacred island in pagan times.

Cornwall in the Bronze Age

I believe that the story of Tristan and Isolt originated in the Bronze Age, so I need to say a little about Bronze Age Cornwall. Like the rest of Britain, Cornwall entered the Bronze Age with the arrival of the Beaker people. One of the greatest concentrations of Beaker pottery in Cornwall was found at St. Keverne on the Lizard peninsula, not far from "Isolt's ford" at Porthallow. A mound at St. Keverne was excavated in 1978, and found to contain about a hundred sherds of decorated Beaker pottery and some flints.[45]

Human bone is rarely found in Cornwall because of the acidic soil, but some Bronze Age burials have been uncovered. One important Early Bronze Age site in west Cornwall is Tregiffian Burial Chamber, a large Late Neolithic or Early Bronze Age entrance grave situated a mile and a half south east of St. Buryan, near the southern coast of the Penwith peninsula, and not far from the Boscawen-un stone circle. The grave consists of a sub-circular mound, 49 feet in diameter with a peripheral kerb of large stones and funerary chamber in its southwest quadrant. Excavations in 1967–8 and 1972 indicated that there may have been two phases to construction. During the first phase the mound was surrounded by a circular kerb of stones but during the second phase these were moved to form an irregular plan in front of the chamber entrance. In addition, a second pit was found containing an intact Collared Urn which held a cremation dating to the Early Bronze Age.[46]

In 1990 a stone covered pit containing a Trevisker Ware vessel was discovered eroding from the cliffs at Harlyn Bay near Padsow on the north Cornish coast and was subsequently excavated. The vessel contained cremated bone from several individuals (perhaps five) with some animal bone, quartz pebbles and a small bronze pendant. A radiocarbon date on the cremated bone fell between 2120–1880 BC. The animal bone is likely to have come from a sheep or goat.[47] Trevisker Ware is Early Bronze Age pottery made from the gabbroic clays of the Lizard peninsula.

Another Bronze Age burial has been found at Gwithian, northwest Cornwall, well to the west of Harlyn Bay. In a settlement which flourished between 1300 and 900 BC, House 1 contained two wooden bowls—both were set into a floor surface but sealed beneath a later floor. One bowl contained unfired clay and granite chips. Next to each bowl were pairs of human (baby) long bones as if specially selected and laid out alongside groups of stone tools. The complete remains of a baby skeleton was found under the floor in the northwest.[48] At the Middle Bronze Age settlement at Trethellan Farm, Newquay, on the north coast of Cornwall, one roundhouse contained an extended inhumation under the central hearth.[49]

Cornwall flourished during the Late Bronze Age, when Cornish tin was much in demand, and the evidence of this comes from Bronze Age hoards. In 1884, six gold bracelets were found at Morvah on the northwestern coast of the Penwith peninsula in Cornwall. Three of the bracelets had distinctive trumpet-like ends, and one also has engraved geometric designs on it. These bracelets were almost certainly made in Ireland, or from Irish gold, between 1000 BC and 800 BC.[50] In 1931 another hoard of gold ornaments was found in a boundary bank or hedge (possibly part of a prehistoric field system) at Towednack near St. Ives. The hoard included two twisted neckrings, four armrings, and two lengths of unfinished gold rod, and probably dates from around 900 BC.[51]

The Prehistoric Origins of Tristan and Isolt

The origin of the name Tristan is uncertain, but in the 19th century, Edward Tyrrell Leith suggested that Tristan was derived from the Vedic god Trita and his Old Persian counterpart Thraetaona.[52] Trita ("Third"), also known as Trita Aptya, is a god in the *Rig Veda* who either kills, or helps Indra to kill, a three-headed six-eyed dragon. Thraetaona (later Feridun) is a character in the Old Persian *Avesta* who kills the dragon Azi Dahaka, which has three mouths, six eyes and three heads. According to Leith,[53] Thraetaona's birth is due to the divine nectar *haoma*, and the same is true of Trita,[54] who also conquers the dragon with the help of *soma*. The classicist Graham Anderson also sees a link between Thraetaona and Tristan, and also draws attention to a late 2nd century work by the Syrian philosopher Iamblichus, *Babyloniaca*, which appears to retell the story of Thraetaona/Feridun, here called Rhodanes.[55] The Tristan story involves killing a dragon, and the magic potion is the equivalent of the divine nectar *soma* or *haoma*. Soma was a Vedic ritual drink frequently mentioned in the *Rigveda* and made by extracting juice from the stalks of a certain plant (exactly which plant is not known, even in India).

We don't know if soma or its equivalent was consumed in Bronze Age Britain, but mead certainly was. An Early Bronze Age vessel from Bulford near Amesbury in Wiltshire shows high levels of chemical compounds that indicate the presence of beeswax in the funerary vessel, suggesting that it could have contained mead.[56] A food vessel from the henge monument at North Mains, Strathallan, in Perth and Kinross, eastern Scotland, was analyzed and found to contain high percentages of *Filipendula* (meadowsweet) pollen and relatively high percentages of cereal pollen[57]:

> high proportion of cereal pollen grains might suggest either a porridge of cereals [...] or a fermented ale, flavoured with meadowsweet flowers or extract. The name "meadowsweet" orginates from mead-sweet as it was used to flavour mead and other drinks. It is distinctly possible therefore that the North Mains food vessel contained a fermented drink.

Merryn Dineley and Graham Dineley also mention the residues found in a Beaker accompanying a skeleton in a stonelined cist at Ashgrove, Fife, in eastern Scotland, where the presence of pollen from immature lime flowers (*Tilia cordata*) and meadowsweet (*Filipendula vulgaris*) indicates a fermented honey drink, mead.[58]

Evidence for the drinking of mead in the Iron Age is much more scarce. The best example comes from a high-status site at Hochdorf near Stuttgart in Germany. The remains of mead were found in an enormous bronze cauldron uncovered in a grave dated to around 550 BC. It is estimated that the cauldron contained 600 pints of mead.[59]

The importance of mead in Dark Age Britain is hinted at in *Y Gododdin*, where its influence is seen as negative, and in the Fortress of Mead-Drunkenness of *The Spoils of Annwn*.

The importance of mead in Ireland is underlined by the figure of Medb in early medieval Irish mythology. Medb is associated with both Connacht in the west of Ireland and Tara in the east; her name is related to Irish *medb* "intoxicating," Welsh *meddw* "intoxicated," and English *mead*. She was queen of Connacht and ruled from Cruachan, now Rathcroghan in County Roscommon, and her story probably dates from the Iron Age. Little is known about the archaeology of Rathcroghan, but in 1981 a limited excavation was carried out on "Dathi's Mound," named after the supposed last pagan king of Ireland. Before excavation, the mound appeared to be an embanked tumulus, but the discovery of a substantial internal ditch indicates that the monument "has affinities with the ring-barrow class." Radiocarbon dates from charcoal suggest that the monument was built between 200 BC and AD 200, in the Irish Iron Age.[60] Interestingly, Rathcroghan is not far from Coggalbeg, where a Bronze Age gold lunula and two gold sun discs were found.

There is also a figure called Medb Lethderg associated with Tara, near the River Boyne in County Meath, which may date from the Neolithic or Bronze Age. The Mound of the Hostages at Tara was excavated in the 1950s by a team of archaeologists who discovered that the mound was in fact a mantle of soil over 3 feet deep which covered a cairn enclosing a passage tomb. Outside the walls of the tomb lay three cists. These cists contained the remains of 55 adults, three children and four infants. The main tomb housed the richest collection of Neolithic and Early Bronze Age burials and artifacts known at the time (and never matched since). It contained an enormous quantity of cremated and unburnt human bone representing more than 250 individuals and artifacts including decorative beads; pendants; bone and antler pins; a ceremonial battleax; bronze daggers; food vessels; and urns.[61]

The Rath na Ríogh ("Fortress of the Kings") at Tara was first excavated in the 1950s and again excavated in 1997. The 1950s excavations had identified a black, charcoal-rich layer, and the 1997 excavation revealed that the source of this black, charcoal-rich layer was debris from a bowl furnace. Throughout the layer, and especially around the immediate area of the furnace, were found quantities of iron slag, tuyère and crucible fragments, some with bronze residue, bronze stems and droplets, and small iron objects which await conservation before identification. The most interesting iron object found is a complete socketed axhead.[62]

Lismullin enclosure lies just over a mile northeast of Tara, and was discovered in 2007 by archaeologists working on the route of a controversial highway. The enclosure consists of an outer circle (outer enclosure), with an external diameter of 87 yards, of two concentric rings of small posts (between 300 and 400 in total); an eastern entrance in the outer circle built of four large posts, as well as an entrance avenue 13 feet in width and 98 feet in length; and an inner circle or ring, 52 feet in diameter, of 60 small posts. The enclosure has been radiocarbon dated to between 520 BC and 370 BC.[63]

It seems likely that Tristan was originally a Bronze Age god associated with the storm god, with killing dragons, and with a magic potion. Isolt, who came from Ireland, may be associated with the prehistoric queen Medb of Rathcroghan and Tara, and therefore with mead and intoxication. These two elements came together to form the story of Tristan and Isolt and their love potion, which may have originated in the Lizard peninsula, which seems to have been a special place in both the Bronze Age and Iron Age.

Arthur and the Druids

In this chapter I have looked at the many possible origins of Arthur, but I have ignored the Druids. Of course, the Romans suppressed the Druids, and with the coming of Christianity, prehistoric paganism vanished forever. However, on the basis of archaeology and later Christian foundations, it is possible to speculate where druidism may have thrived, and this will form the basis of my final chapter. In this chapter I will also consider the link between druidism and Arthur in the form of Math son of Mathonwy, the bear-druid of the Fourth Branch of the *Mabinogion*.

CHAPTER 11

Druids and the Early Medieval World: The Bear-Druid of Welsh Mythology

Looking for Druids in Medieval Britain and Ireland

Tara, Ireland

Were there Druids in Late Bronze Age and Iron Age Britain and Ireland, and if so, where were they? The Druids were famed for their knowledge of astronomy, so we would expect to find Druids in areas where astronomically aligned monuments were built in the Neolithic or Bronze Age. And if these areas were sacred to the Druids, we might expect to find early Christian churches there. One good candidate is Tara in Co. Meath, Ireland, which lies near the River Boyne upstream from Newgrange passage tomb, which is aligned on the rising sun on the day of the midwinter solstice. There is a Neolithic tomb at Tara, an Iron Age iron working site, and an Early Iron Age ceremonial site at Lismullin. The iron working site may be significant: Koch says that the Druids belonged to the class of people called *aes dano*, or "people of the arts," which also included metalworkers. There was a church at Tara by 1190: a charter of 1191–2 provides the earliest documentary evidence of the church, which was among the possessions confirmed to the Knights Hospitallers of St. John of Kilmainham by Pope Innocent II in 1212.[1]

Anglesey, North Wales

There were certainly Druids in Iron Age Anglesey, as the Roman historian Tacitus makes clear. The Neolithic Bryn Celli Ddu was aligned on the midsummer sunrise, there was a rich Bronze Age burial at Bedd Branwen, and there were burnt mounds on or near Anglesey in the Bronze Age. There was a Middle/Late Iron Age deposition site in the lake of Llyn Cerrig Bach, and in the early Christian period there was a monastery at Holyhead, not far from Llyn Cerrig Bach.

The Druids were an Iron Age priesthood with Neolithic roots, so one of the most interesting sites on Anglesey is Castell Bryn Gwyn near Brynsiencyn in the parish of Llanidan, which is located along the Menai Strait. Castell Bryn Gwyn is a near circular earthwork enclosure defined by a massive rampart that remains up to 8 feet 6 inches high, with an internal area in the region of 56–61 yards across. Excavations in 1959–60 demonstrated that the monument had originated as a late Neolithic ritual henge enclosure or similar. It had later been adapted as a defensible circuit, presumably enclosing a settlement. This reuse probably occurred in the later Prehistoric period and its latest phase is associated with Roman pottery of the late 1st century AD.[2] Between 2007 and 2010 archaeologists discovered the remains of a stone circle 328 yards southwest of the Neolithic henge.³ This is just the sort of place where the Druids might have lived before they were wiped out by the Roman army in AD 61.

Monmouthshire, Southeast Wales

In the Early Bronze Age there was a barrow in Crick, Monmouthshire aligned on the midwinter sunrise, and in the Late Bronze Age there was a ramp at nearby Caldicot whose timbers were felled around the time of lunar eclipses. If there were Druids in Monmouthshire, they may well have lived at Llanmelin Wood, an Iron Age hillfort to the north of Caldicot. This is described as "a small but elaborate Iron Age hillfort defended by two, and in some places three, banks." The main hillfort is oval and measures 218 by 142 yards, with a main gateway on the southeast side. Alongside and to the east of the hillfort is a complex annex consisting of two rectangular compartments bounded by a high earthwork along the north, and terminating in a series of linear banks alongside a southeast gateway. The annex measures some 164 yards east-west by 65 yards. Together the hillfort and annex enclose around 7 acres. The hillfort was excavated between 1930 and 1932, and the most interesting discovery from the annex were two human burials, one in the external ditch on the south-west side and one external to the northeast of the annex earthworks.⁴

Llanmelin was succeeded by Roman *Venta Silurum*, which as Caerwent continued to play a significant role in the early medieval period. Over "150 early medieval burials, spanning the period from the 4th to the 9th century AD, have been found in the areas around the present church and outside the east gate" of Caerwent.⁵ Caerwent is documented as the site of a monastery in the 10th century, and in 1992 a pre–Norman disc cross-head was found to the southeast of the church of St. Stephen and St. Tathan, which dates from the 13th century.⁶

Cornwall

The presence of Druids in Iron Age Cornwall is more difficult to prove. In Cornwall, the Age of Megaliths is represented by the Propped Stone on Leskernick Hill, on the northeastern edge of Bodmin Moor, and The Hurlers on Bodmin Moor. The Propped Stone has a peep-hole through which the horizon to the north can be seen, and on the day of the summer solstice, "the dying rays of the midsummer sun shine through the peep-hole just before the sun sinks below the horizon." The Hurlers on Bodmin Moor mark the four cardinal points together with the solstices and equinoxes, and are laid out to resemble Orion's Belt.

In the Iron age, the focus of activity moved away from Bodmin Moor to the hillfort of Castle Killibury near the River Camel, and to The Rumps, a cliff castle to the north of Castle Killibury defended by three banks and ditches enclosing an area of 6.1 acres. The cliff castle was examined between 1963 and 1967, and three phases of building and two periods of occupation were revealed. The initial settled occupation is contemporary with the inner rampart, dated by pottery to the 2nd century BC. The carefully constructed middle rampart which superseded the inner was on the evidence from the excavation, the final period of occupation which ended in the mid 1st century AD.⁷

The religious significance of this area is demonstrated by the fact that in the 5th or early 6th century a Celtic monastery *Lann Docco* was founded by St. Docco at St. Kew, not far from Castle Killibury. It was visited by St. Samson in the 6th century. The church was dedicated to St. Docco until 1440 when it was rededicated to St. Kew. An early Christian memorial stone of the 6th or 7th century, now preserved in the parish church of St. Kew, was recovered in 1924 from the bed of the stream just below the church, where the bridge spans it. It bears the Latin inscription, "IUSTUS," and the ogham inscription "ISTIS."[8] All of these sites, of course, are just a few miles from the early medieval high-status site at Tintagel, where Tristan's uncle King Mark had his court.

Lady St. Mary Church, Wareham, built on the site of an 8th century Anglo-Saxon monastery (author's photograph).

Dorset

In the Neolithic, Dorset Cursus was aligned with the mid-winter sunset, and Maiden Castle near Dorchester was a Neolithic causewayed enclosure that became a hillfort in the Iron Age. Wareham, down the River Frome from Dorchester, was the site of a Middle Bronze Age settlement and burnt mound, and a Late Bronze Age settlement, with extensive pottery making throughout the life of the settlement. If the Druids were "people of the arts," then there were surely Druids in Bronze Age Wareham. Pottery-making resumed at Wareham in the Late Iron Age and Roman period, and after the departure of the Roman legions, Wareham seems to have had a thriving Christian community[9]:

> The site of Wareham seems to have been of significance to early Christian communities and a late Roman or post–Roman "Celtic" or "British" Christian church was established, probably on or near the site of the present church of Lady St. Mary. The evidence for this is a group of five inscribed memorial stones, made from Romano-British architectural fragments (perhaps from a local villa or shipped downriver from Dorchester) and dating to the 7th to 9th centuries, which were found in the fabric of Lady St. Mary church during its rebuilding in 1841–2.

The inscribed memorial stones are in Latin, and most of the names of the people memorialized appear to be Celtic.

There is no mention of the founding of an Anglo-Saxon church at Wareham, but we know from an entry in the *Anglo-Saxon Chronicle* dated 786 that King Beorhtric of

St. Martin's Church, Wareham. The chancel and nave are Anglo-Saxon, probably 11th century. The tower dates from 16th century (author's photograph).

The River Frome at Wareham, near Lady St. Mary Church (author's photograph).

Wessex was buried there in 802,[10] and Asser, in his *Life of Alfred*, refers to a "monasterium of holy virgins" (nunnery) at Wareham, which was attacked by the Danes in 876.[11]

Wiltshire

There were probably Druids in Late Bronze Age Wiltshire. Late Neolithic Stonehenge is aligned on the midsummer sunrise when viewed from within the monument, and on the midwinter sunrise when approaching from the northeast along the Avenue. In the Late Bronze Age, the focus shifted up the Salisbury Avon to the Late Bronze Age/Early Iron Age feasting and ceremonial sites at East Chisenbury, Potterne and All Cannings Cross. These were replaced in the Early/Middle Iron Age by hillforts like Danebury in Hampshire and Yarnbury Castle in Wiltshire, and ritual sites like Wilsford Shaft near Stonehenge. There was also a late Roman midden at Wayside Farm near Devizes which deliberately recalls the much earlier middens at Potterne and All Cannings Cross.

Opposite, top: Porch House, Potterne: Porch House (built around 1480) stands on the site of a 10th century Saxon church, just a few hundred yards from the Early Iron Age midden and feasting site. The top of the tower of the present church is just visible in the distance (author's photograph).

Opposite bottom: The Church of St. Mary, Potterne (13th century), just a short distance from the site of the 10th century Saxon church (author's photograph).

11: Druids and the Early Medieval World

The Church of St. Mary, Potterne (13th century), with a view of the tower (author's photograph).

The religious significance of the area between Amesbury and All Cannings Cross is underlined by two early churches there (among the earliest in Wiltshire). The present church in Potterne, St. Mary's, is 13th century, but in 1962 the site of a 10th century church was found by Mr. N. Davey in his grounds at Porch House, which dates from the late 15th century and may have been built for the Bishop of Salisbury. Excavation revealed that the church was of timber construction and originally consisted of a nave, chancel, and baptistry. At a later stage the nave was extended westwards, chapels were added on the north and south sides and a porch built onto the west end. A recess in the baptistry

The church of St. Mary and St. Melor, Amesbury (12th century), which stands on or near the site of the 10th century Anglo-Saxon monastery (author's photograph).

The River Avon at Amesbury, which flows between the church and Vespasian's Camp hillfort (author's photograph).

is the same size as a 10th century tub font in the present church and it seems probable that this font was originally situated in the timber church. Roman pottery, including samian and New Forest wares, was found in the area of the baptistry together with a quantity of 12th century pottery.[12]

In around 979, Queen Aelfthryth, the second or third wife of King Edgar, founded a Benedictine monastery at Amesbury dedicated to St. Mary and St. Melor.[13] Melor, it seems, was the son of the Duke of Cornouaille in the west of Brittany. When Melor was seven, his father was killed by his brother who wished to seize the throne. Melor's life was spared by his uncle at the request of the clergy, but his right hand and left foot were cut off. The mutilated Melor was fitted with a silver hand and bronze foot and confined to a monastery. At the age of fourteen, Melor began to work miracles. His artificial limbs came to life and functioned as though natural, and he worked other miracles as well, such as calling forth a fountain from the earth by throwing a stone on the ground. On hearing of these events, the uncle bribed Melor's guardian to behead him. After the beheading, angels appeared with lights to guard the body until the deed was discovered. The assassins brought Melor's head to the uncle; during the journey the head spoke to the assassins and produced a fountain to quench their thirst. When the uncle touched the head, he died; white bulls were used to carry the body to its grave. The cult of Melor at Amesbury did not generate much income, and William of Malmesbury said very little about it.[14] The dedication is a most unusual one in Anglo-Saxon England: there are probably only two other churches in Britain dedicated to him, both in Cornwall, at Mylor near Falmouth, and Linkinhorne, between Callington and Launceston. The story of Melor is similar to that of the legendary Irish king Nuada (the god Nodens of Lydney Park in Gloucestershire), who lost a hand or arm in a battle, and had it replaced by a silver hand or arm.

Cambridgeshire

There are also likely to have been Druids in the fens of Cambridgeshire. At Neolithic Godmanchester in Cambridgeshire, posts were aligned on solstices, equinoxes, and major and minor lunar standstills. In the Bronze Age, most activity focused on Peterborough and Flag Fen, where a wooden platform allowed metalwork to be placed in the fen from the 12th to the 5th centuries BC. At the same time, use was made of islands in the fen like Whittlesey, where a number of Bronze Age burnt mounds were uncovered. In the Iron Age the focus shifted to "hillforts" on islands in the Fens like Stonea Camp and Borough Fen enclosure. The religious significance of the Fens is underlined by the early (7th century) foundation of an Anglo-Saxon monastery at Ely, the largest island in the Fens.

North Yorkshire and Lincolnshire

At Thornborough monument complex in North Yorkshire, the eastern end of the main cursus is aligned on the midsummer sunrise, whilst its western terminal would have framed the three setting stars of Orion's main belt around 3300–3000 BC; while the three henges can be associated with the rising of Sirius, and with Orion's Belt. In the Late Bronze Age the timber structure at Thwing in East Yorkshire was oriented to the southeast, to the sunrise on the winter solstice.

Ripon Cathedral, North Yorkshire (western facade), June 26, 2014 (photograph by David Iliff).

Two millennia later the focus of activity switched south to Lincolnshire and the Late Bronze Age feasting site at Washingborough near Lincoln, and the Early/Middle Iron Age causeway at Fiskerton, where timbers were felled at the time of lunar eclipses, and metalwork was later deposited in the River Witham. This seems like a very likely place for Druid activity, and it is in the territory of *Linnuis* (Lindsey) where four of Arthur's battles are recorded in the early 9th century *History of the Britons*. Just as the Lizard peninsula in Cornwall may be the home of Tristan and Isolt, so Lindsey in north Lincolnshire may be the home of Arthur.

I've already mentioned the early monastery at Bardney, downstream from Fiskerton, but there was also an early monastery near the Thornborough monument complex. Ripon in North Yorkshire is downstream from Thornborough, and in 660 a monastery was founded there as a cell of the monastery of Melrose in the Scottish Border, on land granted to the monks by Ealhfrith, king of Deira (Deira was one of the two kingdoms that made up Northumbria). Ripon did not remain long with the monks of Melrose, for Ealhfrith gave the monastery to Wilfrid, the future bishop of Northumbria, who founded a community, probably under the order of St. Benedict, and built a stone church, whose crypt still survives today.[15]

Druids in Welsh Mythology: the Fourth Branch of the Mabinogion

The closest we come to Druids in Welsh mythology is in the Fourth Branch of the *Mabinogion*, entitled *Math Son of Mathonwy*, which is the longest and most complex of the four tales. As the opening lines of the Fourth Branch tell us, Math was lord of Gwynedd, the kingdom in north Wales centered on the island of Anglesey, which remained independent of England until 1282. To put Math in some mythological context, we are told that Pryderi was lord of the twenty-one cantrefs (administrative divisions) in the South, that is, *Deheubarth*, which included the old kingdom of Dyfed in southwest Wales, Ceredigion in west Wales, and Ystrad Tywi, the valley of the River Towy around Carmarthen in south Wales.

As the Fourth Branch opens, we are told that Math had an unusual disability[16]:

> At that time, Math son of Mathonwy could not live except when he had his feet enfolded in the lap of a maiden, unless the commotion of war prevented him. The maiden that was with him was Goewin daughter of Pebin of Dol Pebin in Arfon. She was the most beautiful woman known [around] there in her day.
> Caer Dathyl was his constant abode. He could not do the circuit of the land, but Gilfaethwy son of Don and Gwydion son of Don—his nephews, sons of his sister, and the household with them—would go on the circuit on his behalf.

The location of Caer Dathyl is a mystery. W.J. Gruffydd speculated in 1928 that *Caer Dathyl* might be derived from the name Tuathal (Irish), Tudwal (Welsh), from the Celtic *Toutovalos* "Ruler of the People."[17] The most famous Irish Tuathal is Tuathal Techtmar, a legendary king of Ireland in the late 1st century AD who was overthrown, spent some time in Britain, and later regained his throne, possibly with the help of Romans in Britain. The best known Welsh Tudwal is St. Tudwal, a Breton monk who gave his name to Saint Tudwal's Island East, a small island some 550 yards long by 220 yards wide lying off the south coast of the Llyn Peninsula, southwest of Anglesey. The island was the setting for a monastic settlement from at least the13th century—there are records of an Augustinian priory between 1291 and 1509-11. The island is known to have been farmed in the 18th century and the former chapel may have originated at this time. Excavations on the Priory site in 1959-63 produced Roman material, tentatively associated with a timber structures.[18]

Tudwal also gave his name to the parish of Tudweiliog ("Tudwal's land") in the northern part of the Llyn Peninsula. The church there is dedicated to St. Cwyfan, possibly a Welsh version of the 6th century Irish saint Kevin of Glendalough. Near Tudweiliog is Carn Fadrun, a mountain crowned with a large Iron Age hillfort. The earliest hillfort enclosed an area some 12 acres in extent "defined by a ruinous rampart wall with entrances to the north and south." The later hillfort enclosed a much larger area of roughly 26 acres, defined by a "better preserved rampart circuit, again with entrances to the north and south." The interior of the fort "shows many tumbled stone-walled buildings, some round, some rectangular and some irregular. Some have small walled yards or gardens attached. Similar features are scattered thickly over the steep slopes below the ramparts

St. Beuno's church, Clynnog Fawr, northwest Wales (late 15th–early 16th century) (Rhion Pritchard).

and may well represent activity here from the Iron Age through to the Roman period and possibly later." A castle was built on the highest part of the summit in the 12th century—it was mentioned by Gerald of Wales as newly-built in 1188.[19] If Caer Dathyl is linked to Tudwal, then it may refer to Caer Fadrun, though we can't discount Tudwal's Island East as an otherworldly island residence. This link to the Llyn Peninsula is supported by the theory put forward by Patrick Sims-Williams that the *Mabinogion* was compiled at the monastery of Clynnog Fawr on the Llyn Peninsula.[20] Very little is known about the Clynnog Fawr monastery: John Leland refers to it in his *Itineraries*, written between 1538 and 1543, as "a Monastery sometime of white monks [= Cistercians] suppressed many years ago,"[21] but this is the only evidence we have for its existence.

Why did Math need to keep his feet enfolded in the lap of a maiden? The original Welsh does not say "lap" but *croth* "womb," and the Celtic scholar Proinsias Mac Cana points out that Math had to have his feet in the lap of a virgin "because she embodied the vital and undiminished source of fertility with which he must maintain constant and harmonious contact so as to ensure the fruitful discharge of his royal function."[22] This interpretation is reinforced by the name of his sister and the mother of Gwydion and Gilfaethwy. Don is often compared to the Irish Danu, mother of the Irish gods, the Tuatha De Danann ("Peoples of Danu"), whose name is sometimes linked to the Indo-European root *da-* "to flow; river," found in the River name *Danube*.[23] However, in his discussion of Don, Koch suggests a different etymology for the name *Don*, namely that it is cognate with Old Irish genitive, dative and accusative singular *don* "place, ground, earth, and with Greek *khthon* "earth."[24]

The name Math was first studied by the French historian and philologist Henri d'Arbois de Jubainville in a work published in 1906. He says[25] that the word *math* can be recognized in the term *math-ghamhuin* "bearcub" (literally "calf of bear"), used in the Irish translation of the Bible to render the Hebrew *dob* "bear." According to the *Irish Language Dictionary*, *math* is an archaic word for "bear, replaced in Middle Irish by *mathgamain*.[26] The word *matus* "bear" appears as the first term in the Gaulish men's names *Matugenos* "Son of the Bear," and *Matumurus* "Great like a Bear." The Celtic god *Matunus*, known from an inscription at High Rochester Roman fort in Northumberland, is also derived from this root, and a variant of this, *Matunnos*, provided the second element of the Gallo-Roman name of Langres, *Andematunnum* ("Great Bear"). There is also an Irish proper name *Mac-Mathghamhna*, which today is written as Mac-Mahon, and means "son of the bear." To this list we may add, says Boekhoorn, *Math mac Úmóir in druí*, the druid of the Tuatha De Danann according to the *Book of Invasions*, and *Matgen* ("Son of the Bear"), the *corrguine*, or "sorcerer," of the Tuatha.[27] The word *math* actually means "good," and may be a euphemism for a taboo word, like English *bear*, which originally meant "the brown one."

Math, it seems, was a man with strong powers. Gilfaethwy was in love with Goewin, and began wasting away because he could do nothing about his love. Gwydion noticed the change in Gilfaethwy, and asked him what was wrong:

> "Lord brother," he said "it would not be fruitful for me to tell anyone what has happened to me."
> "What is it, friend?"
> "You know," he said "the ability of Math son of Mathonwy: whatever whisper, however small, that there might be between people, once the wind has met it, he will know it."

This supernatural hearing ability is not unique to Math—it is also found in the story of *Lludd and Llefelys*, which was probably written down between 1225 and 1250, though it may date to the 11th century. In this tale, Lludd (Nodens, the god of Lydney Park) is the son of Beli, and king of the Island of Britain, and Llefelys (Lugus) his brother is king of France, having married the daughter of the former king. During Lludd's reign, three *gormesoedd*, variously translated as "plagues" or "oppressions," fall on the Island of Britain[28]:

> The first was a certain race that came, and was called the Coranians; and so great was their knowledge, that there was no discourse upon the face of the Island, however low it might be spoken, but what, if the wind met it, it was known to them. And through this they could not be injured.

The name Coranians, or *Coraniaid* as they are more correctly known, is generally linked to Welsh *cor(r)* "dwarf"; Koch also suggests a connection with Old Irish *corrguinecht* "magic, wizardry," and *corrguinech* "magician, sorcerer."[29] This of course links Math to *Matgen*, the *corrguine*, or "sorcerer," of the Tuatha, and confirms that Math is also a sorcerer and druid.

It turns out that Gwydion knows that Gilfaethwy is in love with Goewin, and has a plan—he will provoke a war so that Math leaves Goewin alone with Gilfaethwy. So Gwydion approaches Math and tells him that a new kind of creature has appeared in the South called a *pig*, sent to Pryderi by Arawn king of Annwn. Math would like some of these animals, and Gwydion says he will go to Pryderi disguised as a bard and get some pigs. He then went with Gilfaethwy and ten other men to Rhuddlan Teifi near Llandysul in the far south of Ceredigion. Recent historical and archaeological analysis has highlighted the significance of Rhuddlan Teifi, which was documented in the 12th century as a grange (manor house) granted to Talley Abbey in Carmarthenshire. The estate was an

The ruins of Talley Abbey, Carmarthenshire, June 23, 2015 (Mark A. Wilson).

early medieval Welsh royal site of some significance, becoming a Cistercian grange farm in the late 12th century. The estate was so valuable, it was eventually usurped by the large and powerful Cistercian Whitland Abbey near Narberth in Pembrokeshire.[30]

Gwydion, who was the best story-teller in the world, "delighted the court with entertaining recitals and story-telling." He then asked Pryderi if he could have the pigs, but Pryderi said he couldn't give them away until they had bred twice their number—to which Gwydion replied that he would show Pryderi something the next day that he could offer in exchange. Gwydion then went away and

> performed his arts and began to reveal his magic. He conjured up twelve steeds, twelve grey-hounds (each of them black, with a white breast) with twelve collars and twelve leashes on them. Anyone seeing any of [them] would not know they were not of gold; and twelve saddles on the horses: and wherever there would normally be iron on them, it was all gold, and the bridles were of the same workmanship as that.

It is clear that Gwydion, like his uncle Math, is a sorcerer—Koch says the name Gwydion is probably derived from *Widu-genos* "Born of Trees,"[31] and connects him to the Druids, "those who understand wood."

The next morning Gwydion exchanged the pigs for these gifts, together with twelve golden shields that he had made from toadstools. They set off quickly, for as Gwydion said: "The magic will not last from one day to the next," and eventually reached Caer Dathyl. Pryderi, realizing he had been tricked, raised an army to attack Gwynedd. Hearing this, Math and his army set out and went as far as Pennard in Arfon. That night, Gwydion and Gilfaethwy returned to Caer Dathyl, and Gilfaethwy raped Goewin in Math's bed.

The next morning they rejoined Math, and waited "between two fortresses," Maynawr Bennard and Maynawr. A *maynawr* or *maenor* was a collection of villages, and may be derived from Welsh *maen* "stone"[32]—but the location of Maynawr Pennard and Maynawr Coed Alun is uncertain.

Battle was joined, and there was great slaughter on both sides. Pryderi's army retreated to Nant Call (Nant Cyll near Garndolbenmaen) and were harried as far as there. There was a further battle, and Pryderi's army retreated to Dol Penmaen (Dolbenmaen, south of Garndolbenmaen). Pryderi then called for a truce, gave Math 24 hostages, and retreated to Traeth Mawr ("Big Sands"), on the estuary of the River Glaslyn at Porthmadog, to the south of Dolbenmaen. Dolbenmaen may have been well known to those who compiled the *Mabinogion*: there is a medieval castle mount at Dolbenmaen, thought to have been associated with a *llys*, the court of a Gwynedd prince. It was probably a royal residence until it was abandoned by Llywelyn Fawr in 1230, in favor of Criccieth Castle in the south of the Llyn Peninsula.[33] In the shadow of the castle mount is Plas Dolbenmaen, a house first recorded in 1662.[34] Across the road is St. Mary's church, which dates from the 15th century.[35]

As the soldiers of each army came to Uelen Rhyd (Felinrhyd near Maentwrog), they began firing at each other. Finally it was agreed that Gwydion and Pryderi would fight each other in single combat: "Through strength and valour and aggression and magic and enchantment Gwydion prevailed, and Pryderi was killed." He was buried at Maen Tyuynawc (Maentwrog), upstream from Uelen Rhyd (Y Felynrhyd). Interestingly, Nant Cyll and Dolbemmaen are not far from Clynnog Fawr and the Llyn Peninsula where Caer Dathyl may have been located.

Math then returned to Caer Dathyl and was told by Goewin that she could no longer be his foot-holder, since she had been raped by Gilfaethwy with the help of Gwydion. Math said he would make Goewin his wife, and when Gwydion and Gilfaethwy returned from making a circuit of Math's lands, he punished them in an unusual way:

> he took his magic wand and struck Gilfaethwy, turning him into a sizable hind. He seized [Gwydion] quickly—and though he would have liked to escape, he was not able. He was struck with the same magic wand, turning him into a stag.
> "Since you have been in league together, I will make you fare together and be mated. You will have the same nature as the beasts whose shapes you are in; and during this time, they will have offspring—so you will have them too. A year from today, come to me here."

One year later a stag, a hind and a sturdy fawn turned up at the court, and Math raised his wand, and transformed the pair into a wild boar and a sow. A year later, a wild boar, a wild sow and a fine little piglet turned up at the court, and Math transformed the boar and sow into a she-wolf and wolf. After a further year had passed, a wolf, a she-wolf and a sturdy wolf-cub turned up at court. Then Math struck Gwydion and Gilfaethwy with his magic wand, returning them to their own shape.

Now that the old order was restored, Math needed to find a new footholder, and Gwydion suggested his sister Arianrhod. The name *Arianrhod* is usually translated as "Silver Wheel," and Arianrhod linked to the moon. However, in the Fourth Branch the name consistently appears as *Aranrot*; the word *Aran* survives independently in the mountain names *Yr Aran Fawr* (*Arenig Fawr* in Snowdonia to the east of Porthmadog), and *Aran Benllyn*, also in Snowdonia near Dolgellau, as well as in the name of the Isle of Arran in the Firth of Clyde, Scotland. The Celtic scholar Rachel Bromwich says that the meaning of *aran* is uncertain, but "huge," "round" or "humped" would be possible interpretations.[36]

Arianrhod was brought to Math, who asked her to step over his wand to see if she was a virgin:

> Then she stepped over the magic wand, and in that step she dropped a large boy with curly yellow hair. What the boy did was give a loud cry. After the boy's cry, she made for the door, and in the process a little something [dropped] from her. Before anyone could get second look of it, Gwydion picked it up and wrapped a sheet of brocaded silk around it, and hid it away. [The place] where he hid it was in a small chest at the foot of his bed.

The boy with the yellow curly hair was given the name Dylan, and he made for the sea, where he became in effect a sea-god. As for the "little something":

> As Gwydion was waking up in his bed one day, he heard a cry in the chest at his feet. Although it wasn't loud, it was loud enough for him to hear it. He quickly got up and opened the chest. As he opened it, he could see a little boy thrusting his arms out of the folds of the sheet, pushing it away. He took the boy between his hands, and made for the township with him, where he knew there was a woman with [milk in her] breasts. He made a deal a woman to nurture the boy. The boy was reared for that year. And [he grew so fast that] after the period of a year, they would have been impressed by his size even if he had been two years old.

Within a year he was large enough to go to court, and Gwydion acknowledged him when he came to court, and the boy "got to know him, and loved him more than any other person."

One day Gwydion and the boy made for Caer Arianrhod, a rocky island off the coast of Caernarfonshire, opposite the hillfort of Dinas Dinlle ("Fort of Lleu") near Llandwrog and not far from Clynnog Fawr, and was welcomed by Arianrhod. She then enquired who the boy was:

> "This boy is a boy of yours."
> "Alas, man! What has come over you, shaming me [like this], and continuing my shame, and keeping it with you for as long as this?"
> "If your shame is nothing more than my having reared a boy this fine, then a small thing is your shame."
> "What is the name of your boy?" said she.
> "God knows," said he "there is no name upon him yet."
> "Aye," said she "I will swear an oath upon him: he will not get a name until he gets it from me."

Gwydion, not surprisingly, reacted with fury to Arianrhod's oath, and swore that the boy would get a name. The next day he and the boy walked along the ocean and conjured up a ship out of dulse (a kind of red algae that has long been used as a food) and sea-girdle (a variety of brown kelp), and conjured dovan leather out of sea-weed and dulse. He and the boy then sailed to Caer Arianrhod disguised as shoemakers. When Arianrhod discovered they were shoemakers, she ordered some shoes—but the first pair were too large, and the second pair too small. Finally she went out to the boat:

> When she came, he was cutting-out, and the boy was stitching.
> "Aye, Lady," he said "good day to you."
> "God give well to you," said she "it seems strange to me that you are not able to adjust the shoes to my measure."
> "I couldn't," he said "[but] now I can."
> At that, suddenly, there was a wren alighting on the deck of the boat. The boy took aim and hit it between the sinew and the bone of its leg. She laughed.

> "God knows," said she "the fair one strikes it with a skilful hand!"
> "Aye," he replied "and the wrath of God upon you! He has obtained a name, and the name is good enough "Lleu Skillful Hand" he will be from now on."

Lleu is the equivalent of the Celtic god Lugus and the Irish hero Lugh, and this episode is a pale imitation of the episode in Irish mythology in which Lugh kills the giant Balor by casting a spear through his eye. The Celtic god Lugus is well known but less well understood. There are few inscriptions dedicated to Lugus, and the most famous is the one from Uxama (Osma) in Spain, in Latin, which reads: "L. L. Urcico dedicated this, sacred to the Lugoves, to the guild of shoemakers"[37] (which explains why Gwydion and his foster-son were working as shoe-makers). The origins of the name *Lugus* are disputed. Some link it to a word meaning "light," related to Welsh *llug*, "light, radiance, lustre," Welsh *lluched*, "flash of lightning,"[38] while others link it to Welsh *llw*, "oath," Old Irish *luige*, to swear; oath."[39] If Lugus is a god of oaths, then this might explain why Arianrhod swear an oath on Lleu.

Arianrhod's reaction to the boy seems strange, but there may be a good reason. In the genealogy of Brycheiniog (a kingdom in southeast Wales) contained in the Harleian 3859 manuscript, we find the Old Welsh name *Lou Hen map Guidgen*. If this can be interpreted as "Lleu the Old, son of Gwydion," then it means that Gwydion is actually the father of Lleu.[40]

Arianrhod was furious at being deceived by Gwydion and swore another oath on the boy—that he "never take arms until I arm him myself." Some time later Gwydion and Lleu walked as far as Brynn Aryen (Brynaerau, between Llandwrog and Clynnog Fawr), then at the top of Cefyn Cludno (Cefn Clydno) near Capel Uchaf, to the south of Clynnog Fawr, they kitted out some horses and went to Caer Arianrhod. There they disguised themselves as bards, and entertained Arianrhod and her court, and a room was prepared for them. The next morning

> At cock-crow, Gwydion arose. Then he invoked his enchantment and his powers. At the first light of day, there was a multitude of trumpet blasts and shouting resounding throughout the countryside. When day-break came they heard a knocking on the chamber door, and (at that) Aranrhod asking them to open it. The youth got up and opened it. She came inside, a maiden with her.
> "Good men," said she "we are in an evil position."
> "Aye," he replied "we can hear trumpets and shouting. What do you suppose from that?"
> "God knows," said she "we can't even see the colour of the ocean for all the boats crammed-up together [out there]. And the bulk [of them] are heading for land as fast as they can. What should we do?"

At Gwydion's suggestion, Arianrhod got some weapons and armed Lleu. Once Lleu was fully armed, Gwydion told her that they no longer had any need of the weapons—there was not a single boat to be seen. Angry at being tricked again, Arianrhod swore another destiny on Lleu—"that he will never get a wife, from any race that is in the world today!"

Gwydion then approached Math and told him of Arianrhod's oath. Math had a solution:

> "Aye," said Math "we must endeavour, you and I, to conjure a wife for him out of flowers, using our magic and enchantment."
> [Lleu], for his part, was a fully grown man, and the most handsome youth anyone had ever seen.
> Then they took the flowers of the oak, the flowers of the broom, and the flowers of the

The reconstructed wall of Tomen Y Mur roman fort, Gwynedd, Wales, September 1, 2009 (Maxentius2).

meadowsweet—and from those they called forth the fairest and most beautiful woman anyone had ever seen. She was baptised with the baptism they practiced [back] then, and [the name of] "Blodeuedd" was put upon her.

Now that Lleu had a wife, he needed a territory to rule, and Math gave him Dunoding, later called Eifionydd and Ardudwy. Lleu set up his court in Mur Castell, also known as Tomen Y Mur. This is a Roman military settlement 2 miles southeast of Maentwrog, established in the late 1st century and occupied into the 2nd century if not later. The site continued to be important into the early medieval period and the fort defenses may have been refortified, possibly when Norman armies encamped here in the late–11th early–12th century. The "Tomen," the great castle mound, was probably raised in the 12th or 13th century and may have been associated with a *llys* of a local prince.[41]

One day Lleu went to Caer Dathyl, and while he was gone, Blodeuedd heard the blast of a horn, and saw an exhausted stag pursued by dogs and huntsmen. She sent a servant to find out who it was, and he reported that it was Gronw Pebyr, lord of Penllyn, a district above Lake Bala, well to the east of Mur Castell. Gronw may be derived from Proto-Celtic *uironos* "man-slaying," related to Homeric Greek *andro-phonos* "man-slaying," an epithet applied to the Trojan prince Hector.[42] Gronw caught the stag by the River Cynfael (Cynfal), a tributary of the Dwyryd, which flows to the north of Toman Y Mur. As he was passing the gate of the court, Blodeuedd saw him and invited him in. As soon as they saw each other, they fell passionately in love, and it wasn't long before they were discussing how to get rid of Lleu. Gronw advised Blodeuedd to "find out from him by what means his death might come—under the pretence of caring about him." So Blodeuedd said to Lleu that she was worried about his death, in case he died before her, but Lleu reassured her, saying it would not be easy to kill him:

> "It is not easy," he continued "to kill me by a blow . It would be necessary to spend a year making the spear to strike me with—and without making any of it [at any other time] except when one was at mass on Sundays."
> "And is that certain?" she asked.
> "It's certain, God knows," he replied "I cannot be killed inside a house, nor outside," he continued "I cannot be killed on horseback or on foot."
> "Aye," said she "[so] in what way can you be killed?"
> "I'll tell you," he replied. "By making a bath for me by the side of a river, making a curved, slatted roof over the tub, and thatching that well and without [leaving] any gaps. And bringing a buck," he continued "and putting it next to the tub, and me putting one of my feet on the buck's back, and the other one on the side of the tub. Whoever would strike me [while I am] like that would bring about my death."

Blodeuedd told Gronw this, and he spent the next year making a spear. Once the spear was ready, Blodeuedd asked Lleu to demonstrate how he might be killed. She told Gronw to wait by the River Cynfael, and arranged for all the goats in the district to be herded together (Lleu specified a buck, which might mean a goat, but could also mean a young male deer). Then Blodeuedd had the bath and slatted roof prepared—Lleu took a bath, then put one foot on the edge of the bath and one foot on a buck:

> Gronw rose up from the hill that was called Bryn Kyfergyr, went up on one knee, and cast the poison spear and struck him on the side, with the shaft protruding out of him and the head stuck inside. Then [Lleu] took flight in the form of an eagle, and gave a terrible scream, and after that they lost sight of him.

Math and Gwydion received news of what had happened, and Gwydion set out to look for Lleu. He wandered through Gwynedd and Powys, and finally came to Arfon, and to the house of the son of a villain in Maenawr Bennard, where he spent the night. The man there had a sow who wandered about freely during the day, and the next morning, after the sow had been released from her sty, Gwydion followed the sow to Nant Lleu (Nantlle, to the southeast of Llandwrog), where she started grazing:

> Gwydion, for his part, came under the tree, and looked for what the sow was grazing on. He could see the sow was grazing on rotting flesh and maggots. He looked up into the top of the tree. When he looked up, he could see an eagle in the top of the tree. When the eagle shook himself, worms and rotting flesh fell from him, and those the sow was devouring. It occurred to him that the eagle was Lleu, and he sung an englyn:
>
>> "An oak grows between two pools,
>> Dark-black branches sky and glen
>> If I do not tell a lie
>> From the flowers of Lleu this has come!"

The eagle let himself down until he was in the middle of the tree. [Then] Gwydion sang another englyn:

> "An oak grows upon a high plain
> Rain neither wets it, nor drips upon it
> Nine-score strikes has it endured
> In its top, Lleu Skillful-Hand

And then he let himself down until he was on the lowest branch of the tree. Then [Gwydion] sang an englyn:

> Grows an oak upon a steep
> The sanctuary of fair lord
> Unless I speak falsely:
> Lleu will come down into my lap

And he fell onto Gwydion's knee; and then Gwydion struck him with a magic wand, until he was [back] in his own form.

Lleu was in a sorry state, but Gwydion returned with him to Caer Dathyl, and within a year he was restored to health. They then raised an army and Gwydion headed for Mur Castell. Blodeuedd tried to escape, but Gwydion caught up with her, and changed her into an owl. Gronw fled to Penllyn, and Lleu challenged him to come to the River Cynfael and receive a spear from him, just as he had received a spear from Gronw. Gronw, with Lleu's agreement, stood behind a rock, but the spear pierced the rock and killed Gronw.

Druids in Early Medieval Wales

The name *Math* appears to be derived from an ancient word for "bear," and this may have its roots in Neolithic shamanism. Lappland is in northern Finland and Sweden, and when the Lapp shaman "went to the gods in the sky, he adopted the appearance of the bear (the mythical ancestor shaman) to increase his strength."[43] Among the Khanty of western Siberia, the bear "may be a totem and, at the same time a spirit helper of a particular shaman."[44]

Gwydion and Arianrhod are both children of Don, and if *Don* means "earth" as Koch suggests, then this links them to the Druids. According to Caesar the Druids taught that the Gauls were descended from the earth god that he calls Dis Pater, possibly in fact the earth goddess called Litavis, who is associated with an early name for Brittany, and possibly with the Corieltauvi of Leicestershire and Lincolnshire.

Math and Gwydion certainly appear to be Druids, and it is significant that when they create Blodeuedd, they use flowers of the oak, which is famously associated with the Druids, and meadowsweet, used since the Neolithic to flavor mead. Lleu is the god Lugus, and when Gwydion finds him after he is "killed" by Gronw, the eagle Lleu is sitting in an oak tree.

The Druids famously believed in reincarnation, and there are hints of reincarnation when Math transforms Gwydion and Gilfaethwy into animals, and when Lleu changes into an eagle. The Celtic scholar John Koch says that these episodes may be "interpreted as reflecting traditions of transformation and rebirth." Koch also quotes from an Irish theological treatise written around AD 655, called *De mirabilibus sacrae scripturae* ("On the miracles of the holy scripture"), which speaks of "the ridiculous fables of the druids who say that their ancestors flew through the ages in the form of birds."[45]

The Druids of course disappeared with the coming of Christianity, but were not entirely forgotten. St. Illtud is associated with Llantwit Major (*Llanilltud* in Welsh), and is described in the *Life* of St. Samson. The author tells us that "Illtud was of all the Britons the most accomplished in all the Scriptures, namely of the Old and New Testaments, and in those of philosophy of every kind, of geometry namely, and of rhetoric, grammar and arithmetic, and of all the theories of philosophy. And by birth he was a most wise magician, having knowledge of the future."⁴⁶ Presumably, by "magician" the author meant "Druid." Llantwit Major is quite close to the Late Bronze Age/Iron Age feasting site at Llanmaes, which was almost certainly presided over by Druids.

Anne Ross says that druidism seemed to still persist in late 6th century Ireland, well after St. Patrick's mission, as this extract from the *Life* of St. Mochuda shows⁴⁷:

> On a certain day in early springtime there came to tempt him a Druid (*draoi*), who said to him "In the name of your God cause this apple-tree branch to produce foliage." Mochuda knew that it was in contempt of the divine power the Druid proposed this, and the branch put forward leaves on the instant. The Druid demanded "In the name of your God put blossoms on it." Mochuda made the sign of the Cross over the branch and it blossomed presently. The Druid persisted "What profits blossom without fruit?" For the third time Mochuda blessed the branch, and the fruit, fully ripe, fell to earth. The Druid picked up an apple off the ground and, examining it, understood it was quite sour, whereupon he objected. "Such miracles as these are worthless, since the fruit is left uneatable." Mochuda blessed the apples and they became as sweet as honey. And in punishment for his opposition the Druid was deprived of his eyesight for a year. He went away, and at the end of the year he came back to Mochuda and did penance, whereupon he received his sight back again, and he returned home rejoicing.

St. Mochuda is associated with Lismore, Co. Waterford, in the southeast of Ireland.

We also have reports of druids in Scotland around the same time. Ross notes⁴⁸ that Adamnan, in his *Life of St. Columba*, reports that when St. Columba journeyed into the Inverness region of Pictland to convert the pagan Picts, he had to deal with Broichan, the hostile druid of the pagan Pictish king Brude. Brude converted, but Broichan remained hostile until he became ill. St. Columba was summoned—he caused a quartz pebble to be placed in some water, the stone came to the surface, Broichan drank some of the water, and was cured.

In some ways the most enigmatic figure in the Fourth Branch is Arianrhod, who apparently exists only to give birth to Dylan and Lleu, and swear a series of oaths on Lleu. The only female in British mythology associated with oaths is Sulis, the goddess of Roman Bath, who was the recipient of over a hundred curse tablets, and there are certain similarities between Sulis and Arianrhod. Like Sulis, Arianrhod is associated with water: Caer Arianrhod appears to be an island (at least some of the time), and Arianrhod's son Dylan is a sea god. And although Arianrhod does not punish wrongdoers, she does curse her son three times (he of course can be seen as a substitute for whoever it was who made her pregnant). If Arianrhod was originally Aranrot, then "enormous wheel" or "round wheel" might refer to the sun, just as Sulis ("Eye") is indirectly linked to the sun.

As I said, Caer Arianrhod may have been an island (as befits an otherworldly place, its status is rather vague), and the most famous holy island in early medieval Gwynedd is Bardsey Island is off the western tip of the Llyn Peninsula. The earliest reference to a monastery on Bardsey is a record of the death of a monk in 1011. In about 1200 it was reformed or refounded as a priory of Augustianian canons, and up until the dissolution, it was an important pilgrimage center for Wales. St. Cadfan is said to have founded a monastery there, though it may have been a retreat used by monks living on the mainland at Aberdaron or at nearby Capel Anelog, on the eastern slope of a hill called Mynydd Anelog, where two gravestones were found dating from the late 5th or early 6th century.⁴⁹ The gravestones are in Latin: one reads "Here lies the priest Veracius," while the other reads "Here lies the priest Senacus with a multitude of his brothers."⁵⁰

Saints may have taken the place of Druids in the early medieval period, and they may also have inherited some of the attributes of Druids. Beuno is the saint associated with Clynnog Fawr, and a story is told in *Life* of St. Beuno of a very special oak tree[51]:

> Beuno lived on the land he had inherited from his father and built a church there, consecrating it in the name of Christ the Lord. He planted an acorn by the side of his father's grave, which grew into an oak tree of great height and thickness. From the crown of this tree there grew a branch right down to the ground and from the ground back up to the top of the tree so that the bend in the branch was touching the ground. This is how it always remained. If an Englishman passes between the branch and the trunk of the tree, he shall drop dead on the spot, but if a Welshman does so, he shall be none the worse.

We tend to think of Druids as priests, but they were also skilled in medicine. Pliny, in the passage in which he says that Druids pick mistletoe on the sixth day of the moon, explains what mistletoe is used for[52]: "[The Druids] believe that mistletoe given in drink will impart fertility to any animal that is barren, and that it is an antidote for all poisons." In another passage, Pliny discusses a herb called *selago* (lycopodium, or fir clubmoss)[53]:

> Similar to savin is the herb known as "selago." Care is taken to gather it without the use of iron, the right hand being passed for the purpose through the left sleeve of the tunic, as though the gatherer were in the act of committing a theft. The clothing must be white, the feet bare and washed clean, and a sacrifice of bread and wine must be made before gathering it: it is carried also in a new napkin. The Druids of Gaul have pretended that this plant should be carried about the person as a preservative against accidents of all kinds, and that the smoke of it is extremely good for all maladies of the eyes.

This healing role was taken over by medieval saints, among them St. Beuno, who is closely linked to another Welsh saint, Gwenfrewi, better known as Winefride or Winifred and associated with Holywell in Flintshire, northeast Wales. According to the 14th century *Life* of St. Beuno, Winefride was the only child of noble parents, and a virgin. One Sunday, while her parents were at church, the local ruler Caradog tried to rape her. Escaping, Winefride fled towards Beuno's church; but Prince Caradog caught her on the hillside, and cut off her head. Beuno cursed the unrepentant Caradog, who melted away. Happily for Winefride, she miraculously survived this fatal blow[54]:

> Beuno took the girl's head and placed it back with the body, covering the body with his cloak and saying to her mother and father who were mourning for her: "Be quiet for a little while and leave her as she is until the Mass is over." Then Beuno celebrated the sacrifice to God. When the Mass was finished, the girl rose up entirely healed and dried the sweat from her face; God and Beuno healed her. Where her blood fell to earth, a spring was formed, which even today still heals people and animals from their illnesses and injuries.

We don't know what the Druids thought of animals, but we do know that in the Iron Age people were buried with animals—so it is not surprising that many Celtic saints had an affinity with animals. St. Melangell is associated with Pennant Melangell near Llangynog in Powys, east Wales. Pennant Melangell, in the remote Tanat valley, 8 miles northwest of the nearest small town of Llanfyllin, lies on the valley floor where a stream, Nant Ewyn, enters the River Tanat. There is a charming story told in the *Life* of Melangell, which dates to the late 15th or early 16th century.[55] One day a prince of Powys called Brychwel Ysgithrog was out hunting and his dogs went in pursuit of a hare:

> he too gave chase until he came to a certain thicket of brambles, which was large and full of thorns. In this thicket he found a girl of beautiful appearance who, given up to divine

The tower of St. Melangell's Church in Powys, east Wales, October 16, 2009 (Gerald Morgan).

contemplation, was praying with the greatest devotion, with the said hare lying boldly and fearlessly under the hem or fold of her garments, its face toward the dogs.
Then the prince cried "Get it hounds, get it!" but the more he shouted, urging them on, the further the dogs retreated and, howling, fled from the little animal. Finally, the prince, altogether astonished, asked the girl how long she had lived on her own on his lands. in such a lonely spot. In reply the girl said she had not seen a human face for these fifteen years.

St. Brynach is associated with the small village of Nevern on the River Nevern in Pembrokeshire, south west. His 12th century *Life* tells us that he could tame wild animals[56]:

a cow, which he had segregated from the others, as if unique and singular for his need, both on account of the size of her body, because she was larger than the rest, and also on account of the abundance of her milk, he deputed to the custody of a wolf, which in the manner of a well-trained herdsman drove the cow in the morning to the pastures, and in the evening brought her home in safety.

St. Patrick is said to have brought Christianity to Ireland, and Muirchu, in his 7th century *Life* of St. Patrick, tells this story. One day, as Patrick and several companions were surveying land at Armagh where a church was to be built, they climbed to the top of a hill[57]:

They found a deer, with her little fawn, lying in the place where is now an altar of the church of Armagh, and the associates of Patrick rashly wished to slay the fawn, but the Saint was unwilling, and did not permit it; but the Saint himself, holding the fawn, carried it on his shoulders, and the deer following him, even like a most attached sheep, until at

The Church of St. Brynach, Pembrokeshire, February 21, 2007 (LinguisticDemographer).

length he let down the fawn in another wood, situated at the northern side of Armagh, where those persons skilled in such matters say, that some signs of his virtue remain even to this day.

St. Cuthbert was an Anglo-Saxon saint from Northumbria who was educated at Irish monasteries like Melrose in the Scottish borders. Once he was staying at the monastery of St. Abb's Head in Berwickshire, on the southeast coast of Scotland. While he was there, he used to go out alone at night, and one night a brother of the monastery followed him[58]:

> when he left the monastery,[he] went down to the sea, which flows beneath, and going into it, until the water reached his neck and arms, spent the night in praising God. When the

dawn of day approached, he came out of the water, and, falling on his knees, began to pray again. Whilst he was doing this, two quadrupeds, called otters, came up from the sea, and, lying down before him on the sand, breathed upon his feet, and wiped them with their hair after which, having received his blessing, they returned to their native element.

Math and Arthur

Math and Arthur both seem to be linked by the bear. In the case of Math, the word *math* is archaic, and almost certainly belongs to the Iron Age or earlier; while in the case of Arthur, *arth* is the normal word for "bear," and reinforces my belief that Arthur is a product of Roman or post-Roman Britain.

However, there are similarities between the two. Firstly, pigs, which in the Fourth Branch originate in the Otherworld, play an important role in both the Fourth Branch and *Culhwch and Olwen*: in the Fourth Branch, Gwydion obtains Pryderi's pigs by deception and provokes a war, and a sow leads Gwydion to the eagle Lleu; while the high point of *Culhwch and Olwen* is the hunt for the boar Twrch Trwyth. Pigs, of course, were associated with feasting from the Neolithic to the Iron Age.

Secondly, islands play a significant role in both the Fourth Branch and the Arthurian stories: Arianrhod's fortress Caer Arianrhod sometimes appears to be an island, and islands appear in tales of Arthur from *The Spoils of Annwn* to the *History of the Kings of Britain*. As the history of Caldey Island shows, islands were sacred places from the earliest times, and as Stonea Camp and Sutton Common demonstrate, islands in fens and marshes were also sacred places.

Thirdly, Arthur is the protector of his people, which may link him to the god *Toutatis* "Protector of the Tribe," and Caer Dathyl may be derived from Tuathal or Tudwal, that is *Toutovalos* "Ruler of the People." We don't know if Toutatis was widely venerated, but he was certainly popular in Lincolnshire in the Roman period, and is known from Leicestershire, Hertfordshire and Cumbria.

Finally, though Arianrhod of the Fourth Branch and Guinevere of later Arthurian tales may seem like very different characters, there are surprising similarities. In the 12th century *Dialogue of Melwas and Gwenhwyfar*, Guinevere betrays Arthur with Melwas from the Isle of Glass (Glastonbury); Arianrhod is apparently unmarried, but she does betray her son Lleu by seeking to deny him a name, weapons and a wife. Melwas probably lived on Glastonbury Tor, which is a peninsula washed on three sides by the River Brue, and Caer Arianrhod appears to be an island.

These links between Math and Arthur reminds us just how complex the origins of Arthur may be. With Neolithic bears and shamanism, prehistoric sacred islands, and influences from Germanic or Thracian soldiers in Roman times, Arthur seems to have brought together British pagan beliefs spanning a period of at least three millennia. We may never truly know the origins of Arthur, but the search for answers will continue to enthrall those of us who are fascinated by this Dark Age hero.

Chapter Notes

Introduction

1. John Koch, "Eriu, Alba, Letha: When Was a Language Ancestral to Gaelic First Spoken in Ireland?" *Emania* 9 (1991), 17–18.
2. Barry Cunliffe, *Druids: A Very Short Introduction* (Oxford: Oxford University Press, 2010), 38.
3. John Koch, "A Case for Tartessian as a Celtic Language," *Acta Palaeohispanica X: Palaeohispanica* 9 (2009), 341.
4. *Ibid.*, 339.
5. Jane McIntosh, *Handbook to Life in Prehistoric Europe* (Santa Barbara, CA: ABC-CLIO, 2006), 187.
6. Leonardo Garcia Sanjuan, "The Warrior Stelae of the Iberian South-West: Symbols of Power in Ancestral Landscapes," in T. Moore and L. Armada Pita (eds.), *Atlantic Europe in the First Millennium BC: Crossing the Divide* (Oxford: Oxford University Press, 2010), 534–5.
7. Barry Cunliffe, *Britain Begins* (Oxford: Oxford University Press, 2013), 284.
8. John Koch, *O'donnell Lectures 2008*, at the website http://www.wales.ac.uk/Resources/Documents/Research/ODonnell.pdf.
9. John Koch, "A Case for Tartessian as a Celtic Language," 341.
10. John Koch, "Eriu, Alba, Letha: When Was a Language Ancestral to Gaelic First Spoken in Ireland?" 21.
11. Graham Isaac, "The Origins of the Celtic Languages: Language Spread from East to West," in Barry Cunliffe and John T. Koch. *Celtic from the West: Alternative Perspectives from Archaeology, Genetics, Language and Literature* (Oxford: Oxbow Books, 2010), 154–67.
12. John Koch, "Eriu, Alba, Letha: When Was a Language Ancestral to Gaelic First Spoken in Ireland?" 23.
13. *Ibid.*, 24.
14. Julius Pokorny, *Indogermanisches etymologisches Wörterbuch* (Bern: Francke, 1959), 201–202.
15. *Ibid.*, 11.
16. Julius Caesar, *Commentaries on the Gallic War*, trans. W.A. McDevitte and W.S. Bohn (New York: Harper and Brothers, 1869), Book 1, Chapter 1; Book 2, Chapter 4.
17. Book 6, Chapter 13.
18. *Ibid.*, Book 6, Chapter 14.
19. *Ibid.*, Book 6, Chapter 16.
20. *Ibid.*, Book 6, Chapter 17.
21. *Ibid.*, Book 6, Chapter 18.
22. Diodorus Siculus, *Historical Library*, trans. C.H. Oldfather (Cambridge, MA: Harvard University Press), Book 5, Chapter 31.
23. *Ibid.*, Book 5, Chapter 28.
24. *Ibid.*, Book 5, Chapter 29.
25. Strabo, *Geography*, trans. H.L. Jones (Cambridge, MA: Harvard University Press, 1923), Book 4, Chapter 4.
26. Ministère de la Culture et de la Communication, *The Gauls in Provence: The Oppidum of Entremont*, at the website http://www.entremont.culture.gouv.fr/en/index2.html.
27. Tacitus, *Annals*, trans. Alfred John Church and William Jackson Brodribb (New York: Random House, 1942), Book 14, Chapter 30.
28. Coflein (database of the Royal Commission on the Ancient and Historical Monuments of Wales), *Llyn Cerrig Bach*.
29. Strabo, *Geography*, Book 4, Chapter 1.
30. Barry Cunliffe, *Druids: A Very Short Introduction*, 37.
31. *Ibid.*, 51–2.

Chapter 1

1. Chris Scarre, *Monuments and Landscape in Atlantic Europe* (London: Routledge, 2005), 23.
2. Clive Ruggles, *Seven-Stone Antas* (Portugal and Spain), at the website http://www2.cliveruggles.com/index.php/image-coll/category/1-seven-stone-antas.
3. Michael Hoskin, "Studies in Iberian Archaeoastronomy: (9) an Overview," *Archaeoastronomy* 27 (2002), S76-S77.
4. Chris Scarre, *Landscapes of Neolithic Brittany* (Oxford: Oxford University Press, 2011), 103.
5. *Ibid.*, 117.
6. Ministère de la Culture, *Megalithism in Morbihan: Gavrinis*, at the website http://www.culture.gouv.fr/fr/arcnat/megalithes/en/mega/megagav_en.htm.
7. Barry Cunliffe, *Druids: A Very Short Introduction* (Oxford: Oxford University Press, 2010), 44.
8. Martin Brennan, *The Stones of Time: Calendars, Sundials, and Stone Chambers of Ancient Ireland* (Rochester, VT: Inner Traditions International, 1994), 46–8.
9. Historic Scotland, *Calanais Standing Stones*, at the website http://www.historic-scotland.gov.uk/propertyoverview.htm?PropID=PL_051.
10. Gerald Ponting, *2006/7 Southern Moon Skim at the Callanish Stones*, at the website http://home.clara.net/gponting/page42.html.
11. Clive Ruggles, *Ancient Astronomy: An Encyclopedia of Cosmologies and Myth* (Santa Barbara, CA: ABC-CLIO, 2005), 237.
12. Nicholas Higham, M.J. Ryan, *The Anglo-Saxon World* (New Haven, CT: Yale University Press, 2013), 149.
13. Coflein, *Bryn Celli Ddu*.
14. Steve Burrow, "Sensational New Discoveries at Bryn Celli Ddu," *British Archaeology* 89 (July/August 2006).
15. Mike Parker Pearson, "Bluestones at Stonehenge," *British Archaeology* 110 (Jan/Feb 2010).
16. Mike Pitts, *Hengeworld* (London: Arrow Books, 2000), 121.
17. Mike Parker Pearson, "Who Was Buried at Stonehenge?" *Antiquity* 83 (2009), 23–39.
18. Mike Parker Pearson, Josh Pollard, Colin Richards, Julian Thomas, Chris Tilley and Kate Welham, *The Stonehenge Riverside Project 2007: Excavation I*, at the website http://www.shef.ac.uk/archaeolo

gy/research/2.4329/stonehenge07-01.

19. Royal Astronomical Society, *Stonehenge and Ancient Astronomy*, at the website http://www.ras.org.uk/images/stories/ras_pdfs/misc/Stonehenge.LowRes.pdf.

20. Pastscape (English Heritage database), *Durrington Walls*.

21. Mike Parker Pearson, Josh Pollard, Colin Richards, Julian Thomas, Christopher Tilley, Kate Welham and Umberto Albarella, "Materializing Stonehenge: The Stonehenge Riverside Project and New Discoveries," *Journal of Material Culture* 11 (2006), 227–261.

22. Mike Parker Pearson, Josh Pollard, Colin Richards, Julian Thomas, Chris Tilley and Kate Welham, "A New Avenue at Durrington Walls," *Past* 52 (April 2006), 1–2.

23. Mike Parker Pearson, Ros Cleal, Josh Pollard, Colin Richards, Julian Thomas, Chris Tilley, Kate Welham, Andrew Chamberlain, Carolyn Chenery, Jane Evans, Janet Montgomery and Mike Richards, "The Age of Stonehenge," *Antiquity* 81 (2007), 617–639.

24. Christopher Tilley, *Interpreting Landscapes: Geologies, Topographies, Identities; Explorations in Landscape Phenomenology 3* (Walnut Creek, CA: Left Coast Press, 2010), 445.

25. Jim Leary and David Field, "Journeys and Juxtapositions: Marden Henge and the View from the Vale," in Alex M. Gibson (ed.), *Enclosing the Neolithic: Recent Studies in Britain and Europe* (Oxford: Archaeopress, 2012), 58–9.

26. Ibid., 64.
27. Ibid., 60.
28. Ibid., 61.
29. Ibid., 62.
30. Pastscape, *Dorset Cursus*.

31. Martin Green, *The Dorset Cursus*, at the website Digital Digging http://digitaldigging.net/dorset-cursus-monument-map/.

32. Pastscape, *Site VIII*.

33. Clive Ruggles, *Astronomy in Prehistoric Britain and Ireland* (New Haven, CT: Yale University Press, 1999), 127.

34. David Lloyd, "The Astronomy at Godmanchester: A Possible Neolithic Observatory," *Archaeoastronomy* 22 (2009), 34–52.

35. Jan Harding, Ben Johnston and Glyn Goodrick, "Neolithic Cosmology and the Monument Complex of Thornborough, North Yorkshire," *Archaeoastronomy* 20 (2006), 28–9.

36. Jan Harding and Ben Johnson, "Yorkshire's Holy Secret," *British Archaeology* 75 (March 2004).

37. Jan Harding, Ben Johnston and Glyn Goodrick, "Neolithic Cosmology and the Monument Complex of Thornborough, North Yorkshire," 45.

38. Ibid., 47.

39. Hesiod, *Works and Days*, trans. Hugh G. Evelyn-White (London: William Heinemann, 1914), lines 615–620, lines 415–420.

40. Jan Harding, *The Neolithic and Bronze Age Monument Complex of Thornborough, North Yorkshire, and Its Landscape Context: Desk Top Assessment*, at the website http://thornborough.ncl.ac.uk/desktop_assessment/desktop_contents.htm.

41. Canmore, *South Ronaldsay, Isbister*.

42. Mike Pitts, "Flight of the Eagles," *British Archaeology* 86 (January/February 2006).

43. Pastscape, *Willerby Wold Long Barrow*.

44. Coflein, *Parc Le Breos Burial Chamber*.

45. Pastscape, *Ascott-Under-Wychwood*.

46. Pastscape, *West Kennet Long Barrow*.

47. Pastscape, *Windmill Hill Causewayed Enclosure*.

48. Rosamund Cleal, "Great Sites: Windmill Hill," *British Archaeology* 67 (October 2002).

49. Rosamund Cleal, "Human Remains from Windmill Hill and West Kennet Avenue, Avebury Parish, Wiltshire, Held by the Alexander Keiller Museum," in David Thackray and Sebastian Payne, *Draft Report on the Request for the Reburial of Human Remains from the Alexander Keiller Museum at Avebury* (London: National Trust and English Heritage, 2008).

50. Pastscape, *Hambledon Hill*.

51. Pastscape, *Etton Causewayed Enclosure*.

52. Francis Pryor, *Etton: Excavations at a Neolithic Causewayed Enclosure Near Maxey Cambridgeshire, 1982-7* (London: English Heritage, 1998), 271–2.

53. Ibid., 30.
54. Ibid., 68.

55. Robert Hertz, "A Contribution to the Study of the Collective Representation of Death" in Hertz, *Death and the Right Hand*, trans. Rodney and Claudia Needham (Glencoe, IL: The Free Press, 1960), 27–86.

56. Martin Smith, "Bones Chewed by Canids as Evidence for Human Excarnation: A British Case Study," *Antiquity* 80 (2006), 671–685.

57. R. Thomas and L. McFadyen, "Animals and Cotswold-Severn Long Barrows: A Re-Examination," *Proceedings of the Prehistoric Society* 76 (2010), 102–3.

58. Pastscape, *Bowls Barrow*.

59. Pastscape, *Monument No. 215662*.

60. Dale Serjeantson, *Review of Animal Remains from the Neolithic and Early Bronze Age of Southern Britain* (London: English Heritage, 2011), 76.

61. Ibid., 71.

62. Pastscape, *Monument No. 213515*.

63. Pastscape, *Monument No. 1080765*.

64. Axel Pollex, "Comments on the Interpretation of the So-Called Cattle-Burials of Neolithic Central Europe," *Antiquity* 73 (1999), 542–550.

65. Euan Mackie, "The Prehistoric Solar Calendar: An Out-Of-Fashion Idea Revisited with New Evidence," *Time and Mind* 2.1 (March 2009), 13.

Chapter 2

1. Alan Outram, Natalie Stear, Robin Bendrey, Sandra Olsen, Alexei Kasparov, Victor Zaibert, Nick Thorpe, Richard Evershed, "The Earliest Horse Harnessing and Milking," *Science* 6 (March 2009), 1332–1335.

2. Philip L. Kohl, *The Making of Bronze Age Eurasia* (Cambridge: Cambridge University Press, 2007), 84–5.

3. Sarunas Milisauskas, *European Prehistory: A Survey* (New York: Springer, 2011), 236.

4. Edgar C. Polomé and Werner Winter, *Reconstructing Languages and Cultures* (New York: Mouton de Gruyter, 1992), 294.

5. Ibid., 295.

6. Andrew Sherratt, "The Transformation of Early Agrarian Europe: The Later Neolithic and Copper Ages 4500–2500 BC," in Barry Cunliffe (ed.), *The Oxford Illustrated History of Prehistoric Europe* (Oxford: Oxford University Press, 2001), 191.

7. Barry Cunliffe, *Britain Begins* (Oxford: Oxford University Press, 2013), 198.

8. Deutsches Archäologisches Institut, *Zambujal*, at the website http://www.dainst.org/en/project/zambujal?ft=all.

9. Barry Cunliffe, *Britain Begins*, 198.

10. Ibid., 200.
11. Ibid., 200–1.

12. B. Höppner, M. Bartelheim, M. Huijsmans, R. Krauss, K.-P. Martinek, E. Pernicka and R. Schwab, "Prehistoric Copper Production in

the Inn Valley (Austria), and the Earliest Copper in Central Europe," *Archaeometry* 47 (2005), 298–9.

13. Giuliani Morteani and Jeremy P. Northover, *Prehistoric Gold in Europe* (Dordrecht, Netherlands: Springer, 1994), 167.

14. Roland Müller, Gert Goldenberg, Martin Barthelheim, Michael Kunst and Ernst Pernicka, "Zambujal and the Beginnings of Metallurgy in Southern Portugal," in Susan La Niece, Duncan Hook and Paul T. Craddock (eds.), *Metals and Mines: Studies in Archaeometallurgy* (London: Archetype Publications, 2007), 15–16.

15. William O'Brien, "Ross Island, Kerry," *Database of Irish Excavation Reports*, at the website http://www.excavations.ie/report/1993/Kerry/0001504/.

16. *Pentrwyn Bronze Age Metalworking Site, Great Orme*, at the website *Ancient Arts* http://www.ancient-arts.org/Pentrwyn%20Bronze%20Age%20Metalworking%20Site.htm.

17. A.L.F. Rivet and Colin Smith, *The Place-Names of Roman Britain* (London: Batsford, 1979), 333.

18. P. R. Kitson, "British and European River-Names," *Transactions of the Philological Society* 94 (1996), 78.

19. *Ibid.*, 81.

20. Julius Pokorny, *Indogermanisches etymologisches Wörterbuch* (Bern: Francke, 1959), 204–206.

21. P. R. Kitson, "British and European River-Names," 87.

22. *Ibid.*, 88.

23. *Ibid.*, 90.

24. Simon Denison, "Tin Mine Closure Marks More than the End of an Era," *British Archaeology* 33 (April 1998).

25. Wessex Archaeology, *The Amesbury Archer*, at the website http://www.wessexarch.co.uk/projects/amesbury/archer.html.

26. Wessex Archaeology, *The Boscombe Bowmen*, at the website http://www.wessexarch.co.uk/projects/wiltshire/boscombe/bowmen.

27. Pastscape, *Hemp Knoll Barrow*.

28. Pastscape, *Monument No. 347818*.

29. Pastscape, *Monument No. 965142*.

30. Pastscape, *Monument No. 79665*.

31. Yorkshire Archaeological Society, *The Folkton Drums*, at the website http://www.prehistory.yas.org.uk/content/folkton.html.

32. Canmore, *Ashgrove*.

33. James H. Dickson, "Bronze Age Mead," *Antiquity* 52 (1978), 108–113.

34. Wiltshire Heritage Museum, *Bush Barrow*, at the website http://www.wiltshiremuseum.org.uk/galleries/?Action=3&obID=89&prevID=9.

35. I.A. Kinnes, I.H. Longworth, I.M. McIntyre, S.P. Needham and W.A. Oddy, "Bush Barrow Gold," *Antiquity* 62 (1988), 24–39.

36. Pastscape, *Wilsford 7*; *Wilsford 8*.

37. Pastscape, *Clandon Barrow*.

38. Pastscape, *Monument No. 458711*.

39. Pastscape, *Rillaton Barrow*.

40. British Museum, *The Rillaton Gold Cup*, at the website http://www.britishmuseum.org/explore/highlights/highlight_objects/pe_prb/t/the_rillaton_gold_cup.aspx.

41. Andy Chapman, *The Bronze Age Barrow Cemetery at Gayhurst*, at the website http://www.mkheritage.co.uk/sga/Gayhurst/barrow.html.

42. Yorkshire Archaeological Society, *Gristhorpe Man*, at the website http://www.prehistory.yas.org.uk/content/gristhorpe.html.

43. Coflein, *Bedd Branwen*.

44. *The Knowes O' Trotty*, at the Orneyjar website http://www.orkneyjar.com/history/knowestrotty/.

45. Christopher Tilley, *Interpreting Landscapes: Explorations in Landscape Phenomenology 3* (Walnut Creek, CA: Left Coast Press, 2010), 257–60.

46. *Ibid.*, 271.

47. *Ibid.*, 272–3.

48. *Ibid.*, 275.

49. Christopher Tilley, *The East Devon Pebblebed Landscape*, at the website http://www.pebblebedsproject.org.uk/east_devon_pebblebed_landscape.html.

50. Christopher Tilley, *Interpreting Landscapes: Explorations in Landscape Phenomenology 3*, 285.

51. Sue Hamilton, Christopher Tilley and Barbara Bender, "Bronze Age Stone Worlds of Bodmin Moor," *Archaeology International* 3 (1999), 13–14.

52. Barbara Bender, Sue Hamilton and Christopher Tilley, *Stone Worlds: Narrative and Reflexivity in Landscape Archaeology* (Walnut Creek, CA: Left Coast Press, 2008), 172.

53. *Ibid.*, 173.

54. *Ibid.*, 83.

55. Royal Astronomical Society, *Archaeo-Astronomy Steps Out from Shadows of the Past*, at the website http://www.ras.org.uk/news-and-press/news-archive/254-news-2014/2468-archaeo-astronomy-steps-out-from-shadows-of-the-past.

56. Martin J. Powell, "Astronomical Alignments at the Crick Barrow in Gwent, South Wales," *Archaeoastronomy* 26 (1995), S49-S56.

57. Marcus Abbott and Hugo Anderson-Whymark, *Stonehenge Laser Scan: Archaeological Analysis Report* (London: English Heritage, 2012), 33–37.

58. *Boscawen-Un Stone Circle*, at the website http://www.historic-cornwall.org.uk/a2m/bronze_age/stone_circle/boscawen_un/boscawen_un.htm.

59. Thomas Goskar, "The Stonehenge Lasershow," *British Archaeology* 73 (November 2003).

60. Wiltshire Heritage Museum, *Mere G6a*, at the website http://www.wiltshireheritagecollections.org.uk/wiltshiresites.asp?page=selectedplace&mwsquery=%7BPlace%20identity%7D=%7BMere%20G6a%7D.

61. Wiltshire Heritage Museum, *Disk/Gold Sun Disk*, at the website http://www.wiltshireheritagecollections.org.uk/index.asp?page=item&mwsquery.

62. Pastscape, *Jugs Barrow*.

63. Simon Timberlake, Adam Gwilt and Mary Davis, "A Copper Age/Early Bronze Age Gold Disc from Banc Tynddol (Penguelan, Cwmystwyth Mines, Cerdigion)," *Antiquity* 302 (December 2004), at the website http://www.antiquity.ac.uk/projgall/timberlake/.

64. National Museum of Ireland, *Safe Secrets: The Story of the Coggalbeg Hoard*, at the website http://www.museum.ie/en/exhibition/coggalbeg-hoard.aspx.

65. M.L. West, *Indo-European Poetry and Myth* (Oxford: Oxford University Press, 2007), 204.

66. Euan Mackie, "The Prehistoric Solar Calendar: An Out-Of-Fashion Idea Revisited with New Evidence," *Time and Mind* 2.1 (March 2009), 29.

67. Wolfhard Schlosser, "Die Himmelsscheibe Von Nebra—Sonne, Mond Und Sterne," in A.D. Wittmann, G. Wolfschmidt and H.W. Duerbeck (eds.), *Development of Solar Research: Proceedings of the Colloquium Freiburg (Breisgau), September 15, 2003* (Frankfurt am Main, Germany: Verlag Harri Deutsch, 2006), 27.

68. Kristian Kristiansen, "The Nebra Find and Early Indo-European Religion," *Tagungen Des Landesmuseums Für Vorgeschichte Halle* 5 (2010), 431–7.

69. Walter Burkert, *Greek Religion: Archaic and Classical* (Hoboken, NJ: John Wiley & Sons, 2013), 212.

70. Diodorus Siculus, *Historical*

Library, trans. C.H. Oldfather (Cambridge, MA: Harvard University Press), Book 4, Chapter 56.

71. Joanna Brück, "Fire, Earth, Water: An Elemental Cosmography in the European Bronze Age," in Timothy Insoll (ed.), *The Oxford Handbook of the Archaeology of Ritual and Religion* (Oxford: Oxford University Press, 2011), 391–2.

72. Kristian Kristiansen and Thomas Larsson, *The Rise of Bronze Age Society* (Cambridge: Cambridge University Press, 2005), 297.

73. J.M. Edmonds, *Lyra Graeca* (Rockville, MD: Wildside Press, 2007), 317.

74. Faya Causey, *Amber and the Ancient World* (Los Angeles, CA: Getty Publications, 2011), 45–6.

75. Homer, *The Odyssey*, trans. Samuel Butler, at the website http://classics.mit.edu/Homer/odyssey.12.xii.html.

76. Alistair Barclay, "Excavating the Living Dead," *British Archaeology* 115 (November–December 2010).

Chapter 3

1. Pastscape, *Fengate*.
2. Pastscape, *Flag Fen*.
3. Duncan Garrow and Chris Gosden, *Technologies of Enchantment? Exploring Celtic Art: 400 BC to AD 100* (Oxford: Oxford University Press, 2012), 128.
4. Peter Ackroyd, *Thames: Sacred River* (London: Vintage, 2007), 370.
5. Richard Bradley, *The Passage of Arms: An Archaeological Analysis of Prehistoric Hoards and Votive Deposits* (Cambridge: Cambridge University Press, 1990), 108–9.
6. Barry Cunliffe, *Iron Age Communities in Britain* (N.p.: Taylor & Francis e-library, 2005), 8514.
7. Canmore, *Edinburgh, Holyrood Park, Duddingston Loch*.
8. Ashmolean Museum, *Bronze Age Cauldron from Shipton-On-Cherwell*, at the website http://britisharchaeology.ashmus.ox.ac.uk/highlights/cauldron.html.
9. Sheridan Bowman and Stuart Needham, "The Dunaverney and Little Thetford Flesh-Hooks: History, Technology and Their Position Within the Later Bronze Age Feasting Complex," *The Antiquaries Journal* 87 (2007), 55.
10. *Ibid.*, 53.
11. *Ibid.*, 56.
12. *Ibid.*, 66.
13. *Ibid.*, 63.
14. Francis Pryor, *The Flag Fen Basin* (London: English Heritage, 2001), 149.
15. *Ibid.*, 264.
16. *Ibid.*, 289.
17. Gregor Nagy, *Greek Mythology and Poetics* (Ithaca, NY: Cornell University Press, 1992), 93–4.
18. *Ibid.*, 100.
19. *Ibid.*, 101.
20. Richard Bradley, "Danish Razors and Swedish Rocks," *Antiquity* 80 (2006), 372–89.
21. English Heritage, *Burnt Mounds* (London: English Heritage, 2011), 2–3.
22. David Gibson and Mark Knight, *Bradley Fen Excavations Whittlesey, Cambridgeshire 2001–2004* (Cambridge: Cambridge Archaeological Unit, 2006), 12.
23. *Ibid.*, 48.
24. *Ibid.*, 64.
25. *Ibid.*, 20.
26. *Ibid.*, 64.
27. Norfolk Heritage Explorer, *Early Bronze Age Burnt Mound and Inhumation*, at the website http://www.heritage.norfolk.gov.uk/.
28. Lilian Ladle and Ann Woodward, "Bestwall Quarry," *British Archaeology* 115 (Nov/Dec 2010).
29. Jane Kenney, *Recent Excavations at Parc Bryn Cegin, Llandygai, Near Bangor, North Wales* (Bangor, Wales: Gwynedd Archaeological Trust, 2008), 8.
30. *Ibid.*, 9.
31. *Ibid.*, 14.
32. *Ibid.*, 17.
33. *Ibid.*, 51.
34. *Ibid.*, 59–60.
35. *Ibid.*, 66–7.
36. Coflein, *Burnt Mound at Rhos Lligwy*.
37. Coflein, *Lligwy Burial Chamber, Near Moelfre*.
38. Irish Archaeology, *The Enigmatic Fulacht Fiadh or Burnt Mound*, at the website http://irisharchaeology.ie/2012/07/the-enigmatic-fulacht-fiadhburnt-mound/.
39. James Eogan, *Cleansing Body & Soul?* at the website http://www.waterfordcity.ie/n25bypass/cleansing.htm.
40. Heritage Gateway, *Late Bronze Age Riverbank Activity, Washingborough*, at the website http://www.heritagegateway.org.uk/Gateway/Results_Single.aspx?uid=MLI87018&resourceID=1006.
41. Pastscape, *Runnymede Bridge*.
42. David Longley, "Excavations on the Site of a Late Bronze Age Settlement at Runnymede Bridge, Egham," *London Archaeologist* 3 (1976), 10.
43. Stuart Needham and Tony Spence, "Refuse and the Formation of Middens," *Antiquity* 71 (1997), 77–90.
44. David Longley, "Excavations on the Site of a Late Bronze Age Settlement at Runnymede Bridge, Egham," 13.
45. Ralph Merrifield, *London, City of the Romans* (Berkeley and Los Angeles, CA: University of California Press, 1983), 2.
46. David Longley, "Excavations on the Site of a Late Bronze Age Settlement at Runnymede Bridge, Egham," 17.
47. Jacqueline McKinley, "Human Bone," in Andrew Lawson, *Potterne 1982–5* (Salisbury, Wiltshire: Trust for Wessex Archaeology, 2000), 100.
48. Kate Waddington, *Reassembling the Bronze Age: Exploring the Southern British Midden Sites* (PhD diss., Cardiff University, 2009), 145.
49. *Ibid.*, 67.
50. Athenaeus, *Deipnosophists*, trans. C.D. Yonge (London: Henry G. Bohn, 1854), Book 4, Chapters 36–7, at the website http://www.attalus.org/info/athenaeus.html.
51. Christopher Evans, "Delivering Bodies Unto Waters: A Late Bronze Age Mid-Stream Midden Settlement and Iron Age Ritual Complex in the Fens," *The Antiquaries Journal* 93 (2013), 58.
52. *Ibid.*, 61.
53. M.L. West, *Indo-European Poetry and Myth* (Oxford: Oxford University Press, 2007), 174.
54. *Ibid.* 175.
55. *Ibid.*, 177.
56. Julius Pokorny, *Indogermanisches etymologisches Wörterbuch* (Bern: Francke, 1959), 833–834.
57. Raimund Karl, "Emerging Settlement Monumentality in North Wales During the Late Bronze and Iron Age: The Case of Meillionydd," in J.T. Koch, B.W. Cunliffe (eds.), *Celtic from the West Vol. III* (Oxford: Oxbow Books, forthcoming).
58. Coflein, *Castell Henllys*.
59. Pastscape, *Hallygye Fogou*.
60. Mike Pitts, "News: All Cannings Cross," *British Archeology* 74 (January 2004).
61. Nancy Sandars, *Bronze Age Cultures in France* (Cambridge: Cambridge University Press, 1957), 225.
62. Jean-Jacques Hatt, "Circonscription De Strasbourg," *Gallia* 18 (1960), 245–246.
63. Pastscape, *All Cannings Cross*.
64. John Barrett and David McOmish, *All Cannings Cross*, at the website http://www.wiltshire.gov.uk/acc.pdf.
65. John C. Barrett and David McOmish, "The Early Iron Age in Southern Britain: Recent Work at All Cannings Cross, Stanton St. Bernard and East Chisenbury, Wiltshire," in

M.J. Lambert-Roulière, A. Daubigney, P.Y. Milcent, M. Talon and J. Vital (eds.). *De L'âge Du Bronze a L'âge Du Fer En France Et En Europe Occidentale (Xe-Viie Siècle Av. J.C.). La Moyenne Vallée Du Rhône Aux Âges Du Fer. Actes Du Xxxe Colloque International De L'a.F.E.A.F., Co-Organisé Avec L'a.P.R.A.B. (Saint-Romain-En-Gal, 26-28 Mai 2006* (Dijon: Société Archéologique de l'Est, 2009), 567.
66. John Barrett and David McOmish, *All Cannings Cross*.
67. Ian Armit, *Headhunting and the Body in Iron Age Europe* (Cambridge, Cambridge University Press, 2012), 6.
68. Kate Waddington, *Reassembling the Bronze Age* (Thesis submitted to Cardiff University for the degree of Doctor of Philosophy, February 2009), 125-6.
69. *Ibid.*, 127.
70. Pastscape, *Rybury Camp*.
71. Pastscape, *Rybury Causewayed Enclosure*.
72. Andrew Lawson, *Potterne 1982-5* (Salisbury, Wiltshire: Trust for Wessex Archaeology, 2000), 4.
73. Pastscape, *Monument No. 211644*.
74. Barry Cunliffe, *Iron Age Communities in Britain* (Taylor & Francis e-library, 2005), 1795.
75. Andrew Lawson, *Potterne 1982-5*, 105.
76. *Ibid.*, 203.
77. Kate Waddington, *Reassembling the Bronze Age: Exploring the Southern British Midden Sites*, 121.
78. Andrew Lawson, *Potterne 1982-5*, 220-2.
79. *Ibid.*, 219-220.
80. Ian Armit, *Headhunting and the Body in Iron Age Europe* (Cambridge, Cambridge University Press, 2012), 6.
81. Andrew Lawson, *Potterne 1982-5*, 100.
82. Kate Waddington, *Reassembling the Bronze Age: Exploring the Southern British Midden Sites*, 114-5.
83. *Ibid.*, 365-6.
84. *Ibid.*, 368-9.
85. David McOmish, "East Chisenbury: Ritual and Rubbish at the British Bronze Age-Iron Age Transition," *Antiquity* 70 (March 1996), 68-76.
86. P.P. Rhodes, "A Prehistoric and Roman Site at Wittenham Clumps, Berks.," *Oxoniensia* 12 (1948), 18-31.
87. Tim Allen, Kate Cramp, Hugo Lamdin-Whymark and Leo Webley, *Castle Hill and Its Landscape; Archaeological Investigations at the Wittenhams, Oxfordshire* (Oxford, Oxford Archaeology, 2010), 111.
88. *Ibid.*, 177.
89. *Ibid.*, 113.
90. *Ibid.*, 122.
91. *Ibid.*, 125.
92. *Ibid.*, 22-6.
93. Adam Gwilt, Mark Lodwick and Jody Deacon, *Llanmaes Archaeological Fieldwork, Vale of Glamorgan*, at the website https://www.museumwales.ac.uk/1492/.
94. David McOmish, "East Chisenbury: Ritual and Rubbish at the British Bronze Age-Iron Age Transition."
95. Kate Waddington, *Reassembling the Bronze Age: Exploring the Southern British Midden Sites*, 396.
96. *The Boyhood Deeds of Finn Mac Cumhaill*, trans. Tom P. Cross and Clark Harris Slover (New York: Henry Holt & Co., 1936), at the website http://www.maryjones.us/ctexts/f02.html.
97. Mott Macdonald Pettit, *Proposed Power Plant at Derrygreenagh, Co. Offaly*, at the website http://www.derrygreenaghpower.ie/docs/EIS%20Chapters/Chapter%2012%20Cultural%20Heritage.pdf.
98. Kate Waddington, *Reassembling the Bronze Age: Exploring the Southern British Midden Sites*, 393.
99. *Ibid.*, 394.
100. *Ibid.*, 395-6.
101. Pliny the Elder, *Natural History*, trans. John Bostock and H.T. Riley (London: Henry G. Bohn, 1855), Book 16, Chapter 95.
102. Julius Pokorny, *Indogermanisches etymologisches Wörterbuch*, 214-217.
103. *Ibid.*, 1125-1127.
104. Pastscape, *Paddock Hill*.
105. Richard Bradley, *The Idea of Order: The Circular Archetype in Prehistoric Europe* (Oxford: Oxford University Press, 2012), 131.
106. Mike Parker Pearson, "Food, Sex and Death: Cosmologies in the British Iron Age with Particular Reference to East Yorkshire," *Cambridge Archaeological Journal* 9 (1999), 43.
107. *Ibid.*, 44.

Chapter 4

1. M.L. West, *Indo-European Poetry and Myth* (Oxford: Oxford University Press, 2007), 166-7.
2. Lucan, *Civil War*, trans. Sir Edward Ridley (London: Longmans, Green, and Co., 1896), lines 498-501.
3. "Taranis," in *Encyclopédie De l'Arbre Celtique*, at the website http://www.arbre-celtique.com/encyclopedie/taranis-3450.htm.
4. R.G. Collingwood and R.P. Wright, "RIB 452. Altar Dedicated to Jupiter Tanarus Optimus Maximus," in *The Roman Inscriptions of Britain*, at the website http://romaninscriptionsofbritain.org/inscriptions/452.
5. "Taranis," in *Encyclopédie De l'Arbre Celtique*.
6. Miranda Green, "The Worship of the Romano-Celtic Wheel-God in Britain Seen in Relation to Gaulish Evidence," *Latomus* 38 (1979), 347-8.
7. Nicholas Kazanas, "Anatolian Bull and Vedic Horse in the Indo-European Diffusion," in *Indo-Aryan Origins and Other Vedic Issues* (New Delhi, India: Aditya Prakashan, 2009).
8. "Dioskouroi," at the website *Theoi Greek Mythology* http://www.theoi.com/Ouranios/Dioskouroi.html.
9. Barry Cunliffe, "Understanding Hillforts: Have We Progressed?" in Andrew Payne, Mark Corney and Barry Cunliffe (eds.), *The Wessex Hillforts Project* (London: English Heritage, 2006), 152.
10. *Ibid.*, 158.
11. *Ibid.*, 159.
12. Julius Pokorny, *Indogermanisches etymologisches Wörterbuch* (Bern: Francke, 1959), 260.
13. Xavier Delamarre, *Dictionnaire De La Langue Gauloise* (Paris: Errance, 2008), 155-6.
14. Calvert Watkins and Lisi Oliver (ed.), *Selected Writings: Culture and Poetics* (Innsbruck, Austria: Institut für Sprachwissenschaft der Universität Innsbruck, 1994), 752.
15. The Liss Triangle Centre, *A Potted History of Liss*, at the website https://www.liss-triangle-centre.org.uk/pages/wp-content/uploads/2013/10/A-Potted-History-of-Liss.pdf.
16. Barry Cunliffe, *Iron Age Communities in Britain* (Taylor & Francis e-library, 2005), 6354.
17. Clwyd-Powys Archaeological Trust, *The Breiddin*, at the website http://www.cpat.org.uk/keysites/breiddin/breiddin.htm.
18. Clwyd-Powys Archaeological Trust, *Defensive and Military Landscapes*, at the website http://www.cpat.org.uk/projects/longer/histland/holywell/hodefend.htm.
19. Coflein, *Dinorben, Destroyed Hillfort*.
20. Clwyd-Powys Archaeological Trust, *The Iron Age, 600 BC-AD 50*, at the website http://www.cpat.org.uk/cpat/past/iron/iron.htm.
21. Ian Armit, *Headhunting and the Body in Iron Age Europe* (Cambridge: Cambridge University Press, 2012), 8.
22. Pastscape, *Blewburton Hill*.
23. A.E.P. Collins, "Excavations on Blewburton Hill, 1948 and 1949," *Berkshire Archaeological Journal* 53 (1952-3), 4-29.

24. D. Blair Gibson, *From Chiefdom to State in Early Ireland* (Cambridge: Cambridge University Press, 2012), 32–4.
25. Barry Cunliffe, *Iron Age Communities in Britain*, 6804.
26. Ibid., 6810.
27. Ibid., 6821.
28. Julius Pokorny, *Indogermanisches etymologisches Wörterbuch*, 1069–1070.
29. Walter O. Kaelber, "'Tapas,' Birth, and Spiritual Rebirth in the Veda," *History of Religions* 15 (1976), 343–4.
30. Roger D. Woodard, *Myth, Ritual, and the Warrior in Roman and Indo-European Antiquity* (Cambridge: Cambridge University Press, 2013), 252–3.
31. Maud Cunnington, "Lidbury Camp," *Wiltshire Archaeological and Natural History Magazine* 40 (1917), 17–19.
32. Ibid., 22.
33. Ibid., 25.
34. Maud Cunnington, "Excavations in Yarnbury Castle Camp," *Wiltshire Archaeological and Natural History Magazine* 46 (1933), 203.
35. Pastscape, *Yarnbury Castle*.
36. Maud Cunnington, "Excavations in Yarnbury Castle Camp," 207.
37. Kurt Hunter-Mann, "Excavations at Vespasians's Camp Iron Age Hillfort, 1987," *Wiltshire Archaeological and Natural History Magazine* 92 (1999), 47.
38. Jodie Lewis, "Upwards at 45 Degrees: The Use of Vertical Caves During the Neolithic and Early Bronze Age on Mendip, Somerset," *Capra* 2 (2000), at the website http://capra.group.shef.ac.uk/2/upwards.html.
39. Pastscape, *Wilsford Shaft*.
40. Paul Ashbee, Martin Bell and Edwina Proudfoot, *Wilsford Shaft: Excavations 1960–62* (London: English Heritage, 1989), 126.
41. Ibid., 68.
42. Pastscape, *Danebury*.
43. Barry Cunliffe, "Landscape with People," in Kate Flint and Howard Morphy (eds.), *Culture, Landscape and the Environment* (Oxford: Oxford University Press, 2001), 126.
44. Ibid., 128.
45. Miranda Green, *Animals in Celtic Life and Myth* (London: Routledge, 1998), 119.
46. Barry Cunliffe, *Danebury: An Iron Age Hillfort in Hampshire Vol. 6. A Hillfort Community in Perspective* (York: Council for British Archaeology, 1995), 77.
47. Dale Serjeantson and James Morris, "Ravens and Crows in Iron Age and Roman Britain," *Oxford Journal of Archaeology* 30 (2011), 91.
48. Pastscape, *Maiden Castle*.
49. Christine Hamlin, *The Material Expression of Social Change* (PhD diss., University of Wisconsin-Milwaukee, 2007), 80–1.
50. Pastscape, *Cadbury Castle*.
51. John C. Barrett, P.M.W. Freeman and Ann Woodward, *Cadbury Castle, Somerset: The Later Prehistoric and Early Historic Archaeology* (London: English Heritage, 2014), 206.
52. Pastscape, *Nottingham Hill*.
53. R.W.B. Morris and A. Marshall, "A Cup- and Ring-Marked Stone from Nottingham Hill, Gotherington," *Transactions of the Bristol and Gloucestershire Archaeological Society* 101 (1983), 172–3.
54. Tim Allen, Kate Cramp, Hugo Lamdin-Whymark and Leo Webley, *Castle Hill and Its Landscape; Archaeological Investigations at the Wittenhams, Oxfordshire* (Oxford, Oxford Archaeology, 2010), 26.
55. Ibid., 32–3.
56. Pastscape, *Stonea Camp*.
57. Pastscape, *Borough Fen Enclosure*.
58. Pastscape, *Hunsbury Hill Complex*.
59. Northamptonshire Archaeological Society, *Whittlebury Hillfort*, at the website http://northants-archaeology.org.uk/Whittlebury.htm.
60. University of Leicester, *Burrough Hill Iron Age Hillfort*, at the website http://www2.le.ac.uk/departments/archaeology/research/projects/burrough-hill.
61. University of Leicester, *University of Leicester Archaeologists Discover Bronze Remains of Iron Age Chariot*, at the website http://www2.le.ac.uk/offices/press/press-releases/2014/october/university-of-leicester-archaeologists-discover-bronze-remains-of-iron-age-chariot.
62. English Heritage, *History of Old Oswestry Hillfort*, at the website http://www.english-heritage.org.uk/visit/places/old-oswestry-hill-fort/history/.
63. Pastscape, *The Wrekin*.
64. Chris Ellis and Andrew Powell, *An Iron Age Settlement Outside Battlesbury Hillfort, Warminster and Sites Along the Southern Range Road* (Salisbury: Wessex Archaeology, 2008), 50.
65. Ibid., 135–6.
66. Jacqueline McKinley, "Human Remains," in Chris Ellis and Andrew Powell, *An Iron Age Settlement Outside Battlesbury Hillfort, Warminster and Sites Along the Southern Range Road*, 71–6.
67. Ibid., 81–2.
68. Chris Ellis and Andrew Powell, *An Iron Age Settlement Outside Battlesbury Hillfort, Warminster and Sites Along the Southern Range Road*, 34–5.
69. Catriona Gibson and Stephanie Knight, "A Middle Iron Age Settlement at Weston Down Cottages, Weston Colley, Near Winchester, Hampshire," *Proceedings of the Hampshire Field Club and Archaeological Society* 62 (2007), 13.
70. Ibid., 16–17.
71. Pastscape, *Monument No. 210038*.
72. G.J. Wainwright, *Gussage All Saints: An Iron Age Settlement in Dorset* (London: Her Majesty's Stationery Office, 1979), 33–4.
73. Ibid., 153.
74. Chris Webster, *The Archaeology of South West England*, at the website http://www1.somerset.gov.uk/archives/hes/downloads/swarfweb.pdf.
75. Arthur Bulleid and Harold St. George Gray, *The Glastonbury Lake Village* (Glastonbury: The Glastonbury Antiquarian Society, 1917), 405.
76. Ibid., 676.
77. Leonora O'Brien, *Blood, Seeds and Soil: Bronze Age, Iron Age and Anglo-Saxon Settlement and Burial at Harston Mill, Cambs.*, at the website https://www.academia.edu/1701365/Blood_seeds_and_soil_Iron_Age_storage_pit_burials_at_Harston_Mill_Cambridgeshire.
78. Christopher Evans, "Delivering Bodies Unto Waters: A Late Bronze Age Mid-Stream Midden Settlement and Iron Age Ritual Complex in the Fens," *The Antiquaries Journal* 93 (2013), 63.
79. Ibid., 63–7.
80. Ibid., 67.
81. Ibid., 76.
82. Heritage Council, *Dun Aonghasa, Inis Mor, Co. Galway*, at the website http://heritagecouncil.ie/unpublished_excavations/section11.html.
83. Pastscape, *Trevelgue Head*.
84. Royal Commission on the Ancient and Historical Monuments of Wales, *Hidden Histories Episode Five: Iron Age People Living on the Edge*, at the website http://www.rcahmw.gov.uk/HI/ENG/Heritage+of+Wales/Hidden+Histories+II/Hidden+Histories+2+Episode+5/.
85. Barry Cunliffe, "Atlantic Sea-Ways," *Revista De Guimarães, Volume Especial* (1999), 93–105.
86. Plutarch, "The Obsolescence of Oracles," in *Moralia* Vol V, trans. Frank Cole Babbitt (Cambridge, MA: Harvard University Press, 1936), Chapter 18.

87. A.R. Burn, "Holy Men on Islands in Pre-Christian Britain," *Glasgow Archaeological Journal* 1 (1969), 2.
88. Rebecca Redfern, "New Evidence for Iron Age Secondary Burial Practice and Bone Modification from Gussage All Saints and Maiden Castle (Dorset, England)," *Oxford Journal of Archaeology* 27 (2008), 286.
89. Ibid., 291.
90. Silius Italicus, *Punica*, trans. J.D. Duff (Cambridge, MA: Harvard University Press, 1961), Book 3.
91. Gabriel Sopeña, "Celtiberian Ideologies and Religion," *E-Keltoi Journal of Interdisciplinary Celtic Studies*, Volume 6 (2005).
92. Francisco Marco Simon, "Images of Transition: Ways of Death in Celtic Hispania," *Proceedings of the Prehistoric Society* 74 (2008), 61–2.
93. Ian Armit, *Headhunting and the Body* (Cambridge: Cambridge University Press, 2012), 146, 156.
94. Julius Pokorny, *Indogermanisches etymologisches Wörterbuch*, 775–777.
95. Ibid., 315–316.
96. Gananath Obeyesekere, *Imagining Karma: Ethical Transformations in Amerindian, Buddhist and Greek Rebirth* (Oakland: University of California Press, 2002), 44–5.
97. Ibid., 45.
98. Ann Fienup-Riordan, *Boundaries and Passages: Rule and Ritual in Yup'ik Eskimo Oral Tradition* (Norman: University of Oklahoma Press, 1995), 211.
99. Ibid., 106.
100. Ibid., 107.
101. *Giraldus Cambrensis: The Topography of Ireland*, trans. Thomas Forester (Cambridge, Ontario: In parentheses Publications, 2000), 35.
102. Chris Lynn, *Navan Fort: Archaeology and Myth* (Dublin, Ireland: Wordwell, 2003).
103. Irish Archaeology, *A Barbary Ape Skull from Navan Fort, Co. Armagh*, at the website http://irisharchaeology.ie/2014/05/a-barbary-ape-skull-from-navan-fort-co-armagh/.
104. Poem/Story 112, *Metrical Dindshenchas*, at the website Corpus of Electronic Texts http://www.ucc.ie/celt/online/T106500D/text112.html.
105. Ian Johnston, *The Iliad* (Arlington, VA: Richer Resources Publications, 2007), 218–9.
106. Robert Turcan, *The Cults of the Roman Empire* (Hoboken, NJ: Wiley, 1997), 248–9.
107. Ann Ross, *Pagan Celtic Britain* (Chicago, IL: Academy Chicago Publishers, 1996), 80.
108. Ibid., 83.
109. Myles Dillon, "The Wasting Sickness of Cu Chulainn," *Scottish Gaelic Studies* 7 (1953), 56.
110. Mariko Namba Walter and Eva Jane Neumann Fridman (eds.), *Shamanism: An Encyclopedia of World Beliefs, Practices and Culture* (Santa Barbara, CA: ABC-CLIO, 2004), 220.
111. Z. Kyrgyz, *On the Music of Shamanism in the Tuvinian Culture* (Kyzyl, Russia: International Science Center Khomei of the Ministry of Culture of the Republic of Tuva, 1993).

Chapter 5

1. Barry Cunliffe, *Iron Age Communities in Britain* (Taylor & Francis e-library, 2005), 1640.
2. René Joffroy, "La tombe à char hallstattienne de Vix," *Comptes-Rendus Des Séances De l'Académie Des Inscriptions Et Belles-Lettres* 97 (1953), 169–179.
3. *Volute Krater: Female Burial, Vix, Burgundy*, at the website http://www.unc.edu/celtic/catalogue/grave/VixKrater.html.
4. Barry Cunliffe, "Iron Age Societies in Western Europe and Beyond, 800–140 BC," in Barry Cunliffe (ed.), *The Oxford Ilustrated History of Prehistoric Europe* (Oxford: Oxford University Press, 2001), 348.
5. René Joffroy and Denise Bretz-Mahler, "Les Tombes À Char De La Tène Dans L'est De La France," *Gallia* 17 (1959), 32.
6. Ibid., 34–5.
7. Ibid., 9–11.
8. Ibid., 30.
9. Pastscape, *Monument No. 64320*.
10. Pastscape, *Monument No. 79342*.
11. British Museum, *The Kirkburn Sword*, at the website http://www.britishmuseum.org/explore/highlights/highlight_objects/pe_prb/t/the_kirkburn_sword.aspx.
12. Pastscape, *Garton Slack*.
13. Pastscape, *Monument No. 64755*.
14. Barry Cunliffe, *Iron Age Communities in Britain*, 10043–4.
15. Ian Stead, "Chalk Figurines of the Parisi," *The Antiquaries Journal* 68 (1988), 9–29.
16. Stuart Piggott, *Early Celtic Art* (Piscataway, NJ: Transaction Publishers, 2008), 7.
17. British Museum, *The Wetwang Chariot Burial*, at the website https://www.britishmuseum.org/explore/online_tours/britain/the_wetwang_chariot_burial/the_wetwang_chariot_burial.aspx.
18. Pastscape, *Monument No. 64640*.
19. Barry Cunliffe, *Iron Age Communities in Britain*, 1628.
20. Pastscape, *Danes Graves*.
21. Pastscape, *Monument No. 910763*.
22. Mike Parker Pearson, "Food, Sex and Death: Cosmologies in the British Iron Age with Particular Reference to East Yorkshire," *Cambridge Archaeological Journal* 9 (1999), 53.
23. Mike Parker Pearson, Niall Sharples and Jacqui Mulville, "Brochs and Iron Age Society: A Reappraisal," *Antiquity* 70 (March 1996), 57–67.
24. Yorkshire Archaeological Society, *The Ferry Fryston Chariot*, at the website http://www.prehistory.yas.org.uk/content/ferryfryston.html.
25. Canmore, *Newbridge Industrial Estate*.
26. Ian Stead, *Iron Age Cemeteries in East Yorkshire* (London: English Heritage, 1991), 33.
27. Julius Pokorny, *Indogermanisches etymologisches Wörterbuch* (Bern: Francke, 1959), 1080–1085.
28. Heritage Gateway, *Fiskerton Causeway*, at the website http://www.heritagegateway.org.uk/Gateway/Results_Single.aspx?uid=MLI52904&resourceID=1006.
29. Julia Farley, "Transformations of Scale: The Deposition of Miniature Weaponry in Iron Age Lincolnshire," *PALLAS: Revue D'études Antiques* 86 (2011), 103.
30. Christopher Gosden, Sally Crawford, Katharina Ulmschneider (eds.), *Celtic Art in Europe: Making Connections* (Oxford: Oxbow Books, 2014), 293.
31. S. Parry and S. McGrail, "A Prehistoric Plank Boat Fragment and a Hard from Caldicot Castle Lake, Gwent, Wales," *The International Journal of Nautical Archaeology* 20 (1991), 321.
32. Mike Parker Pearson, Andrew Chamberlain, Naomi Field and Jim Rylatt, "Déposition Votive Et Éclipses Lunaires En Angleterre Et Sur Le Continent," in Ph. Barral, A. Daubigney, C. Dunning, G. Kaenel, M.J. Roulière-Lambert, *L'âge Du Fer Dans L'arc Jurassien Et Ses Marges* (Besançon: Presses universitaires de Franche-Comté, 2007), 444.
33. Ibid., 444–5.
34. Axel G. Posluschny, "From Landscape Archaeology to Social Archaeology: Finding Patterns to Explain the Development of Early Celtic 'Princely Sites' in Middle Europe," in J.T. Clark and E. Hagemeister (eds.), *Digital Discovery. Exploring New Frontiers in Human Heritage* (Budapest: Archaeolingua, 2007), 124.

35. Cunliffe, *Druids: A Very Short Introduction* (Oxford: Oxford University Press, 2010), 72.
36. Julius Caesar, *Commentaries on the Gallic War*, trans. W.A. McDevitte and W.S. Bohn (New York: Harper and Brothers, 1869), Book 7, Chapter 3.
37. T.D. Kendrick, *Druids and Druidism* (Mineola, NY: Dover Publications, 2003), 136.
38. Julius Pokorny, *Indogermanisches etymologisches Wörterbuch*, 413–414.
39. Brian M. Fagan and Charlotte Beck, *The Oxford Companion to Archaeology* (Oxford: Oxford University Press, 1996), 379.
40. Anne-Marie Romeuf, "Les Ex-Voto En Bois De Chamalières (Puy-De-Dôme) Et Des Sources De La Seine (Côte-D'or): Essai De Comparaison," *Gallia* 44 (1986), 65–7.
41. Barry Cunliffe, "Understanding Hillforts: Have We Progressed?" in Andrew Payne, Mark Corney, Barry Cunliffe (eds.), *The Wessex Hillforts Project* (London: English Heritage, 2006), 162.
42. John Koch, *Celtic Culture*: a historical encyclopedia (Santa Barbara, CA: ABC-CLIO, 2006), 199.
43. Ministère de la Culture et de la Communication, *Les Gaulois D'acy-Romance*, at the website http://www.gaulois.ardennes.culture.fr/#/fr/annexe/accueil/tab/04/t=Accueil.
44. Pastscape, *Monument No. 465335*.
45. British Museum, *Finds from a Late Iron Age Cremation Burial*, at the website http://www.britishmuseum.org/explore/highlights/highlight_objects/pe_prb/f/late_iron_age_burial_finds.aspx.
46. Pastscape, *Lexden Tumulus*.
47. Barry Cunliffe, *Iron Age Communities in Britain*, 3176.
48. Peter C. Jupp and Clare Gittings, *Death in England* (Manchester: Manchester University Press, 1999), 49.
49. Eric Hostetter and Thomas Noble Howe, *The Romano-British Villa at Castle Copse, Great Bedwyn* (Bloomington: Indiana University Press, 1997), 26.
50. Pastscape, *Monument No. 228524*.
51. Pastscape, *Monument No. 1128248*.
52. English Heritage, *Gussage Style Settlements: General Description*, at the website http://www.eng-h.gov.uk/mpp/mcd/sub/guss3.htm.
53. A. Selkirk, "John Collis," *Current Archaeology* 123 (1991), 116–123.
54. Matt Leivers and Catriona Gibson, *A Later Bronze Age Settlement and Iron Age Cemetery. Excavations at Adanac Park, Nursling, Hampshire 2008* (Salisbury: Wessex Archaeology, 2010).
55. Anthony King and Grahame Soffe, "Internal Organisation and Deposition at the Iron Age Temple on Hayling Island (Hampshire)," in J. Collis (ed.), *Society and Settlement in Iron Age Europe* (Sheffield: Sheffield Academic Press, 2001), 111–124.
56. Julius Pokorny, *Indogermanisches etymologisches Wörterbuch*, 123–124.
57. Jean Louis Brunaux and Patrice Méniel, "Le Sanctuaire De Gournay-Sur-Aronde (Oise): Structures Et Rites, Les Animaux Du Sacrifice," *Revue Archéologique De Picardie* 1–2 (1983), 165–173.
58. English Heritage, *Enclosed Oppida*, at the website http://www.eng-h.gov.uk/mpp/mcd/encop.htm.
59. Michael Fulford, *City of the Dead: Calleva Atrebatum*, at the website http://www.bbc.co.uk/history/ancient/archaeology/city_dead_01.shtml.
60. Barry Cunliffe, *Iron Age Communities in Britain*, 3492.
61. Dave Allen, "Buried in Time—Late Iron Age," *Hampshire Archaeology: Musings from a Hampshire Archaeologist*, January 12, 2015, at the website https://hampshirearchaeology.wordpress.com/2015/01/12/buried-in-time-late-iron-age/.
62. Pastscape, *Hengistbury Head*.
63. British Museum, *Chiseldon Cauldrons: Unearthing and Conserving An Iron Age Feast*, at the website http://www.britishmuseum.org/research/research_projects/all_current_projects/chiseldon_cauldrons.aspx.
64. Pastscape, *Monument No. 1501997*.
65. Julie Lovell, Jane Timby, Gail Wakeham and Michael J. Allen, "Iron Age to Saxon Farming Settlement at Bishop's Cleeve, Gloucestershire: Excavations South of Church Road, 1998 and 2004," *Transactions of the Bristol and Gloucestershire Archaeoligical Society* 125 (2007), 99.
66. Tom Moore, "The Iron Age," in N. Holbrook and J.Jurica, *Twenty-Five Years of Archaeology in Gloucestershire* (Cirencester, UK: Cotswold Archaeology, 2006), 76.
67. Pastscape, *Monument No. 116361*.
68. Pastscape, *Sharpstones Hill*.
69. Pastscape, *Clun-Clee Ridgeway*.
70. Evan Gwilym Hughes, "An Iron Age Barrow Burial at Bromfield, Shropshire," *Proceedings of the Prehistoric Society* 60 (1994), 395–402.
71. Pastscape, *Monument No. 108613*.
72. Frank Hargrave, "The Hallaton Treasure: Evidence of a New Kind of Shrine?" *Current Archaeology* 236 (2009).
73. Vicki Score and Jennifer Browning, *Hoards, Hounds and Helmets: An Iron Age Shrine at Hallaton, Leicestershire*, at the website https://ulasnews.wordpress.com/projects/the-hallaton-treasure/.
74. David Hall and John Coles, *Fenland Survey: An Essay in Landscape and Persistence* (London: English Heritage, 1994), 98.
75. Pastscape, *Monument No. 383123*.
76. Martin Henig, *Religion in Roman Britain* (London: Batsford, 1984), 5.
77. Barbara Green and Ian Stead, "The Snettisham Treasure," *Current Archaeology* (May 24, 2007).
78. John Davies, "Norfolk: Land of Boudicca," *Current Archaeology* 235 (2009).
79. Heritage Gateway, *Late Iron Age Settlement in Old Sleaford*, at the website http://www.heritagegateway.org.uk/Gateway/Results_Single.aspx?uid=MLI60583&resourceID=1006.
80. Robert Van de Noort, Henry P. Chapman and John R. Collis (eds.), *Sutton Common: The Excavation of An Iron Age "Marsh-Fort"* (London: Council for British Archaeology, 2007).
81. Antony Dickson and Guy Hopkinson, *Holes in the Landscape: Seventeen Years of Archaeological Investigations at Nosterfield Quarry, North Yorkshire*, at the website http://www.archaeologicalplanningconsultancy.co.uk/thornborough/pdf/holes_in_the_landscape.pdf.

Chapter 6

1. A.L.F. Rivet and Colin Smith, *The Place-Names of Roman Britain* (London: Batsford, 1979), 342.
2. David Mills, *A Dictionary of British Place-Names* (Oxford: Oxford University Press, 2011), 156; Julius Pokorny, *Indogermanisches etymologisches Wörterbuch* (Bern: Francke, 1959), 203, 78–81.
3. A.L.F. Rivet and Colin Smith, *The Place-Names of Roman Britain*, 391–2.
4. Julius Pokorny, *Indogermanisches etymologisches Wörterbuch*, 1146–1147.
5. A.L.F. Rivet and Colin Smith, *The Place-Names of Roman Britain*, 291–2.
6. Julius Pokorny, *Indogerman-

isches etymologisches Wörterbuch, 1090.

7. A.L.F. Rivet and Colin Smith, *The Place-Names of Roman Britain*, 445–6.

8. Ibid., 427.

9. Julius Pokorny, *Indogermanisches etymologisches Wörterbuch*, 854–857.

10. Catherine Royer-Hemet (ed.), *Canterbury: A Medieval City* (Newcastle upon Tyne: Cambridge Scholars Publishing, 2010), 3.

11. Johannes Hoops (ed.), *Reallexikon Der Germanischen Altertumskunde Band 16* (Berlin: Walter de Gruyter, 2000), 445.

12. Julius Pokorny, *Indogermanisches etymologisches Wörterbuch*, 534; Xavier Delamarre, *Dictionnaire De La Langue Gauloise* (Paris: Errance, 2008), 311.

13. Xavier Delamarre, "Gallo-Britonnica," *Zeitschrift Für Celtische Philologie* 54 (2004), 131–2.

14. Pastscape, *Londinium*.

15. Museum of London, "Ritual Practices," in *Londinium Lite*, at the website http://archive.museumoflondon.org.uk/Londinium/analysis/religiouslife/rites/17+ritual.htm.

16. K. S. Painter, "A Bronze Ox-Head from Somerset," *The Antiquaries Journal* 43 (1963), 291.

17. Portable Antiquities Scheme, *Bucket*, at the website https://finds.org.uk/database/artefacts/record/id/70768.

18. Miranda Green, *The Gods of Roman Britain* (Princes Risborough, Buckinghamshire, UK: Shire Publications, 2003), 63.

19. A.L.F. Rivet and Colin Smith, *The Place-Names of Roman Britain*, 368.

20. Julius Pokorny, *Indogermanisches etymologisches Wörterbuch*, 880.

21. Miranda Green, *The Celtic World* (London: Routledge, 1996), 125.

22. John Rhys, "All Around the Wrekin," *Y Cymmrodor* 21 (1908), 1–62.

23. Xavier Delamarre, "Gallo-Brittonica [11–21]," *Zeitschrift Für Celtische Philologie* 55 (2006), 31.

24. Julius Pokorny, *Indogermanisches etymologisches Wörterbuch*, 574–577.

25. A.L.F. Rivet and Colin Smith, *The Place-Names of Roman Britain*, 324.

26. Portable Antiquities Scheme, *Mount*, at the website https://finds.org.uk/database/search/results/q/bulls+head+vessel+cheshire.

27. Gathering the Jewels: The website for Welsh cultural history, *Bronze Ox-Head Bucket-Mount Buried in a Grave in Welshpool*, http://education.gtj.org.uk/en/item1/28763.

28. Portable Antiquities Scheme, *Mount*, at the website https://finds.org.uk/database/artefacts/record/id/235509.

29. Anne Ross, "The Human Head in Insular Pagan Celtic Religion," *Proceeding of the Society of Antiquaries of Scotland* 91 (1957/8), 17–18.

30. Ibid., 19.

31. British Museum, *Horned Helmet*, at the website http://www.britishmuseum.org/explore/highlights/highlight_objects/pe_prb/h/horned_helmet.aspx.

32. A.L.F. Rivet and Colin Smith, *The Place-Names of Roman Britain*, 443.

33. John Koch, *Celtic Culture: A Historical Encyclopedia* (Santa Barbara, CA: ABC-CLIO, 2006), 482.

34. A.L.F. Rivet and Colin Smith, *The Place-Names of Roman Britain*, 373.

35. Julius Pokorny, *Indogermanisches etymologisches Wörterbuch*, 504.

36. Pastscape, *Mickelmoor Hill Settlement*.

37. Barry Cunliffe, *Iron Age Communities in Britain* (Taylor & Francis e-library, 2005), 1874.

38. Ibid., 3847.

39. Conseil général des Hauts-de-Seine, *Nanterre Et Les Parisii*, at the website http://www.nanterre.net/parisii/visite/documents/Cahier_pedagogique.pdf.

40. John Koch and Antone Minard, *The Celts: History, Life and Culture* (Santa Barbara, CA: ABC-CLIO, 2012), 91.

41. Xavier Dlamarre, *Dictionnaire De La Langue Gauloise*, 246.

42. Alexander Falileyev, "Parisii," *Dictionary of Continental Place-Names* (Aberystwyth, Wales: CMCS Publications, 2010).

43. Pastscape, *Petuaria Roman Town*.

44. Adrian M. Chadwick, *The Iron Age and Romano-British Periods in West Yorkshire* (Wakefield, UK: West Yorkshire Archaeology Advisory Service, 2009), 114.

45. Peter Halkon, "Britons and Romans in an East Yorkshire Landscape, UK," *Bollettino Di Archeologia on Line* Volume Speciale, 2010, 36.

46. Julius Pokorny, *Indogermanisches etymologisches Wörterbuch*, 299–301.

47. John Koch, *Celtic Culture: A Historical Encyclopedia* (Santa Barbara, CA: ABC-CLIO, 2006), 284.

48. "Stanwick" at the webite *Oppida: Premières Villes Au Nord Des Alpes*, http://www.oppida.org/page.php?lg=fr&rub=00&id_oppidum=155.

49. Colin Haselgrove, "Stanwick," *Current Archaeology* 10 (1990), 380–385.

50. British Museum, *Horse Harness from the Stanwick Hoard*, at the website http://www.britishmuseum.org/explore/highlights/highlight_objects/pe_prb/h/stanwick_hoard_horse_harness.aspx.

51. Patrizia de Bernardo Stempel, "The Phonetic Interface of Celtic Word Formation in Continental Celtic," in Juan Luis Garcia Alonso (ed.), *Continental Celtic Word Formation: The Onomastic Data* (Salamanca, Spain: Ediciones Universidad de Salamanca, 2013), 70.

52. John Koch, *Celtic Culture*, 638.

53. Julius Pokorny, *Indogermanisches etymologisches Wörterbuch*, 199–200.

54. Rodney Castleden, *King Arthur: The Truth Behind the Legend* (London: Routledge, 2003), 57.

55. Portable Antiquities Scheme, *Mount*, at the website https://finds.org.uk/database/artefacts/record/id/415555.

56. Pastscape, *Tintagel Island*.

57. Ken Dark, *Britain and the End of the Roman Empire* (Stroud, Gloucestershire: The History Press, 2006), 153–4.

58. Pastscape, *Monument No. 431901*.

59. Pastscape, *Monument No. 456729*.

60. Julius Pokorny, *Indogermanisches etymologisches Wörterbuch*, 909–910.

61. Ibid., 911.

62. Ibid., 910.

63. Rachel Bromwich, *Trioedd Ynys Prydein: The Triads of the Island of Britain* (Cardiff, UK: University of Wales Press, 2014), 256.

64. Ibid., 12.

65. Pastscape, *Durocornovium*.

66. Ranko Matasovic, "'Sun' and 'Moon' in Celtic and Indo-European," *Celto-Slavica* 2 (2009), 154–162.

67. Sandra Billington and Miranda Green, *The Concept of the Goddess* (London: Routledge, 2002), 35.

68. Pastscape, *Monument No. 203800*.

69. British Museum, *Bronze Spoons*, at the website http://www.britishmuseum.org/explore/highlights/highlight_objects/pe_prb/b/bronze_spoons.aspx.

70. David Hall and John Coles, *Fenland Survey: An Essay in Landscape and Persistence* (London: English Heritage, 1994), 109.

71. Pastscape, *Monument No. 1331890*.

72. English Heritage, *Pre-Christian Cemeteries* (London: English Heritage, 2011), 4.
73. Dorothy Watts, *Religion in Late Roman Britain* (London: Routledge, 1998), 74.
74. Jacqueline McKinley, "Human Bone," in Kirsten Egging Dinwiddy, *A Late Roman Cemetery at Little Keep. Dorchester, Dorset*, at the website http://www.wessexarch.co.uk/files/Little_Keep_Dorchester_64913.pdf.
75. Giles Clarke, *Pre-Roman and Roman Winchester: The Roman Cemetery at Lankhills* (Oxford: Oxford University Press, 1979), 141.
76. Ibid., 142.
77. Ibid., 192.
78. "Winterbourne Down," *Wiltshire Archaeological and Natural History Magazine* 58 (1962), 470.
79. Ossafreelance, *Osteological Analysis of Human Remains from Sainsbury's Site, St. Johns, Worcester*, at the website http://www.ossafreelance.co.uk/PastProjects/WCM101591Sainsburysstjohns.pdf.
80. T. Anderson, "Two Decapitations from Roman Towcester," *Journal of Osteoarchaeology* 11 (2001), 400–405.
81. Neil McGavin, "A Roman Cemetery and Trackway at Stanton Harcourt," *Oxoniensia* 45 (1980), 112–123.
82. John Valentin and Stephen Robinson, "Excavations in 1999 on Land Adjacent to Wayside Farm, Nursteed Road, Devizes," *Wiltshire Archaeological and Natural History Magazine* 95 (2002), 152.
83. Ibid., 153.
84. Ibid., 194, 208.
85. Ibid., 184.
86. Ibid., 195–6.
87. Ibid., 207.
88. Ibid., 167.
89. Pastscape, *Monument No. 216158*.
90. Pastscape, *Monument No. 208294*.
91. British Museum, *Ashwell Roman Treasure and Excavation*, at the website http://www.britishmuseum.org/research/research_projects/all_current_projects/ashwell_roman_treasure.aspx.
92. British Museum, *The Barkway Hoard*, at the website http://www.britishmuseum.org/explore/highlights/highlight_objects/pe_prb/t/the_barkway_hoard.aspx.
93. "Lydney," at the website *Curse Tablets from Roman Britain*, http://curses.csad.ox.ac.uk/sites/lydney-deity.shtml.
94. David Hall and John Coles, *Fenland Survey: An Essay in Landscape and Persistence* (London: English Heritage, 1994), 114.
95. Christopher Evans, "Delivering Bodies Unto Waters: A Late Bronze Age Mid-Stream Midden Settlement and Iron Age Ritual Complex in the Fens," *The Antiquaries Journal* 93 (2013), 69.
96. Barry C. Burnham and J.S. Wacher, *The Small Towns of Roman Britain* (London: Batsford, 1990), 346–7.
97. Jan Harding and Frances Healy, *The Raunds Area Project: A Neolithic and Bronze Age Landscape in Northamptonshire* (London: English Heritage, 2013), 196–7.
98. Iain Ferris, *Romano-British Religious Sites in the West Midlands Region*, at the website http://www.birmingham.ac.uk/schools/historycultures/departments/caha/research/arch-research/wmrrfa/seminar3.aspx.
99. Steve Roskams, Cath Neal and Ruth Leary, "A Late Roman Well at Heslington East: Ritual or Routine Practices?" *Internet Archaeology* 34 (2013), http://dx.doi.org/10.11141/ia.34.5.
100. Pastscape, *Benwell Roman Temple*.
101. Pastscape, *Coventinas Well*.
102. Lindsay Allason-Jones, "Coventina's Well," in Sandra Billington and Miranda Green, *The Concept of the Goddess*, 107–8.
103. Ibid., 112.
104. Dale Serjeantson, "Deer, Picks and People," *Deer: Journal of the Deer Society* 16 (2012), 31.
105. Ibid., 32.

Chapter 7

1. Gildas, *On the Ruin and Conquest of Britain*, trans. Hugh Williams (London: Cymmrodorion, 1899), Chapters 22–3.
2. N.J. Higham, *The English Conquest* (Manchester: Manchester University Press, 1994), 40.
3. Gildas, *On the Ruin and Conquest of Britain*, Chapter 24.
4. Michelle Ziegler, "Artur Mac Aedan of Dal Riata," *The Heroic Age* Issue 1 (Spring/Summer 1999).
5. John Koch and Antone Minard, *The Celts: History, Life, and Culture* (Santa Barbara, CA: ABC-CLIO, 2012), 742.
6. John Stone, "Some Discoveries at Ratfyn," *Wiltshire Archaeological and Natural History Magazine* 47 (1935), 66.
7. Martin Green, "Down Farm," *Current Archaeology* 138 (April/May 1994), 216–225.
8. Stephen Birch, *Uamh An Ard Achadh (High Pasture Cave), Strath, Isle of Skye: Interim Report—November 2004*, at the website http://www.high-pasture-cave.org/index.php/the_work/article/fieldwork_2004.
9. J. Anderson, "Notices of Nine Brochs Along the Caithness Coast from Keiss Bay to Skirza Head, Excavated by Sir Francis Tress Barry, Bart., MP., of Keiss Castle, Caithness," *Proceedings of the Society of Antiquaries of Scotland* 35 (1901), 112–148.
10. Canmore, *Keiss, Kirk Tofts, "Road" Broch*.
11. Brendon Wilkins, "Under the Uplands: Cave Archaeology in the Yorkshire and Lancashire Dales," *Current Archaeology* 261 (Nov 2011), 13–15.
12. Naomi Sykes, *Beastly Questions: Animal Answers to Archaeological Issues* (London: Bloomsbury Publishing, 2014), 69.
13. Martin Schönfelder, "Bear-Claws in Germanic Graves," *Oxford Journal of Archaeology* 13.2 (1994), 217–227.
14. Tom Sjöblom, "The Great Mother: The Cult of the Bear in Celtic Traditions," *Studia Celtica Fennica* III (2006), 71–78.
15. Etienne Rynne, "Celtic Stone Idols in Ireland," in Charles Thomas, *The Iron Age in the Irish Sea Province* (London: Council for British Archaeology, 1972).
16. Finbar McCormick, "Early Evidence for Wild Animals in Ireland," in Norbert Benecke (ed.), *The Holocene History of the European Vertebrate Fauna* (Rahden, Germany: Verlag Marie Leidorf, 1999), 359.
17. James MacKillop, *A Dictionary of Celtic Mythology* (Oxford: Oxford University Press, 2004), 25.
18. Ibid., 171–2.
19. Miranda Green, *Animals in Celtic Life and Myth* (London: Routledge, 1998), 217–8.
20. Michael Speidel, *Ancient Germanic Warriors* (London: Taylor & Francis, 2002), 14.
21. Ibid., 36.
22. Donald Haase, *The Greenwood Encyclopedia of Folktales and Fairy Tales* (Portsmouth, NH: Greenwood Publishing Group, 2007), 103.
23. Christopher R. Fee and David A. Leeming, *Gods, Heroes and Kings* (Oxford: Oxford University Press, 2001), 107.
24. Robert Dennis Fulk, *Interpretations of Beowulf: A Critical Anthology* (Bloomington, IN: Indiana University Press, 1991), 185.
25. Richard Hinckley Allen, *Star Names: Their Lore and Meaning* (Mineola, NY: Dover Publications, 1963), 99.

26. David R. Slavic and Palmer Bovie, *Three Comedies by Titus Maccius Plautus* (Baltimore, MD: Johns Hopkins University Press, 1995), 223.
27. Aratus, *Phaenomena*, at the website http://www.theoi.com/Text/AratusPhaenomena.html.
28. Marina Smyth, *Understanding the Universe in Seventh-Century Ireland* (Woodbridge, Suffolk: Boydell & Brewer, 1996), 138–9.
29. Thomas Green, *A Bibliographic Guide to Welsh Arthurian Literature*, at the website http://www.arthuriana.co.uk/notes&queries/N&Q1_ArthLit.pdf.
30. Roger White and Hal Dalwood, *Archaeological Assessment of Wroxeter*, at the website http://archaeologydataservice.ac.uk/archiveDS/archiveDownload?t=arch-435-1/dissemination/pdf/PDF_REPORTS_TEXT/SHROPSHIRE/WROXETER_REPORT.pdf.
31. Thomas Green, *A Bibliographic Guide to Welsh Arthurian Literature*.
32. Pastscape, *Catterick Roman Town*.
33. Barry C. Burnham and J.S. Wacher, *The Small Towns of Roman Britain* (London: Batsford, 1990), 116–7.
34. Pastscape, *Monument No. 1200574*.
35. Canmore, *Edinburgh Castle*.
36. Nennius, *History of the Britons*, trans. J.A. Giles (London: Henry G. Bohn, 1848), at the website http://d.lib.rochester.edu/camelot/text/nennius-history-of-the-britons.
37. Xavier Delamarre, *Dictionnaire De La Langue Gauloise* (Paris: Errance, 2008), 96.
38. Nennius, *History of the Britons*.
39. John Morris, *Nennius: British History and the Welsh Annals* (Chichester, UK: Phillimore & Co. Ltd., 1980), 35.
40. Thomas Green, *Lincolnshire and the Arthurian Legend*, at the website http://www.arthuriana.co.uk/notes&queries/N&Q3_ArthLincs.pdf.
41. Pastscape, *The Berth*.
42. Thomas Green, *A Bibliographic Guide to Welsh Arthurian Literature*.
43. Wessex Archaeology, *Binchester Roman Fort, County Durham* (Salisbury, UK: Wessex Archaeology, 2008), 9–10.
44. David Mason, *Binchester Roman Fort Excavation Project: Results of 2011 Season*, at the website http://www.durham.gov.uk/media/1565/Binchester-Roman-Fort-Excavation-Project-Results-of-2011-season/pdf/Archaeology_issue_7_binchester_article.pdf.
45. Pastscape, *Deva*.
46. Pastscape, *Chester Amphitheatre*.
47. C.P. Lewis and A.T. Thacker (eds.), *A History of the County of Chester: Volume 5 Part 1, the City of Chester: General History and Topography*, at the website http://www.british-history.ac.uk/vch/ches/vol5/pt1.
48. In *A Song for Urien* (*Book of Taliesin* 36), Taliesin mentions the "battle of Cellawr Brewyn."

Chapter 8

1. Sarah Higley, trans., "The Spoils of Annwn," The Camelot Project at the University of Rochester, http://www.lib.rochester.edu/camelot/.
2. John Koch, *Celtic Culture: a historical encyclopedia* (Santa Barbara, CA: ABC-CLIO, 2006), 1610.
3. Will Parker, *The Mabinogi of Pwyll*, at the website www.mabinogi.net.
4. Patrick Sims-Williams, *Irish Influence on Medieval Welsh Literature* (Oxford: Oxford University Press, 2010), 59.
5. *Geographical Distribution of Epona* at the website www.epona.net.
6. Hilda Ellis Davidson, *Roles of the Northern Goddess* (Taylor & Francis e-library, 2001), 40.
7. Ibid., 41.
8. Manfred Lurker, *The Routledge Dictionary of Gods and Goddesses* (London: Routledge, 2004), 58.
9. Hilda Ellis Davidson, *Roles of the Northern Goddess*, 43.
10. Ray Howell, *Searching for the Silures: An Iron Age Tribe in South-East Wales* (Stroud, Gloucestershire: The History Press, 2006), 25.
11. F.E. Romer, *Pomponius Mela's Description of the World* (Ann Arbor: University of Michigan Press, 1998), 115.
12. Will Parker, *The Mabinogi of Branwen*, at the website www.mabinogi.net.
13. Heritage of Wales News, *Remote Island Reveals Fascinating Prehistoric Past*, at the website http://heritageofwalesnews.blogspot.co.uk/2012/10/remote-island-reveals-prehistoric-past.html.
14. Dale Serjantson and James Morris, "Ravens and Crows in Iron Age and Roman Britain," *Oxford Journal of Archaeology* 30 (2011), 85–107.
15. "Y Gododdin," trans. Joseph Clancy, *Earliest Welsh Poetry* (London: Macmillan, 1970), at the website http://www.maryjones.us/ctexts/a01b.html.
16. Nennius, *History of the Britons*, in J.A. Giles, *Six Old English Chronicles* (London: Henry G. Bohn, 1848), at the website http://legacy.fordham.edu/halsall/basis/nennius-full.asp.

Chapter 9

1. Mark Adderley, *What Man Is the Gatekeeper/Porter?* at the website http://www.markadderley.net/arthur/welsh-arthur/pagur.html.
2. "Triad 6," *The Welsh Triads*, at the website http://norin77.50megs.com/triads.htm.
3. "Culhwch and Olwen," in Gwyn Jones and Thomas Jones (eds.), *The Mabinogion* (London: Everyman, 1949).
4. Julius Caesar, *Commentaries on the Gallic War*, trans. W.A. McDevitte and W.S. Bohn (New York: Harper and Brothers, 1869), Book 1, Chapter 1.
5. Alexei Kondratiev, "Lugus: The Many-Gifted Lord," *An Tribhís Mhór: The IMBAS Journal of Celtic Reconstructionism* 1 (1997).
6. Robin Birley, *Vindolanda: A Roman Frontier Fort on Hadrian's Wall* (Stroud, Gloucestershire: Amberley Publishing, 2012), 97.
7. "Triad 1," *The Welsh Triads*, at the website http://norin77.50megs.com/triads.htm.
8. Rachel Bromwich, *Trioedd Ynys Prydein: The Triads of the Island of Britain* (Cardiff, UK: University of Wales Press, 2014), 4.
9. Mike McCarthy, "Rheged: An Early Historic Kingdom Near the Solway," *Proceedings of the Society of Antiquarians of Scotland* 132 (2002), 357–381.
10. Jack Hunter, *The Lost Town of Innermessan* at www.scottishcorpus.ac.uk.
11. Historic Scotland, *Kirkmadrine Early Christian Stones*, at the website http://www.historic-scotland.gov.uk/propertyresults/propertydetail.htm?PropID=PL_188.
12. John Koch, *Celtic Culture* (Santa Barbara, CA: ABC-CLIO, 2006), 1722.
13. J.A. Giles, "Geoffrey of Monmouth's British History," in *Six Old English Chronicles* (London: Henry G. Bohn, 1848), Book 8, Chapter 14.
14. Ibid., Book 8, Chapter 15.
15. Edward Gibbon, *The History of the Decline and Fall of the Roman Empire*, ed. David Womersley (London: Penguin, 2000), 577.
16. Jeffrey John Dixon, *The Glory of Arthur* (Jefferson, NC: McFarland, 2014), 98.
17. John Koch, *Celtic Culture*, 1722.

18. J.A. Giles, "Geoffrey of Monmouth's British History," in *Six Old English Chronicles*, Book 8, Chapter 19.

19. Charles Thomas, "The Hill-Fort at St. Dennis," *Cornish Archaeology* 4 (1965), 31–35.

20. "Triad 56," *The Welsh Triads*, at the website http://norin77.50megs.com/triads.htm.

21. "Ogyrven," in *Jones Celtic Encyclopedia* at www.maryjones.us.

22. *The Annales Cambriae*, trans. James Ingram (London: Everyman Press, 1912).

23. Caitlin R. Green, *Pre-Galfridian Arthurian Characters*, at the website http://www.arthuriana.co.uk/n&q/figures.htm.

24. J.A. Giles, "Geoffrey of Monmouth's British History," in *Six Old English Chronicles*, Book 10, Chapter 12.

25. Thomas Green, *A Bibliographic Guide to Welsh Arthurian Literature*, at the website http://www.arthuriana.co.uk/notes&queries/N&Q1_ArthLit.pdf.

26. Caradoc of Llancarfan, *Life of Gildas*, trans. Hugh Williams (London: Cymmrodorion, 1899).

27. Geoffrey of Monmouth, *Life of Merlin*, trans. John Jay Perry (Urbana, IL: The University of Illinois, 1925).

28. Thomas Green, *A Bibliographic Guide to Welsh Arthurian Literature*.

29. William Jenkins Rees and Thomas Wakeman, *Lives of the Cambro-British Saints* (London: Longman & Co., 1853), 398.

30. Pastscape, *Monument No. 188644*.

31. William Jenkins Rees and Thomas Wakeman, *Lives of the Cambro-British Saints*, 341–2.

32. *Ibid.*, 508–9.

33. Gerald of Wales, *On the Instruction of Princes*, trans. John William Sutton, at the website http://d.lib.rochester.edu/camelot/text/gerald-of-wales-arthurs-tomb.

34. William of Malmesbury, *Chronicle of the Kings of England*, trans. J.A.Giles (London: Henry G. Bohn, 1847), 315.

35. Thomas Malory, *Le Morte D'arthur*, at the website http://www.gutenberg.org/files/1252/1252-h/1252-h.htm.

36. J. Armitage Robinson, *Two Glastonbury Legends* (Cambridge: Cambridge University Press, 1926), 51–2.

37. Thomas Green, *A Gazetteer of Arthurian Onomastic and Topographic Folklore*, at the website http://www.arthuriana.co.uk/notes&queries/N&Q2_ArthFolk.pdf.

38. Thomas Green, *A Bibliographic Guide to Welsh Arthurian Literature*.

Chapter 10

1. P.H. Sawyer, *From Roman Britain to Norman England* (London: Routledge, 2002), 66.

2. Caitlin R. Green, *The Historicity and Historicisation of Arthur*, at the website http://www.arthuriana.co.uk/historicity/arthur.htm.

3. Livius.org, *Diploma*, at the website http://www.livius.org/di-dn/diploma/diploma.html.

4. Roman Britain Organisation, *Corinnium Dobunnorum*, at the website http://www.roman-britain.org/places/corinium.htm.

5. Roman Footprints, *Camulodunum*, at the website http://roman-footprints.com/britannia-england-east/colchester/.

6. Thomas Lloyd, Julian Orbach, Robert Scourfield, *Pembrokeshire* (New Haven, CT: Yale University Press, 2004), 141.

7. Marilyn Dunn, *Emergence of Monasticism* (Malden, MA and Oxford, UK: Blackwell, 2000, 2003), 139.

8. Polly Groom and Will Steele, *Caldey Island: Tir Gofal Farm Historic Environment Report*, at the website http://www.herwales.co.uk/her/groups/DAT/media/DAT%20Reports/39860%20TG%20Caldey.pdf.

9. Trevor D. Ford (ed), *Limestones and Caves of Wales* (Cambridge: Cambridge University Press, 2011), 84.

10. Coflein, *Caer Gybi Roman Fort*.

11. John Roberts, *Land at Ty Mawr Holyhead Anglesey* (Bangor, Wales: Gwynedd Archaeological Trust, 2006), 4.

12. Canmore, *Iona, Early Christian Monastery*.

13. Compute Scotland, "Radiocarbon Dating Gets Iona Its Bronze Age Links," at the website http://www.computescotland.com/radiocarbon-dating-gets-iona-its-bronze-age-links-2275.php.

14. Headland Archaeology, *Recent Excavations on Inchmarnock & the Identification of An Early Monastic School-House*, at the website http://www.headlandarchaeology.com/Images/news/downloads/IMK99-Webnews.pdf.

15. Canmore, *Inchmarnock, Northpark*.

16. Alison Sheridan, "Radiocarbon Dates Arranged Through National Museums Scotland During 2006/7," *Discovery and Excavation in Scotland* 8 (2007), 220–1.

17. Dom Michael Barrett, "March: St. Marnock or Marnan," *A Calendar of Scottish Saints* (Fort Augustus: Abbey Press, 1919).

18. Charles Thomas, "Beacon Hill Re-Visited," *Annual Report of the Lundy Field Society* 42 (1992), 43–4.

19. Pastscape, *Beacon Hill Iron Age Settlement*.

20. Rhona Finlayson and Caroline Hardie, *Holy Island: Northumberland Extensive Urban Survey* (Morpeth, UK: Northumberland County Council, 2009).

21. Pastscape, *Glastonbury Tor*.

22. Martin Grimmer, "Saxon Bishop and Celtic King," *Heroic Age* 4 (2001).

23. Pastscape, *Earthworks on Glastonbury Tor*.

24. Miranda Richardson, *An Archaeological Assessment of Lyng and Athelney* (Taunton, UK: Somerset County Council, 2003), 3–4.

25. Pastscape, *Muchelney Abbey*.

26. Pastscape, *Ely Cathedral*.

27. Pastscape, *Ramsey Abbey*.

28. John R. Black, "Tradition and Transformation in the Cult of St. Guthlac in Early Medieval England," *The Heroic Age* 10 (May 2007).

29. Pastscape, *Bardney Abbey*.

30. Pastscape, *Castle Killibury*.

31. Ray Howell, *Searching for the Silures An Iron Age Tribe in South-East Wales* (Stroud, Gloucestershire: The History Press, 2006), 96.

32. Andrew Seaman, "Dinas Powys in Context: Settlement and Society in Post-Roman Wales," *Studia Celtica* 47 (2013), 7.

33. Christopher Snyder, *Age of Tyrants: Britain and the Britons A.D. 400–600* (University Park, PA: Pennsylvania State University Press, 2003), 191.

34. Canmore, *Trusty's Hill, Anwoth*.

35. Guard Archaeology, *The Galloway Picts Project*, at the website http://www.guard-archaeology.co.uk/news12/gallowayNews.html.

36. Caitlin R. Green, *The Other Early Arthurian Cycle: The Tale of Tristan and Isolt*, at the website http://www.arthuriana.co.uk/n&q/tristan.htm.

37. Nicholas Orme, *The Saints of Cornwall* (Oxford: Oxford University Press, 2002), 156.

38. Pastscape, *Liskeard*.

39. Pastscape, *King Donierts Stone and Other Half Stone*.

40. Pastscape, *Castle Dore*.

41. Pastscape, *Helston Town*.

42. Pastscape, *Lankidden*.

43. Pastscape, *St. Michaels Mount Monastery*.

44. "Bronze Age Hoard from St. Michael's Mount Now on Display," *Past Horizons* (13.6.2011).
45. Pastscape, *Monument No. 426787*.
46. Pastscape, *Tregiffian Burial Chamber*.
47. Andy M. Jones, Jane Marley, Henrietta Quinnell, Steve Hartgroves, *On the Beach: New Discoveries at Harlyn Bay, Cornwall* (York, Archaeology Data Service, 2010), doi:10.5284/1000384.
48. Jacqueline A. Nowakowski, *Excavations of a Bronze Age Landscape and a Post-Roman Industrial Settlement 1953–1961, Gwithian, Cornwall* (Truro, Cornwall: Truro County Council, 2007), 30.
49. Pastscape, *Monument No. 968564*.
50. Pastscape, *Monument No. 424253*.
51. Pastscape, *Monument No. 423260*.
52. Edward Tyrrell Leith, *On the Legend of Tristan* (Bombay, India: Education Society, 1868), 26–9.
53. *Ibid.*, 27.
54. *Ibid.*, 28.
55. Graham Anderson, *King Arthur in Antiquity* (London: Routledge, 2004), 110–111.
56. Lucija Soberl, Richard P. Evershed and Joshua Pollard, *Cooking for the Dead: Investigation of Organic Residues Preserved in Early Bronze Age Funerary Pottery from South-West Britain*, at the website https://www.academia.edu/233371/Cooking_for_the_Dead.
57. S. Bohncke, "The Pollen Analysis of Deposits in a Food Vessel from the Henge Monument and North Mains," in Gordon J. Barclay, "Sites of the Third Millennium BC to the First Millennium AD at North Mains, Strathallan, Perthshire," *Proceedings of the Society of Antiquaries of Scotland* 113 (1983), 180.
58. Merryn Dineley and Graham Dineley, "Neolithic Ale: Barley as a Source of Sugars for Fermentation," in A. Fairbairn (ed.), *Plants in the Neolithic and Beyond* (Oxford: Oxbow Books, 2000).
59. Bettina Arnold, "Power Drinking in Iron Age Europe," *British Archaeology* 57 (February 2001).
60. John Waddell, "Excavation at 'Dathi's Mound,' Rathcroghan, Co. Roscommon," *The Journal of Irish Archaeology* 4 (1988), 34.
61. University College Dublin, *Excavation Findings from 3500 BC Passage Tomb at the Mound of the Hostages Published*, at the website http://www.ucd.ie/news/mar06/030306_mound_of_the_hostages.htm.
62. Database of Irish Excavation Reports, *Rath Na Riogh, Tara*, at the website http://www.excavations.ie/report/1997/Meath/0002968/.
63. *Archaeology: Lismullin Henge* at the website https://lismullinhenge.wordpress.com/.

Chapter 11

1. Meath County Council, *Draft Tara Skryne Landscape Conservation Area*, at the website http://www.meath.ie/CountyCouncil/Publications/PlanningPublications/TaraSkryneLandscapeConservationArea/File,41581,en.pdf.
2. Coflein, *Castell Bryn Gwyn*.
3. Gwynedd Archaeological Trust, *A Re-Discovered Stone Circle, Bryn Gwyn, Anglesey*, at the website http://www.heneb.co.uk/cadwprojs/cadwreview2010-11/funrit10-11.html.
4. Coflein, *Llanmelin Wood Hillfort*.
5. Wessex Archaeology, *Caerwent Roman Town*, at the website http://www.wessexarch.co.uk/system/files/68736_Caerwent%20Monmouthshire.pdf.
6. John Newman, *Gwent/Monmouthshire* (London: Penguin, 2000), 149.
7. Pastscape, *The Rumps*.
8. Pastscape, *Church of St. Kew*.
9. Dorset County Council, *Dorset Historic Towns Survey: Wareham*, at the website https://www.dorsetforyou.com/article/398181/Wareham-historic-towns-survey.
10. Michael Swanton, *Anglo-Saxon Chronicle* (New York, NY: Psychology Press, 1998), 52.
11. Asser., *Life of Alfred*, in J.A. Giles, *Six Old English Chronicles* (London: Henry G. Bohn, 1848), 58.
12. Pastscape, *Monument No. 211665*.
13. Pastscape, *Amesbury Abbey*.
14. Patricia Healy Wasyliw, *Martyrdom, Murder and Magic* (New York: Peter Lang, 2008), 78–9.
15. Pastscape, *Ripon Minster*.
16. Will Parker, *The Mabinogi of Math*, at the website www.mabinogi.net.
17. W.J. Gruffydd, *Math Vab Mathonwy: An Inquiry into the Origins and Development of the Fourth Branch of the Mabinogi* (Cardiff: University of Wales Press Board, 1928), 43.
18. Coflein, *St. Tudwal's Island*.
19. Coflein, *Caer Fadrun*.
20. Patrick Sims-Williams, "Clas Beuno and the Four Branches of the Mabinogi," in Bernhard Maier and Stefan Zimmer (eds.), *150 Jahre "Mabinogion": Deutsche-Walische Kulturbeziehungen* (Buchreihe der Zeitscrift für celtische Philologie 19, Tübingen: Niemeyer, 2001), 111–127.
21. Rev. P.B. Williams, "Historical Account of the Monasteries and Abbeys in Wales," *Transactions of the Cymmrodorion* 2 (1828), 237.
22. Charles William Sullivan, *The Mabinogi: A Book of Essays* (New York: Garland Press, 1996), 354.
23. Julius Pokorny, *Indogermanisches etymologisches Wörterbuch* (Bern: Francke, 1959), 175.
24. John Koch, *Celtic Culture* (Santa Barbara, CA: ABC-CLIO, 2006), 606–7.
25. Henri d'Arbois de Jubainville, *Les Druides Et Les Dieux Celtiques À Forme D'animaux* (Paris: Librairie Honoré Champion, 1906), 160–2.
26. *Electronic Dictionary of the Irish Language*, at the website http://edil.qub.ac.uk/dictionary/results-new.php?srch=math&&dictionary_choice=edil_2012&&limit=10.
27. Dimitri Nikolai Boekhoorn, *Mythical, Legendary and Supernatural Bestiary in Celtic Tradition: From Oral to Written Literature* (PhD diss., Université Rennes 2/University College Cork, 2008), 82.
28. *Lludd and Llefelys*, trans. Lady Charlotte Guest, at the website http://www.maryjones.us/ctexts/lludd.html.
29. John Koch, *Celtic Culture*, 484.
30. University of Wales, *Archaeology of the Mabinogion*, at the website http://www.uwtsd.ac.uk/research/environment-archaeology-history-and-anthropology/archaeology-of-the-mabinogion/.
31. John Koch, *Celtic Culture*, 867.
32. A.W. Wade Evans (ed.), *Welsh Medieval Law* (Oxford: Clarendon Press, 1909). 344.
33. Castles of Wales, *Dolbenmaen Motte*, at the website http://www.castlewales.com/dolbmen.html.
34. Coflein, *Plas Dolbenmaen*.
35. Coflein, *St. Mary's Church, Dolbenmaen*.
36. Rachel Bromwich, *Trioedd Ynys Prydein: The Triads of the Island of Britain* (Cardiff, UK: University of Wales Press, 2014), 277.
37. Will Parker, *Lugus: The Gaulish Mercury*, at the website http://www.mabinogion.info/lugus.htm.
38. Julius Pokorny, *Indogermanisches etymologisches Wörterbuch*, 687–690.
39. *Ibid.*, 687.
40. John Koch, *Celtic Culture*, 867.
41. Coflein, *Tomen Y Mur Roman Military Settlement*.
42. John Koch, "Some Suggestions and Etymologies Reflecting Upon the Mythology of the Four Branches," *Proceedings of the Harvard Celtic Colloquium* 9 (1989), 6.

43. Mariko Namba Walter and Eva Jane Neumann Fridman (eds.), *Shamanism: An Encyclopedia of World Beliefs, Practices and Culture* (Santa Barbara, CA: ABC-CLIO, 2004), 494.

44. *Ibid.*, 13.

45. John Koch, *Celtic Culture*, 1486.

46. Reverend Canon Dr. Patrick Thomas, *Illtud*, at the website.

47. Anne Ross, "Ritual and the Druids," in Miranda Green (ed.), *The Celtic World* (Abingdon, UK: Routledge, 1995), 423.

48. *Ibid.*, 429.

49. Elizabeth Rees, *Celtic Sites and Their Saints: A Guidebook* (London: Burns & Oates, 2003), 94.

50. Celtic Inscribed Stones Project, *Capel Anelog*, at the website http://www.ucl.ac.uk/archaeology/cisp/database/site/adarn.html.

51. "Life of St. Beuno," in Oliver Davies, *Celtic Spirituality* (Mahwah, NJ: Paulist Press, 1999), 212.

52. Pliny the Elder, *Natural History*, trans. John Bostock and H.T. Riley (London: Henry G. Bohn, 1855), Book 16, Chapter 45.

53. *Ibid.*, Book 24, Chapter 62.

54. "Life of St. Beuno," in Oliver Davies, *Celtic Spirituality*, 34.

55. "The Life of St. Melangell," in Oliver Davies, *Celtic Spirituality*, 219.

56. A.W. Wade-Evans, *Vitae Sanctorum Britanniae Et Genealogiae* (Cardiff: University of Wales Press, 1944), at the website http://www.maryjones.us/ctexts/brynach.html.

57. Muirchu moccu Machtheni, *Life of St. Patrick*, in William Bethan, *Irish Antiquarian Researches* (Dublin: William Curry Jun. and Co., 1827).

58. Bede, "The Life and Miracles of St. Cuthbert," Chapter 10, in *Ecclesiastical History of the English Nation*, trans. J.A. Giles (London: J.M. Dent; New York, E.P. Dutton, 1910).

Bibliography

Abbott, Marcus, and Hugo Anderson-Whymark. *Stonehenge Laser Scan: Archaeological Analysis Report.* London: English Heritage, 2012.

Ackroyd, Peter. *Thames: Sacred River.* London: Vintage, 2007.

Adderley, Mark. *What Man Is the Gatekeeper/Porter?* http://www.markadderley.net/arthur/welsh-arthur/pagur.html.

Allason-Jones, Lindsey. "Coventina's well." In *The Concept of the Goddess.* Edited by S. Billington and M. Green. London: Routledge, 2002.

Allen, Dave. "Buried in Time—Late Iron Age." *Hampshire Archaeology: Musings from a Hampshire Archaeologist.* https://hampshirearchaeology.wordpress.com/2015/01/12/buried-in-time-late-iron-age/.

Allen, Richard Hinckley. *Star Names: Their Lore and Meaning.* Mineola, NY: Dover Publications, 1963.

Allen, T., K. Cramp, H. Lamdin-Whymark, and L. Welbley. *Castle Hill and Its Landscape: Archaeological Investigations at the Wittenhams, Oxfordshire.* Oxford, UK: Oxford Archaeology, 2010.

Anderson, Graham. *King Arthur in Antiquity.* London: Routledge, 2004.

Anderson, J. "Notices of Nine Brochs Along the Caithness Coast from Keiss Bay to Skirza Head, Excavated by Sir Francis Tress Barry, Bart., Mp., of Keiss Castle, Caithness." *Proceedings of the Society of Antiquaries of Scotland* 35 (1901): 112–148.

Anderson, T. "Two Decapitations from Roman Towcester." *Journal of Osteoarchaeology* 11 (2001): 400–405.

The Annales Cambriae. Translated by James Ingram. London: Everyman Press, 1912.

Aratus. *Phaenomena.* http://www.theoi.com/Text/AratusPhaenomena.html.

L'arbre celtique. *Encyclopédie De L'arbre Celtique.* http://encyclopedie.arbre-celtique.com/encyclopedie.php.

Armit, Ian. *Headhunting and the Body in Iron Age Europe.* Cambridge, UK: Cambridge University Press, 2012.

Arnold, Bettina. "Power Drinking in Iron Age Europe." *British Archaeology* 57 (February 2001).

Ashbee, P., M. Bell, and E. Proudfoot. *Wilsford Shaft: Excavations 1960-62.* London: English Heritage, 1989.

Ashmolean Museum. *Bronze Age Cauldron from Shipton-On-Cherwell.* http://britisharchaeology.ashmus.ox.ac.uk/highlights/cauldron.html.

Athenaeus. *Deipnosophists.* Translated by C.D. Yonge. London: Henry G. Bohn, 1854. http://www.attalus.org/info/athenaeus.html.

Barclay, Alistair. "Excavating the Living Dead." *British Archaeology* 115 (November–December 2010).

Barrett, Dom Michael. "March: St. Marnock or Marnan." In *A Calendar of Scottish Saints.* Fort Augustus: Abbey Press, 1919.

Barrett, John, and David McOmish. *All Cannings Cross.* http://www.wiltshire.gov.uk/acc.pdf.

Barrett, John C., Freeman, P.M.W. and Woodward, Ann. *Cadbury Castle, Somerset: The Later Prehistoric and Early Historic Archaeology.* London: English heritage, 2014.

Barrett, John C., and David McOmish. "The Early Iron Age in Southern Britain: Recent Work at All Cannings Cross, Stanton St. Bernard and East Chisenbury, Wiltshire." *De L'âge Du Bronze a L'âge Du Fer En France Et En Europe Occidentale (Xe-Viie Siècle Av. J.C.). La Moyenne Vallée Du Rhône Aux Âges Du Fer. Actes Du Xxxe Colloque International De L'a.F.E.A.F., Co-Organisé Avec L'a. P.R.A.B. (Saint-Romain-En-Gal, 26–28 Mai 2006.* Edited by M.J. Lambert-Roulière, A. Daubigney, P.Y. Milcent, M. Talon and J. Vital. Dijon, France: Société Archéologique de l'Est, 2009.

Bede. "The Life and Miracles of St. Cuthbert." In *Ecclesiastical History of the English Nation.* Translated by J.A Giles. London: J.M. Dent; New York, NY: E.P. Dutton, 1910.

Bender, B., S. Hamilton, and C. Tilley. *Stone Worlds: Narrative and Reflexivity in Landscape Archaeology.* Walnut Creek, CA: Left Coast Press, 2008.

Bernardo Stempel, Patrizia de. "The Phonetic Interface of Celtic Word Formation in Continental Celtic." In *Continental Celtic Word Formation: The Onomastic Data.* Edited by Juan Luis Garcia Alonso. Salamanca, Spain: Ediciones Universidad de Salamanca, 2013.

Billington, Sandra, and Miranda Green. *The Concept of the Goddess.* London: Routledge, 2002.

Birch, Steven. *Uamh An Ard Achadh (High Pasture Cave), Strath, Isle of Skye: Interim Report—November 2004.* http://www.high-pasture-cave.org/index.php/the_work/article/fieldwork_2004.

Birley, Robin. *Vindolanda: A Roman Frontier Fort on*

Hadrian's Wall. Stroud, Gloucestershire, UK: Amberley Publishing, 2012.

Black, John R. "Tradition and Transformation in the Cult of St. Guthlac in Early Medieval England." *The Heroic Age* 10 (May 2007).

Boekhoorn, Dimitri Nikolai. *Mythical, Legendary and Supernatural Bestiary in Celtic Tradition: From Oral to Written Literature*. PhD diss., Université Rennes 2/University College Cork, 2008.

Bohncke, S. "The Pollen Analysis of Deposits in a Food Vessel from the Henge Monument and North Mains," in Gordon J. Barclay, "Sites of the Third Millennium BC to the First Millennium AD at North Mains, Strathallan, Perthshire." *Proceedings of the Society of Antiquaries of Scotland* 113 (1983): 178–180.

Bowman, Sheridan, and Stuart Needham. "The Dunaverney and Little Thetford Flesh-Hooks: History, Technology and Their Position Within the Later Bronze Age Feasting Complex." *The Antiquaries Journal* 87 (2007): 53–108.

The Boyhood Deeds of Finn Mac Cumhaill. Translated by Tom P. Cross and Clark Harris Slover. New York, NY: Henry Holt & Co., 1936. http://www.maryjones.us/ctexts/f02.html.

Bradley, Richard. "Danish Razors and Swedish Rocks." *Antiquity* 80 (2006): 372–389.

Bradley, Richard. *The Idea of Order: The Circular Archetype in Prehistoric Europe*. Oxford, UK: Oxford University Press, 2012.

Bradley, Richard. *The Passage of Arms: An Archaeological Analysis of Prehistoric Hoards and Votive Deposits*. Cambridge, UK: Cambridge University Press, 1990.

Brennan, Martin. *The Stones of Time: Calendars, Sundials, and Stone Chambers of Ancient Ireland*. Rochester, VT: Inner Traditions International, 1994.

British Museum. *Ashwell Roman Treasure and Excavation*. http://www.britishmuseum.org/research/research_projects/all_current_projects/ashwell_roman_treasure.aspx.

British Museum. *The Barkway Hoard*. http://www.britishmuseum.org/explore/highlights/highlight_objects/pe_prb/t/the_barkway_hoard.aspx.

British Museum. *Bronze Spoons*. http://www.britishmuseum.org/explore/highlights/highlight_objects/pe_prb/b/bronze_spoons.aspx.

British Museum. *Chiseldon Cauldrons: Unearthing and Conserving An Iron Age Feast*. http://www.britishmuseum.org/research/research_projects/all_current_projects/chiseldon_cauldrons.aspx.

British Museum. *Finds from a Late Iron Age Cremation Burial*. http://www.britishmuseum.org/explore/highlights/highlight_objects/pe_prb/f/late_iron_age_burial_finds.aspx.

British Museum. *Horned Helmet*. http://www.britishmuseum.org/explore/highlights/highlight_objects/pe_prb/h/horned_helmet.aspx.

British Museum. *Horse Harness from the Stanwick Hoard*. http://www.britishmuseum.org/explore/highlights/highlight_objects/pe_prb/h/stanwick_hoard_horse_harness.aspx.

British Museum. *The Kirkburn Sword*. http://www.britishmuseum.org/explore/highlights/highlight_objects/pe_prb/t/the_kirkburn_sword.aspx.

British Museum. *The Rillaton Gold Cup*. http://www.britishmuseum.org/explore/highlights/highlight_objects/pe_prb/t/the_rillaton_gold_cup.aspx.

British Museum. *The Wetwang Chariot Burial*. https://www.britishmuseum.org/explore/online_tours/britain/the_wetwang_chariot_burial/the_wetwang_chariot_burial.aspx.

Bromwich, Rachel. *Trioedd Ynys Prydein: The Triads of the Island of Britain*. Cardiff, UK: University of Wales Press, 2014.

Brück, Joanna. "Fire, Earth, Water: An Elemental Cosmography in the European Bronze Age." In *The Oxford Handbook of the Archaeology of Ritual & Religion*. Edited by Timothy Insoll, 387–404. Oxford, UK: Oxford University Press, 2011.

Brunaux, Jean-Louis, and Patrice Méniel. "Le Sanctuaire De Gournay-Sur-Aronde (Oise): Structures Et Rites, Les Animaux Du Sacrifice." *Revue Archéologique De Picardie* 1–2 (1983): 165–173.

Bulleid, Arthur, and Harold St. George Gray. *The Glastonbury Lake Village*. Glastonbury: The Glastonbury Antiquarian Society, 1917.

Burkert, Walter. *Greek Religion: Archaic and Classical*. Hoboken, NJ: John Wiley & Sons, 2013.

Burn, A.R. "Holy Men on Islands in Pre-Christian Britain." *Glasgow Archaeological Journal* 1 (1969): 2–6.

Burnham, Barry, and J.S. Wacher. *The Small Towns of Roman Britain*. London: Batsford, 1990.

Burrow, Steve. "Sensational New Discoveries at Bryn Celli Ddu." *British Archaeology* 89 (July/August 2006).

Caradoc of Llancarfan. *Life of Gildas*. Translated by Hugh Williams. London: Cymmrodorion, 1899.

Castleden, Rodney. *King Arthur: The Truth Behind the Legend*. London: Routledge, 2003.

Castles of Wales. *Dolbenmaen Motte*. http://www.castlewales.com/dolbmen.html.

Causey, Faya. *Amber and the Ancient World*. Los Angeles, CA: Getty Publications, 2011.

Celtic Inscribed Stones Project. *Capel Anelog*. http://www.ucl.ac.uk/archaeology/cisp/database/site/adarn.html.

Centre for the Study of Ancient Documents. *Curse Tablets from Ancient Britain: Archaeological Sites*. http://curses.csad.ox.ac.uk.

Chadwick, Adrian M. *The Iron Age and Romano-British Periods in West Yorkshire*. Wakefield, UK: West Yorkshire Archaeology Advisory Service, 2009.

Chapman, Andy. *The Bronze Age Barrow Cemetery at Gayhurst*. http://www.mkheritage.co.uk/sga/Gayhurst/barrow.html.

Clarke, Giles. *Pre-Roman and Roman Winchester. the Roman Cemetery at Lankhills*. Oxford, UK: Oxford University Press, 1979.

Cleal, Rosamund. "Great Sites" Wndmill Hill." *British Archaeology* 67 (October 2002).

Cleal, Rosamund. "Human Remains from Windmill

Hill and West Kennet Avenue, Avebury Parish, Wiltshire, Held by the Alexander Keiller Museum." In *Draft Report on the Request for the Reburial of Human Remains from the Alexander Keiller Museum at Avebury*. Edited by David Thackray and Sebastian Payne. London: National Trust and English Heritage, 2008.

Clwyd-Powys Archaeological Trust. *The Breiddin*. http://www.cpat.org.uk/keysites/breiddin/breiddin.htm.

Clwyd-Powys Archaeological Trust. *Defensive and Military Landscapes*. http://www.cpat.org.uk/projects/longer/histland/holywell/hodefend.htm.

Clwyd-Powys Archaeological Trust. *The Iron Age, 600 BC–AD 50*. http://www.cpat.org.uk/cpat/past/iron/iron.htm.

Collingwood, R.G., and R.P. Wright. *The Roman Inscriptions of Britain*. http://romaninscriptionsofbritain.org/.

Collins, A.E.P. "Excavations on Blewburton Hill, 1948 and 1949." *Berkshire Archaeological Journal* 53 (1952–3): 4–29.

Compute Scotland. "Radiocarbon Dating Gets Iona Its Bronze Age Links." http://www.computescotland.com/radiocarbon-dating-gets-iona-its-bronze-age-links-2275.php.

Conseil général des Hauts-de-Seine, *Nanterre Et Les Parisii*. http://www.nanterre.net/parisii/visite/documents/Cahier_pedagogique.pdf.

Corpus of Electronic Texts. *Metrical Dindshenchas*. http://www.ucc.ie/celt/online/T106500D/text112.html.

Cunliffe, Barry. "Atlantic Sea-Ways." *Revista De Guimarães, Volume Especial* (1999): 93–105.

Cunliffe, Barry. *Britain Begins*. Oxford, UK: Oxford University Press, 2013.

Cunliffe, Barry. *Danebury: An Iron Age Hillfort in Hampshire Vol. 6. A Hillfort Community in Perspective*. York, UK: Council for British Archaeology, 1995.

Cunliffe, Barry. *Druids: A Very Short Introduction*. Oxford, UK: Oxford University Press, 2010.

Cunliffe, Barry. *Iron Age Communities in Britain*. Taylor & Francis e-library, 2005.

Cunliffe, Barry. "Iron Age Societies in Western Europe and Beyond, 800–140 BC." In *The Oxford Ilustrated History of Prehistoric Europe*. Edited by Barry Cunliffe. Oxford, UK: Oxford University Press, 2001.

Cunliffe, Barry. "Landscape with People." In *Culture, Landscape and the Environment*. Edited by Kate Flint and Howard Morphy. Oxford, UK: Oxford University Press, 2001.

Cunliffe, Barry. "Understanding Hillforts: Have We Progressed?" In *The Wessex Hillforts Prokect*. Edited by Andrew Payne, Mark Corney and Barry Cunliffe. London: English Heritage, 2006.

Cunnington, Maud. "Excavations in Yarnbury Castle Camp." *Wiltshire Archaeological and Natural History Magazine* 46 (1933): 198–213.

Cunnington, Maud. "Lidbury Camp." *Wiltshire Archaeological and Natural History Magazine* 40 (1917): 12–36.

D'Arbois de Jubainville, Henri. *Les Druides Et Les Dieux Celtiques À Forme D'animaux* Paris: Librairie Honoré Champion, 1906.

Dark, Ken. *Britain and the End of the Roman Empire*. Stroud, Gloucestershire: The History Press, 2006.

Database of Irish Excavation Reports. *Rath Na Riogh*. http://www.excavations.ie/report/1997/Meath/0002968/.

Davidson, Hilda Ellis. *Roles of the Northern Goddess*. Taylor & Francis e-library, 2001.

Davies, John. "Norfolk: Land of Boudicca." *Current Archaeology* 235 (2009).

Davies, Oliver. *Celtic Spirituality*. Mahwah, NJ: Paulist Press, 1999.

Delamarre, Xavier. *Dictionnaire De La Langue Gauloise*. Paris, France: Errance, 2008.

Delamarre, Xavier. "Gallo-Brittonica. Transports, Richesse Et Générosité Chez Les Anciens Celtes." *Zeitschrift Für Celtische Philologie* 54 (2004): 121–132.

Delamarre, Xavier. "Gallo-Brittonica (Suite 11–21)." *Zeitschrift Für Celtische Philologie* 55 (2006): 29–41.

Denison, Simon. "Tin Mine Closure Marks More than the End of an Era." *British Archaeology* (April 1998).

Deutsches Archäologisches Institut, *Zambujal*. http://www.dainst.org/en/project/zambujal?ft=all.

Dickson, Antony, and Guy Hopkinson. *Holes in the Landscape: Seventeen Years of Archaeological Investigations at Nosterfield Quarry, North Yorkshire*. http://www.archaeologicalplanningconsultancy.co.uk/thornborough/pdf/holes_in_the_landscape.pdf.

Dickson, James H. "Bronze Age Mead." *Antiquity* 52 (1978): 108–113.

Dillon, Myles. "The Wasting Sickness of Cu Chulainn." *Scottish Gaelic Studies* 7 (1953).

Dineley, Merryn, and Graham Dineley. "Neolithic Ale: Barley as a Source of Sugars for Fermentation." In *Plants in the Neolithic and Beyond*. Edited by A. Fairbairn. Oxford: Oxbow Books, 2000.

Dinwiddy, Kisten Egging. *A Late Roman Cemetery at Little Keep. Dorchester, Dorset*. http://www.wessexarch.co.uk/files/Little_Keep_Dorchester_64913.pdf.

Diodorus Siculus. Historical Library. Translated by C.H. Oldfather. Cambridge, MA: Harvard University Press, 1935. http://penelope.uchicago.edu.

Dorset County Council. *Dorset Historic Towns Survey: Wareham*. https://www.dorsetforyou.com/article/398181/Wareham—historic-towns-survey.

Dunn, Marilyn. *Emergence of Monasticism*. Malden, MA and Oxford, UK: Blackwell, 2000, 2003.

Edmonds, J.M. *Lyra Graeca*. Rockville, MD: Wildside Press, 2007.

Ellis, Chris, and Andrew Powell. *An Iron Age Settlement Outside Battlesbury Hillfort, Warminster and Sites Along the Southern Range Road*. Salisbury, UK: Wessex Archaeology, 2008.

English Heritage. *Burnt Mounds*. London: English Heritage, 2011.

English Heritage. *Enclosed Oppida.* http://www.eng-h.gov.uk/mpp/mcd/encop.htm.

English Heritage. *Gussage Style Settlement: General Description.* http://www.eng-h.gov.uk/mpp/mcd/sub/guss3.htm.

English Heritage. *History of Old Oswestry Hillfort.* http://www.english-heritage.org.uk/visit/places/old-oswestry-hill-fort/history/.

English Heritage. *Pre-Christian Cemeteries.* London: English Heritage, 2011.

Eogan, James. *Cleansing Body and Soul?* http://www.waterfordcity.ie/n25bypass/cleansing.htm.

Evans, Christopher. "Delivering Bodies Unto Waters: A Late Bronze Age Mid-Stream Midden Settlement and Iron Age Ritual Complex in the Fens." *The Antiquaries Journal* 93 (2013): 55–79.

Fagan, Brian M., and Charlotte Beck. *The Oxford Companion to Archaeology.* Oxford, UK: Oxford University Press, 1996.

Falileyev, Alexander. *Dictionary of Continental Place-Names.* Aberyswyth, Wales: CMCS Publications, 2010.

Farley, Julia. "Transformations of Scale: The Deposition of Miniature Weaponry in Iron Age Lincolnshire." *Pallas: Revue D'études Antiques* 86 (2011): 97–121.

Fee, Christopher R., and David A. Leeming. *Gods, Heroes and Kings.* Oxford, UK: Oxford University Press, 2001.

Ferris, Iain. *Romano-British Religious Sites in the West Midlands Region.* http://www.birmingham.ac.uk/schools/historycultures/departments/caha/research/arch-research/wmrrfa/seminar3.aspx.

Fienup-Riordan, Ann. *Boundaries and Passages: Rule and Ritual in Yup'ik Eskimo Oral Tradition.* Norman: University of Oklahoma Press, 1995.

Finlayson, Rhona, and Caroline Hardie. *Holy Island: Northumberland Extensive Urban Survey.* Morpeth, UK: Northumberland County Council, 2009.

Ford, Trevor D. *Limestones and Caves of Wales.* Cambridge, UK: Cambridge University Press, 2011.

Fulford, Michael. *City of the Dead: Calleva Atrebatum.* http://www.bbc.co.uk/history/ancient/archaeology/city_dead_01.shtml.

Fulk, Robert Dennis. *Interpretations of Beowulf: A Critical Anthology.* Bloomington: Indiana University Press, 1991.

Garcia Sanjuan, Leonardo. "The Warrior Stelae of the Iberian South-West: Symbols of Power in Ancestral Landscapes." In *Atlantic Europe in the First Millennium BC: Crossing the Divide.* Edited by T. Moore and L. Armada Pita. Oxford, UK: Oxford University Press, 2010.

Garrow, Duncan, and Chris Gosden. *Technologies of Enchantment? Exploring Celtic Art: 400 BC to AD 100.* Oxford, UK: Oxford University Press, 2012.

Gathering the Jewels: The website for Welsh cultural history. *Bronze Ox-Head Bucket-Mount Buried in a Grave in Welshpool.* http://education.gtj.org.uk/en/item1/28763.

Geoffrey of Monmouth. *Life of Merlin.* Translated by John Jay Perry. Urbana: The University of Illinois, 1925.

Gerald of Wales, *Giraldus Cambrensis: The Topography of Ireland.* Translated by Thomas Forester. Cambridge, Ontario: In parentheses Publications, 2000.

Gerald of Wales. *On the Instruction of Princes.* Translated by John William Sutton. http://d.lib.rochester.edu/camelot/text/gerald-of-wales-arthurs-tomb.

Gibson, Catriona, and Stephanie Knight. "A Middle Iron Age Settlement at Weston Down Cottages, Weston Colley, Near Winchester, Hampshire." *Proceedings of the Hampshire Field Club and Archaeological Society* 62 (2007): 5–36.

Gibbon, Edward. *The History of the Decline and Fall of the Roman Empire.* Edited by David Womersley. London: Penguin, 2000.

Gibson, David, and Mark Knight. *Bradley Fen Excavations Whittlesey, Cambridgeshire 2001–2004.* Cambridge, UK: Cambridge Archaeological Unit, 2006.

Gibson, D. Blair. *From Chiefdom to State in Early Ireland.* Cambridge, UK: Cambridge University Press, 2012.

Gildas. *On the Ruin and Conquest of Britain.* Translated by Hugh Williams. London: Cymmrodorion, 1899.

Giles, J.A. "Asser's Life of Alfred." In *Six Old English Chronicles.* London: Henry G. Bohn, 1848.

Giles, J.A. "Geoffrey of Monmouth's British History." In *Six Old English Chronicles.* London: Henry G. Bohn, 1848.

Gosden, C., S. Crawford, and K. Ulmschneider. *Celtic Art in Europe: Making Connections.* Oxford, UK: Oxbow Books, 2014.

Goskar, Thomas. "The Stonehenge Lasershow." *British Archaeology* 73 (November 2003).

Green, Barbara, and Ian Stead. "The Snettisham Treasure." *Current Archaeology* (May 24, 2007).

Green, Caitlin R. *The Historicity and Historicisation of Arthur.* http://www.arthuriana.co.uk/historicity/arthur.htm.

Green, Caitlin R. *The Other Early Arthurian Cycle: The Tale of Tristan and Isolt.* http://www.arthuriana.co.uk/n&q/tristan.htm.

Green, Caitlin R. *Pre-Galfridian Arthurian Characters.* http://www.arthuriana.co.uk/n&q/figures.htm.

Green, Martin. *The Dorset Cursus.* http://digitaldigging.net/dorset-cursus-monument-map/.

Green, Martin. "Down Farm." *Current Archaeology* 138 (April/May 1994): 216–225.

Green, Miranda. *Animals in Celtic Life and Myth.* London: Routledge, 1998.

Green, Miranda. *The Celtic World.* London: Routledge, 1996.

Green, Miranda. *The Gods of Roman Britain.* Princes Risborough, Buckinghamshire, UK: Shire Publications, 2003.

Green, Miranda. "The Worship of the Romano-Celtic Wheel-God in Britain Seen in Relation to Gaulish Evidence." *Latomus* 38 (1979): 345–367.

Green, Thomas. *A Bibliographic Guide to Welsh Arthurian Literature*. http://www.arthuriana.co.uk/notes&queries/N&Q1_ArthLit.pdf.

Green, Thomas. *A Gazetteer of Arthurian Onomastic and Topographic Folklore*. http://www.arthuriana.co.uk/notes&queries/N&Q2_ArthFolk.pdf.

Green, Thomas. *Lincolnshire and the Arthurian Legend*. http://www.arthuriana.co.uk/notes&queries/N&Q3_ArthLincs.pdf.

Grimmer, Martin. "Saxon Bishop and Celtic King." *Heroic Age* 4 (2001).

Groom, Polly, and Will Steele. *Caldey Island: Tir Gofal Farm Historic Environment Report*. http://www.herwales.co.uk/her/groups/DAT/media/DAT%20Reports/39860%20TG%20Caldey.pdf.

Gruffydd, W.J. *Math Vab Mathonwy: An Inquiry into the Origins and Development of the Fourth Branch of the Mabinogi*. Cardiff, Wales: University of Wales Press Board, 1928.

Guard Archaeology. *The Galloway Picts Project*. http://www.guard-archaeology.co.uk/news12/gallowayNews.html.

Guest, Lady Charlotte. *Lludd and Llefelys*. http://www.maryjones.us/ctexts/lludd.html.

Gwilt, A., M. Lodwick, and J. Deacon. *Llanmaes Archaeological Fieldwork, Vale of Glamorgan*. https://www.museumwales.ac.uk/1492/.

Gwynedd Archaeological Trust. *A Re-Discovered Stone Circle, Bryn Gwyn, Anglesey*. http://www.heneb.co.uk/cadwprojs/cadwreview2010-11/funrit10-11.html.

Haase, Donald. *The Greenwood Encyclopedia of Folktales and Fairy Tales*. Portsmouth, NH: Greenwood Publishing Group, 2007.

Halkon, Peter. "Britons and Romans in an East Yorkshire Landscape, UK." *Bollettino Di Archeologia on Line* Volume Speciale (2010): 24–40.

Hall, David and Coles, John. *Fenland Survey: An Essay in Landscape and Persistence*. London: English Heritage, 1994.

Hamilton, S., C. Tilley, and B. Bender. "Bronze Age Stone Worlds of Bodmin Moor." *Archaeology International* 3 (1999): 13–17.

Hamlin, Christine. *The Material Expression of Social Change*. PhD diss., University of Wisconsin–Milwaukee, 2007.

Harding, Jan, and Francis Healy. *The Raunds Area Project: A Neolithic and Bronze Age Landscape in Northamptonshire*. London: English Heritage, 2013.

Harding, Jan, and Ben Johnston. "Yorkshire's Holy Secret." *British Archaeology* 75 (March 2004).

Harding, Jan, Ben Johnston and Glyn Goodrick. "Neolithic Cosmology and the Monument Complex of Thornborough, North Yorkshire." *Archaeoastronomy* 20 (2006): 28–53.

Hargrave, Frank. "The Hallaton Treasure: Evidence of a New Kind of Shrine." *Current Archaeology* 236 (2009).

Haselgrove, Colin. "Stanwick." *Currrent Archaeology* 10 (1990): 380–385.

Hatt, Jean-Jacques. "Circonscription De Strasbourg." *Gallia* 18 (1960): 213–246.

Headland Archaeology. *Recent Excavations on Inchmarnock & the Identification of An Early Monastic School-House*. http://www.headlandarchaeology.com/Images/news/downloads/IMK99-Webnews.pdf.

Henig, Martin. *Religion in Roman Britain*. London: Batsford, 1984.

Heritage Council. *Inis Mor, Co. Galway*. http://heritagecouncil.ie/unpublished_excavations/section11.html.

Heritage Gateway. *Fiskerton Causeway*. http://www.heritagegateway.org.uk/Gateway/Results_Single.aspx?uid=MLI52904&resourceID=1006.

Heritage Gateway. *Late Bronze Age Riverbank Activity, Washingborough*. http://www.heritagegateway.org.uk/Gateway/Results_Single.aspx?uid=MLI87018&resourceID=1006.

Heritage Gateway. *Late Iron Age Settlement in Old Sleaford*. http://www.heritagegateway.org.uk/Gateway/Results_Single.aspx?uid=MLI60583&resourceID=1006.

Heritage of Wales News. *Remote Island Reveals Fascinating Prehistoric Past*. http://heritageofwalesnews.blogspot.co.uk/2012/10/remote-island-reveals-prehistoric-past.html.

Hertz, Robert. "A Contribution to the Study of the Collective Representation of Death." In *Death and the Right Hand*. Translated by Rodney and Claudia Neeham. Glencoe, IL: The Free Press, 1960.

Hesiod. *Works and Days*. Translated by Hugh G. Evelyn-White. London: William Heinemann, 1914.

Higham, N.J. *The English Conquest*. Manchester, UK: Manchester University Press, 1994.

Higham, Nicholas, and M.J. Ryan. *The Anglo-Saxon World*. New Haven, CT: Yale University Press, 2013.

Higley, Sarah, trans. "The Spoils of Annwn." The Camelot Project at the University of Rochester. http://www.lib.rochester.edu/camelot/.

Historic England, *Pastscape*. http://www.pastscape.org.uk/.

Historic Scotland. *Calanais Standing Stones*. http://www.historic-scotland.gov.uk/propertyoverview.htm?PropID=PL_051.

Historic Scotland. *Kirkmadrine Early Christian Stones*. http://www.historic-scotland.gov.uk/propertyresults/propertydetail.htm?PropID=PL_188.

Homer. *The Odyssey*. Translated by Samuel Butler. http://classics.mit.edu/Homer/odyssey.12.xii.html.

Hoops, Johannes. *Reallexikon Der Germanischen Altertumskunde Band 16*. Berlin, Germany: Walter de Gruyter, 2000.

Höppner, B., M. Bartelheim, M. Huijsmans, R. Krauss, K.-P. Martinek, E. Pernicka, and R. Schwab. "Prehistoric Copper Production in the Inn Valley (Austria), and the Earliest Copper in Central Europe." *Archaeometry* 47 (2005): 293–315.

Hoskin, Michael. "Studies in Iberian Archaeoastronomy: (9) an Overview." *Archaeoastronomy* 27 (2002): S75-S82.

Hostetter, Eric, and Thomas Noble Howem. *The Romano-British Villa at Castle Copse, Great Bedwyn*. Bloomington: Indiana University Press, 1997.

Howell, Ray. *Searching for the Silures: An Iron Age*

Tribe in South-East Wales. Stroud, Gloucestershire, UK: The History Press, 2006.
Hughes, Evan Gwilym. "An Iron Age Barrow Burial at Bromfield, Shropshire." *Proceedings of the Prehistoric Society* 60 (1994): 395–402.
Hunter, Jack. *The Lost Town of Innermessan.* www.scottishcorpus.ac.uk.
Hunter-Mann, Kurt. "Excavations at Vespasian's Camp Iron Age Hillfort, 1987." *Wiltshire Archaeological and Natural History Magazine* 92 (1999): 39–52.
Irish Archaeology. *A Barbary Ape Skull from Navan Fort, Co. Armagh*. http://irisharchaeology.ie/2014/05/a-barbary-ape-skull-from-navan-fort-co-armagh/.
Irish Archaeology. *The Enigmatic Fulacht Fiadh or Burnt Mound*. http://irisharchaeology.ie/2012/07/the-enigmatic-fulacht-fiadhburnt-mound/.
Isaac, Graham. "The Origins of the Celtic Languages: Language Spread from East to West." In *Celtic from the West: Alternative Perspectives from Archaeology, Genetics, Language and Literature*. Edited by Barry Cunliffe and John T. Koch, 154–67. Oxford, UK: Oxbow Books, 2010.
Joffroy, René, and Denise Bretz-Mahler. "Les Tombes À Char De La Tène Dans L'est De La France." *Gallia* 17 (1959): 5–36.
Johnston, Ian. *The Iliad*. Arlington, VA: Richer Resources Publications, 2007.
Jones, A.M., J. Marley, H. Quinnell, and S. Hartgroves. *On the Beach: New Discoveries at Harlyn Bay, Cornwall*. York, UK: Archaeology Data Service, 2010. doi:10.5284/1000384.
Jones, Gwyn, and Thomas Jones. *The Mabinogion*. London: Everyman, 1994.
Jones, Mary. *Jones Celtic Encyclopedia*. www.maryjones.us.
Julius Caesar. *Commentaries on the Gallic War*. Translated by W.A. McDevitte and W.S.Bohn. New York: Harper & Brothers, 1869. http://classics.mit.edu.
Jupp, Peter C. and Clare Gittings. *Death in England*. Manchester, UK: Manchester University Press, 1999.
Kaelber, Walter O. "'Tapas,' Birth, and Spiritual Rebirth in the Veda." *History of Religions* 15 (1976): 343–386.
Karl, Raimund. "Emerging Settlement Monumentality in North Wales During the Late Bronze and Iron Age: The Case of Meillionydd." In *Celtic from the West Vol. III*. Oxford, UK: Oxbow Books, forthcoming.
Kazanas, Nicholas. "Anatolian Bull and Vedic Horse in the Indo-European Diffusion." In *Indo-Aryan Origins and Other Vedic Issues*. New Delhi, India: Aditya Prakashan, 2009.
Kendrick, T.D. *Druids and Druidism*. Mineola, NY: Dover Publications, 2003.
Kenney, Jane. *Recent Excavations at Parc Bryn Cegin, Llandygai, Near Bangor, North Wales*. Bangor, Wales: Gwynedd Archaeological Trust, 2008.
King, Anthony, and Graham Soffe. "Internal Organisation and Deposition at the Iron Age Temple on Hayling Island (Hampshire)." In *Society and Settlement in Iron Age Europe*. Edited by J. Collis. Sheffield, UK: Sheffield Academic Press, 2001.
Kinnes, I.A., I.H. Longworth, I.M. McIntyre, S.P. Needham, and W.A Oddy. "Bush Barrow Gold." *Antiquity* 62 (1988): 24–39.
Kitson, P.R. "British and European River-Names." *Transactions of the Philological Society* 94 (1996): 73–118.
Koch, John. "A Case for Tartessian as a Celtic Language." *Acta Palaeohispanica X: Palaeohispanica* 9 (2009): 339–351.
Koch, John. *Celtic Culture: A Historical Encyclopedia*. Santa Barbara, CA: ABC-CLIO, 2006.
Koch, John. "Eriu, Alba, Letha: When Was a Language Ancestral to Gaelic First Spoken in Ireland?" *Emania* 9 (1991): 17–27.
Koch, John. *O'donnell Lectures 2008*. http://www.wales.ac.uk/Resources/Documents/Research/ODonnell.pdf.
Koch, John. "Some Suggestions and Etymologies Reflecting Upon Mythology of the Four Branches." *Proceedings of the Harvard Celtic Colloquium* 9 (1989): 1–10.
Koch, John, and Antone Minard. *The Celts: History, Life and Culture*. Santa Barbara, CA: ABC-CLIO, 2012.
Kohl, Philip L. *The Making of Bronze Age Eurasia*. Cambridge, UK: Cambridge University Press, 2007.
Kondratiev, Alexei. "Lugus: The Many-Gifted Lord." *An Tríbhís Mhór: The IMBAS Journal of Celtic Reconstructionism* 1 (1997).
Kristiansen, Kristian. "The Nebra Find and Early Indo-European Religion." *Tagungen Des Landesmuseum Für Vorgeschichte Halle* 5 (2010): 431–7.
Kristiansen, Kristian and Thomas Larsson. *The Rise of Bronze Age Society*. Cambridge, UK: Cambridge University Press, 2005.
Kyrgyz, Z. *On the Music of Shamanism in the Tuvinian Culture*. Kyzyl, Russia: International Science Center *Khomei* of the Ministry of Culture of the Republic of Tuva, 1993.
Ladle, Lilian, and Ann Woodward. "Bestwall Quarry." *British Archaeology* 115 (Nov/Dec 2010).
Lawson, Andrew. *Potterne 1982–5*. Salisbury, Wiltshire: Trust for Wessex Archaeology, 2000.
Leary, Jim and David Field. "Journeys and Juxtapositions: Marden Henge and the View from the Vale." In *Enclosing the Neolithic: Recent Studies in Britain and Europe*. Edited by Alex M. Gibson, 55–65. Oxford, UK: Archaeopress, 2012.
Leith, Edward Tyrell. *On the Legend of Tristan*. Bombay, India: Education Society, 1868.
Leivers, Matt, and Catriona Gibson. *A Later Bronze Age Settlement and Iron Age Cemetery. Excavations at Adanac Park, Nursling, Hampshire 2008*. Salisbury, UK: Wessex Archaeology, 2010.
Lewis, C.P., and A.T. Thacker. *A History of the County of Chester: Volume 5 Part 1, the City of Chester: General History and Topography*. http://www.british-history.ac.uk/vch/ches/vol5/pt1.
Lewis, Jodie. "Upwards at 45 Degrees: The Use of Vertical Caves During the Neolithic and Early

Bronze Age on Mendip, Somerset." *Capra* 2 (2000). http://capra.group.shef.ac.uk/2/upwards.html.

The Liss Triangle Centre. *A Potted History of Liss.* https://www.liss-triangle-centre.org.uk/pages/wp-content/uploads/2013/10/A-Potted-History-of-Liss.pdf.

Livius.org. *Diploma.* http://www.livius.org/di-dn/diploma/diploma.html.

Lloyd, David. "The Astronomy at Godmanchester: A Possible Neolithic Observatory." *Archaeoastronomy* 22 (2009): 34–52.

Lloyd, T., J. Orbach, and R. Scourfield. *Pembrokeshire.* New Haven, CT: Yale University Press, 2004.

Longley, David. "Excavations on the Site of a Late Bronze Age Settlement at Runnymede Bridge, Egham." *London Archaeologist* 3 (1976): 10–17.

Lovell, J., J. Timby, G. Wakeman, and Michael J. Allen. "Iron Age to Saxon Farming Settlement at Bishop's Cleeve, Gloucestershire: Excavations South of Church Road, 1998 Ans 2004." *Transactions of the Bristol and Gloucestershire Archaeological Society* 125 (2007): 95–129.

Lucan. *Civil War.* Translated by Sir Edward Ridley. London: Longmans, Green, and Co., 1996.

Lurker, Manfred. *The Routledge Dictionary of Gods and Goddesses.* London: Routledge, 2004.

Lynn, Chris. *Navan Fort: Archaeology and Myth.* Dublin, Ireland: Wordwell, 2003.

McCarthy, Mike. "Rheged: An Early Historic Kingdom Near the Solway." *Proceedings of the Society of Antiquaries of Scotland* 132 (2002): 357–381.

McCormick, Finbar. "Early Evidence for Wild Animals in Ireland." In *The Holocene History of the European Vertebrate Fauna.* Edited by Norbert Benecke. Rahden, Germany: Verlag Marie Leidorf, 1999.

McGavin, Neil. "A Roman Cemetery and Trackway at Stanton Harcourt." *Oxoniensia* 45 (1980): 112–123.

McIntosh, Jane. *Handbook to Life in Prehistoric Europe.* Santa Barbara, CA: ABC-CLIO, 2006.

MacKie, Euan. "The Prehistoric Solar Calendar: An Out-Of-Fashion Idea Revisited with New Evidence." *Time and Mind* 2.1 (March 2009): 9–46.

MacKillop, James. *A Dictionary of Celtic Mythology.* Oxford, UK: Oxford University Press, 2004.

McOmish, David. "East Chisenbury: Ritual and Rubbish at the British Bronze Age-Iron Age Transition." *Antiquity* 70 (March 1996): 68–76.

Malory, Thomas. *Le Morte D'arthur.* http://www.gutenberg.org/files/1252/1252-h/1252-h.htm.

Mason, David. *Binchester Roman Fort Excavation Project: Results of 2011 Season.* http://www.durham.gov.uk/media/1565/Binchester-Roman-Fort-Excavation-Project-Results-of-2011-season/pdf/Archaeology_issue_7_binchester_article.pdf.

Matasovic, Ranko. "'Sun' and 'Moon' in Celtic and Indo-European." *Celto-Slavica* 2 (2009): 152–162.

Meath County Council. *Draft Tara Skryne Landscape Conservation Area.* http://www.meath.ie/CountyCouncil/Publications/PlanningPublications/TaraSkryneLandscapeConservationArea/File,41581,en.pdf.

Merrifield, Ralph. *London: City of the Romans.* Berkeley and Los Angeles: University of California Press, 1983.

Milisauskas, Sarunas. *European Prehistory: A Survey.* New York: Springer, 2011.

Mills, David. *A Dictionary of British Place-Names.* Oxford, UK: Oxford University Press, 2011.

Ministère de la Culture et de la Communication. *Les Gaulois D'acy-Romance.* http://www.gaulois.ardennes.culture.fr/#/fr/annexe/accueil/tab/04/t=Accueil.

Ministère de la Culture et de la Communication. *The Gauls in Provence: The Oppidum of Entremont.* http://www.entremont.culture.gouv.fr/en/index2.html.

Ministère de la Culture et de la Communication. *Megalithism in Morbihan: Gavrinis.* http://www.culture.gouv.fr/fr/arcnat/megalithes/en/mega/megagav_en.htm.

Moore, Tom. "The Iron Age." In *Twenty-Five Years of Archaeology in Gloucestershire.* Edited by N. Holbrook and J. Jurica. Cirencester, UK: Cotswold Archaeology, 2006.

Morris, John. *Nennius: British History and the Welsh Annals.* Chichester, UK: Phillimore & Co. Ltd., 1980.

Morris, R.W.B., and A. Marshall. "A Cup- and Ring-Marked Stone from Nottingham Hill, Gotherington." *Transactions of the Bristol and Gloucestershire Archaeological Society* 101 (1983): 171–174.

Morteani, Giuliani, and Jeremy P. Northover. *Prehistoric Gold in Europe.* Dordrecht, Netherlands: Springer, 1994.

Mott Macdonald Pettitt. *Proposed Power Plant at Derrygreenagh, Co. Offaly.* http://www.derrygreenaghpower.ie/docs/EIS%20Chapters/Chapter%2012%20Cultural%20Heritage.pdf.

Muirchu moccu Machtheni, *Life of St. Patrick.* In *Irish Antiquarian Researches.* Edited by William Bethan. Dublin, Ireland: William Curry Jun. and Co., 1827. http://www.maryjones.us/ctexts/patrick-armagh1-muirchu.html.

Müller, R., G. Goldenberg, M. Barthelheim, M. Kunst, and E. Pernicka. "Zambujal and the Beginnings of Metallurgy in Southern Portugal." In *Metal and Mines: Studies in Archaeometallurgy.* Edited by Susan La Niece, Duncan Hook and Paul T. Craddock, 15–26. London: Archetype Publications, 2007.

Museum of London. "Ritual Practices." *Londinium Lite.* http://archive.museumoflondon.org.uk/Londinium/analysis/religiouslife/rites/17+ritual.htm.

Nagy, Gregor. *Greek Mythology and Poetics.* Ithaca, NY: Cornell University Press, 1992.

National Museum of Ireland. *Safe Secrets: The Story of the Coggalbeg Hoard.* http://www.museum.ie/en/exhibition/coggalbeg-hoard.aspx.

Needham, Stuart and Tony Spence. "Refuse and the Formation of Middens." *Antiquity* 71 (1997): 77–90.

Nennius. *History of the Britons.* Translated by J.A. Giles. London: Henry G. Bohn, 1848. http://d.lib.rochester.edu/camelot/text/nennius-history-of-the-britons.

Newman, John. *Gwent/Monmouthshire*. London: Penguin, 2000.
Noort, Robert Van de, Henry P. Chapman, and John R. Collis. *Sutton Common: The Excavation of An Iron Age "Marsh-Fort."* London: Council for British Archaeology, 2007.
Norfolk Heritage Explorer. *Early Bronze Age Burnt Mound and Inhumation*. http://www.heritage.norfolk.gov.uk/.
Northamptonshire Archaeological Society. *Whittlebury Hillfort*. http://northants-archaeology.org.uk/Whittlebury.htm.
Nowakowski, Jacqueline A. *Excavations of a Bronze Age Landscape and a Post-Roman Industrial Settlement 1953–1961, Gwithian, Cornwall*. Truro, Cornwall: Truro County Council, 2007.
Obeyesekere, Gananath. *Imagining Karma: Ethical Transformations in Amerindian, Buddhist and Greek Rebirth*. Oakland: University of California Press, 2002.
O'Brien, Leonora. *Blood, Seeds and Soil: Bronze Age, Iron Age and Anglo-Saxon Settlement and Burial at Harston Mill, Cambs*. https://www.academia.edu/1701365/Blood_seeds_and_soil_Iron_Age_storage_pit_burials_at_Harston_Mill_Cambridgeshire.
O'Brien, William. "Ross Island, Kerry." *Database of Irish Excavation Reports*. http://www.excavations.ie/report/1993/Kerry/0001504/.
Orme, Nicholas. *The Saints of Cornwall*. Oxford, UK: Oxford University Press, 2002.
Ossafreelance. *Osteological Analysis of Human Remains from Sainsbury's Site, St. Johns, Worcester*. http://www.ossafreelance.co.uk/PastProjects/WCM101591Sainsburysstjohns.pdf.
Outram, A., et al. "The Earliest Horse Harnessing and Milking." *Science* 6 (March 2009): 1332–1335.
Painter, K.S. "A Bronze Ox-Head from Somerset." *The Antiquaries Journal* 43 (1963): 291–2.
Parker, Will. *The Celtic Lugus*. http://www.mabinogion.info/lugus.htm.
Parker, Will. *The Mabinogi of Branwen*. www.mabinogi.net.
Parker, Will. *The Mabinogi of Math*. www.mabinogi.net.
Parker, Will. *The Mabinogi of Pwyll*. www.mabinogi.net.
Parker Pearson, Mike. " Bluestones at Stonehenge." *British Archaeology* 110 (Jan/Feb 2010).
Parker Pearson, Mike. "Food, Sex and Death: Cosmologies in the British Iron Age with Particular Reference to East Yorkshire." *Cambridge Archaeological Journal* 9 (1999): 43–69.
Parker Pearson, M., A. Chamberlain, N. Field, and J. Rylatt. "Déposition Votive Et Éclipses Lunaires En Angleterre Et Sur Le Continent." In *L'âge Du Fer Dans L'arc Jurassien Et Ses Marges*. Edited by Ph. Barral, A. Daubigney, C. Dunning, G. Kaenel, M.J. Roulière-Lambert. Besançon, France: Presses universitaires de Franche-Comté, 2007.
Parker Pearson, M., et al. "Who Was Buried at Stonehenge?" *Antiquity* 83 (2009): 23–39.
Parker Pearson, M., et al. "The Age of Stonehenge." *Antiquity* 81 (2007): 617–639.
Parker Pearson, M., et al. "Materializing Stonehenge: The Stonehenge Riverside Project and New Discoveries." *Journal of Material Culture* 11 (2006): 227–261.
Parker Pearson, M., et al. "A New Avenue at Durrington Walls." *Past* 52 (April 2006): 1–2.
Parker Pearson, M., et al. *The Stonehenge Riverside Project: Excavation I*. http://www.shef.ac.uk/archaeology/research/2.4329/stonehenge07-01.
Parker Pearson, M., N. Sharples, and J. Mulville. "Brochs and Iron Age Society: A Reappraisal." *Antiquity* 70 (March 1996): 57–67.
Parry, S., and S. McGrail. "A Prehistoric Plank Boat Fragment and a Hard from Caldicot Castle Lake, Gwent, Wales." *The International Journal of Nautical Archaeology* 20 (1991): 21–27.
Piggott, Stuart. *Early Celtic Art*. Piscataway, NJ: Transaction Publishers, 2008.
Pitts, Mike. "Flight of the Eagles." *British Archaeology* 86 (January/February 2006).
Pitts, Mike. *Hengeworld*. London: Arrow Books, 2000.
Pitts, Mike. "News: All Cannings Cross." *British Archaeology* 74 (January 2004).
Pliny the Elder. *Natural History*. Translated by John Bostock and H.T. Riley. London: Henry G. Bohn, 1855.
Plutarch. "The Obsolescence of Oracles." In *Moralia* Vol. V. Translated by Frank Cole Babbitt. Cambridge, MA: Harvard University Press, 1936.
Pokorny, Julius. *Indogermanisches etymologisches Wörterbuch*. Bern, Switzerland: Francke, 1959. http://www.indoeuropean.nl.
Pollex, Axel. "Comments on the Interpretation of the So-Called Cattle Burials of Neolithic Central Europe." *Antiquity* 73 (1999): 542–550.
Polomé, Edgar C., and Werner Winter. *Reconstructing Languages and Cultures*. New York, NY: Mouton de Gruyter, 1992.
Ponting, Gerald. *2006/7 Southern Moon Skim at the Callanish Stones*. http://home.clara.net/gponting/page42.html.
Portable Antiquities Scheme. *Bucket*. https://finds.org.uk/database/artefacts/record/id/70768.
Portable Antiquities Scheme. *Bucket*. https://finds.org.uk/database/search/results/q/ox+shropshire.
Portable Antiquities Scheme. *Mount*. https://finds.org.uk/database/artefacts/record/id/415555.
Portable Antiquities Scheme. *Mount*. https://finds.org.uk/database/search/results/q/bulls+head+vessel+cheshire.
Posluschny, Axel G. "From Landscape Archaeology to Social Archaeology: Finding Patterns to Explain the Development of Early Celtic 'Princely Sites' in Middle Europe." In *Digital Discovery. Exploring New Frontiers in Human Heritage*. Edited by J.T. Clark and E. Hagemeister. Budapest, Hungary: Archaeolingua, 2007.
Powell, Martin J. "Astronomical Alignments at the Crick Barrow in Gwent, South Wales." *Archaeoastronomy* 26 (1995): S49-S56.

Pryor, Francis. *Etton: Excavations at a Neolithic Causewayed Enclosure Near Maxey Cambridgeshire 1982-7*. London: English Heritage, 1998.
Pryor, Francis. *The Flag Fen Basin*. London: English Heritage, 2009.
Redfern, Rebecca. "New Evidence for Iron Age Secondary Burial Practice and Bone Modification from Gussage All Saints and Maiden Castle (Dorset, England)." *Oxford Journal of Archaeology* 27 (2008): 281-301.
Rees, Elizabeth. *Celtic Sites and Their Saints: A Guidebook*. London: Burns & Oates, 2003.
Rees, William Jenkins, and Thomas Wakeman. *Lives of the Cambro-British Saints*. London: Longman & Co., 1853.
Rhodes, P.P. "A Prehistoric and Roman Site at Wittenham Clumps, Berks." *Oxoniensia* 12 (1948): 18-31.
Richardson, Miranda. *An Archaeological Assessment of Lyng and Athelney*. Taunton, UK: Somerset County Council, 2003.
Rhys, John. "All Around the Wrekin." *Y Cymmrodor* 21 (1908): 1-62.
Rivet, A.L.F. and Colin Smith. *The Place-Names of Roman Britain*. London: Batsford, 1979.
Roberts, John. *Land at Ty Mawr Holyhead Anglesey*. Bangor, Wales: Gwynedd Archaeological Trust, 2006.
Robinson, J. Armitage. *Two Glastonbury Legends*. Cambridge, UK: Cambridge University Press, 1926.
Roman Britain Organisation. *Corinium Dobunnorum*. http://www.roman-britain.org/places/corinium.htm.
Roman Footprints. *Camulodunum*. http://roman-footprints.com/britannia-england-east/colchester/.
Romer, F.E. *Pomponius Mela's Description of the World*. Ann Arbor, MI: University of Michigan Press, 1998.
Romeuf, Anne-Marie. "Les Ex-Voto En Bois De Chamalières (Puy-De-Dôme) Et Des Sources De La Seine (Côte D'or)· Essai De Comparaison." *Gallia* 44 (1986): 65-89.
Roskams, S., C. Neal, and R. Leary. "A Late Roman Well at Heslinton East: Ritual or Routine Practices?" *Internet Archaeology* 34 (2013). http://dx.doi.org/10.11141/ia.34.5.
Ross, Ann. "The Human Head in Insular Pagan Celtic Religion." *Proceedings of the Society of Antiquaries of Scotland* 91 (1957-8): 10-43.
Ross, Ann. *Pagan Celtic Britain*. Chicago, IL: Academy Chicago Publishers, 1996.
Ross, Ann. "Ritual and the Druids." In *The Celtic World*. Edited by Miranda Green. Abingdon, UK: Routledge, 1995.
Royal Astronomical Society. *Archaeo-Astronomy Steps Out from the Shadows of the Past*. http://www.ras.org.uk/news-and-press/news-archive/254-news-2014/2468-archaeo-astronomy-steps-out-from-shadows-of-the-past.
Royal Astronomical Society. *Stonehenge and Ancient Astronomy*. http://www.ras.org.uk/images/stories/ras_pdfs/misc/Stonehenge.LowRes.pdf.
Royal Commission on the Ancient and Historical Monuments of Wales. *Coflein*. http://www.coflein.gov.uk/.
Royal Commission on the Ancient and Historical Monuments of Wales. *Hidden Histories Episode Five: Iron Age People Living on the Edge*. http://www.rcahmw.gov.uk/HI/ENG/Heritage+of+Wales/Hidden+Histories+II/Hidden+Histories+2+Episode+5/.
Royer-Hemet, Catherine. *Canterbury: A Medieval City*. Newcastle upon Tyne, UK: Cambridge Scholars Publishing, 2010.
Ruggles, Clive. *Ancient Astronomy: An Encyclopedia of Cosmologies and Myth*. Santa Barbara, CA: ABC-CLIO, 2005.
Ruggles, Clive. *Astronomy in Prehistoric Britain and Ireland*. New Haven, CT: Yale University Press, 1999.
Ruggles, Clive. *Seven-Stone Antas (Portugal and Spain)*. http://www2.cliveruggles.com/index.php/image-coll/category/1-seven-stone-antas.
Rynne, Etienne. "Celtic Stone Idols in Ireland. in the *Iron Age in the Irish Sea Province*. Edited by Charles Thomas. London: Council for British Archaeology, 1972.
Sandars, Nancy. *Bronze Age Cultures in France*. Cambridge, UK: Cambridge University Press, 1957.
Sawyer, P.H. *From Roman Britain to Norman England*. London: Routledge, 2002.
Scarre, Chris. *Landscapes of Neolithic Brittany*. Oxford: Oxford University Press, 2011.
Scarre, Chris. *Monuments and Landscapes in Atlantic Europe*. London: Routledge, 2005.
Schlosser, Wolfhard. "Die Himmelsscheibe Von Nebra—Sonne, Mond Und Sterne." In *Development of Solar Research: Proceedings of the Colloquium Freiburg (Breisgau), September 15, 2003*. Edited by A.D. Wittmann, G. Wolfschmidt and H.W. Duerbeck. Frankfurt am Main, Germany: Verlag Harri Deutsch, 2006.
Schönfelder, Martin. "Bear-Claws in Germanic Graves." *Oxford Journal of Archaeology* 13.2 (1994): 217-227.
Score, Vicki, and Jennifer Browning. *Hoards, Hounds and Helmets: An Iron Age Shrine at Hallaton, Leicestershire*. https://ulasnews.wordpress.com/projects/the-hallaton-treasure/.
Seaman, Andrew. "Dinas Powys in Context: Settlement and Society in Post-Roman Wales." *Studia Celtica* 47 (2013): 1-23.
Selkirk, A. "John Collis." *Current Archaeology* 123 (1991): 116-123.
Serjeantson, Dale. "Deer, Picks and People." *Deer: Journal of the Deer Society* 16 (2001): 30-33.
Serjeantson, Dale. *Review of Animal Remains from the Neolithic and Early Bronze Age of Southern Britain*. London: English Heritage, 2011.
Serjeantson, Dale and Morris, James. "Ravens and Crows in Iron Age and Rman Britain." *Oxford Journal of Archaeology* 30 (2011): 85-107.
Sheridan, Alison. "Radiocarbon Dates Arranged Through National Museums Scotland During 2006/7." *Discovery and Excavation in Scotland* 8 (2007): 220-1.

Sherratt, Andrew. "The Transformation of Early Agrarian Europe: The Later Neolithic and Copper Ages 4500–2500 BC." In *The Oxford Illustrated History of Prehistoric Europe*. Edited by Barry Cunliffe, 167–201. Oxford, UK: Oxford University Press, 2001.

Silius Italicus. *Punica*. Translated by J.D. Duff. Cambridge, MA: Harvard University Press, 1961.

Simms-Williams, Patrick. "Clas Beuno and the Four Branches of the Mabinogi." In *150 Jahre "Mabinogion": Deutsche-Walische Kulturbeziehunge*. Edited by B. Maier and S. Zimmer. Buchreihe der Zeitschrift für celtische Philologie 19, Tübingen: Niemeyer, 2001.

Simms-Williams, Patrick. *Irish Influence on Medieval Welsh Literature*. Oxford, UK: Oxford University Press, 2010.

Simon, Francisco M., "Images of Transition: Ways of Death in Celtic Hispania," *Proceedings of the Prehistoric Society* 74 (2008): 53–68.

Sjöblom, Tom. "The Great Mother: The Cult of the Bear in Celtic Traditions." *Studia Celtica Fennica* III (2006): 71–78.

Slavie, David R., and Palmer Bovie. *Three Comedies by Titus Maccius Plautus*. Baltimore, MD: Johns Hopkins University Press, 1995.

Smith, Martin. "Bones Chewed by Canids as Evidence for Human Excarnation: A British Case Study." *Antiquity* 80 (2006): 671–685.

Smyth, Marina. *Understanding the Universe in Seventh-Century Ireland*. Woodbridge, Suffolk, UK: Boydell & Brewer, 1996.

Sullivan, Charles William. *The Mabinogi: A Book of Essays*. New York: Garland Press, 1996.

Snyder, Christopher. *Age of Tyrants: Britain and the Britons A.D. 400–600*. University Park: Pennsylvania State University Press, 2003.

Soberl, L., R.P. Evershed, and J. Pollard. *Cooking for the Dead: Investigation of Organic Residues Preserved in Early Bronze Age Funerary Pottery from South-West Britain*. https://www.academia.edu/233371/Cooking_for_the_Dead.

Sopeña, Gabriel. "Celtiberian Ideologies and Religion," *E-Keltoi Journal of Interdisciplinary Celtic Studies*, Volume 6 (2005).

Speidel, Michael. *Ancient Germanic Warriors*. London: Taylor & Francis, 2002.

Stead, Ian. "Chalk Figurines of the Parisi." *The Antiquaries Journal* 68 (1988): 9–29.

Stead, Ian. *Iron Age Cemeteries in East Yorkshire*. London: English Heritage, 1991.

Stone, John. "Some Discoveries at Ratfyn." *Wiltshire Archaeological and Natural History Magazine* 47 (1935): 55–67.

Strabo. *Geography*. Translated by H.L. Jones. Cambridge, MA: Harvard University Press, 1932. http://penelope.uchicago.edu.

Swanton, Michael. *Anglo-Saxon Chronicle*. New York: Psychology Press, 1998.

Sykes, Naomi. *Beastly Questions: Animal Answers to Archaeological Issues*. London: Bloomsbury Publishing, 2014.

Tacitus. *Annals*. Translated by Alfred John Church and William Jackson Brodribb. New York: Random House, 1942. http://www.perseus.tufts.edu.

Theoi Project. *Theoi Greek Mythology*. http://www.theoi.com/.

Thomas, Charles. "Beacon Hill Re-Visited." *Annual Report of the Lundy Field Society* 42 (1992): 43–54.

Thomas, Charles. "The Hill-Fort at St. Dennis." *Cornish Archaeology* 4 (1965): 31–35.

Thomas, Reverend Canon Dr. Patrick. *Illtud*. http://llanilltud.org.uk/wp-content/uploads/2014/12/Illtud-Lectures-by-Revd-Patrick-Thomas-edited.pdf.

Thomas, R., and L. McFadyen. "Animals and Cotswold-Severn Long Barrows: A Re-Examination." *Proceedings of the Prehistoric Societ* 76 (2010): 95–113.

Tilley, Christopher. *The East Devon Pebblebed Landscape*. http://www.pebblebedsproject.org.uk/east_devon_pebblebed_landscape.html.

Tilley, Christopher. *Interpreting Landscapes: Geologies, Topographies, Identities; Explorations in Landscape Phenomenology 3*. Walnut Creeek, CA: Left Coast Press, 2010.

Timberlake, S., A. Gwilt, and M. Davis. "A Copper Age/Early Bronze Age Gold Disc from Banc Tynddol (Penguelan, Cwmystwyth Mines, Ceredigion)." *Antiquity* 302 (December 2004). http://www.antiquity.ac.uk/projgall/timberlake/.

Turcan, Robert. *The Cults of the Roman Empire*. Hoboken, NJ: Wiley, 1997.

University College Dublin. *Excavation Findings from 3500 BC Passage Tomb at the Mound of the Hostages Published*. http://www.ucd.ie/news/mar06/030306_mound_of_the_hostages.htm.

University of Leicester. *Burrough Hill Iron Age Hillfort*. http://www2.le.ac.uk/departments/archaeology/research/projects/burrough-hill.

University of Leicester. *University of Leicester Archaeologists Discover Bronze Remains of Iron Age Chariot Burial*. http://www2.le.ac.uk/offices/press/press-releases/2014/october/university-of-leicester-archaeologists-discover-bronze-remains-of-iron-age-chariot.

University of Wales. *Archaeology of the Mabinogion*. http://www.uwtsd.ac.uk/research/environment-archaeology-history-and-anthropology/archaeology-of-the-mabinogion/.

Valentin, John, and Stephen Robinson. "Excavations in 1999 on Land Adjacent to Wayside Farm, Nursteed Road, Devizes." *Wiltshire Archaeological and Natural History Magazine* 95 (2002): 147–213.

Waddell, John. "Excavation at 'Dathi's Mound,' Rathcroghan, Co. Roscommon." *The Journal of Irish Archaeology* 4 (1988): 23–36.

Waddington, Kate. *Reassembling the Bronze Age: Exploring the Southern British Midden Sites*. PhD diss., Cardiff University, 2009.

Wade-Evans, A.W. *Vitae Sanctorum Britanniae Et Genealogiae*. Cardiff: University of Wales Press, 1944. http://www.maryjones.us/ctexts/brynach.html.

Wade-Evans, A.W. *Welsh Medieval Law*. Oxford, UK: Clarendon Press, 1909.

Wainwright, G.J. *Gussage All Saints: An Iron Age Settlement in Dorset*. London: Her Majesty's Stationery Office, 1979.

Walter, Mariko Namba and Eva Jane Neumann. *Shamanism: An Encyclopedia of World Beliefs, Practices and Culture*. Santa Barbara, CA: ABC-CLIO, 2004.

Wasyliw, Patricia Healy. *Martyrdom, Murder and Magic*. Ney York: Peter Lang, 2008.

Watkins, Calvert, and Lisi Oliver. *Selected Writings: Culture and Poetics*. Innsbruck, Austria: Institut für Sprachwissenschaft der Universität Innsbruck, 1994.

Watts, Dorothy. *Religion in Late Roman Britain*. London: Routledge, 1998.

Webster, Chris. *The Archaeology of South West England*. http://www1.somerset.gov.uk/archives/hes/downloads/swarfweb.pdf.

The Welsh Triads. http://norin77.50megs.com/triads.htm.

Wessex Archaeology. *The Amesbury Archer*. http://www.wessexarch.co.uk/projects/amesbury/archer.html.

Wessex Archaeology. *Binchester Roman Fort, County Durham*. Salisbury, UK: Wessex Archaeology, 2008.

Wessex Archaeology. *The Boscombe Bowmen*. http://www.wessexarch.co.uk/projects/wiltshire/boscombe/bowmen.

Wessex Archaeology. *Caerwent Roman Town*. http://www.wessexarch.co.uk/system/files/68736_Caerwent%20Monmouthshire.pdf.

West, M.L. *Indo-European Poetry and Myth*. Oxford, UK: Oxford University Press, 2007.

White, Roger, and Hal Dalwood. *Archaeological Assessment of Wroxeter*. http://archaeologydataservice.ac.uk/archiveDS/archiveDownload?t=arch-435-1/dissemination/pdf/PDF_REPORTS_TEXT/SHROPSHIRE/WROXETER_REPORT.pdf.

Wilkins, Brendon. "Under the Uplands: Cave Archaeology in the Yorkshire and Lancashire Dales." *Current Archaeology* 261 (Nov 2011): 13–15.

William of Malmesbury. *Chronicle of the Kings of England*. Translated by J.A. Giles. London: Henry G. Bohn, 1847.

Williams, Rev. P.B. "Historical Account of the Monasteries and Abbeys in Wales," *Transactions of the Cymmrodorion* 2.4 (1828): 203–262.

Wiltshire Heritage Museum. *Bush Barrow*. http://www.wiltshiremuseum.org.uk/galleries/?Action=3&obID=89&prevID=9.

Wiltshire Heritage Museum. *Disk/Gold Sun Disk*. http://www.wiltshireheritagecollections.org.uk/index.asp?page=item&mwsquery.

Wiltshire Heritage Museum. *Mere G6a*. http://www.wiltshireheritagecollections.org.uk/wiltshiresites.asp?page=selectedplace&mwsquery=%7BPlace%20identity%7D=%7BMere%20G6a%7D.

Woodard, Roger D. *Myth, Ritual, and the Warrior in Roman and Indo-European Antiquity*. Cambridge, UK: Cambridge University Press, 2013.

"Y Gododdin." In *Earliest Welsh Poetry*. Translated by Joseph Clancy. London: Macmillan, 1970. http://www.Maryjones.Us/Ctexts/A01b.Html.

Yorkshire Archaeological Society. The *Ferry Fryston Chariot*. http://www.Prehistory.Yas.Org.Uk/Content/Ferryfryston.Html.

Yorkshire Archaeological Society. The *Folkton Drums*. http://www.Prehistory.Yas.Org.Uk/Content/Folkton.Html.

Yorkshire Archaeological Society. *Gristhorpe Man*. http://www.Prehistory.Yas.Org.Uk/Content/Gristhorpe.Html.

Ziegler, Michelle. "Artur Mac Aedan of Dal Riata." *The Heroic Age* 1 (Spring/Summer 1999).

Index

Aldborough, North Yorkshire 146–147
All Cannings Cross, Wiltshire 67–69
Almendres cromlech 15
amber 51, 70
Ambrosius Aurelianus 163, 175, 195
Amesbury abbey, Wiltshire 231–232
Amesbury Archer 38
Anglesey, north Wales 8, 11, 18, 44, 60–61, 181, 182, 208, 224–225
Antenociticus ((god) 159
anthropomorphic short swords 113
Apam Napat (god) 58
Arcturus (star) 169–170, 196
Arianrhod daughter of Don 238–240, 244
Arras, East Yorkshire 111, 112
Arthur's battles 173–175
Arthur's Palace, Scotland 202
Artio (goddess) 167
Artur, son of Aedan mac Gabran 164
Ascott-under-Wychwood, Oxfordshire 28
Ashgrove Farm, Fife, Scotland 40
Athelney, Somerset 212
Avalon 198–199, 200
ax carvings 48–49
Aylesford, Kent 121
Aylesford-Swarling culture 121

Badbury barrow, Dorset 49
Bagendon, Gloucestershire 127
Baldock, Hertfordshire 122
Bardney Abbey, Lincolnshire 215
bards 10
Bardsey Island, Gwynedd 244
Barnack, Cambridgeshire 39
Bath, Somerset 151–152
Battlesbury Bowl, Wiltshire 95–96
Beaker burials 38–40
bear skin burials 165
bear skin hoods 167–168
bears 164, 167, 236
Bear's Son tales 168–169
Bedd Branwen, Anglesey 44, 182
Bedwyr 186–187, 188–189
Bell-Beaker Culture 35–40, 220
Beltane 32, 48
Berth hillfort, Shropshire 174
Binchester Roman fort 174
Bishop's Cleeve, Gloucestershire 127

Blewburton Hill, Oxfordshire 82
Borough Fen enclosure, Cambridgeshire 92
Boscombe Bowmen 38–39
Boscombe Down, Wiltshire 38–39, 52
Boskednan stone circle, Cornwall 23
Bradley Fen, Cambridgeshire 59
Bran the Blessed 181–183
Breiddin hillfort, Powys 81
Brigantes 147
Bromfield, Shropshire 128–129
Brough-on-Humber, East Yorkshire 145–146
Bryn Celli Ddu, Anglesey 18–20
burnt mounds 58–62
Burrough Hill, Leicestershire 93–94
Bush Barrow, Wiltshire 40–42, 49
Bush Barrow lozenge 42, 181

Cadbury Castle, Somerset 90–91
Caerloggas barrow, Cornwall 38
Caerwent, Monmouthshire 147–148, 225
Caistor St. Edmunds, Norfolk 144–145
Caldey Island, Pembrokeshire 206–208
Caldicot, Monmouthshire 117
Callanish, Outer Hebrides 17
Cambridge 152–153, 158
Canterbury, Kent 137–138
Carhampton, Somerset 199
Carlisle, Cumbria 147
Carmarthen 148
Carn Fadrun hillfort, Gwynedd 234–235
Carnac, Brittany 16
Carnutes 119
Castell Henllys, Pembrokeshire 66
Castle Dore, Cornwall 219
Castle Killibury, Cornwall 215
Catterick, North Yorkshire 171–172
cattle 31–32, 39, 43, 51–52, 109–110, 155, 158, 159, 185
cauldrons 55, 56, 72, 79, 122, 126, 180, 181, 182, 191
Cei 186–187, 188–189
Celliwig 187, 192, 194
Celtiberians 104
Celts 5–8

chalk figurines 113
chariot burials 111–112
Chester 174–175
Chichester, West Sussex 137
Chiseldon, Wiltshire 126
Cirencester, Gloucestershire 140–141
Clandon barrow, Dorset 42
Clun-Clee Ridgeway 128
Clynnog Fawr monastery, Gwynedd 235, 245
coastal promontory forts 100–101, 103, 220
Colchester, Essex 138
Coligny calendar 118
Corded Ware Culture 34–35
Cornovii 140, 141–142, 148, 151, 159–160
Coveney, Cambridgeshire 129
Coventina's well, Northumberland 159
Cowlam, East Yorkshire 113
Crick Barrow, Monmouthshire 47–48
Cronus (god) 103, 202, 206, 210
Crowland Abbey, Lincolnshire 213–214
Cynddylan of Powys 170

Danebury hillfort, Hampshire 87–88, 184
Danes' Graves, East Yorkshire 114
Devon Pebble Beds 44–46
Dinas Powys hillfort, Vale of Glamorgan 215
Dinorben hillfort, Conwy 82
Dis (Dis Pater) 9, 74
Divine Twins 51, 107
dogs 30–31, 104, 129, 156, 158, 172, 177
Domellick, Cornwall 196–197
Don Quixote 204
Doniert stone 219
Dorchester, Dorset 135, 154
Dorchester-on-Thames, Oxfordshire 25
Dorset cursus 24–25
Druids 8–13, 73, 75, 118–120, 146, 224–234, 243–248
Drustanus stone 217
Dumnonii 134
Dun Aonghasa, Ireland 100–101
Durrington Walls, Wiltshire 23

275

earth-goddess 65–67
East Chisenbury, Wiltshire 71
Edinburgh 172, 186
Ely Abbey, Cambridgeshire 212–213
Entremont, France 10
Epona (goddess) 179
equinox, spring/autumn 17, 25, 32, 46, 47, 73, 77, 225
Etton causewayed enclosure, Cambridgeshire 29–30
excarnation 30–31, 75, 103–105
Exeter, Devon 134

feasting 23, 24, 29, 56, 62–65, 67–75
Feltwell, Norfolk 56, 57, 59
Ferry Fryston, West Yorkshire 114–115
fire, ritual 84
Fiskerton, Lincolnshire 116–117
Flag Fen, Cambridgeshire 53–54
flesh-hooks 56–57
Flimson Bay fort, Pembrokeshire 101–102
Folkton, North Yorkshire 39–40

Garton Slack, East Yorkshire 112–113
Gawain 201
Gayhurst Quarry, Buckinghamshire 43
Gildas 162–163, 198
Glastonbury, Somerset 97–99, 198, 200–201
Glastonbury Tor, Somerset 211–212
Gloucester 141, 190
Godmanchester, Cambridgeshire 25
Godwin Ridge, Cambridgeshire 65, 99–100
gold discs (Bronze Age) 49–50, 184
Gorlois, duke of Cornwall 196
Gournay-sur-Aronde shrine, France 123–124
Great Orme copper mine, Llandudno 37
Gristhorpe, North Yorkshire 43–44
Gussage All Saints, Dorset 96–97, 104
Gwales/Grassholm, Pembrokeshire 183
Gwenhwyfar/Guanhumara/Guinevere 188, 197–198
Gwithian, Cornwall 220
Gwydion son of Don 236–238, 239–240, 242–243
Gwyn son of Nudd 188, 190

Haddenham Roman temple, Cambridgeshire 157
Hallaton, Leicestershire 129
Hambledon Hill, Dorset 29
Harlyn Bay, Cornwall 220
Harston Mill, Cambridgeshire 99
Hayling Island shrine, Hampshire 122–123
head cult 10, 68, 70, 87–88, 140, 154–155, 182–183
Helston, Cornwall 67, 219
Hemp Knoll Barrow, Wiltshire 39

Hengistbury Head, Dorset 42, 126
High Peak, Devon 45
hillforts 80–81
Holt, Worcestershire 127–128
Holy Island, Anglesey 208
horned god 142–143, 159, 160
horses 34, 58, 79–80, 82, 106–109, 130, 132, 158, 159, 178–180, 181
Hunsbury Hill, Northamptonshire 92
The Hurlers (Cornwall) 46–47

Ilchester, Somerset 135
Imbolc 32
Inchmarnock, Scotland 209–210
Indo-European languages 37
Innermessan, Dumfries and Galloway 194
Iona, Scotland 208–209
Irthlingborough, Northamptonshire 39, 158
islands 103, 180, 181, 183, 198–199, 206–215, 244
Isolt's Ford, Cornwall 217

Kirkburn sword 112
Kirkmadrine church, Dumfries and Galloway 194
Knowes of Trotty, Orkney 44

Lankidden cliff castle, Cornwall 220
La Tène, Switzerland 119
Leicester 144
Leskernick Hill, Cornwall 46–47, 225
Lexden Tumulus, Colchester 121–122
Lidbury Camp, Wiltshire 84–85
Lincoln 145, 173
Lindisfarne, Northumberland 211
Liskeard, Cornwall 219
Litavis (goddess) 66, 74
Llandegai, Gwynedd 60
Llanmaes, Vale of Glamorgan 72–73
Llanmelin hillfort, Monmouthshire 148, 225
Lleu Skillful Hand 240–243
Lludd and Llefelys 236
Llyn Cerrig Bach, Anglesey 11
Llyn Fawr hoard 55
Loch Ryan, Dumfries and Galloway 194
London 140
Loughcrew passage tombs, Ireland 17
Lugnasadh 32, 48
Lugus (god) 240
lunar eclipse 117
Lundy Island, Devon 210–211
Lydney Park Roman temple, Gloucestershire 157

Mabinogion 177–179, 181–183, 234–243
Mabon son of Modron 189–190, 192, 205
Macha (goddess) 107

Maeshowe, Orkney 17–18
Maiden Castle, Dorset 88–90, 104
Malory, Sir Thomas 201
Maponos (god) 119, 189
Marden henge, Wiltshire 23–24
Marlborough bucket 122
Math son of Mathonwy 234–236
Matres/Matronae (triple goddesses) 197
Matrona (goddess) 189
mead 180, 184–185, 221–222
meadowsweet 40, 221, 241
Medb (goddess) 222
Mercury (god) 8, 115, 141, 153
Mere gold disc 49
middens 63, 67, 69, 71, 72, 73, 155
Mildenhall, Wiltshire 141
mistletoe 245
Modred/Mordred 197
Moel y Gaer hillfort, Flintshire 81–82
Mooghaun hillfort, Ireland 82–83
moon 17, 24, 50, 117–118

Navan fort/*Emain Macha*, Ireland 107, 165
Nebra sky disc 50
Nettleton Roman temple, Wiltshire 156
Newbridge, Edinburgh 115
Newgrange, Ireland 16–17
nine priestesses of Sena 180–181, 199
Nodens (god) 157, 188, 191
North Grimston, North Yorkshire 113
Nottingham Hill, Gloucestershire 91

Old Kea monastery, Cornwall 219
Old Oswestry hillfort, Shropshire 94–95
Oram's Arbour, Winchester 124–125
Orion 26, 47, 225
Oven of King Arthur, Dartmoor 201–202
Owslebury, Hampshire 122

Paddock Hill, East Yorkshire 75–77
Parc Le Breos, Swansea 27–28
Parisi(i) 145–146
pigs/boars 23, 24, 29, 43, 72, 87, 88, 99, 112, 113, 114, 129, 166, 187, 189, 191–192, 236, 248
Pitton, Wiltshire 154
Potterne, Wiltshire 69–71, 229–232
Pryderi 176, 179, 180, 236–238
Pwyll 176, 177–179

Ramsey, Cambridgeshire 213
Rathcrogan, Ireland 222
ravens/crows 57, 184, 204
reincarnation 9, 10, 105–106, 202, 243
Rhiannon 178–179
Rhinns of Galloway, Scotland 194, 216
Ridgeway 127
Rillaton, Cornwall 42–43

Index

Ripon monastery, North Yorkshire 233-234
Ross Island copper mine, Ireland 37
roundhouses, Iron Age 76-77
Rudston, East Yorkshire 114
The Rumps (Cornwall) 225
Runnymede Bridge, Surrey 63-64
Rybury Camp hillfort, Wiltshire 69

St. Albans, Hertfordshire 138-140
St. Beuno 245
St. Brynach 246
St. Cadoc 199
St. Carantoc 199
St. Columba 208-209, 244
St. Cuthbert 247-248
St. David's, Wales 193-194
St. Illtud 243-244
St. Kentigern 194
St. Keverne, Cornwall 220
St. Kew monastery, Cornwall 225-226
St. Melangell 245-246
St. Michael's Mount, Cornwall 217, 220
St. Mochuda 244
St. Padarn 199-200
St. Patrick 246-247
St. Winefride 245
Salisbury, Wiltshire 150
Samhain 32, 74
Sandy Lane, Wiltshire 151
sea god 101-103
Senuna (goddess) 156
seven-stone *antas* 15-16
shamanism 109-110
sheep/goats 109-110, 114, 157, 158
Shrewsbury, Shropshire 128
Silchester, Hampshire 124, 137, 187
Sirius (star) 16
sky god 78
Sleaford, Lincolnshire 131
Snettisham Treasure 130
solar calendar 32
solstice, summer/winter 16-17, 18, 22, 23, 24, 25, 32, 45-46, 47, 48, 73-74, 77, 225
soma 221
Source des Roches, France 119
Sources de la Seine, France 119
spoons 152, 184
Stanton Harcourt, Oxfordshire 155
Stanwick Camp, North Yorkshire 147
Stanzas of the Graves 202
Stonea Camp, Cambridgeshire 92
Stonea Roman settlement, Cambridgeshire 153
Stonehenge, Wltshire 20-22, 40, 48, 228
Sulis (goddess) 151-152, 244
Sutton Common, South Yorkshire 131-132
swans 51, 57
Swarling, Kent 121

Tara, Ireland 222, 224
Taranis (god) 78-79
Thames 54-55
Thetford, Norfolk 129-130
Thornborough complex, North Yorkshire 25-26, 132
Thracian Horseman 108-109, 205
Tintagel, Cornwall 148-150, 164, 196, 197, 216, 217
Tomb of the Eagles, Orkney 27
Toutatis (god) 115, 144, 157, 203, 206
Towcester, Northamptonshire 154-155
Tregiffian Burial Chamber, Cornwall 220
Trevelgue Head, Cornwall 101
Tristan and Isolt 216-223
Trita/Thraetaona (god) 221
Trundholm sun-horse 50
Trusty's Hill, Dumfries and Galloway 215-216

Urien Rheged 175
Ursa Major (Great Bear) 169, 196, 205
Uther Pendragon 195-197

Vespasian's Camp, Wiltshire 86
Viables Farm, Basingstoke 125-126
vitrified hillforts 83

Wanborough, Wiltshire 151
Wareham, Dorset 59-60, 150, 226-228
Washingborough, Lincolnshire 62-63
Wayside Farm, Devizes 155
Welwyn Garden City, Hertfordshire 122
West Harling, Norfolk 145
West Kennet Long Barrow, Wiltshire 28
Westhampnett, Chichester 122
Weston Colley, Hampshire 96
Wetwang Slack, East Yorkshire 113
Whittlebury hillfort, Northamptonshire 92-93
Willerby Wold Long Barrow, North Yorkshire 27
Wilsford barrows, Wiltshire 42
Wilsford Shaft, Wiltshire 86-87
Winchester, Hampshire 135-136, 154
Windmill Hill, Wiltshire 29
witches 192-193
Wittenham Clumps, Oxfordshire 72, 91-92
wonders of Britain 172
Worcester 154
Wrekin hillfort, Shropshire 95
Wroxeter, Shropshire 141, 158, 170-171

Y Gododdin 171, 184, 215, 222
Yarnbury Castle, Wiltshire 85-86
York 146, 158

Zambujal, Portugal 35, 36-37

www.ingramcontent.com/pod-product-compliance
Ingram Content Group UK Ltd.
Pitfield, Milton Keynes, MK11 3LW, UK
UKHW050539150426
5217IPUK00026B/1999